Volume VI.
The Sermons of John Donne

JOHN DONNE, AET. CA. 45

[The original of this portrait, artist unknown, is in the National Portrait Gallery, London. It shows him at the age of forty-four or forty-five. Before it reached the National Portrait Gallery, it was for many years at Brandon House, Suffolk, and seems to be one of a number of portraits that were collected by the Rev. Jonathan Tyers Barrett, D.D. (1783 or 1784 to 1851), Rector of Attleborough, while he resided at Brandon House. For further details see the "bibliographical note" by Geoffrey Keynes prefixed to John Sparrow's edition of Donne's Devotions (Cambridge University Press, 1923). For permission to reproduce this portrait we are indebted to Mr. C. K. Adams, Director of the National Portrait Gallery.—THE EDITORS]

THE
SERMONS
OF
JOHN DONNE

Edited,
with Introductions
and Critical Apparatus, by

EVELYN M. SIMPSON
and
GEORGE R. POTTER

In Ten Volumes

VI.

UNIVERSITY OF CALIFORNIA PRESS
BERKELEY AND LOS ANGELES
1962

UNIVERSITY OF CALIFORNIA PRESS

BERKELEY AND LOS ANGELES, CALIFORNIA

❖

CAMBRIDGE UNIVERSITY PRESS

LONDON, ENGLAND

Table of Contents

Volume VI

PAGE

List of Illustrations

Volume VI

Introduction

THE SERMONS included in this volume cover the period from May, 1623, to January, 1626, that is, the last two years of the reign of James I, his death, and the accession of Charles I, followed by the marriage of Charles to Henrietta Maria, and the terrible outbreak of plague in the summer and autumn of 1625. For the most part the historical background was gloomy. In the summer of 1623 the negotiations for the marriage of Charles to the Spanish Infanta were in full swing, and the projected match was most unpopular in England. Donne's friend, Sir Robert Ker or Karr, was among the courtiers who followed Charles and Buckingham to Spain, and a letter which Donne wrote to him while he was there enables us to date approximately the sermon which we print as No. 1 of this volume. In this letter, which Gosse misdated as having been written in February or March, 1624,[1] we find Donne writing thus: "But yet, *Oriens nomen ejus,* the East is one of Christ's names, in one Prophet; And, *Filius Orientis est Lucifer,* the East is one of the Devill's names, in another, and these two differ diametrically."[2] He continues by pointing out that if a flat map is pasted on a round globe, the farthest east and the farthest west meet and are all one. A little later he says apologetically, "Sir, I took up this paper to write a letter, but my imaginations were full of a sermon before, for I write but a few hours before I am to preach, and so instead of a letter I send you a homily."

The sermon which we print here echoes these words very closely. "In a flat Map, there goes no more, to make West East, though they be distant in an extremity, but to paste that flat Map upon a round body, and then West and East are all one.... The name of Christ is *Oriens, The East;* And yet Lucifer himselfe is called *Filius Orientis, The Son of the East."* Though the sermon is undated, we can ascribe it with some confidence, in view of the striking resemblance of the wording, to the period of the letter to Ker. Mr. I. A. Shapiro[3] dates

---

[1] Gosse, *Life and Letters of John Donne* (1899), II, 189, 191–192.

[2] Tobie Matthew, *Letters,* 1660, p. 305.

[3] Mr. Shapiro, who is preparing an edition of Donne's letters, has kindly sent us his views on the dating of the letter and sermon.

the letter between March and September, 1623, since Charles and Buckingham were in Spain between those dates and returned to England on October 5. In view of other indications in the letter, he is inclined to think that it was written before rather than after July. Since it was Donne's custom to spend most of July, August, and September preaching in his country parishes and visiting his friends, and since, as far as we know, he never prepared any of these country sermons for publication, we have an additional reason for assigning this sermon to a date in April, May, or June, 1623.

The sermon itself is a good average specimen of Donne's middle period. It is not connected with the sermon which immediately precedes it in the Folio, which has the title "Preached to the King at White-hall, upon the occasion of the Fast, April 5, 1628," though that sermon took as its text two verses from the same penitential psalm on which Donne was now preaching. There is, however, some slight connection between the present sermon and the group of undated sermons on the Sixth Psalm, which are Nos. 50–53 in the Folio. This is shown by Donne's remarks on page 40: "But why is it so long before *David* leads us to that consideration? Why hath he deferred so primary a duty, to so late a place, to so low a roome, to the end of the Psalme? The Psalme hath a Deprecatory part, that God would forbeare him, and a Postulatory part, that God would heare him, and grant some things to him, and a Gratulatory part, a sacrifice of thankesgiving." Donne then gives a few sentences to the "Deprecatory" and the "Postulatory" parts which had been the subject of Nos. 50–53. In No. 51, preaching on verses 2 and 3 of the psalm, he had remarked: "This whole Psalm is prayer; And the whole prayer is either Deprecatory, as in the first verse, or Postulatory ... And in that Postulatory part of *Davids* prayer, which goes through six verses of this Psalme, we consider the Petitions, and the Inducements." Thus the present sermon, which deals with the "Gratulatory part," completes the series, and must have been later than the others. It is, however, well able to stand by itself, and may have been preached at some considerable interval after them.

It contains many points of interest, as when Donne remarks that David postponed his expression of thanksgiving "because being reserved to the end, and close of the Psalme, it leaves the best impression in the memory. And therefore it is easie to observe, that in all Metricall compositions, of which kinde the booke of Psalmes is, the force of the whole piece, is for the most part left to the shutting up; the whole frame of the Poem is a beating out of a piece of gold, but the last clause is as the impression of the stamp, and that is it that makes it currant." This is true of a number of Donne's best poems, and at once we remember such characteristic concluding lines as

> Thy firmnes makes my circle just,
> And makes me end, where I begunne.[4]

or

> Hope not for minde in women; at their best
> Sweetnesse and wit, they'are but *Mummy,* possest.[5]

Donne speaks of thanksgiving as the only return which we can make to God for His love to us. "The love of God is not a contract, a bargaine, he looks for nothing againe, and yet he looks for thanks, for that is nothing, because there is nothing done in it, it is but speaking; ... God looks for nothing, nothing to be done in the way of exact recompence, but yet, as he that makes a Clock, bestowes all that labour upon the severall wheeles, that thereby the Bell might give a sound, and that thereby the hand might give knowledge to others how the time passes; so this is the principall part of that thankfulnesse, which God requires from us, that we make open declarations of his mercies, to the winning and confirming of others."

A little later he speaks of the continual presence of God with the faithful on earth. "He that goes about his worldly businesse, and goes about them in Gods name, in the feare and favour of God, remaines in Gods presence still. ... No descent into hell, of what kinde soever you conceive that descent into hell to have been, put the Son of God out of heaven, by descending into hell; no *Discede,* no Leave, no Commandement that God gives us, to doe the works of our calling here, excludes us from him; but as the Saints of God shall follow the Lamb, wheresoever he goes in heaven, so the Lamb of God shall follow his Saints, wheresoever they goe upon earth, if they walk sincerely."

---

[4] *A Valediction: forbidding mourning* (Grierson, I, 51).
[5] *Loves Alchymie* (Grierson, I, 40).

There is now an interval of ten months in our dated sermons. This is due first to the usual summer vacation, and then to the serious illness which Donne contracted in the late autumn. We know from a letter of Chamberlain[6] to Carleton, of October 25, 1623, that two days earlier Donne had preached at St. Paul's after the admission of a number of eminent lawyers as Serjeants-at-law at the Temple. The sermon has not been preserved, unless it is one of those in the Folios without a heading or date. The whole procession walked through heavy rain "dabbling and bareheaded" from the Inns of Court to St. Paul's, and it may be that Donne caught a chill which predisposed him to the sickness which afflicted him during November and December. Walton describes this as "a dangerous sickness, which inclined him to a Consumption," but by this Walton means merely a wasting disease, not tuberculosis. Gosse's account is even more misleading. He takes it to be an unusually violent attack of what he describes as Donne's chronic disease, of which he says "its crises were apt to be brought on by anxiety or excess of intellectual work, as well as by cold.... We are tempted to suppose that Donne had suffered from what we now call typhoid fever in his youth, and that it had left behind a chronic tendency to gastritis. Whatever medical name we call it by, it was evidently a burning away of the internal organs, which gradually consumed, and at last destroyed him."[7] This is at variance with our only trustworthy source of evidence, Donne's own account of this sickness in the *Devotions upon Emergent Occasions* which he composed during his convalescence, and caused to be published early in 1624. According to Donne the onset of the disease was very sudden. In Meditation 1 he says: "this minute I was well, and am ill, this minute. I am surpriz'd with a sodaine change, and alteration to worse, and can impute it to no cause, nor call it by any name." In Meditation 2 he analyses his symptoms further. He has lost his appetite, and everything tastes insipid; his knees are weak and give way; he sweats from his forehead to the soles of his feet, and he finds him-

[6] *The Letters of John Chamberlain,* ed. N. E. McClure (published by the American Philosophical Society, Philadelphia, 1939, as No. XII of their *Memoirs*), Vol. II, p. 518.

[7] Gosse, *Life and Letters,* II, 181. See E. M. Simpson, *A Study of the Prose Works of John Donne,* 2d ed., 1948, pp. 241–242.

self unable to sleep. A message is sent for the physician, and meanwhile he is left alone by his friends, for fear of infection (Meditation 5). When the physician arrives, he takes a grave view of the case, and Donne detects this, in spite of the physician's attempt to disguise it. "I feare the more, because he disguises his fear, and I see it with the more sharpnesse, because hee would not have me see it" (Meditation 6). He turns to God, and prays that he may submit everything to the will of God. The King hears of Donne's severe illness, and sends his own physician to consult with Donne's doctor (Meditation 8). They prescribe physic, and Donne accepts it gladly (Meditation 9), but the disease grows worse, so that the physicians prescribe the fashionable remedy of applying pigeons cut in half "to draw the vapors from the Head" (Meditation 12).[8] In Meditation 13, we are told that the sickness "declares the infection and malignity thereof by spots." Donne cannot sleep by day or night, and the bells of the neighboring church seem by their tolling to summon him to prepare for death (Meditations 15–18). At last, however, he begins to recover, and the physicians immediately apply their favorite purgatives (Meditations 19, 20). He is told by them that he may get out of bed, but he finds that he can hardly stand. Finally he recovers, and employs his convalescence in arranging his devotions during his sickness into a little volume to be published immediately.

The evidence proves that Donne suffered from a violent fever, which ran its course in about three weeks. It left him extremely weak, but after a protracted convalescence he was able to resume his usual duties, and on Easter Day, 1624, he preached at St. Paul's. His health was restored so that for another six years he was able to live an active, energetic life. There is nothing to justify Gosse's hypothesis of a chronic disease aggravated by a neurotic temperament. What is noteworthy is the sane and commonsense view which Donne took of his illness. He recognized that he was acutely ill, summoned the doctor and obeyed his instructions, prepared himself for the possibility of death, but hoped for recovery, and rejoiced when he found that the sickness had abated. It was natural and right that he should wish to

---

[8] Pepys in his Diary for October 19, 1663, records that "the Queene ... was so ill as to be shaved, and pidgeons put to her feet, and to have the extreme unction given her by the priests."

live, for he was the father of a family of young people who had lost their mother a few years previously, and he was also the Dean, but lately appointed, of the cathedral church of St. Paul's. At the same time, his recovery was probably helped by his confidence that, whether he lived or died, he was in the hands of God (see Expostulation 4). On his sickbed he wrote the well-known *Hymne to God the Father:*

> Wilt thou forgive that sinne where I begunne,
>   Which was my sin, though it were done before?
> Wilt thou forgive that sinne, through which I runne,
>   And do run still: though still I do deplore?
>   When thou hast done, thou hast not done,
>   For I have more.
>
> Wilt thou forgive that sinne which I have wonne
>   Others to sinne? and made my sinne their doore?
> Wilt thou forgive that sinne which I did shunne
>   A yeare, or two: but wallowed in, a score?
>   When thou hast done, thou hast not done,
>   For I have more.
>
> I have a sinne of feare, that when I have spunne
>   My last thred, I shall perish on the shore;
> But sweare by thy selfe, that at my death thy sonne
>   Shall shine as he shines now, and heretofore;
>   And, having done that, Thou hast done,
>   I feare no more.

After quoting this *Hymne,* Walton adds that Donne "caus'd it to be set to a most grave and solemn Tune, and to be often sung to the *Organ* by the *Choristers* of St. *Pauls* Church, in his own hearing, especially at the Evening Service; and at his return from his Customary Devotions in that place, did occasionally say to a friend, *The words of this Hymne have restored to me the same thoughts of joy that possess my Soul in my sickness when I composed it. And, O the power of Church-musick! that Harmony added to it has raised the Affections of my heart, and quickened my graces of zeal and gratitude; and I observe, that I alwayes return from paying this publick duty of Prayer and Praise to God, with an unexpressible tranquillity of mind, and a willingness to leave the world.*"[9] Grierson[10] gives a con-

---

[9] Walton, *Lives* (1670), Life of Donne, p. 55.
[10] II, 252–253.

temporary musical setting from Egerton MS 2013 by John Hillton, organist of St. Margaret's Church, Westminster, who died in 1657.

It is against this background of a vigorous life interrupted by serious sickness and then restored to renewed activity that we should view this volume of Donne's sermons, which contains much of his best work. The first dated sermon which he preached after his recovery was that which he delivered at St. Paul's on Easter Day, March 28, 1624 (No. 2 in this volume). He took as his text a verse from one of his favourite books, the Apocalypse or Revelation of St. John, "Blessed and holy is he that hath part in the first Resurrection." Though he made no direct allusion to his illness, he was in fact carrying on a line of thought which we find in Expostulation and Prayer 21 of the *Devotions* which he had written so lately. There he had taken his own rising from his bed of sickness as an earnest of a resurrection from sin in this life, and a resurrection of body and soul hereafter. "... wee shall have a *Resurrection* in *Heaven;* the knowledge of that thou castest by another *glasse* upon us here; we *feele* that we have a *Resurrection* from *sinne;* and that by another *glasse* too; wee see wee have a *Resurrection* of the *body,* from the *miseries* and *calamities* of this life. This *Resurrection* of my *body,* shewes me the *Resurrection* of my *soule;* and both *here* severally, of both together hereafter." A few pages later he had written "... thou hast not onely afforded mee, the abilitie to rise out of this *bed* of *wearinesse* and *discomfort,* but hast also made this *bodily rising,* by thy *grace,* an *earnest* of a *second* resurrection from *sinne,* and of a *third,* to *everlasting glory.*"

In this Easter sermon Donne takes as one branch of his exposition the resurrection of the soul from sin. "Of these words of this first Resurrection (which is not the last, of the body, but a spirituall Resurrection) there are three expositions authorized by persons of good note in the Church.... Secondly, that it is a Resurrection from the death of sin, of actuall, and habituall sin; so it belongs to every particular penitent soul; and *Blessed art thou, blessed am I, if we have part in this first Resurrection.*" Later in the sermon he applies the text to the state of the glorified soul in heaven: "But then in her [the soul's] Resurrection, her measure is enlarged, and filled at once; There she reads without spelling, and knowes without thinking, and concludes without arguing; she is at the end of her race, without running; In her triumph, without fighting; In her Haven, without sayling ... What a death is this life? what a resurrection is this death? For though this world be a sea, yet (which is most strange) our Harbour is larger then the sea; Heaven infinitely larger then this world.... Beloved, I thinke you could be content to heare, I could be content to speake of this Resurrection, our glorious state, by the low way of the grave, till God by that gate of earth, let us in at the other of precious Stones."[11]

Another passage in this sermon offers a parallel to Expostulation 4 of the *Devotions*. There Donne had written, when his friends sent for the doctor, "*My God, my God,* how soone wouldest thou have me goe to the *Phisician,* and how far wouldest thou have me go with the *Phisician?* I know thou hast made the *Matter,* and the *Man,* and the *Art,* and I goe not from *thee* when I go to the *Phisician.*... And it is the voyce of the Wise man, both for the *matter, phisicke* it selfe, *The Lorde hath created Medicines out of the Earth, and hee that is wise, shall not abhorre them* [marginal reference, Ecclus. 38.4], And for the *Arte,* and the *Person, The Phisician cutteth off a long disease.* In all these voyces, thou sendest us to those helpes, which thou hast afforded us in that. But wilt not thou avowe that voyce too, *Hee that hath sinned against his Maker, let him fall into the hands of the Phisician* [marginal reference, *Ecclus.* 38.15].

So more briefly in this sermon: "As we are bid to honour the Physitian, and to use the Physitian, but yet it is said in the same Chapter, He that sinneth before his Maker, let him fall into the hands of the Physitian [marginal references, *Ecclus.* 38.1 and 15]; It is a blessing to use him, it is a curse to rely upon him ..."[12]

Finally, at the close of the sermon, Donne urges on his hearers the view which he had taken during his own illness: "Stay therefore patiently, stay chearfully Gods leasure till he call; but not so over-chearfully, as to be loath to go when he cals." And he ends by reaffirming his intense belief in Christ, the Resurrection and the Life: "Reliefe in persecution by power, reconciliation in sin by grace, dissolution, and transmigration to heaven by death, are all within this first Resurrection: But that which is before them all, is Christ Jesus.... He was our Creation, he was our Redemption, he is our Resurrection."[13]

---

[11] Pp. 76–77. [12] P. 70. [13] P. 79.

This sermon was followed by two others which Donne thought worthy of preservation. These are his first and second sermons preached as Vicar of St. Dunstan's-in-the-West, on April 11 and April 25, respectively. The reversion of this living had been given to Donne soon after he took holy orders, by Richard, third Earl of Dorset. At that time the Vicar was an old man, who had held the living since 1575, Dr. Thomas White, the founder of Sion College, and of the Professorship of Moral Philosophy at Oxford. He died on March 1, 1623/1624, and Donne succeeded him without any delay. He appointed a curate, Matthew Griffiths, to do the ordinary clerical duties, and installed him in the vicarage, but took pains to preach fairly regularly in the church. Among his parishioners was Izaak Walton, who had a linen-draper's shop in Fleet Street, west of Chancery Lane. He was a great admirer of Donne's "powerful preaching," and he described himself as Donne's *"Convert"* in the *Elegy* which he contributed to the edition of Donne's *Poems* in 1633, and which he revised and reprinted for his enlarged *Life of Donne* in the editions of 1658 and 1670.

The style of the first sermon at St. Dunstan's is different from that of Donne's eloquent discourses at St. Paul's. Dr. Jessopp wrote of it: "The sermon is a kind of manifesto setting forth the preacher's view of the reciprocal duties of the pastor and his flock. It was evidently composed with great care, and is expressed in language almost homely in its simplicity, very unlike the ordinary style of Donne's most studied sermons delivered on important occasions";[14] and he quotes some phrases from the concluding paragraphs: "If the Pastor *love,* there will bee a *double labour;* if the People *love,* there will bee double respect.... For where the Congregation loves the Pastor, hee will forbeare bitter reproofes, and wounding increpations, and where the Pastor loves his Congregation, his *Rebukes,* because they proceed out of *love,* will bee acceptable, and well interpreted by them.... *love* being the *root* of all, the *fruit* of all may be peace, *love* being the *soul* of all, the *body* of all may be unity; which the Lord of unity, and concord, grant to us all, for his Sonne Christ Jesus sake."[15]

The second sermon at St. Dunstan's (No. 4 in this volume) is also

[14] A. H. Jessopp, *John Donne,* p. 164.
[15] P. 94.

in Donne's plainer manner, but it has many happy short sentences such as, *"Militia, vita;* our whole life is a warfare; God would not chuse *Cowards";*[16] or again, "A man may thread Sermons by half dozens a day, and place his merit in the number, a man may have been all day in the perfume and incense of preaching, and yet have receivd none of the *savor of life unto life.* Some things an Ape can do as wel as a Man; some things an Hypocrite as wel as a Saint."[17] Sometimes Donne obtains his effect by quoting or translating an unfamiliar reading from the Vulgate: "(as the vulgat reads that place) *Gods secret discourse is with the single heart."*[18] He ends with these words: "The love of God begins in fear, and the fear of God ends in love; and that love can never end, for God is love."[19]

Sermon 5 is an undated Whitsunday sermon which we have assigned conjecturally to 1624. Like many other of the Whitsunday sermons, it is much less eloquent than the Christmas and Easter sermons. It contains a reference to the Paracelsian doctrine of the balsam, in which Donne believed. "Every thing hath in it, as Physitians use to call it, *Naturale Balsamum,* A naturall Balsumum, which, if any wound or hurt which that creature hath received, be kept clean from extrinsique putrefaction, will heale of it self."[20] This should be compared with a passage in an undated sermon preached at Whitehall: "... that *Balsamum naturale,* which *Paracelsus* speaks of, that naturall *Balme* which is in every body, and would cure any wound, if that wound were kept clean, and recover any body, if that body were purged."[21] There are many references in Donne's poems and prose works to the doctrines of Paracelsus,[22] that enigmatic figure, half

---

[16] P. 108.

[17] Pp. 101–102.

[18] P. 97. The reference is to *Prov.* 3.32.

[19] P. 113.

[20] P. 116.

[21] *Fifty Sermons,* p. 214; second sermon on *Ezekiel* 34.19.

[22] Donne possessed a copy of the *Chirurgia Magna* of Paracelsus (Keynes, *Bibliography of Donne,* 2d ed., p. 178). He refers to this book in *Biathanatos,* p. 216, and calls Paracelsus an "excellent Chirurgian." There are other references to him on pp. 172, 215 of *Biathanatos,* in *Essays in Divinity,* p. 15, and in *Letters* (1651), p. 15. For the poems see *Loves Alchymie* (Grierson, I, 39), and *To Sr Henry Wotton* (Grierson, I, 182, on which see Grierson's note).

scientist, half charlatan, whose vigorous attacks on the traditional medical lore of the Galenists created such a ferment of thought in the sixteenth century. The doctrine of the balsam is to be found in *Paracelsi Opera Omnia* (Geneva, 1658), II, 91: "For there are spirits celestial and infernal of human beings, and of metals, of plants, of stones.... Wherefore you may know that the spirit is in very truth the life and balsam of all corporeal things." Also *ibid.,* I, 368: "This chain of Venus, indeed, is nothing else than a constancy of human balsam which brings it about that the physical body will not decay."[23]

On Trinity Sunday, a week later, Donne returned to St. Dunstan's. Here again he preached a sermon of instruction in doctrine, without much eloquence. In speaking of the difficulty of the doctrine of the Trinity he uses the term "slippery," which he had employed some years previously in his poem *The Litanie.* There he had written:

> O Blessed glorious Trinity,
> Bones to Philosophy, but milke to faith,
> Which, as wise serpents, diversly
> Most slipperinesse, yet most entanglings hath.[24]

In the sermon he says: "...that is true which *S. Augustine* sayes,... there is not so steepy a place to clamber up, nor so slippery a place to fall upon, as the doctrine of the Trinity ..."[25]

On another page there is a reminiscence of what he had written in *Essays in Divinity*[26] about the knowledge of God given in Nature, that Book of Creatures, *Liber Creaturarum,* as Raymond of Sabund called it. In the *Essays* Donne had devoted almost a page to Raymond's praise of the Book of Creatures, but here he is careful to explain the inferiority of the knowledge derived from Nature to that derived from the Word of God.

"We consider two other wayes of imprinting the knowledge of God in man; first in a darke and weake way, the way of Nature, and the book of Creatures...The voyce of the Creature alone, is but a

---

[23] For these references I am indebted to W. A. Murray, "Donne and Paracelsus: An Essay in Interpretation," *Review of English Studies,* XXV, 118, 119.

[24] *Poems,* ed. Grierson, I, 339.

[25] P. 139.

[26] Edition of 1651, pp. 7–8.

faint voyce, a low voyce ... As a stick bears up, and succours a vine, or any plant, more precious then it selfe, but yet gave it not life at first, nor gives any nourishment to the root now: so the assistance of reason, and the voyce of the Creature, in the preaching of Nature, works upon our faith, but the roote, and the life is in the faith it selfe; The light of nature gives a glimmering before, and it gives a reflexion after faith, but the meridianall noone is in faith."[27]

On June 13, Donne preached "to the Earl of Exeter, and his company, in his Chappell at Saint John's." This sermon is remarkable for a passage in which Donne shows a breadth of sympathy unusual in an age so full of theological hatred and uncharitableness: "... there are an infinite number of *Stars* more then we can distinguish, and so, by Gods grace, there may be an infinite number of soules saved, more then those, of whose salvation, we discerne the *ways,* and the *meanes.* Let us embrace the way which God hath given us, which is, the knowledge of his Sonne, *Christ Jesus:* what other way God may take with others, how he wrought upon *Iob,* and *Naaman,* and such others as were not in the *Covenant,* let us not inquire too curiously, determine too peremptorily, pronounce too uncharitably: God be blessed, for his declaring his good-wil towards *us,* and *his will be done* his way upon others."[28] He then proceeds to argue that even those texts which are ordinarily understood to mean that few of the Jews will be saved, may "receive a charitable interpretation, and extension. God says, in *Ieremy, I will take you, one out of a City, and two out of a family;* yet he says, he wil do this therefore, *because he is married to them;* so that this seems to be an act of his love; And therefore, I had rather take it, that God would take a particular care of them, *one by one,* then that he would take in but *one and one ...*"

From the Jews, Donne proceeds to a consideration of the width of God's mercy toward all branches of the Christian Church. "Gods mercy was not confined, nor determined upon the *Iews: Other sheep have I, which are not of this fold,* says *Christ, them also I must bring in ...I must bring them;* who are they? *Many shall come from the east, and from the west, and shall sit downe with Abraham, Isaac, and Iacob, in the kingdom of heaven;* from the *Eastern* Church, and from

[27] Pp. 142–143.
[28] Pp. 161–162.

the *Western* Church too, from the *Greek* Church, and from the *Latine* too, and, (by Gods grace) from them that *pray not in Latine too,* from *every Church,* (so it be truly, and fundamentally a Church) *Many shall come;* How many? *a multitude that no man can number...*"[29]

After this there is an interval of six months for which we have no dated sermons. We know, however, that in September Donne visited Knole, and presumably he preached either in the parish church of Sevenoaks, of which he was rector, or, less probably, in the private chapel of the great house. In a letter to his brother-in-law, Sir Nicholas Carew, dated September 1, 1624, Donne states that on the following Saturday he is to accompany the new Earl of Dorset to Knole.[30] In previous years Donne had been the guest of that ill-assorted couple, Richard, the third Earl, and his wife, who before her marriage was Lady Anne Clifford, daughter of George, Earl of Cumberland, from whom she inherited large estates in Westmoreland. On March 26, 1624, Richard had died at the early age of thirty-five. He had been one of the greatest spendthrifts of the age, and died leaving £60,000 of debt, the equivalent of more than half a million pounds sterling at the present time. He was "so great a lover of scholars and soldiers, as that with an excessive bounty towards them, or indeed any of worth that were in distress, he did much to diminish his estate, as also with excessive prodigality in housekeeping, and other noble ways at court, as tilting, masqueing, and the like."[31] It was he who had bestowed on Donne the reversion of the living of St. Dunstan's in the West, of which he was the patron, but he died before Donne preached his first sermon in that church. The new Earl, Edward Sackville, Richard's younger brother, though he was less prodigal in his hospitality, was as kind to Donne as his brother had been. The heavy load of debt which his brother had left behind encumbered the estate for a number of

[29] P. 163.

[30] British Museum Additional MS 29598, fol. 13: "He [Dorset] remembers himselfe to be in your debt, for a free curtesy that you did him out of your parke, and he reserves a stagge for you in return of that fauor.... Vpon Saterday we make account to go to Knolle together."

[31] Lady Anne Clifford, quoted by V. Sackville-West, *Knole and the Sackvilles,* p. 59. For further details concerning Anne Clifford, see the Introductions to the sermons of Volume I of the present edition of Donne's sermons, pp. 129–130.

years,[32] but by prudent management, and by obtaining from the King a grant of "certain islands on the south of New England, viz.: Long Island, Cole Island, Sandy Point, Hell Gates, Martin's Vineyard, Elizabeth Islands, Block Island, with other islands near thereunto,"[33] he soon increased his income substantially. He became a Commissioner for planting Virginia, and in time was made Lord Chamberlain and Lord Privy Seal.[34]

By the end of October, Donne had finished his country visits and was back in the Deanery of St. Paul's, for from it he wrote an elaborate and beautiful letter to Lady Kingsmill on the death of her husband.[35] He probably continued to preach at St. Dunstan's during the autumn and winter, for Walton tells us that it was his custom when in health to preach "once a week, if not oftner." He did not, however, choose to write up his notes of these sermons, unless any of the three undated sermons described as "preached at St. Dunstan's" should be inserted here. He was careful to preserve the full collection of his Christmas and Easter sermons at St. Paul's, and the Christmas Day sermon for 1624 (No. 8 in this volume) contains one of his most exquisite passages, in which he dilates on his favorite theme, the boundless and ever-present mercy of God:

"God made Sun and Moon to distinguish seasons, and day, and night, and we cannot have the fruits of the earth but in their seasons: But God hath made no decree to distinguish the seasons of his mercies; In paradise, the fruits were ripe, the first minute, and in heaven it is alwaies Autumne, his mercies are ever in their maturity.... He

---

[32] *Ibid.*, p. 91: "The total income for the year 1628 from Knole and Sevenoaks was £100. 18s. 6d.—a fifth part of which was derived from the sale of rabbits."

[33] *Ibid.*, pp. 92–93. Miss Sackville-West rightly remarks that the petition for this grant "takes one's breath away with its magnificent insolence," and that five hundred acres of land near Sevenoaks, which Sackville acquired at the same time, "dwindles suddenly beside this formidable tenure."

[34] *Ibid.*, p. 90. In the Van Dyck portrait at Knole he is a splendid figure in his flame-colored doublet, wearing the blue ribbon of the Garter, with his sword and key of office.

[35] *Letters* (1651), pp. 7–10. The letter is dated "At my poor house at S. Paul's, 26 Octob. 1624."

brought light out of darknesse, not out of a lesser light; he can bring thy Summer out of Winter, though thou have no Spring; though in the wayes of fortune, or understanding, or conscience, thou have been benighted till now, wintred and frozen, clouded and eclypsed, damped and benummed, smothered and stupified till now, now God comes to thee, not as in the dawning of the day, not as in the bud of the spring, but as the Sun at noon to illustrate all shadows, as the sheaves in harvest, to fill all penuries, all occasions invite his mercies, and all times are his seasons."[36]

This is only a fragment of a long passage which should be read slowly and carefully to relish its full flavor. George Saintsbury singled it out as "a passage than which I hardly know anything more exquisitely rhythmed in the whole range of English from Ælfric to Pater."[37]

Donne achieves some of his effect here by the use of alliteration. In the first sentence quoted we have three alliterative sounds: *s* in "*S*un ... *s*easons ... *s*easons ... *s*easons"; *m* in "*M*oon ... *m*ercies ... *m*inute ... *m*ercies ... *m*aturity"; and *d* in "*d*istinguish ... *d*ay ... *d*ecree ... *d*istinguish." More subtle is the effect produced by the use of heavy consonantal groups and thick vowel sounds in "clouded and eclypsed, damped and benummed, smothered and stupified." Here the slow, heavy syllables suggest the bewilderment of the frozen soul, which is contrasted with the sense of life and movement conferred by the bestowal of God's mercy, suggested by the light anapaestic rhythm of "not as in the dawning of the day, not as in the bud of the spring," a clause which leads up in turn to the full splendour of the climax, "as the Sun at noon to illustrate [the second syllable is stressed] all shadows, as the sheaves in harvest, to fill all penuries."

We are not to think of Donne as elaborately working out a series of rhetorical effects. He was a poet, and whenever he was deeply moved, as here by his contemplation of the amazing mercy of God, he chose with a poet's instinct the right sounds and rhythms to express the emotion which he wished to convey.

This magnificence of diction is not sustained throughout the ser-

---

[36] P. 172.
[37] *History of English Prose Rhythm*, pp. 162–163.

mon, which contains a number of dull and tedious pages. In this it is characteristic of Donne's work as a whole, whether in prose or verse, for he is one of the most uneven of writers.

On New Year's Day, 1624/1625, Donne preached at St. Dunstan's. The winter was a sickly one, with "spotted fever" prevalent, so that Parliament was prorogued from November 2 to February 16, on account of "a general sickness and disease which proves mortal to many and infectious to more," which had dispersed itself in the City and Westminster.[38] There is an ominous reference in this sermon: "And, then, when the infection is got into a House, who can say, it shall end here in this Person, and kill no more; or it shall end this weeke, and last no longer?"[39] Since New Year's Day is the Feast of the Circumcision, Donne devotes his sermon (No. 9) to an exposition of the meaning of circumcision as ordained for the Jews, and then to the need for a spiritual circumcision among Christians. This last consists in confession of sin, contrition for and detestation of those sins which are confessed, and restitution to any who may have been wronged. On the subject of contrition Donne has a characteristic passage: "A house is not clean, though all the Dust be swept together, if it lie still in a corner, within Dores; A Conscience is not clean, by having recollected all her sinnes in the *Memory,* for they may fester there, and *Gangreen* even to *Desperation,* till she have emptied them in the bottomlesse Sea of the bloud of Christ Jesus, and the mercy of his Father, by *this* way of *Confession.* But a house is not clean neither, though the Dust be thrown out, if there hang *Cobwebs* about the Walls, in how dark corners soever. A Conscience is not clean, though the sins, brought to our memory by this Examination, be cast upon Gods mercy, and the merits of his Sonne, by *Confession,* if there remaine in me, but a *Cobweb,* a little, but a sinfull delight in the *Memory* of those sins, which I had formerly committed.... Therefore is there a *cleansing* required in this Circumcision ... Now there is no clensing of *our* bloud, but by *his* bloud; and the infusion, and application of his bloud, is in the seale of the *Sacrament;* so that that soule onely is so clensed, as is required in this spirituall circumcision, that preserves it

---

[38] F. P. Wilson, *The Plague in Shakespeare's London,* p. 129.
[39] P. 188.

selfe alwayes, or returns speedily, to a disposition of a worthy receiving of that holy and blessed Sacrament ..."[40]

The next sermon (No. 10) was delivered on January 30, the Sunday following the Feast of the Conversion of St. Paul. It opens with a quotation from that noble passage in Ecclesiasticus, "Let us now praise famous Men, and our Fathers that begat us. The Lord hath wrought great glory by them, through his power from the beginning," and applies the words to "our blessed and glorious Apostle S. *Paul,* whose Conversion the Church celebrates now." Here it is worth remarking that Donne knew the Apocryphal books well, and that this book of Ecclesiasticus was apparently his favorite. Though he was careful never to choose a text for a sermon from the Apocrypha, he made as much use of the book of Ecclesiasticus[41] as of most of the canonical books of the Old Testament, with the exception of Genesis, the Psalms, Isaiah, Jeremiah, Ezekiel, and Job.

The whole sermon is a grand panegyric on St. Paul, full of eloquence, and should be read from beginning to end. Two of the finest passages may be quoted here. Speaking of God's method in converting St. Paul by casting him to the earth, and striking him with blindness, he says: "and he [God] hath not discovered, but made that Northerne passage, to passe by the frozen Sea of calamity, and tribulation, to Paradise, to the heavenly Jerusalem. There are fruits that ripen not, but by frost; There are natures, (there are scarce any other) that dispose not themselves to God, but by affliction. And as Nature lookes for the season for ripening, and does not all before, so Grace looks for the assent of the soule, and does not perfect the whole worke, till that come. It is Nature that brings the season, and it is Grace that brings the assent; but till the season for the fruit, till the assent of the soule come, all is not done."[42]

A little later Donne turns aside to the thought of death, which was never far from his mind. The verbal music of these sentences is worth careful analysis.

"Death is not a banishing of you out of this world; but it is a visita-

---

[40] Pp. 199–200.
[41] For examples, see *Essays in Divinity* (1651), pp. 53, 54, 67, 71, 137, *LXXX Sermons,* pp. 63, 110, 157, 187, 237, 371, 604, 658.
[42] Pp. 212–213.

tion of your kindred that lie in the earth; neither are any nearer of kin to you, then the earth it selfe, and the wormes of the earth. You heap earth upon your soules, and encumber them with more and more flesh, by a superfluous and luxuriant diet; You adde earth to earth in new purchases, and measure not by Acres, but by Manors, nor by Manors, but by Shires; And there is a little Quillet, a little Close, worth all these, A quiet Grave. And therefore, when thou readest, That God makes thy bed in thy sicknesse, rejoyce in this, not onely that he makes that bed, where thou dost lie, but that bed where thou shalt lie; That that God, that made the whole earth, is now making thy bed in the earth, a quiet grave, where thou shalt sleep in peace, till the Angels Trumpet wake thee at the Resurrection, to that Judgement where thy peace shall be made before thou commest, and writ, and sealed, in the blood of the Lamb."[43]

On the first Friday in Lent Donne preached as usual at Whitehall. He took as his subject Christ's reply to the young ruler who asked what he should do to inherit eternal life. This was a sermon which excited Coleridge's intense admiration. Of one passage he remarked with a certain *naïveté:* "The whole paragraph is pure gold. Without being aware of this passage in Donne I expressed the same conviction, or rather declared the same experience, in the Appendix to the Statesman's Manual."[44] A little later, when Donne declares that nothing is essentially good but God, and that there is nothing in the world which does not in some measure partake of that goodness, Coleridge expresses his delight.

"All excellent, and [paragraph] D. most so. Thus, our old divines showed the depth of their love and appreciation of the Scriptures, and thus led their congregations to feel and see the same. Here is Donne's authority (*Deus non est ens, etc.*) for what I have so earnestly endeavoured to show, that *Deus est ens super ens,* the ground of all being, but therein likewise absolute Being, in that he is the eternal self-affirmant, the I Am in that I Am; and that the key of this mystery is given to us in the pure idea of the will, as the alone *Causa Sui.* O!

---

[43] P. 213.

[44] *Notes on the English Divines,* I, 105. The passage to which Coleridge refers is on p. 227, beginning, "He was no ignorant man, and yet he acknowledged that he had somewhat more to learn of Christ, then he knew yet."

compare this manhood of our Church divinity with the feeble dotage of the Paleyan school, the 'natural' theology, or watchmaking scheme, that knows nothing of the maker but what can be proved out of the watch."[45]

It was the philosophy of this sermon rather than its literary quality that appealed to Coleridge. There is less eloquence here than in the previous sermon, but it is one of the most thoughtful of Donne's discourses. For a modern reader ignorant of scholastic philosophy Donne's account of the nature of evil is difficult to grasp. His dependance on St. Thomas Aquinas must be emphasised, for Donne assumes a certain amount of knowledge in his hearers and readers.[46]

"For, when it is ordinarily inquired in the Schoole, whether any thing be essentially good, it is safely answered there, that if by essentially we mean independantly, so good as that it can subsist of it self, without dependance upon, or relation to any other thing, so there is nothing essentially good: But if by essentially good, we mean that whose essence, and beeing is good, so everything is essentially good. And therefore when the *Manichees* pressed S. *Augustine* with that, *Vnde malum?* If there be not an ill God, as wel as a good, *unde malum,* from whom, or from whence proceed all that ill that is in the world? S. *Augustine* saies ... Why, what is there, that you can call evill? I know no such thing; so that, if there be such a God, that God hath no creature. For, as poisons conduce to Physick, and discord to Musick, so those two kinds of evill, into which we contract all others, are of good use, that is, *malum pœnæ,* the evill of punishment, affliction, adversity, and *malum culpæ,* even sin it selfe, from which, the punishment flowes."[47]

Donne has little difficulty in arguing that "affliction, poverty, sicknesse, imprisonment, banishment, and such, are not evill," for wise men of all ages have looked on such misfortunes as the physic of the soul, and Christians believe with St. Paul that all things work together for good to those that love God. *Malum culpæ,* however, presents a

---

[45] *Notes on the English Divines,* I, 107–108. The passage referred to is on p. 231.
[46] Since this sermon was preached at Whitehall, not at St. Paul's or St. Dunstan's, Donne took for granted (perhaps unwisely) a higher degree of education in his hearers.
[47] P. 237.

much more formidable obstacle. Donne, following St. Thomas Aquinas, argues thus: "You know, I presume, in what sense we say in the Schoole, *Malum nihil,* and *Peccatum nihil,* that evill is nothing, sin is nothing; that is, it hath no reality, it is no created substance, it is but a privation, as a shadow is, as sicknesse is; so it is nothing."[48] Aquinas states, "Evil is distinct both from simple being, and from simple not-being, because it is neither a habit, nor a pure negation, but a privation ... Evil imports the absence of good. But not every absence of good is evil. For absence of good can be taken in a privative and a negative sense. Absence of good taken negatively is not evil ... But the absence of good taken in a privative sense is an evil; as, for instance, the privation of sight is called blindness."[49]

Donne recognises that this definition, however valuable it may be for the philosopher, is of little help to the ordinary man, so he proceeds: "But if I cannot finde a foundation for my comfort, in this subtilty of the Schoole, That sin is nothing, (no such thing as was created or induced by God, much lesse forced upon me by him, in any coactive Decree) yet I can raise a second step for my consolation in this, that be sin what it will in the nature thereof, yet my sin shall conduce and cooperate to my good. So *Ioseph* saies to his Brethren, *You thought evill against me, but God meant it unto good:* which is not onely good to *Ioseph,* who was no partaker in the evill, but good even to them, who meant nothing but evill."[50]

Thus Donne carries on and amplifies in this sermon a line of reasoning which he had hinted at in one of his early paradoxes, "That Good is more common than Evill." It is important to grasp the fact that in spite of all his morbidity Donne's thought from first to last is fundamentally optimistic. He believes that goodness will ultimately triumph, and that it does not simply blot out evil, but makes use of it and incorporates it in the finished design. This is the meaning of a passage in Paradox 4: "And as *Imbroderers, Lapidaries,* and other Artisans, can by all things adorne their workes ... so *Good* ... refuses no aid, no

---

[48] P. 238.

[49] *Summa Theologica,* Ia, Qu. xlviii, art. 2, ad. 1, and art. 3. See also *Contra Gentiles,* Lib. iii, cap. vi: "Now every privation, understood in the strict, proper sense, is of what a man is apt, and ought to have. The notion of evil, therefore, consists in privation thus understood."

[50] Pp. 238–239.

not of her utter contrary *Evill,* that she may bee the more *common* to vs . . .["51]

This faith that even man's sin can be fashioned by the Divine goodness to form part of a higher and more beautiful whole finds expression in several of the sermons. *"God's work is perfect;* How appeares that? *For all his ways are Iudgement,* sayes *Moses* in his victorious song. This is Perfection, That he hath established an order, a judgement . . . That even disorders are done in order, that even our sins some way or other fall within the providence of God."[52] So in a loftier strain, in a sermon preached near the end of his life, he took up the words of Job, "O earth, cover not thou my blood": "And truly, so may I, so may every soule say, that is rectified, refreshed, restored, re-established by the seales of Gods pardon, and his mercy, so the world would take knowledge of the consequences of my sins, as well as of the sins themselves, and read my leafes on both sides, and heare the second part of my story, as well as the first; so the world would look upon my temporall calamities, the bodily sicknesses, and the penuriousnesse of my fortune contracted by my sins, and upon my spirituall calamities, dejections of spirit, sadnesse of heart, declinations towards a diffidence and distrust in the mercy of God, and then, when the world sees me in this agony and bloody sweat, in this agony and bloody sweat would also see the Angels of heaven ministering comforts unto me . . . so they would know as well what God hath done for my soule, as what my soule and body have done against my God; so they would reach me throughout, and look upon me altogether, I would joyne with *Iob* in his confident adjuration, *O Earth cover not thou my blood;* Let all the world know all the sins of my youth, and of mine age too, and I would not doubt, but God should receive more glory, and the world more benefit, then if I had never sinned."[53]

In March, 1624/1625, Donne wrote the last of his funeral elegies at the insistent request of his friend and patron, Sir Robert Ker, later Earl of Ancrum, on the occasion of the death of the Marquess of Hamilton. In the letter to Ker which accompanied the poem Donne

---

[51] *Iuvenilia* (1st ed.), sig. C1 verso. We have adopted the reading "aid" from the manuscripts in place of "end" in the quarto.

[52] *LXXX Sermons,* p. 369; second sermon on *John* 16.8-11.

[53] *LXXX Sermons,* p. 132; sermon on *Job* 16.17-19.

wrote, "I presume you rather try what you can doe in me, then what I can doe in verse; you know my uttermost when it was best, and even then I did best when I had least truth for my subjects. In this present case there is so much truth as it defeats all Poetry. Call therefore this paper by what name you will, and, if it bee not worthy of him, nor of you, nor of mee, smother it, and bee that the sacrifice. If you had commanded mee to have waited on his body to Scotland and preached there, I would have embraced the obligation with more alacrity; But, I thanke you that you would command me that which I was loath to doe..."[54] The poem was entitled "An hymne to the Saints, and to Marquesse Hamylton." Some lines in it find a parallel in various passages of the sermons:

> And if, faire soule, not with first *Innocents*
> Thy station be, but with the *Pænitents,*
> (And, who shall dare to aske then when I am
> Dy'd scarlet in the blood of that pure Lambe,
> Whether that colour, which is scarlet then,
> Were black or white before in eyes of men?)
> When thou rememb'rest what sins thou didst finde
> Amongst those many friends now left behinde,
> And seest such sinners as they are, with thee
> Got thither by repentance, Let it bee
> Thy wish to wish all there, to wish them cleane;
> With *him* a *David,* her a *Magdalen.*[55]

This should be compared with a passage in the Whitsunday sermon which we have assigned to 1625: "...yet when I shall come to the next world, I shall finde...*Mary Magdalen* that had been, I know not what sinner; and *David* that had been all; I leave none so ill in this world, but I may carry one that was, or finde some that had been as ill as they, in heaven; and that blood of Christ Jesus, which hath brought them thither, is offered to them that are here, who may be successors in their repentance, as they are in their sins."[56]

On March 27, a few weeks after Hamilton's death, King James died. On April 2, Donne received a royal command from the new king, Charles the First, to preach before him on the afternoon of Sunday,

---

[54] *Poems,* ed. Grierson, I, 288.

[55] *Ibid.,* I, 289, 290.

[56] Pp. 327–328. See also *XXVI Sermons,* p. 111; sermon on *Matthew* 9.13.

April 3. This was but short notice for so important an occasion, and Donne wrote to his friend Sir Robert Ker begging him to let him spend a little time in his rooms at court before the service, so that he might prepare himself for the ordeal.[57] Ker answered kindly, and invited Donne to dine with him, but Donne refused, writing: "But, in good faith, I do not eat before nor can after, till I have been at home; so much hath my this years debility disabled me, even for receiving favours. After the Sermon, I will steal into my Coach home, and pray that my good purpose may be well accepted, and my defects graciously pardoned."[58]

The King listened to the sermon attentively and devoutly, so the courtiers observed. He was very pale and grave, and all watched him eagerly, for the accession of a new sovereign might mean a reversal of policy both in Church and State. However, he soon signified his approval of Donne's sermon (No. 12 in this volume), and accompanied the message with a command that it should be published. This was done speedily, and it appeared as "The first sermon preached to King Charles, At Saint James: 3° April 1625," the publisher being Thomas Jones, and the printer A. M. (Augustin Matthewes). It was not reprinted in the folios, nor by Alford. Hence it is one of the least familiar of Donne's sermons, even to those who have access to the Folios. The text is chosen from Psalm 11.3: "If the Foundations be destroyed, what can the righteous doe?" Donne reassures his hearers that in truth the foundations of neither Church nor State have been destroyed. Christ is the foundation of the Church, and therefore it cannot be overthrown. The foundation of the State is the Law, and to each hearer Donne says: "Let the *Law* bee sacred to thee, and the Dispensers of the *Law,* reverend; Keepe the *Law,* and the *Law* shall keepe thee; And so *Foundations* being never destroyed, the Righteous shall doe still, as they have done, enjoy their Possessions, and Honours, and themselves, by the overshadowing of the *Lawe,* which is the *Foundation* of the second *House,* the *State.*"[59] It would have been well for the young King if he had remembered this respect for the Law in later years, but at the moment he was full of good resolutions, and his sub-

---

[57] *Letters* (1651), pp. 313, 314. (Gosse, *Life and Letters,* II, 219.)
[58] *Letters,* p. 311. (Gosse, II, 220.)
[59] P. 259.

OLD ST. PAUL'S: THE CHOIR, FACING EAST
From an engraving by Hollar, 1656. Reproduced in Arthur M. Hind's
Wenceslaus Hollar (1922).

jects were pleased with him, for his projected marriage with Henrietta Maria was far more popular than the detested Spanish match, which James the First had first designed, and had then broken off.

The sermon (No. 13) preached at St. Paul's "in the Evening, upon Easter-day, 1625" is a good example of Donne's quieter manner. It contains no prose poems such as the paean on God's mercy which distinguishes the Christmas sermon of 1624, but it is full of intellectual vigor and sound sense. It is marked by some of Donne's acutest remarks on the relation of body and soul. Donne has sometimes been accused of an undue depreciation of the body in his sermons, but here he lays emphasis on the dignity of the body and its high value in God's sight.

"That God, all Spirit, served with Spirits, associated to Spirits, should have such an affection, such a love to this body, this earthly body, this deserves this wonder. The Father was pleased to breathe into this body, at first, in the Creation; The Son was pleased to assume this body himself, after, in the Redemption; The Holy Ghost is pleased to consecrate this body, and make it his Temple, by his sanctification ..."[60] This leads him to condemn an excessive asceticism, by which men torture their own bodies, and a harshness which leads men to work their servants or laborers too hard. He condemns the weakening and deforming of the body by lust and intemperance, and also the excessive adorning of the body by the use of paint and cosmetics. He has also a word of rebuke for parsimonious "Heires and Executors" who neglect "the respect and duties, belonging to the dead bodies of Gods Saints, in a decent and comely accompanying them to convenient Funerals," and who "pretend better employments of that, which would be, (say they) vainly spent so."[61] He sums up this section of his sermon in a forceful paragraph: "... marvell at this, at the wonderfull love of God to the body of man, and thou wilt favour it so, as not to macerate thine owne body, with uncommanded and inhumane flagellations, and whippings, nor afflict their bodies, who are in thy charge, with inordinate labour; thou wilt not dishonour this body, as it is Christs body, nor deforme it, as it is thine owne, with intemperance, but thou wilt behave thy selfe towards it

---

[60] Pp. 265–266.
[61] P. 269.

so, as towards one, whom it hath pleased the King to honour, with a resurrection ..."[62]

There is one part of this discussion of the dignity of the body which shows Donne's interest in the social and moral aspect of a legal practice which, though it still survived in the reign of Charles the First, and was not finally discontinued until 1640,[63] was beginning to trouble the consciences of sensitive souls. This was the practice of using torture to extort a confession from a prisoner—a practice so universal throughout the Middle Ages that it is strange to think that as far back as St. Augustine Christians had seen the folly and injustice of the method. Donne justifies his own attack on the practice by the example of his favorite saint: "S. *Augustine* moves a question, and institutes a disputation, and carries it somewhat problematically, whether torture be to be admitted at all, or no. That presents a faire probability, which he sayes against it: we presume, sayes he, that an innocent man should be able to hold his tongue in torture; That is no part of our purpose in torture, sayes he, that hee that is innocent, should accuse himselfe, by confession, in torture. And, if an innocent man be able to doe so, why should we not thinke, that a guilty man, who shall save his life, by holding his tongue in torture, should be able to doe so? And then, where is the use of torture?"[64]

Donne continues with Augustine's exposition of the injustice of this horrible practice: "And whereas, many times, the passion of the Judge, and the covetousnesse of the Judge, and the ambition of the Judge, are calamities heavy enough, upon a man, that is accused, in this case of torture, *Ignorantia Iudicis est calamitas plerumque innocentis,* sayes that Father, for the most part, even the ignorance of the Judge, is the greatest calamity of him that is accused: If the Judge knew that he were innocent, he should suffer nothing; If he knew he were guilty, he should not suffer torture; but because the Judge is ignorant, and knowes nothing, therefore the Prisoner must bee racked, and tortured, and mangled, sayes that Father."[65]

---

[62] P. 271.

[63] "It has never been abolished by Act of Parliament in England, for ... it has never been the law of our country: when used it was always carried out by the order of the King as one of the rights he claimed as pertaining to his position." L. A. Parry, *History of Torture in England,* pp. 32–33.

[64] P. 266.

[65] P. 267.

We may wonder that Donne should need to support his argument by the authority of St. Augustine, but we must remember that he had been a law student at Lincoln's Inn, and that he was familiar with the usual legal prejudice in favor of an established practice, which has made the path of legal reform so thorny and difficult.

The sermon as a whole, like all Donne's Easter sermons, is firmly based on that article of the Christian faith as expressed in the Apostles' Creed, "I believe in the resurrection of the body." This particular sermon is not concerned with Christ's own resurrection from the dead. We note that it was preached on the evening of Easter Day, and probably the morning preacher at St. Paul's had dealt already with that side of the Easter message. Donne concerns himself here with two kinds of resurrection which the Christian believer is to experience—a resurrection of the soul from sin, which takes place in this life, and a resurrection of the body after death, for which he must await the Last Day.

A few days later, Donne preached at Denmark House, shortly before the body of King James was removed from it for burial. Denmark House was in Westminster, and had formerly been known as Somerset House, after its earlier owner, the Protector Somerset. In 1596, Queen Elizabeth granted the keeping of the house to her kinsman, Lord Hunsdon, for life. Later, James I gave it to his Queen, Anne of Denmark, and commanded that it be called Denmark House. Of Donne's sermon (No. 14) Dr. Jessopp wrote, "A greater contrast than this beautiful sermon offers to the fulsome and almost profane oration which the Bishop of Lincoln (Williams) delivered at Westminster Abbey can hardly be imagined."[66] Indeed it is only by comparing Donne's sermons with those of his immediate contemporaries that we can realize how comparatively sober and restrained was the eulogy which Donne delivered on the dead king.

Donne chose a text from Canticles, "Goe forth ye Daughters of Sion, and behold King Solomon, with the Crown, wherewith his mother crowned him, in the day of his espousals and in the day of the gladnesse of his heart." The choice suggests a delicate allusion to the fact that James for his learning and his pacific policy had been called "the British Solomon," but Donne devotes most of his sermon to

[66] Jessopp, *John Donne*, p. 17.

Old St. Paul's, from Bankside
Detail from an engraving by Hollar, 1647. Reproduced in Arthur M.
Hind's *Wenceslaus Hollar* (1922).

Christ as prefigured by Solomon. "...*Behold King Solomon; Solomon* the sonne of *David*, but not the Son of *Bathsheba*, but of a better Mother, the most blessed *Virgin Mary*. For, *Solomon*, in this text, is not a *proper* Name, but an *Appellative;* a significative word: *Solomon* is *pacificus*, the *Peacemaker*, and our peace is made in, and by Christ Jesus...Now, as Saint *Paul* says, that *he would know nothing but Christ*...and then he would know nothing of Christ, but *him crucifyed*...so we seek no other glasse, to see our selves in, but Christ, nor any other thing in this glasse, but his *Humiliation*. What need we? Even that, his lowest humiliation, his death, is expressed here, in three words of exaltation, It is a *Crown*, it is a *Mariage*, it is the *gladnesse of heart: Behold King Salomon crowned* ..."[67] It is only at the close that Donne turns to the commemoration of the dead King, and then in a sufficiently dignified manner. "But then the hand of God, hath *not set up*, but *laid down another Glasse*, wherein thou maist see thy self...Christ, who was the other glasse, *is like thee in every thing*, but not absolutely, for *sinne* is *excepted;* but in this glasse presented now (*The Body of our Royall*, but *dead Master and Soveraigne*) we cannot, we doe not except sinne....Those therefore that are like thee in all things, subject to humane *infirmities*, subject to *sinnes*, and yet are translated, and *translated* by *Death*, to everlasting *Joy*, and *Glory*, are nearest and clearest glasses for thee, to see thy self in; and such is this glasse, which God hath proposed to thee, in this house. And therefore, change the word of the Text, in a letter or two, from *Egredimini*, to *Ingredimini;* never go forth to see, but *Go in and see a Solomon crowned with his mothers crown* ..."[68]

On May 8, Donne preached the first of his "Prebend Sermons." As Dean Donne was one of the thirty prebendaries of St. Paul's, "The Psalter was divided up among the thirty prebendaries, each of whom was supposed to recite his five psalms daily, and to make them his special subject of meditation. Donne took his place in the Chapter as prebendary of Chiswick, and his five psalms were the 62nd to the 66th. inclusive."[69]

This was a congenial task for Donne, who has told us that the Psalms were his favorite reading in the Old Testament. "I acknowl-

[67] Pp. 286–287.
[68] Pp. 289–290.
[69] Jessopp, *John Donne*, p. 141.

edge, that my spirituall appetite carries me still, upon the *Psalms of David,* for a first course, for the Scriptures of the Old Testament: and upon the *Epistles of Saint Paul,* for a second course, for the New, and my meditations even for these *publike exercises* to Gods Church, re-turne oftnest to these two." He justifies this preference by the examples of St. Augustine and St. Chrysostom, and adds, "I may have another more particular reason, because they are Scriptures, written in such forms, as I have been most accustomed to; Saint *Pauls* being Letters, and *Davids* being Poems; for, God gives us, not onely that which is meerly necessary, but that which is convenient too."[70]

Donne began this sermon (No. 15) by praising the Psalter as a whole, and by explaining to his congregation that he proposed from time to time to preach on texts taken from his five special psalms "for some testimony, that those my five Psalmes returne often into my meditation." Though he took as his text the ninth verse, which speaks of men as "lighter than vanity," he gave utterance to an eloquent description of man as "a great thing, a noble Creature" in his relation to God's purpose: "... When we see Man made The Love of the Father, The Price of the Sonne, The Temple of the Holy Ghost, The Signet upon Gods hand, The Apple of Gods eye, Absolutely, uncon-ditionally we cannot annihilate man, not evacuate, not evaporate, not extenuate man to the levity, to the vanity, to the nullity of this Text (*Surely men altogether, high and low, are lighter then vanity.*) For, man is not onely a contributary Creature, but a totall Creature; He does not onely make one, but he is all; He is not a piece of the world, but the world it selfe; and next to the glory of God, the reason why there is a world."[71]

Donne preached again on Whitsunday, which fell on June 5, but our assumption that the sermon which we have printed as No. 16 belongs here, is conjectural. It belongs to this period, and it has certain links with other sermons of this year, especially with that preached on March 4 (No. 11), in which Donne had dwelt on the essential goodness of God and on the fact that everything made by God is good. Here Donne says: "Thou canst not be so absolutely, so intirely, so

---

[70] *Fifty Sermons,* pp. 151 (wrongly numbered as 159)–152; sermon on *Psalms* 38.2.

[71] Pp. 297–298.

essentially sinfull, as God is absolutely, and intirely, and essentially mercifull. Doe what thou canst, there is still some goodnesse in thee; that nature that God made, is good still; Doe God what hee will, hee cannot strip himselfe, not devest himselfe of mercy."[72] Moreover, the passage in which David and Mary Magdalen are linked together[73] is reminiscent of the *Hymne to the Saints, and to Marquess Hamylton,* written in March 1624/1625. There is also a return to Donne's polemical manner, which suits with the fact that after the abandonment of the Spanish marriage project and the outbreak of war with Spain the penal laws against recusants were put in force again. This seems to be the meaning of Donne's words in this sermon: "...But then, this is our comfort still, that where their perversnesse shall endanger either Church or State, both the State and Church may ... and will return to those means which God allows them for their preservation, that is, *To whet the edge of the Iron,* in execution of the laws."[74]

After this we have an interval of six months before the Christmas Day sermon, 1625 (No. 17). This year there was a special reason for a longer interval than the usual summer recess. London was visited by an epidemic of plague, which was probably more terrible than any except the Great Plague of 1665. During April and May there had been a steady increase in the number of deaths recorded, and in June the mortality rose much more rapidly.[75] Nevertheless, the arrival of the new Queen, Henrietta Maria, from France, and the opening of Parliament kept many people in London during June. Charles the First met his bride at Dover on June 13, and three days later they entered London by water. The citizens were ordered to indulge in suitable rejoicings, bonfires were lit in the streets, and the City bells rang continuously for seven hours.[76] Parliament assembled on June 18, sat for three weeks, and was adjourned on July 11 to meet at Oxford on August 1, though most members had left London a week or more before the adjournment,[77] owing to their fear of the plague.

---

[72] Pp. 329–330.

[73] See above, p. 22.

[74] P. 322.

[75] For a detailed account of the epidemic see F. P. Wilson, *The Plague in Shakespeare's London,* pp. 132–173.

[76] *Ibid.,* p. 135.

[77] S. P. Dom. Chas. I, Vol. IV, Doc. 29.

Trinity Term had been adjourned on June 18, and six days later all trials by jury were abandoned.[78] In July more than 5,000 people died of the plague in London itself, and in August the number rose to 19,000. The mortality was proportionally as great in what were then the outlying districts of Westminster, Lambeth, Stepney, and Islington.[79]

The general terror was increased by lack of any proper understanding of the cause of an epidemic of plague. The plague bacillus was not isolated till as late as 1894, and it was only then that the discovery was made that bubonic plague is a disease of rats, and that the infection is transmitted from rat to rat and from rat to man by the bite of rat fleas. The plague may be transmitted from place to place by fleas which are carried by people on their persons or in their baggage. In the seventeenth century no one in England suspected the rat as a cause of infection. Some thought that the plague was due to sin, and that it might be likened to God's arrow flying through the air. Others held that the cause was to be found in the planets. According to them, the plague of 1625 "was the consequence of a great *Conjunction* of *Saturn, Jupiter,* and *Mars,* in the Celestial Sign *Leo,* a sign of the fiery triplicity, and representing the heart in the *Microcosme.*"[80] Another theory assigned the plague to the corruption of the air "by a hidden and secret propertie," and this took place especially when the air was hot and moist. There was, however, a general consensus that whatever might be the cause of the plague, it was transmitted by infected persons to those who were well; that segregation was the remedy in the first place, and if the epidemic became general, flight from the city was the only wise course. This was the view of the authorities, and elaborate plague orders were issued to secure segregation. The Court and Parliament took the lead in forsaking London. A solemn fast was held on July 2, 1625, and the King himself, with the Lords of the Upper House and the Judges, heard two sermons in the Abbey, while the House of Commons heard three sermons, the first of three hours, and the other two of two hours each, in St. Margaret's, Westminster. After this ordeal most of the members left London without waiting for the formal adjournment on July 11, and the Court moved

[78] Wilson, *op. cit.,* p. 136.
[79] *Ibid.,* p. 137.
[80] John Gadbury, *London's Deliverance predicted,* quoted by F. P. Wilson, *op. cit.,* p. 6.

first to Hampton Court, which became infected, then to Oatlands, to Windsor, and finally to Woodstock near Oxford, where it remained while Parliament sat at Oxford during the first part of August. Rich and poor fled from stricken London, so that at last almost all the shops were shut and the streets were as deserted at mid-day as they were ordinarily at three o'clock in the morning. The usual sounds of cheerful traffic were stilled, and "in their stead were heard the howling of dogs, the raving of the sick, and the mourning of the bereaved.... In Cheapside it was almost impossible to change a piece of gold, and if spice were needed to make comfortable Broth, it was not to be had: for all the grocers had fled."[81]

Meanwhile, the scum of the great city, the criminals and the vagabonds, set about looting the empty houses. Donne has a vivid passage on this in his "First Sermon after our Dispersion, by the Sickness" (No. 18): "... even in this City, no doubt but the hand of God fell upon thousands in this deadly infection, who were no more affected with it, then those *Egyptians,* to cry out, *Omnes Moriemur,* We can but die, and we must die: And ... *Let us eat and drink, and take our pleasure,* and make our profits, *for to morrow we shall die,* and so were cut off by the hand of God, some even in their robberies, in halfempty houses; and in their drunkenness in voluptuous and riotous houses; and in their lusts and wantonness in licentious houses; and so took in infection and death, like *Judas's* sop, death dipt and soaked in sin. Men whose lust carried them into the jaws of infection in lewd houses, and seeking one sore perished with another; men whose rapine and covetousness broke into houses, and seeking the Wardrobes of others, found their own winding-sheet, in the infection of that house where they stole their own death; men who sought no other way to divert sadness, but strong drink in riotous houses, and there drank up *Davids* cup of Malediction, the cup of Condemned men, of death, in the infection of that place."[82]

He has also left us an account of the flight of the citizens in a letter written to Sir Thomas Roe on November 25, 1625: "... the Citizens fled away, as out of a house on fire, and stuffed their pockets with their best ware, and threw themselves into the highways, and were not received, so much as into barns, and perished so, some of them

---

[81] Wilson, *op. cit.,* pp. 151–152.
[82] P. 359.

with more money about them than would have bought the village where they died. A Justice of peace—into his Examination it fell—told me of one that died so, with 1400 l. about him. I scattered my family, and ... removed for a time to Chelsea, where within a few weeks the infection multiplied so fast, as that it was no good Manners to go to any other place, and so I have been in a secular Monastery ... the infection hath made this village so infamous as that I go not to Court, though it be at Hampton."[83]

At Chelsea, Donne stayed in the house of his good friends Sir John and Lady Danvers. Before her second marriage Lady Danvers had been Magdalen Herbert, mother of George Herbert and of Lord Herbert of Cherbury. Donne employed his enforced leisure and seclusion by going through the notes of his sermons, and writing them out in full for the use of his elder son John, who was at this time an undergraduate of Christ Church, Oxford, and who was beginning to show signs of intellectual promise by contributing Latin poems to three volumes which were published in 1623, 1624, and 1625, respectively.

In December, Donne wrote to Sir Henry Goodyer contradicting a report of his own death: "The report of my death hath thus much of truth in it, that though I be not dead, yet I am buried; within a few weeks after I immured my self in this house, the infection strook into the town, into so many houses, as that it became ill manners to make any visits. Therefore I never went to *Knoll,* nor *Hanworth,* nor *Kenton,* nor to the Court, since the Court came into these quarters, nor am yet come to *London;* therefore I am little able to give you account of high stages. ... Mr. *George Herbert* is here at the receipt of your letter, and with his service to you, tells you that all of *Uvedall* House are well."[84] This seems to be the first mention of George Herbert in any of Donne's writings.

On Christmas Day Donne preached at St. Paul's (No. 17). He opened his sermon with an eloquent passage on the nature of eternity, and the eternal generation of the Son of God. On the whole, however, the sermon is less interesting than most of Donne's Christmas ser-

[83] *S. P. Dom. Chas. I,* Vol. X, Doc. 28. The letter is quoted in full by Gosse, *Life and Letters of John Donne,* II, 222–225.
[84] *Letters* (1651), pp. 233–236. (Gosse, II, 226–228.)

mons, and Coleridge severely criticized the puerility of some of its statements. Thus on the remark (on p. 334) about a "barbarous and inhumane custome" of the Jews, he wrote: "Is it possible that Donne could have given credit to this absurd legend? It was, I am aware, not an age of critical *acumen*.... Still, that a man like Donne should have imposed on himself such a set of idle tales, as he has collected in the next paragraph for facts of history, is scarcely credible; that he should have attempted to impose them on others, is most melancholy."[85]

Donne made no mention of the plague in this discourse. He reserved his reflections for the sermon which he preached three weeks later at St. Dunstan's (No. 18), which is entitled "The First Sermon after our Dispersion, by the Sickness." It is a powerful discourse on the text "For there was not a house where there was not one dead." There are in it some gruesome passages, such as: "... consider upon what ground you tread; upon ground so holy, as that all the ground is made of the bodies of Christians, and therein hath received a second consecration. Every puff of wind within these walls, may blow the father into the sons eys, or the wife into her husbands, or his into hers, or both into their childrens, or their childrens into both. Every grain of dust that flies here, is a piece of a Christian; you need not distinguish your Pews by figures; you need not say, I sit within so many of such a neighbour, but I sit within so many inches of my husbands, or wives, or childes, or friends grave. Ambitious men never made more shift for places in Court, then dead men for graves in Churches; and as in our later times, we have seen two and two almost in every Place and Office, so almost every Grave is oppressed with twins ... so in this lamentable calamity, the dead were buried, and thrown up again before they were resolved to dust, to make room for more."[86] This is doleful enough, but Donne passes from his morbid contemplation of the dead to give consolation to the mourners: "... we forbid not that office of the eye, that holy tenderness, to weep for them that are so dead. But there was a part in every one of them, that could not die; which the God of life, who breathed it into them, from his own mouth, hath suck'd into his own bosome.... When time shall be no more, when death shall be no more, they shall renew,

---

[85] Coleridge, *Notes on the English Divines*, I, 76.
[86] P. 362.

or rather continue their being. ... And our afternoon shall be as long as Gods forenoon; for, as God never saw beginning, so we shall never see end; but they whom we tread upon now, and we whom others shall tread upon hereafter, shall meet at once, where, though we were dead, dead in our several houses, dead in a sinful *Egypt,* dead in our family, dead in our selves, dead in the Grave, yet we shall be received, with that consolation, and glorious consolation, you were dead, but are alive. *Enter ye blessed into the Kingdom, prepared for you, from the beginning.*"[87]

_____

[87] Pp. 362–364.

The Sermons

Number 1.

Preached upon the Penitentiall Psalmes.
[April, May, or June, 1623]

PSAL. 6.8, 9, 10. *DEPART FROM ME, ALL YE WORKERS OF INIQUITIE; FOR THE LORD HATH HEARD THE VOYCE OF MY WEEPING.*

THE LORD HATH HEARD MY SUPPLICATION; THE LORD WILL RECEIVE MY PRAYER.

LET ALL MINE ENEMIES BE ASHAMED AND SORE VEXED: LET THEM RETURNE AND BE ASHAMED SUDDENLY.

THIS IS *Davids* profligation and discomfiture of his enemies; this is an act of true honour, a true victory, a true triumph, to keepe the field, to make good one station, and yet put the enemy to flight. A man may perchance be safe in a Retrait, but the honour, the victory, the triumph lies in enforcing the enemy to fly. To that is *David* come here, to such a thankfull sense of a victory; in which we shall first consider *Davids* thankfulnesse, that is, his manner of declaring Gods mercy, and his security in that mercy; which manner is, that he durst come to an open defiance, and protestation, and hostility, without modifications, or disguises, *Depart from me all yee workers of iniquity.* And then, secondly, we shall see his reason, upon which he grounded this confidence, and this spirituall exultation, which was a pregnant reason, a reason that produced another reason; *The Lord hath heard my supplication, the Lord will heare my prayer;* upon no premises doth any conclusion follow, so logically, so sincerely, so powerfully, so imperiously, so undeniably, as upon this, *The Lord hath, and therefore the Lord will.* But then what was

39

this prayer? that wee may know, whether it were a prayer to be drawne into practise, and imitation, or no. It is not argument enough, ²⁰ that it was so, because God heard it then; for we are not bound, nay, we are not allowed to pray all such prayers, as good men have prayed, and as God hath heard. But here the prayer was this, *Let all mine enemies be ashamed, and sore vexed, let them returne, and be ashamed suddenly.* But this is a malediction, an imprecation of mischiefe upon others; and will good men pray so? or will God heare that? Because that is an holy probleme, and an usefull intergatory, we shall make it a third part, or a conclusion rather, to enquire into the nature, and into the avowablenesse, and exemplarinesse of this, in which *David* seemes to have been transported with some passion.

Divisio ³⁰ So that our parts will be three, the building it selfe, *Davids* thankesgiving in his exultation, and declaration, *Depart from mee all yee workers of iniquitie;* and then the foundation of this building, *For God hath heard, and therefore God will heare;* and lastly, the prospect of this building, *David* contemplates and lookes over againe the prayer that he had made, and in a cleare understanding, and in a rectified Conscience, he finds that he may persist in that prayer, and he doth so: *Let all mine enemies be ashamed, and sore vexed, let them returne, and be ashamed suddenly.*

I. Part   First then we consider *Davids* thankfulnesse: But why is it so long ⁴⁰ before *David* leads us to that consideration? Why hath he deferred so primary a duty, to so late a place, to so low a roome, to the end of the Psalme? The Psalme hath a Deprecatory part, that God would forbeare him, and a Postulatory part, that God would heare him, and grant some things to him, and a Gratulatory part, a sacrifice of thanksgiving. Now the Deprecatory part is placed in the first place, *Vers.* I. For if it were not so, if we should not first ground that, *That God should not rebuke us in his anger, nor chasten us in his hot displeasure,* but leave our selves open to his indignation, and his judgements, wee could not live to come to a second petition; our sinnes, ⁵⁰ and judgements due to our sinnes, require our first consideration; therefore *David* begins with the deprecatory prayer, That first Gods anger may be removed: but then, that deprecatory prayer, wherein he desired God to forbeare him, spends but one verse of the Psalme; *David* would not insist upon that long: When I have penitently con-

fest my sinnes, I may say with *Iob, My flesh is not brasse, nor my bones* [Job 6.12]
stones, that I can beare the wrath of the Lord; but yet I must say with
Iob too, *If the Lord kill me, yet will I trust in him.* God hath not [Job 13.15]
asked me, What shall I doe for thee, but of himselfe he hath done
more, then I could have proposed to my selfe in a wish, or to him in
60 a prayer. Nor will I aske God, *Quousque,* how long shall my foes
increase? how long wilt thou fight on their side against me? but
surrender my selfe entirely, in an *adveniat regnum,* and a *fiat voluntas, thy kingdome come,* and *thy will be done. David* makes it his
first worke, to stay Gods anger in a deprecatory prayer, but he stayes
not upon that long, he will not prescribe his Physitian, what he shall
prescribe to him, but leaves God to his own medicines, and to his
own methode. But then the Postulatory prayer, what he begs of God,
employes six verses: as well to shew us, that our necessities are many;
as also that if God doe not answer us, at the beginning of our prayer,
70 our duty is still to pursue that way, to continue in prayer. And then
the third part of the Psalme, which is the Gratulatory part, his giving of thanks, is, shall we say deferred, or rather reserved to the end
of the Psalme, and exercises onely those three verses which are our
Text. Not that the duty of thanksgiving is lesse then that of prayer;
for if we could compare them, it is rather greater; because it con-
tributes more to Gods glory, to acknowledge by thanks, that God
hath given, then to acknowledge by prayer, that God can give. But
therefore might *David* be later and shorter here, in expressing that
duty of thanks, first, because being reserved to the end, and close of
80 the Psalme, it leaves the best impression in the memory. And therefore it is easie to observe, that in all Metricall compositions, of which
kinde the booke of Psalmes is, the force of the whole piece, is for the
most part left to the shutting up; the whole frame of the Poem is a
beating out of a piece of gold, but the last clause is as the impression
of the stamp, and that is it that makes it currant. And then also, because out of his abundant manner of expressing his thankfulnesse to
God, in every other place thereof, his whole booke of Psalmes is
called, *Sepher tehillim,* a booke of praise and thanksgiving, he might
reserve his thanks here to the last place; And lastly, because naturall
90 and morall men are better acquainted with the duty of gratitude, of
thanksgiving, before they come to the Scriptures, then they are with

the other duty of repentance, which belongs to Prayer; for in all *Solomons* bookes, you shall not finde halfe so much of the duty of thankfulnesse, as you shall in *Seneca* and in *Plutarch*. No book of Ethicks, of morall doctrine, is come to us, wherein there is not, almost in every leafe, some detestation, some Anathema against ingratitude; but of repentance, not a word amongst them all. And therefore in that dutie of prayer, which presumes repentance, (for he must stand *Rectus in curia* that will pray) *David* hath insisted longest; and be-

100 cause he would enter, and establish a man, upon a confidence in God, he begins with a deprecation of his anger; for but upon that ground, no man can stand; and because he would dismisse him with that which concerns him most, he chooseth to end in a Thanksgiving.

Gratiæ actæ

Therefore at last he comes to his thanks. Now this is so poore a duty, if we proportion it to the infinitenesse of Gods love unto us, our

Bernar.

thanks, as we may justly call it nothing at all. But *Amor Dei affectus, non contractus,* The love of God is not a contract, a bargaine, he looks for nothing againe, and yet he looks for thanks, for that is nothing, because there is nothing done in it, it is but speaking; *Gratias dicere,*

August.

110 *est gratias agere,* To utter our thanks to God, is all our performance

Philo Iudæ.

of thankfulnesse. It is not so amongst us; *Vix, aut nunquam apud nos purum, & merum beneficium;* Every man that gives, gives out

Martial

of designe, and as it conduces to his ends: *Donat in hamo,* There is a hook in every benefit, that sticks in his jawes that takes that benefit, and drawes him whither the Benefactor will. God looks for nothing, nothing to be done in the way of exact recompence, but yet, as he that makes a Clock, bestowes all that labour upon the severall wheeles, that thereby the Bell might give a sound, and that thereby the hand might give knowledge to others how the time passes; so this is the

120 principall part of that thankfulnesse, which God requires from us, that we make open declarations of his mercies, to the winning and confirming of others.

Discedite

This *David* does in this noble and ingenuous publication, and prot- estation, I have strength enough, and company enough, power enough, and pleasure enough, joy enough, and treasure enough, honour enough, and recompence enough in my God alone, in him I shall surely have all which you can pretend to give, and therefore *Discedite à me, Depart from me all ye workers of iniquity;* Here is then first,

a valediction, a parting with his old company, but it is a valediction,
¹³⁰ with a malediction, with an imprecation of Gods Justice, upon their
contempts and injuries. There was in the mouth of Christ, sometimes,
such a *Discede,* such an *Abito,* as that farewell was a welcome; as
when he said to the Ruler, *Abito, Goe thy way, thy son liveth;* And
when he said to the woman, *Goe in peace, thy faith hath saved thee.*
This going was a staying with him still; Here the *Abite,* and *Venite*
was all one. He that goes about his worldly businesse, and goes about
them in Gods name, in the feare and favour of God, remaines in
Gods presence still. When the Angels of God are sent to visit his
children, in the middest of Sodome, or where they lie, and languish
¹⁴⁰ in sordid and nasty corners, and in the loathsomenesse of corrupt
and infectious diseases, or where they faint in miserable dungeons,
this Commission, this *Discedite,* goe to that Sodome, to that Spittle,
to that Dungeon, puts not those Angels out of the presence of God.
No descent into hell, of what kinde soever you conceive that descent
into hell to have been, put the Son of God out of heaven, by descending into hell; no *Discede,* no Leave, no Commandement that God
gives us, to doe the works of our calling here, excludes us from him;
but as the Saints of God shall follow the Lamb, wheresoever he goes
in heaven, so the Lamb of God shall follow his Saints, wheresoever
¹⁵⁰ they goe upon earth, if they walk sincerely. Christ uses not then as
yet, as long as we are in this world, this *Discede* of *David,* to bid any
man, any sinner to depart from him: But there shall come a time,
when Christ shall take *Davids Discede,* the words of this Text into
his mouth, with as much and more bitternesse then *David* does here,
Nescivi vos, I never knew yee, and therefore *Depart from me yee*
workers of iniquity.

So have you his Protestation, his Proclamation, They must avoid;
but who? Who be these that *David* dismisses here? Take them to
be those of his owne house, his Servants, and Officers in neare places,
¹⁶⁰ whose service he had used to ill purposes, (as *Davids* Person, and
Rank, and History directs us upon that Consideration) and we shall
finde all such persons, wrapt up in this danger, that they dare not
discharge themselves, they dare not displace, nor disgrace those men,
to whom by such imployments, they have given that advantage over
themselves, as that it is not safe to them, to offend such a servant.

John 4.50
Luke 7.50

[Apoc. 14.4]

[Mat. 7.23]

Servi sui

Polybius — *Naturâ nec hostem habet, nec amicum rex,* says a wise Statesman; In nature, (that is, in the nature of greatnesse, and, as great) great persons consider no man to be so much a friend, nor to be so much an enemy, but that they will fall out with that friend, and be recon-

170 ciled to that enemy, to serve their own turne, sayes that Statesman. But yet when great Persons trust servants with such secret actions, as may bring them into contempt at home, or danger abroad, by those vices, if they should be published, they cannot come when they would, to this *Discedite, Depart from me all ye workers of iniquity.*

We have this evidently, and unavoidably, we cannot but see it, and say it, in this example which is before us, even in King *David.* He had imployed *Ioab* in such services, as that he stood in feare of him, and

2 Sam. 19. [5–7] — indured at his hands that behaviour, and that language, *Thou hast shamed this day the faces of all thy servants that have saved thy life,*

180 *and thy sons, and daughters, and wives, and concubines, thou regardest neither thy Princes, nor servants; but come out, and speak comfortably unto them, for I sweare by the Lord, except thou doe come out, there will not tarry one man with thee this night.* David indured all this, for he knew that *Ioab* had that letter in his Cabbinet, which he writ to him for the murther of *Vriah,* and he never came to

I Kings 2.[6] — this *Discedite,* to remove *Ioab* from him in his life, but gave it in Commandement to his Son, *Let not Ioabs hoary head goe downe to the grave in peace:* Here is the misery of *David,* he cannot discharge himselfe of that servant when he will, and here the misery of that

190 servant, that at one time or other he will; and he is a short liv'd man, whose ruine a jealous Prince studies. Because the Text invited us, commanded, and constrained us to do so, we put this example in a Court, but we need not dazle our selves with that height; every man in his own house may finde it, that to those servants, which have served him in ill actions, he dares not say, *Discedite, Depart from me ye workers of iniquity.*

Tentatores — Thus then it is; if those whom *David* dismisses here, were his owne servants, it was an expressing of his thankfulnesse to God, and a duty that lay upon him, to deliver himselfe of such servants. But other

200 Expositors take these men, to be men of another sort, men that came

Psal. 69.26 — to triumph over him in his misery, men that *Persecuted him whom God had smitten, and added to the sorrow of him whom God had*

wounded, as himselfe complaines; men that pretended to visit him, yet when they came, *They spoke lies, their hearts gathered iniquity* Psal. 41.6 *to themselves, and when they went abroad they told it;* Men that said to one another, *When shall he dye, and his name perish?* Here also Ver. 5 was a Declaration of the powerfulnesse of Gods Spirit in him, that he could triumph over the Triumpher, and exorcise those evill spirits, and command them away, whose comming was to dishonour God,
210 in his dishonour; and to argue and conclude out of his ruine, that either his God was a weake God, or a cruell God, that he could not, or would not deliver his servants from destruction.

That *David* could command them away, whose errand was to blaspheme God, and whose staying in a longer conversation, might have given him occasion of new sins, either in distrusting Gods mercy towards himselfe, or in murmuring at Gods patience towards them, or perchance in being uncharitably offended with them, and expressing it with some bitternesse, but that in respect of himselfe, and not of Gods glory only, this *Discedite,* Depart from me all such men as do
220 sin in your selves, and may make me sin too, was an act of an heavenly courage, and a thankfull testimony of Gods gracious visiting his soule, inabling him so resolutely to teare himselfe from such persons, as might lead him into tentation.

Neither is this separation of *David,* and this company, partiall; he *Omnes* does not banish those that incline him to one sin, a sin that perchance he is a weary of, or growne unable to proceed in, and retained them that concurre with him in some fresh sin, to which he hath a new appetite. *David* doth not banish them that suckt his Subjects blood, or their money, and retained them that solicite, and corrupt their
230 wives, and daughters; he doth not displace them, who served the vices of his predecessor, and supply those places with instruments of new vices of his owne, but it is *Discedite omnes, Depart all yee workers of iniquity.* Now beloved, when God begins so high as in Kings, he makes this duty the easier to thee; to banish from thee, *All the workers of iniquity.* It is not a *Discede,* that will serve to banish one, and retaine the rest, Nor a *Discedite,* to banish the rest, and retaine one, but *Discedite omnes, Depart all,* for that sinne staies in state, that staies alone, and hath the venome, and the malignity of all the rest contracted in it. It is nothing for a sick man that hath lost his taste, to

²⁴⁰ say, *Discedat gula,* Depart voluptuousnesse; nothing in a consumption
to say, *Discedat luxuria,* Depart wantonnesse; nothing for a Client *in
Forma pauperis,* to say, *Discedat corruptio,* I will not bribe; but
Discedant omnes, Depart all, and all together ye workers of iniquity.

Operantes   But yet *Davids* generall discharge had, and ours must have, a re-
striction, a limitation; it is not (as S. *Ierom* notes upon this place)
Omnes qui operati, but *Omnes operantes,* not all that have wrought
iniquity, but all that continue in doing so still. *David* was not inex-
orable towards those that had offended; what an example should he
have given God against himselfe, if he had beene so? wee must not
²⁵⁰ despise, nor defame men, because they have committed some sin.
When the mercie of God hath wrought upon their sin in the remission
thereof, that leprosie of *Naaman* cleaves to us, their sinne is but trans-
ferred to us, if we will not forgive that which God hath forgiven, for
it is but *Omnes operantes,* all they that continue in their evill wayes.
Rom. 16.17   All these must depart: how far? first, they must be avoided, *Declinate,* saith S. *Paul, I beseech you brethren, marke them diligently
which cause division and offences, and avoid them.* And this corrects
our desire in running after such men, as come with their owne inventions, Schismaticall Separatists, *Declinate,* avoid them; if hee be
²⁶⁰ no such, but amongst our selves, a brother, but yet a worker of iniquity,
I Cor. 5.11   *If any one that is called a brother, be a Fornicator, or covetous, with
such a one eate not.* If we cannot starve him out, wee must thrust him
out; Put away from among you, that wicked man. No conversation at
all is allowed to us, with such a man, as is obstinate in his sin, and
2 Iohn 1.10   incorrigible; no not to bid him God speed, *For he that biddeth him
God speed, is partaker of his evill deeds.* In this divorce, both the
Mat. 5.29–30   generality, and the distance is best exprest by Christ himselfe, *If thine
eye, thine hand, thy foote offend thee, amputandi & projiciendi,* with
what anguish or remorse soever it be done, they must bee *cut off,* and
²⁷⁰ being cut off, *cast away;* it is a divorce and no super-induction, it is a
separating, and no redintegration. Though thou couldest be content
to goe to Heaven with both eyes, (thy selfe, and thy companion) yet
better to goe into Heaven with one, thy selfe alone, then to endanger
thy selfe to be left out for thy companions sake.

Discedite   To conclude this first part, *David* does not say, *Discedam,* but
Discedite, he does not say, that he will depart from them, but he com-

mands them to depart from him. Wee must not thinke to depart from the offices of society, and duties of a calling, and hide our selves in Monasteries, or in retired lives, for feare of tentations; but when a tentation
²⁸⁰ attempts us, to come with that authority, and that powerfull exorcisme of *Nazianzen, Fuge, recede, ne te cruce Christi, ad quam omnia contremiscunt, feriam,* Depart from me, lest the Crosse of Christ, in my hand, overthrow you. For a sober life, and a Christian mortification, and discreet discipline, are crosses derived from the Crosse of Christ Jesus, and animated by it, and may be alwaies in a readinesse to crosse such tentations. In the former descriptions of the manner of our behaviour towards workers of iniquity, there is one *Declinate,* one word that implies a withdrawing of our selves; for that must be done, not out of the world, but out of that ill ayre, we must not put our
²⁹⁰ selves in danger, nor in distance of a tentation; but all the other words, are words of a more active vehemence, *Amputate,* and *Projicite;* it is *Discedite,* and not *Discedam,* a driving away, and not a running away.

    Wee proceed now in our second part, to the reasons of *Davids* confidence, and his opennesse, and his publique declaration; why *David* was content to be rid of all his company; and it was, because he had better; he sayes, *The Lord had heard him;* and first, *He had heard, vocem fletus, the voice of his weeping.* Here is an admirable readinesse in God, that heares a voyce in that, which hath none. They have described God by saying he is all eye, an universall eye, that pierceth
³⁰⁰ into every darke corner; but in darke corners, there is something for him to see; but he is all eare too, and heares even the silent, and speechlesse man, and heares that in that man, that makes no sound, his teares. When *Hezekias* wept, he was turned to the wall, (perchance, because he would not be seene) and yet God bad the Prophet *Esay* tell him, *Vidi lacrymam;* though the text say, *Hezekias wept sore,* yet *Vidit lacrymam,* God saw every single teare, his first teare, and was affected with that. But yet this is more strange; God heard his teares. And therefore the weeping of a penitent sinner, is not improperly called, *Legatio lacrymarum,* An embassage of teares; To Embas-
³¹⁰ sadours belongs an audience, and to these Embassages God gives a gracious audience; *Abyssus abyssum invocat, One depth cals upon another;* And so doth one kinde of teares call upon one another. Teares of sorrow call upon teares of joy, and all call upon God, and bring him

2 Part

Esay 38.
[2–5]

Gregor.

Psal 42.7

to that ready hearing which is implied in the words of this text,
Shamang; a word of that largenesse in the Scriptures, that sometimes
in the Translation of the Septuagint, it signifies hearing, *Shamang,* is
audit, God gives eare to our teares; sometimes it is beleeving, *Shamang,* is *Credit,* God gives faith, and credit to our teares; sometimes
it is Affecting, *Shamang,* is *Miseretur,* God hath mercy upon us for
³²⁰ our teares; sometimes it is Effecting, *Shamang,* is *Respondet,* God
answers the petition of our teares; and sometimes it is Publication,
Shamang, is *Divulgat,* God declares and manifests to others, by his
blessings upon us, the pleasure that he takes in our holy and repentant
teares. And therefore *Lacrymæ fœnus,* sayes S. *Basil,* Teares are that
usury, by which the joyes of Heaven are multiplied unto us; the
preventing Grace, and the free mercy of God, is our stock, and principall; but the Acts of obedience, and mortification, fasting, and
praying, and weeping, are *Fœnus,* (sayes that blessed Father) the
interest, and the increase of our holy joy.

³³⁰   That which we intend in all this, is, that when our heart is well
disposed toward God, God sees our prayers, as they are comming in
the way, before they have any voyce, in our words. When Christ came
to *Lazarus* house, before *Mary* had asked any thing at his hands, as
soone as she had wept, Christ was affected, *He groaned in the spirit,
he was troubled,* and *he wept* too; and he proceeded to the raysing of
Lazarus, before shee asked him; her eyes were his glasse, and he saw
her desire in her tears. There is a kind of simplicity in teares, which
God harkens to, and beleeves. *We know not what we should pray for
as we ought. Quid? nescimus orationem dominicam?* Can we not say
³⁴⁰ the Lords Prayer, sayes S. *Augustin?* Yes, we can say that; but
Nescimus tribulationem prodesse, sayes he, we doe not know the
benefit, that is to be made of tribulation, and tentation, *Et petimus
liberari ab omni malo,* we pray to be delivered from all evill, and we
meane all tribulation, and all tentation, as though all they were alwaies
evill; but in that there may be much error: The sons of *Zebedee*
prayed, but ambitiously, and were not heard; S. *Paul* prayed for the
taking away of the provocation of the flesh, but inconsiderately, and
mist; the Apostles made a request, for fire against the Samaritans,
but uncharitably, and were reproved. But when *Iehosaphat* was come
³⁵⁰ to that perplexity by the Moabites, that he knew not what to doe, nor

Iohn 11.
[33–35]

Rom. 8.26

Mat. 20.22
2 Cor. 12.8
[Luke 9.54–
56]
2 Chro.
20.12

what to say, *Hoc solum residui habemus,* sayes he, *ut oculos nostros dirigamus ad te,* This we can doe, and we need doe no more, wee can turne our eyes to thee. Now whether he directed those eyes in looking to him, or in weeping to him, God heares the voyce of our looks, God heares the voyce of our teares, sometimes better then the voyce of our words; for it is the *Spirit it selfe that makes intercession for us,* Rom. 8.26 *Gemitibus inenarrabilibus,* In those *groanes,* and so in those teares, which we *cannot utter; Ineloquacibus,* as *Tertullian* reads that place, devout, and simple teares, which cannot speak, speake aloud in the 360 eares of God; nay, teares which we cannot utter; not onely not utter the force of the teares, but not utter the very teares themselves. As God sees the water in the spring in the veines of the earth, before it bubble upon the face of the earth; so God sees teares in the heart of a man, before they blubber his face; God heares the teares of that sorrowfull soule, which for sorrow cannot shed teares.

From this casting up of the eyes, and powring out the sorrow of the *Supplicatio* heart at the eyes, at least, opening God a window, through which he may see a wet heart through a dry eye; from these overtures of repentance, which are as those unperfect sounds of words, which Parents 370 delight in, in their Children, before they speake plaine, a penitent sinner comes to a verball, and a more expresse prayer. To these prayers, these vocall and verball prayers from *David,* God had given eare, and from this hearing of those prayers was *David* come to this thankfull confidence, *The Lord hath heard, the Lord will heare.* Now, Beloved, this prayer which *David* speaks of here, which our first translation calls a *Petition,* is very properly rendred in our second translation, a *Supplication;* for Supplications were *à Suppliciis;* Supplications amongst the Gentiles were such sacrifices, as were made to the gods, out of confiscations, out of the goods of those men, upon whom the 380 State had inflicted any pecuniary or capitall punishment. *Supplicationes, à Suppliciis;* and therefore this prayer which *David* made to God, when his hand was upon him, in that heavy correction, and calamitie, which occasioned this Psalme, is truly and properly called a *Supplication,* that is, a Prayer, or Petition, that proceeds from suffering.

And if God have heard his supplication, if God have regarded him then, when he was in his displeasure, if God have turned to him, when

he was turned from him, and stroakt him with the same hand that
struck him, God will much more perfect his own worke, and grant his
390 prayer after; if God would endure to looke upon him in his deformitie,
he will delight to looke upon him then, when he hath shed the light
and the lovelinesse of his owne countenance upon him: It is the

Rom. 5.10

Apostles argument, as well as *Davids, If when we were enemies, we
were reconciled to God, by the death of his Sonne, much more being
reconciled, we shall be saved by his life.* When *David* found, that God
had heard his *Supplications,* the voyce of his suffering, of his punishment, he was sure he would heare his *Prayer,* the voyce of his thankfulnesse too.

Oratio

And this was *Davids* second reason, for his alacrity, and confidence,
400 that God would never be weary of hearing, he had heard him, and he
would heare him still, he had heard the *Supplication,* and he would
heare his *Prayer;* for this word, which signifies *Prayer* here, is derived
from *Palal,* which signifies properly *Separare:* As his *Supplication* was
acceptable, which proceeded *à Suppliciis,* from a sense of his afflictions;
so this *Prayer,* which came *Post separationem,* after he had separated,
and divorced himselfe from his former company, after his *Discedite,*
his discharging of all the workers of iniquitie, must necessarily be
better accepted at Gods hand. He that heares a Suppliant, that is, a
man in misery, and does some small matter for the present ease of that
410 man, and proceeds no farther, *Ipsum quod dedit, perit,* That which
he gave is lost, it is drowned by that floud of misery that overflows and
surrounds that wretched man, he is not the better to morrow for to
dayes almes, *Et vitam producit ad miseriam,* that very almes prolongs
his miserable life still; without to dayes almes, he should not have
had a to morrow to be miserable in. Now, *Christ* onely is the *Samari-*

Luk. 10.33

tane which perfected his cure upon the wounded man: *He saw him,*
sayes the text, so did the rest that passed by him; but, *He had compassion on him;* so he might, and yet actually have done him no
good; but, *He went to him;* so he might too, and then out of a delicate-
420 nesse or fastidiousnesse, have gone from him againe; but (to contract)
he bound up his wounds, he powred in oyle and wine, he put him
upon his own beast, he brought him to an Inne, made provision for
him, gave the Host money before-hand, gave him charge to have a care
of him, and (which is the perfection of all, the greatest testimony of

our *Samaritans* love to us) he promised to come againe, and at that
comming, he does not say, *He will pay,* but *He will recompence,*
which is a more abundant expressing of his bountie. Christ loves not
but in the way of marriage; if he begin to love thee, he tells thee,
Sponsabo te mihi, I will marry thee unto me, and *Sponsabo in æter-*
⁴³⁰ *num, I will marry thee for ever.* For it is a marriage that prevents all
mistakings, and excludes all impediments, *I will marry thee in righteousnesse, and in judgement, and in loving kindnesse, and in mercies,
and in faithfulnesse;* many, and great assurances. And as it is added,
Seminabo te mihi, which is a strange expressing of Gods love to us,
I will sow thee unto me in the earth; when I have taken thee into my
husbandry, thou shalt increase, and multiply, *Seminabo te,* and all that
thou doest produce, shall be directed upon me, *Seminabo te mihi, I will
sowe thee to my selfe:* therefore thy soule may be bold to joyne with
David in that thankfull confidence, *He hath heard my supplication,*
⁴⁴⁰ and therefore *He will heare my prayer;* He lookt upon me in the dust
of the earth, much more will he doe so, having now laid me upon
Carpets; he lookt upon me in my sores, sores of mine enemies malice,
and sores of mine own sinnes, much more will he doe so now, when
he hath imprinted in me the wounds of his own Sonne; for those that
were so many wounds upon him, are so many starres upon me; He
lookt upon me, may *David* say, when I followed the Ewes great with
young, much more will he doe so now, now when by his directions,
I lead out his people, great with enterprizes, and victories against his
enemies. First *David* comes to that holy noblenesse, he dares cast off
⁴⁵⁰ ill instruments, and is not afraid of conspiracy; he dares divorce himselfe from dangerous company, and is not afraid of melancholy; he
dares love God, and is not afraid of that jealousie, that he is too religious to be imployed, too tender conscienced to be put upon businesse; he dares reprehend them that are under his charge, and is not
afraid of a recrimination; he dares observe a Sabbath, he dares startle
at a blasphemy, he dares forbeare countenancing a prophane or a
scurrill jest with his praise, he dares be an honest man; which holy
confidence constituted our first part, *Depart from mee all yee workers
of iniquity;* And then he grounds this confidence upon an undeceiv-
⁴⁶⁰ able Rocke, upon Gods seale, *God hath heard me, therefore God will
heare mee.* And when God heares, God speaks too, and when God

Hosea 2.19

speaks, God does too, and therefore I may safely proceede as I doe, which was our second Consideration. And then the third, which remains, is, that upon this, he returnes to the consideration, what that was, that he had done; he had either imprecated, or denounced, at least, heavy judgements upon his enemies; and he finds it avowable, and justifiable to have done so; and therefore persists in it, *Let all mine enemies be ashamed, and sore vexed; let them returne, and be ashamed suddenly.*

3 Part   470   All cleane beasts had both these marks, they divided the hoofe, and they chewed the cud: All good resolutions, which passe our prayer, must have these two marks too, they must divide the hoofe, they must make a double impression, they must be directed upon Gods glory, and upon our good, and they must passe a rumination, a chawing of the cud, a second examination, whether that prayer were so conditioned or no. We pray sometimes out of sudden and indigested apprehensions; we pray sometimes out of custome, and communion with others; we pray sometimes out of a present sense of paine, or imminent danger; and this prayer may divide the hoofe; It may looke 480 towards Gods glory, and towards our good; but it does not chew the cud too; that is, if I have not considered, not examined, whether it doe so or no, it is not a prayer that God will call a sacrifice. You see Christ

[Mat.26.39] brought his own Prayer, *Si possibile, If it be possible &c.* through such a rumination, *Veruntamen, yet not my will &c.* As many a man sweares, and if he be surprized, and askt, what did you say, he does not remember his owne oath, not what he swore; so many a man prayes, and does not remember his own prayer. As a Clock gives a warning before it strikes, and then there remains a sound, and a tingling of the bell after it hath stricken: so a precedent meditation, 490 and a subsequent rumination, make the prayer a prayer; I must think before, what I will aske, and consider againe, what I have askt; and upon this dividing the hoofe, and chewing the cud, *David* avowes to his own conscience his whole action, even to this consummation thereof, *Let mine enemies be ashamed &c.*

Imprecatoria   Now these words, whether we consider the naturall signification of the words, or the authority of those men, who have been Expositors upon them, may be understood either way, either to be *Imprecatoria,* words of Imprecation, that *David* in the Spirit of anguish wishes that

these things might fall upon his enemies, or els *Prædictoria,* words of
500 Prediction, that *David* in the spirit of Prophecy pronounces that these
things shall fall upon them.

If they be *Imprecatoria,* words spoken out of his wish, and desire,
then they have in them the nature of a curse: And because *Lyra* takes
them to be so, a curse, he referres the words *Ad Dæmones,* To the
Devill: That herein *David* seconds Gods malediction upon the Serpent, and curses the Devill, as the occasioner and first mover of all
these calamities; and sayes of them, *Let all our enemies be ashamed,
and sore vexed &c.* Others referre these words to the first Christian
times, and the persecutions then, and so to be a malediction, a curse
510 upon the Jewes, and upon the Romans, who persecuted the Primitive
Church then, *Let them be ashamed &c.* And then *Gregory Nyssen*
referres these words to more domesticall and intrinsicke enemies, to
Davids owne concupiscences, and the rebellions of his owne lusts, *Let
those enemies be ashamed &c.* For all those who understand these
words to be a curse, a malediction, are loath to admit that *David* did
curse his enemies, meerly out of a respect of those calamities which
they had inflicted upon him. And that is a safe ground; no man may
curse another, in contemplation of himselfe onely, if onely himselfe
be concerned in the case. And when it concernes the glory of God, our
520 imprecations, our maledictions upon the persons, must not have their
principall relation, as to Gods enemies, but as to Gods glory; our end
must be, that God may have his glory, not that they may have their
punishment. And therefore how vehement soever *David* seeme in this
Imprecation, and though he be more vehement in another place, *Let*   Psal. 83.17
*them be confounded, and troubled for ever, yea, let them be put to
shame, and perish,* yet that perishing is but a perishing of their purposes, let their plots perish, let their malignity against thy Church be
frustrated; for so he expresses himselfe in the verse immediately before, *Fill their faces with shame;* but why? and how? *That they may*
530 *seeke thy Name, O Lord;* that was Davids end, even in the curse;
David wishes them no ill, but for their good; no worse to Gods
enemies, but that they might become his friends. The rule is good,
which out of his moderation S. *Augustine* gives, that in all Inquisitions,
and Executions in matters of Religion, (when it is meerly for Religion
without sedition) *Sint qui pœniteant,* Let the men remaine alive, or

else how can they repent? So in all Imprecations, in all hard wishes, even upon Gods enemies, *Sint qui convertantur,* Let the men remaine, that they may be capable of conversion; wish them not so ill, as that God can shew no mercy to them; for so the ill wish falls upon God
540 himselfe, if it preclude his way of mercy upon that ill man. In no case must the curse be directed upon the person; for when in the next Psalme to this, *David* seemes passionate, when hee asks that of God there, which he desires God to forbear in the beginning of this Psalme, when his *Ne arguas in ira, O Lord rebuke not in thine anger,* is turned

[Psa. 7.6] to a *Surge Domine in ira, Arise O Lord in thine anger;* S. *Augustine* begins to wonder, *Quid? illum, quem perfectum dicimus, ad iram provocat Deum?* Would *David* provoke God, who is all sweetnesse, and mildnesse, to anger against any man? No, not against any man; but *Diaboli possessio peccator,* Every sinner is a slave to his beloved
550 sin; and therefore, *Misericors orat, adversus eum, quicunque orat,* How bitterly soever I curse that sin, yet I pray for that sinner. *David* would have God angry with the Tyran, not with the Slave that is oppressed; with the sin, not with the soule that is inthralled to it. And so, as the words may be a curse, a malediction in *Davids* mouth, we may take them into our mouth too, and say, *Let those enemies be ashamed, &c.*

If this then were an Imprecation, a malediction, yet it was Medicinall, and had *Rationem boni,* a charitable tincture, and nature in it;
Prædictoria he wished the men no harm, as men. But it is rather *Prædictorium,* a
560 Propheticall vehemence, that if they will take no knowledge of Gods declaring himselfe in the protection of his servants, if they would not consider that God had heard, and would heare, had rescued, and would rescue his children, but would continue their opposition against him, heavy judgements would certainly fall upon them; Their punishment should be certaine, but the effect should be uncertaine; for God only knowes, whether his correction shall work upon his enemies, to their mollifying, or to their obduration. Those bitter, and waighty
Psal. 109 imprecations which *David* hath heaped together against *Iudas,* seeme
Acts 1.16 to be direct imprecations; and yet S. *Peter* himselfe calls them Proph-
570 esies; *Oportet impleri Scripturam; They were done,* sayes he, *that the Scripture might be fulfilled;* Not that *David* in his owne heart did wish all that upon *Iudas;* but only so, as fore-seeing in the Spirit of

Prophesying, that those things should fall upon him, he concurred with the purpose of God therein, and so farre as he saw it to be the will of God, he made it his will, and his wish. And so have all those judgements, which we denounce upon sinners, the nature of Prophesies in them; when we reade in the Church, that Commination, *Cursed is the Idolater,* This may fall upon some of our owne kindred; and *Cursed is he that curseth Father or Mother,* This may fall upon some of our owne children; and *Cursed is he that perverteth judgement,* This may fall upon some powerfull Persons, that we may have a dependance upon; and upon these we doe not wish that Gods vengeance should fall; yet we Prophesie, and denounce justly, that upon such, such vengeances will fall; and then, all Prophesies of that kinde are alwaies conditionall; they are conditionall, if we consider any Decree in God; they must be conditionall in all our denunciations; if you repent, they shall not fall upon you, if not, *Oportet impleri Scripturam, The Scripture must be fulfilled;* We doe not wish them, we do but Prophesie them; no, nor we doe not prophesie them; but the Scriptures have pre-prophesied them before; they will fall upon you, as upon *Iudas,* in condemnation, and perchance, as upon *Iudas,* in desperation too.

Davids purpose then being in these words to work to their amendment, and not their finall destruction, we may easily and usefully discerne in the particular words, a milder sense then the words seeme at first to present. And first give me leave by the way, only in passing, by occasion of those words which are here rendred, *Convertentur, & Erubescent,* and which in the Originall, are *Iashabu,* and *Ieboshu,* which have a musicall, and harmonious sound, and agnomination in them, let me note thus much, even in that, that the Holy Ghost in penning the Scriptures delights himself, not only with a propriety, but with a delicacy, and harmony, and melody of language; with height of Metaphors, and other figures, which may work greater impressions upon the Readers, and not with barbarous, or triviall, or market, or homely language: It is true, that when the Grecians, and the Romanes, and S. *Augustine* himselfe, undervalued and despised the Scriptures, because of the poore and beggerly phrase, that they seemed to be written in, the Christians could say little against it, but turned still upon the other safer way, wee consider the matter, and not the phrase,

Mollior sensus

⁶¹⁰ because for the most part, they had read the Scriptures only in Translations, which could not maintaine the Majesty, nor preserve the ele-
gancies of the Originall.

Their case was somewhat like ours, at the beginning of the Reformation; when, because most of those men who laboured in that Reformation, came out of the Romane Church, and there had never read
the body of the Fathers at large; but only such ragges and fragments
of those Fathers, as were patcht together in their Decretat's, and
Decretals, and other such Common placers, for their purpose, and to
serve their turne, therefore they were loath at first to come to that
⁶²⁰ issue, to try controversies by the Fathers. But as soon as our men that
imbraced the Reformation, had had time to reade the Fathers, they
were ready enough to joyne with the Adversary in that issue: and
still we protest, that we accept that evidence, the testimony of the
Fathers, and refuse nothing, which the Fathers unanimly delivered,
for matter of faith; and howsoever at the beginning some men were
a little ombrageous, and startling at the name of the Fathers, yet since
the Fathers have been well studied, for more then threescore yeares,
we have behaved our selves with more reverence towards the Fathers,
and more confidence in the Fathers, then they of the Romane per-
⁶³⁰ swasion have done, and been lesse apt to suspect or quarrell their
Books, or to reprove their Doctrines, then our Adversaries have been.
So, howsoever the Christians at first were fain to sink a little under
that imputation, that their Scriptures have no Majesty, no eloquence,
because these embellishments could not appeare in Translations, nor
they then read Originalls, yet now, that a perfect knowledge of those
languages hath brought us to see the beauty and the glory of those
Books, we are able to reply to them, that there are not in all the world
so eloquent Books as the Scriptures; and that nothing is more demon-
strable, then that if we would take all those Figures, and Tropes, which
⁶⁴⁰ are collected out of secular Poets, and Orators, we may give higher,
and livelier examples, of every one of those Figures, out of the Scriptures, then out of all the Greek and Latine Poets, and Orators; and
they mistake it much, that thinke, that the Holy Ghost hath rather
chosen a low, and barbarous, and homely style, then an eloquent, and
powerfull manner of expressing himselfe.

Erubescent   To returne and to cast a glance upon these words in *Davids* predic-

tion, upon his enemies, what hardnesse is in the first, *Erubescent, Let them be ashamed:* for the word imports no more, our last Translation sayes no more, neither did our first Translators intend any more, by
⁶⁵⁰ their word, *Confounded;* for that is, confounded with shame in themselves. This is *Virga disciplinæ,* sayes S. *Bernard;* as long as we are ashamed of sin, we are not growne up, and hardned in it; we are under correction; the correction of a remorse. As soone as *Adam* came to be ashamed of his nakednesse, he presently thought of some remedy; if one should come and tell thee, that he looked through the doore, that he stood in a window over against thine, and saw thee doe such or such a sin, this would put thee to a shame, and thou wouldest not doe that sin, till thou wert sure he could not see thee. O, if thou wouldest not sin, till thou couldst think that God saw thee
⁶⁶⁰ not, this shame had wrought well upon thee. There are complexions that cannot blush; there growes a blacknesse, a sootinesse upon the soule, by custome in sin, which overcomes all blushing, all tendernesse. White alone is palenesse, and God loves not a pale soule, a soule possest with a horror, affrighted with a diffidence, and distrusting his mercy. Rednesse alone is anger, and vehemency, and distemper, and God loves not such a red soule, a soule that sweats in sin, that quarrels for sin, that revenges in sin. But that whitenesse that preserves it selfe, not onely from being died all over in any foule colour, from contracting the name of any habituall sin, and so to be called such or such a
⁶⁷⁰ sinner, but from taking any spot, from comming within distance of a tentation, or of a suspition, is that whitenesse, which God meanes, when he sayes, *Thou art all faire my Love, and there is no spot in thee.*   Cant. 4.7
Indifferent looking, equall and easie conversation, appliablenesse to wanton discourses, and notions, and motions, are the Devils single money, and many pieces of these make up an Adultery. As light a thing as a Spangle is, a Spangle is silver; and Leafe-gold, that is blowne away, is gold; and sand that hath no strength, no coherence, yet knits the building; so doe approaches to sin, become sin, and fixe sin. To avoid these spots, is that whitenesse that God loves in the
⁶⁸⁰ soule. But there is a rednesse that God loves too; which is this Erubescence that we speak of; an aptnesse in the soule to blush, when any of these spots doe fall upon it.

God is the universall Confessor, the generall Penitentiary of all the

world, and all dye in the guilt of their sin, that goe not to Confession to him. And there are sins of such waight to the soule, and such intangling, and perplexity to the conscience, in some circumstances of the sin, as that certainly a soule may receive much ease in such cases, by confessing it selfe to man. In this holy shamefastnesse, which we intend in this outward blushing of the face, the soule goes to confes-
690 sion too. And it is one of the principall arguments against Confessions by Letter, (which some went about to set up in the Romane Church) that that took away one of the greatest evidences, and testimonies of their repentance, which is this Erubescence, this blushing, this shame after sin; if they should not be put to speak it face to face, but to write it, that would remove the shame, which is a part of the repentance. But that soule that goes not to confession to it selfe, that hath not an internall blushing after a sin committed, is a pale soule, even in the palenesse of death, and senslesnesse, and a red soule, red in the defiance of God. And that whitenesse, to avoid approaches to sin, and
700 that rednesse, to blush upon a sin, which does attempt us, is the complexion of the soule, which God loves, and which the Holy Ghost

Cant. 5.10   testifies, when he sayes, *My Beloved is white and ruddy.* And when these men that *David* speaks of here, had lost that whitenesse, their innocency, for *David* to wish that they might come to a rednesse, a shame, a blushing, a remorse, a sense of sin, may have been no such great malediction, or imprecation in the mouth of *David,* but that a man may wish it to his best friend, which should be his own soule, and say, *Erubescam,* not let mine enemies, but let me be ashamed with such a shame.

Contur-   710   In the second word, *Let them be sore vexed,* he wishes his enemies
bentur   no worse then himselfe had been: For he had used the same word of

Ver. 2 & 3   himselfe before, *Ossa turbata, My bones are vexed,* and *Anima turbata, My soule is vexed;* and considering, that *David* had found this vexation to be his way to God, it was no malicious imprecation, to wish that enemy the same Physick that he had taken, who was more sick of the same disease then he was. For this is like a troubled Sea after a tempest; the danger is past, but yet the billow is great still: The danger was in the calme, in the security, or in the tempest, by mis-interpreting Gods corrections to our obduration, and to a re-
720 morselesse stupefaction; but when a man is come to this holy vexa-

tion, to be troubled, to be shaken with a sense of the indignation of God, the storme is past, and the indignation of God is blowne over. That soule is in a faire and neare way, of being restored to a calmnesse, and to reposed security of conscience, that is come to this holy vexation.

In a flat Map, there goes no more, to make West East, though they be distant in an extremity, but to paste that flat Map upon a round body, and then West and East are all one. In a flat soule, in a dejected conscience, in a troubled spirit, there goes no more to the making of
730 that trouble, peace, then to apply that trouble to the body of the Merits, to the body of the Gospel of Christ Jesus, and conforme thee to him, and thy West is East, thy Trouble of spirit is Tranquillity of spirit. The name of Christ is *Oriens, The East;* And yet Lucifer himselfe is called *Filius Orientis, The Son of the East.* If thou beest fallen by *Lucifer,* fallen to *Lucifer,* and not fallen as *Lucifer,* to a senslesnesse of thy fall, and an impenitiblenesse therein, but to a troubled spirit, still thy Prospect is the East, still thy Climate is heaven, still thy Haven is Jerusalem; for, in our lowest dejection of all, even in the dust of the grave, we are so composed, so layed down, as that
740 we look to the East; If I could beleeve that Trajan, or Tecla, could look East-ward, that is, towards Christ, in hell, I could beleeve with them of Rome, that Trajan and Tecla were redeemed by prayer out of hell. God had accepted sacrifices before; but no sacrifice is called *Odor quietis,* It is not said, *That God smelt a savor of rest,* in any sacrifice, but that which *Noah* offered, after hee had beene variously tossed and tumbled, in the long hulling of the Arke upon the waters. A troublesome spirit, and a quiet spirit, are farre asunder; But a troubled spirit, and a quiet spirit, are neare neighbours. And therefore *David* meanes them no great harme, when hee sayes, *Let them*
750 *be troubled;* For, Let the winde be as high as it will, so I sayle before the winde, Let the trouble of my soule be as great as it will, so it direct me upon God, and I have calme enough.

And this peace, this calme is implyed in the next word, *Convertantur,* which is not, *Let them be overthrowne,* but *Let them returne,* let them be forced to returne; he prayes, that God would do something to crosse their purposes; because as they are against God, so they are against their owne soules. In that way where they are, he

Zach. 6.12.
[Vulg.]
Esay 14.12

Gen. 8.21

Convertantur

[Lam. 5.21]

sees there is no remedy; and therefore he desires that they might be *Turned* into another way; What is that way? This. *Turne us O Lord,*
760 *and we shall be turned;* That is, turned the right way; Towards God. And as there was a promise from God, to heare his people, not onely when they came to him in the Temple, but when they turned towards that Temple, in what distance soever they were, so it is alwaies accompanied with a blessing, occasionally to turne towards God; But this prayer, *Turne us, that we may be turned,* is, that we may be, that is, remaine turned, that we may continue fixed in that posture. *Lots* Wife turned her selfe, and remained an everlasting monument of Gods anger; God so turne us alwaies into right wayes, as that we be not able to turne our selves out of them. For God hath *Viam rectam,*
770 *& bonam,* as himselfe speakes in the Prophet, A right way, and then a good way, which yet is not the right way, that is, not the way which God of himselfe would go. For his right way is, that we should still keepe in his way; His good way is, to beat us into his right way againe, by his medicinall corrections, when we put our selves out of his right way. And that, and that onely *David* wishes, and we wish, That you may *Turne,* and *Be turned;* stand in that holy posture, all the yeare, all the yeares of your lives, That your Christmas may be as holy as your Easter, even your Recreations as innocent as your Devotions, and every roome in the house as free from prophanenesse as the
780 Sanctuary. And this he ends as he begun, with another *Erubescant,* Let them be ashamed, and that *Valde velociter, Suddenly:* for *David* saw, that if a sinner came not to a shame of sin quickly, he would quickly come to a shamelesnesse, to an impudence, to a searednesse, to an obduration in it.

Now beloved, this is the worst curse that comes out of a holy mans mouth, even towards his enemie, that God would correct him to his amendment. And this is the worst harme that we meane to you, when we denounce the judgements of God against sin and sinners, *Vt erubescatis,* that we might see blood in your faces, the blood of your
790 Saviour working in that shame for sin. That that question of the Prophet might not confound you, *Were they ashamed when they committed abomination? nay, they were not ashamed; Erubescere nesciebant,* they were never used to shame, they knew not how to be ashamed. *Therefore,* sayes he, *they shall fall amongst them that fall,*

Ier. 6.15

they shall do as the world does, sin as their neighbours sin, and fall as they fall, irrepentantly here, and hereafter irrecoverably. And then, *Vt conturbati sitis,* that you may be troubled in your hearts, and not cry Peace, Peace, where there is no peace, and flatter your selves, because you are in a true Religion, and in the right way; for a Child
800 may drowne in a Font, and a Man may be poysoned in the Sacrament, much more perish, though in a true Church. And also *Vt revertamini,* that you may returne againe to the Lord, returne to that state of purenesse, which God gave you in Baptisme, to that state, which God gave you the last time you received his body and blood so as became you. And then lastly, *Vt erubescatis velociter,* that you may come to the beginning of this, and to all this quickly, and not to defer it, because God defers the judgement. For to end this with S. *Augustines* words, upon this word *Velociter, Quandocunque venit, celerrimè venit, quod desperatur esse venturum:* How late soever it come, that comes
810 quickly, if it come at all, which we beleeved would never come. How long soever it be, before that judgement come, yet it comes quickly, if it come before thou looke for it, or be ready for it. Whosoever labours to sleepe out the thought of that day, *His damnation sleepeth* [2 Pet. 2.3] *not,* sayes the Apostle. It is not onely, that his damnation is not dead, that there shall never be any such day, but that it is no day asleepe: every midnight shall be a day of judgement to him, and keepe him awake; and when consternation, and lassitude lend him, or conterfait to him a sleep, as S. *Basil* sayes of the righteous, *Etiam somnia justorum preces sunt,* That even their Dreames are prayers, so this in-
820 corrigible sinners Dreames shall be, not onely presages of his future, but acts of his present condemnation.

Number 2.

Preached at S. Pauls, upon Easter-day,
in the Evening. 1624.

APOC. 20.6. *BLESSED AND HOLY IS HE THAT*
HATH PART IN THE FIRST RESURRECTION.

IN THE first book of the Scriptures, that of Genesis, there is danger
in departing from the letter; In this last book, this of the Revelation, there is as much danger in adhering too close to the letter.
The literall sense is always to be preserved; but the literall sense is
not always to be discerned: for the literall sense is not always that,
which the very Letter and Grammer of the place presents, as where
it is literally said, *That Christ is a Vine,* and literally, *That his flesh
is bread,* and literally, *That the new Ierusalem is thus situated, thus
built, thus furnished:* But the literall sense of every place, is the prin-
¹⁰ cipall intention of the Holy Ghost, in that place: And his principall
intention in many places, is to express things by allegories, by figures; so that in many places of Scripture, a figurative sense is the
literall sense, and more in this book then in any other. As then to
depart from the literall sense, that sense which the very letter presents, in the book of Genesis, is dangerous, because if we do so there,
we have no history of the Creation of the world in any other place
to stick to; so to binde our selves to such a literall sense in this book,
will take from us the consolation of many spirituall happinesses, and
bury us in the carnall things of this world.

²⁰   The first error of being too allegoricall in Genesis, transported
divers of the ancients beyond the certain evidence of truth, and the
second error of being too literall in this book, fixed many, very many,
very ancient, very learned, upon an evident falshood; which was, that
because here is mention *of a first Resurrection, and of raigning with
Christ a thousand years after that first Resurrection,* There should

[Ioh. 15.1
6.51]

62

be to all the Saints of God, a state of happinesse in this world, after
Christs comming, for a thousand yeares; In which happy state, though
some of them have limited themselves in spirituall things, that they
should enjoy a kinde of conversation with Christ, and an impecca-
30 bility, and a quiet serving of God without any reluctations, or concupiscences, or persecutions; yet others have dreamed on, and enlarged
their dreames to an enjoying of all these worldly happinesses, which
they, being formerly persecuted, did formerly want in this world, and
then should have them for a thousand yeares together in recompence.
And even this branch of that error, of possessing the things of this
world, so long, in this world, did very many, and very good, and
very great men, whose names are in honour, and justly in the Church
of God, in those first times stray into; and flattered themselves with
an imaginary intimation of some such thing, in these words, *Blessed*
40 *and holy is he, that hath part in the first Resurrection.*

Thus far then the text is literall, That this Resurrection in the text, *Divisio*
is different from the generall Resurrection. The first differs from the
last: And thus far it is figurative, allegoricall, mysticall, that it is a
spirituall Resurrection, that is intended. But wherein spirituall? or
of what spirituall Resurrection? In the figurative exposition of those
places of Scripture, which require that way oft to be figuratively
expounded, that Expositor is not to be blamed, who not destroying
the literall sense, proposes such a figurative sense, as may exalt our
devotion, and advance our edification; And as no one of those Ex-
50 positors did ill, in proposing one such sense, so neither do those
Expositors ill, who with those limitations, that it destroy not the literall sense, that it violate not the analogy of faith, that it advance
devotion, do propose another and another such sense. So doth that
preacher well also, who to the same end, and within the same limit,
makes his use of both, of all those expositions; because all may stand,
and it is not evident in such figurative speeches, which is the literall,
that is, the principall intention of the Holy Ghost.

Of these words of this first Resurrection (which is not the last, of
the body, but a spirituall Resurrection) there are three expositions au-
60 thorized by persons of good note in the Church. First, that this first Alcazar
Resurrection, is a Resurrection from that low estate, to which persecution had brought the Church; and so it belongs to this whole State,

August. &
nostri

Ribera

[Ioh. 11.25]

I. Part
From
persecution

and Church, and *Blessed are we who have our part in this first Resur-rection.* Secondly, that it is a Resurrection from the death of sin, of actuall, and habituall sin; so it belongs to every particular penitent soul; and *Blessed art thou, blessed am I, if we have part in this first Resurrection.* And then thirdly, because after this Resurrection, it is said, *That we shall raign with Christ a thousand yeares,* (which is a certain for an uncertain, a limited, for a long time) it hath also been
70 taken for the state of the soul in heaven, after it is parted from the body by death; for though the soul cannot be said properly to have a Resurrection, because properly it cannot die, yet to be thus delivered from the danger of a second death, by future sin, to be removed from the distance, and latitude, and possibility of tentations in this world, is by very good Expositors called a Resurrection; and so it belongs to all them who are departed in the Lord; *Blessed and holy is he that hath part in this first Resurrection.* And then the occasion of the day, which we celebrate now, being the Resurrection of our Lord and Saviour Christ Jesus, invites me to propose a fourth sense, or rather
80 use of the words; not indeed as an exposition of the words, but as a convenient exaltation of our devotion; which is, that this first Resur-rection should be the first fruits of the dead; The first Rising, is the first Riser, Christ Jesus: for as Christ sayes of himself, that *He is the Resurrection,* so he is the first Resurrection, the root of the Resurrec-tion, he upon whom our Resurrection, all ours, all our kindes of Resurrections are founded; and so it belongs to State and Church, and particular persons, alive, and dead; *Blessed and holy is he that hath part in this first Resurrection.*

And these foure considerations of the words; A Resurrection from
90 persecution, by deliverance; a Resurrection from sin, by grace; a Resurrection from tentation to sin, by the way of death, to the glory of heaven; and all these, in the first Resurrection, in him that is the roote of all, in Christ Jesus, These foure steps, these foure passages, these foure transitions will be our quarter Clock, for this houres exercise.

First then, we consider this first Resurrection, to be a Resurrection from a persecution for religion, for the profession of the Gospell, to a forward glorious passage of the Gospell. And so a learned Ex-positor in the Romane Church carries the exposition of this whole

¹⁰⁰ place (though not indeed the ordinary way, yet truly not incom-
modiously, not improperly) upon that deliverance, which God afforded his Church, from those great persecutions, which had otherwise
supplanted her, in her first planting, in the primitive times. Then
sayes he (and in part well towards the letter of the place) *The devill*   [Apoc. 20.2]
was chained for a thousand yeares, and then we began *to raign with
Christ for a thousand yeares;* reckoning the time from that time, when
God destroyed Idolatry more fully, and gave peace and rest, and free
exercise of the Christian religion, under the Christian Emperours,
till Antichrist in the height of his rage shall come, and let this thou-
¹¹⁰ sand yeares prisoner Satan loose, and so interrupt our thousand yeares
raign with Christ, with new persecutions. In that persecution was
the death of the Church, in the eye of the world; In that deliverance
by Christian Emperours was the Resurrection of the Church; And
in Gods protecting her ever since is the chaining up of the devill, and
our raigning with Christ for those thousand yeares.

    And truly, beloved, if we consider the low, the very low estate of
Christians in those persecutions, tryed ten times in the fire, ten severall and distinct persecutions, in which ten persecutions, God may
seem to have had a minde to deale eavenly with the world, and to lay
¹²⁰ as much upon his people whom he would try then, as he had laid
upon others, for his people before, and so to equall the ten plagues
of Ægypt, in ten persecutions, in the primitive Church; if we consider that low, that very low estate, we may justly call their deliverance a Resurrection. For as God said to Jerusalem, *I found thee in*   [Ezek. 16.6
thy blood, and washed thee, so Christ Jesus found the Church, the   and 9]
Christian Church in her blood, and washed her, and wiped her;
washed her in his own blood, which washes white, and wiped her
with the garments of his own righteousnesse, that she might be acceptable in the sight of God, and then wiped all teares from her eyes,
¹³⁰ took away all occasions of complaint, and lamentation, that she might
be glorious in the eyes of man, and chearefull in her own; such was
her Resurrection.

    We wonder, and justly, at the effusion, at the pouring out of blood,
in the sacrifices of the old Law; that that little countrey scarce bigger
then some three of our Shires, should spend more cattle in some few
dayes sacrifice at some solemnities, and every yeare in the sacrifices

of the whole yeare, then perchance this kingdome could give to any
use. Seas of blood, and yet but brooks, tuns of blood, and yet but
basons, compared with the sacrifices, the sacrifices of the blood of
140 men, in the persecutions of the Primitive Church. For every Oxe of
the Jew, the Christian spent a man, and for every Sheep and Lamb,
a Mother and her childe; and for every heard of cattle, sometimes a
towne of Inhabitants, sometimes a Legion of Souldiers, all martyred
at once; so that they did not stand to fill their Martyrologies with
names, but with numbers, they had not roome to say, such a day, such
a Bishop, such a day, such a Generall, but the day of 500. the day of
5000. Martyrs, and the martyrdome of a City, or the Martyrdome
of an Army; This was not a red Sea, such as the Jews passed, a Sinus,
a Creek, an Arm, an Inlet, a gut of a Sea, but a red Ocean, that over-
150 flowed, and surrounded all parts; and from the depth of this Sea God
raised them; and such was their Resurrection. Such, as that they which
suffered, lay, and bled with more ease, then the executioner stood
and sweat; and embraced the fire more fervently, then he blew it;
and many times had this triumph in their death, that even the executioner himself, was in the act of execution converted to Christ, and
executed with them; such was their Resurrection.

   When the State of the Jews was in that depression, in that con-
culcation, in that consternation, in that extermination in the captivity of Babylon, as that God presents it to the Prophet in that Vision,
[Ezek. 37.3]   160 in the field of dry bones, so, *Fili hominis, Son of man, as thou art a
reasonable man, dost thou think these bones can live, that these men
can ever be re-collected to make up a Nation?* The Prophet saith,
Domine tu scis, Lord thou knowest; which is, not only thou knowest
whether they can, or no, but thou knowest clearly they can; thou
canst make them up of bones again, for thou madest those bones of
earth before. If God had called in the Angels to the making of man
at first, and as he said to the Prophet, *Fili hominis, Son of man, as
thou art a reasonable man,* so he had said to them, *Filii Dei,* as you
are the Sons of God, illumined by his face, do you think, that this
170 clod of red earth can make a man, a man that shall be equall to you,
in one of his parts, in his soul, and yet then shall have such another
part, as that he, whom all you worship, my essentiall Son shall assume, and invest that part himself, can that man made of that body,

and that soul, be made of this clod of earth? Those Angels would have said, *Domine tu scis,* Lord thou must needs know, how to make as good creatures as us of earth, who madest us of that which is infinitely lesse then earth, of nothing, before. To induce, to facilitate these apprehensions, there were some precedents, some such thing had been done before. But when the Church was newly conceived, 180 and then lay like the egge of a Dove, and a Gyants foot over it, like a worm, like an ant, and hill upon hill whelmed upon it, nay, like a grain of corn between the upper and lower Mill-stone, ground to dust between Tyrans and Heretiques, when as she bled in her Cradle, in those children whom *Herod* slew, so she bled upon her crutches, in those decrepit men whom former persecutions and tortures had creepled before, when East and West joyned hands to crush her, and hands, and brains, joyned execution to consultation to annihilate her; in this wane of the Moon, God gave her an instant fulnesse; in this exinanition, instant glory; in this grave, an instant Resurrection.

190   But beloved, the expressing the pressing of their depressions, does but chafe the Wax; the Printing of the seale, is the reducing to your memory, your own case: and not that point in your case, as you were for a few yeares under a sensible persecution of fire, and prisons; that was the least part of your persecution; for it is a cheap purchase of heaven, if we may have it for dying; To sell all we have to buy   Mat. 13.44 that field where we know the treasure is, is not so hard, as not to know it; To part with all, for the great Pearle, not so hard a bargaine, as not to know that such a Pearle there might have beene had; we could not say heaven was kept from us, when we might have it 200 for a Fagot, and when even our enemies helpt us to it: but your greater affliction was, as you were long before, in an insensiblenesse, you thought your selves well enough, and yet were under a worse persecution of ignorance, and of superstition, when you, in your Fathers, were so farre from expecting a resurrection, as that you did not know your low estate, or that you needed a Resurrection; And yet God gave you a Resurrection from it, a reformation of it.

    Now, *who have their parts in this first resurrection?* or upon what conditions have you it? We see in the fourth verse, *They that are beheaded for the witnesse of Iesus;* that is, that are ready to be so, 210 when the glory of Jesus shall require that testimony. In the meane time, as it followes there, *They that have not worshipped the Beast;* that is, not applied the Honour, and the Allegiance due to their Soveraign, to any forraign State; nor the Honor due to God, that is, infallibility, to another Prelate; *That have not worshipped the Beast, nor his Image,* sayes the Text; that is, that have not been transported with vain imaginations of his power, and his growth upon us here, which hath been so diligently Painted, and Printed, and Preached, and set out in the promises, and practises of his Instruments, to delude slack, and easie persons: And then, as it is added there, *That have* ²²⁰ *not received his mark upon their foreheads;* That is, not declared themselves Romanists apparently; *nor in their hands,* sayes the Text; that is, which have not under-hand sold their secret endeavours, though not their publique profession, to the advancement of his cause. These men, who are ready to be beheaded for Christ, and have not worshipped the Beast, nor the Image of the Beast, nor received his mark upon their foreheads, nor in their hands, these have their parts in this first resurrection. These are *blessed,* and *holy,* sayes our Text; Blessed, because they have meanes to be holy, in this resurrection; For the Lamb hath unclasped the book; the Scriptures are open; ²³⁰ which way to holinesse, our Fathers lacked; And then, our blessednesse is, that we shall raigne a thousand yeares with Christ: Now since this first resurrection, since the reformation we have raigned so with Christ, but 100. yeares: But if we persist in a good use of it, our posterity shall adde the Cypher, and make that 100. 1000. even to the time, when Christ Jesus shall come againe, and as he hath given us the first, so shall give us the last resurrection; and to that come Lord Jesus, come quickly; and till that, continue this.

2. Part

A peccato

This is the first resurrection, in the first acceptation, a resurrection from persecution, and a peaceable enjoying of the Gospell: And in ²⁴⁰ a second, it is a resurrection from sin; and so it hath a more particular

Aug.

appropriation to every person. So S. *Augustine* takes this place, and with him many of the Fathers, and with them, many of the sons of the Fathers, better sons of the Fathers, then the Romane Church will confesse them to be, or then they are themselves, The Expositors of the Reformed Church: They, for the most part, with S. *Augustine,*

Gregor.

take this first resurrection, to be a resurrection from sin. *Inter abjectos abjectissimus peccator:* No man falls lower, then he that falls into

a course of sin; Sin is a fall; It is not onely a deviation, a turning out
of the way, upon the right, or the left hand, but it is a sinking, a
²⁵⁰ falling: In the other case, of going out of the way, a man may stand
upon the way, and inquire, and then proceed in the way, if he be
right, or to the way, if he be wrong; But when he is fallen, and lies
still, he proceeds no farther, inquires no farther. To be too apt to conceive scruples in matters of religion, stops, and retards a man in the
way; to mistake some points in the truth of religion, puts a man for
that time in a wrong way; But to fall into a course of sin, this makes
him unsensible of any end, that he hath to goe to, of any way that he
hath to goe by. God hath not removed man, not with-drawne man
from this Earth; he hath not given him the Aire to flie in, as to Birds,
²⁶⁰ nor Spheares to move in, as to Sun and Moone; he hath left him
upon the Earth; and not onely to tread upon it, as in contempt, or
in meere Dominion, but to walk upon it, in the discharge of the
duties of his calling; and so to be conversant with the Earth, is not
a falling. But as when man was nothing but earth, nothing but a
body, he lay flat upon the earth, his mouth kissed the earth, his hands
embraced the earth, his eyes respected the earth; And then God
breathed the breath of life into him, and that raised him so farre
from the earth, as that onely one part of his body, (the soles of his
feet) touches it, And yet man, so raised by God, by sin fell lower to
²⁷⁰ the earth againe, then before, from the face of the earth, to the womb,
to the bowels, to the grave; So God, finding the whole man, as low
as he found *Adams* body then, fallen in Originall sin, yet erects us
by a new breath of life, in the Sacrament of Baptisme, and yet we
fall lower then before we were raised, from Originall into Actuall,
into Habituall sins; So low, as that we think not, that we need, know
not, that there is a resurrection; and that is the wonderfull, that is the
fearfull fall.

Though those words, *Quomodo cecidisti de Cælo, Lucifer, How*   Esay 14.12
art thou fallen from heaven O Lucifer, the Son of the morning? be
²⁸⁰ ordinarily applied to the fall of the Angels, yet it is evident, that they
are literally spoken of the fall of a man: It deserves wonder, more then
pity, that man, whom God had raised, to so Noble a heighth in him,
should fall so low from him. Man was borne to love; he was made
in the love of God; but then man falls in love; when he growes in

love with the creature, he falls in love: As we are bid to honour the
Physitian, and to use the Physitian, but yet it is said in the same
Chapter, He that sinneth before his Maker, let him fall into the hands
of the Physitian; It is a blessing to use him, it is a curse to rely upon
him, so it is a blessing to glorifie God, in the right use of his creatures,
²⁹⁰ but to grow in love with them, is a fall: For we love nothing that is
so good as our selves; Beauty, Riches, Honour, is not so good as man;
Man capable of grace here, of glory hereafter. Nay as those things,
which we love, in their nature, are worse then we which love them,
so in our loving them, we endeavour to make them worse then they
in their own nature are; by over-loving the beauty of the body, we
corrupt the soule, by overloving honour, and riches, we deflect, and
detort these things, which are not in their nature ill, to ill uses, and
make them serve our ill purposes: Man falls, as a fall of waters, that
throwes downe, and corrupts all that it embraces. Nay beloved, when
³⁰⁰ a man hath used those wings, which God hath given him, and raised
himselfe to some heighth in religious knowledge, and religious practise, as *Eutichus,* out of a desire to hear *Paul* preach, was got up into
a Chamber, and up into a window of that Chamber, and yet falling
asleep, fell downe dead; so we may fall into a security of our present
state, into a pride of our knowledge, or of our purity, and so fall
lower, then they, who never came to our heighth. So much need have
we of a resurrection.

So sin is a fall, and every man is affraid of falling, even from his
temporall station; more affraid of falling, then of not beeing raised.
³¹⁰ And *Qui peccat, quatenus peccat, fit seipso deterior:* In every sin a
man falls from that degree which himselfe had before; In every sin,
he is dishonoured, he is not so good a man, as he was; impoverished,
he hath not so great a portion of grace as hee had; Infatuated, hee
hath not so much of the true wisedome of the feare of God, as he had;
disarmed, he hath not that interest and confidence in the love of God,
that he had: and deformed, he hath not so lively a representation of
the Image of God, as before. In every sin, we become prodigals, but
in the habit of sin, we become bankrupts, affraid to come to an account. A fall is a fearfull thing, that needs a raising, a help; but sin
³²⁰ is a death, and that needs a resurrection; and a resurrection is as great
a work, as the very Creation it selfe. It is death *in semine,* in the roote,

Ecclus. 38.1
V. 15

Acts 20.9

Mors

Clem. Alex.

it produces, it brings forth death; It is death *in arbore,* in the body, in it selfe; death is a divorce, and so is sin; and it is death *in fructu,* in the fruit thereof; sin plants spirituall death, and this death produces more sin, Obduration, Impenitence, and the like.

Be pleased to returne, and cast one halfe thought upon each of these: Sin is the roote of death; *Death by sin entred, and death passed upon all men, for all men have sinned.* It is death because we shall dye for it. But it is death in it selfe, We are dead already, dead in it;
³³⁰ *Thou hast a name, that thou livest, and art dead,* was spoken to a whole Church. It is not evidence enough, to prove that thou art alive, to say, I saw thee at a Sermon; that spirit, that knowes thy spirit, he that knowes whether thou wert moved by a Sermon, melted by a Sermon, mended by a Sermon, he knows whether thou be alive or no.

That which had wont to be said, That dead men walked in Churches, is too true; Men walk out a Sermon, or walk out after a Sermon, as ill as they walked in; they have a name that they live, and are dead: *But the houre is come, and now is, when the dead shall heare the voyce of the Son of God:* That is, at these houres they may
³⁴⁰ heare, if they will, and till they doe heare, they are dead. Sin is the root of death, the body of death, and then it is the fruit of death. S. *Augustine* confesses of himselfe, that he was *Allisus intra parietes in celebritate solemnitatum tuarum,* that in great meetings upon solemne dayes, in the Church, there, within the walls of Gods house, *Egit negotium procurandi fructus mortis,* he was not buying and selling doves, but buying and selling soules, by wanton lookes, cheapning and making the bargaine of the fruits of death, as himselfe expresses it. Sin is the root, and the tree, and the fruit of death; The mother of death, death it selfe, and the daughter of death; and from this death,
³⁵⁰ this threefold death, death past in our past sins, present death in our present insensiblenesse of sin, future death in those sins, with which sins God will punish our former, and present sins, (if he proceed meerly in justice) God affords us this first resurrection.

How? Thus. Death is the Divorce of body and soule; Resurrection is the Re-union of body and soule: And in this spirituall death, and resurrection, which we consider now, and which is all determined in ˙the soule it selfe, Grace is the soule of the soule, and so the departing of grace, is the death, and the returning of grace is the resurrection of

Rom. 5.12

Apoc. 3.1

Iohn 5.25

August.

Resurrectio

this sinfull soule. But how? By what way, what meanes? Consider
³⁶⁰ *Adam; Adam* was made to enjoy an immortality in his body; He
induced death upon himselfe: And then, as God having made Marriage for a remedy against uncleannesse, intemperate men make even
Marriage it selfe an occasion of more uncleannesse, then if they had
never married; so man having induced and created death, by sin,
God takes death, and makes it a means of the glorifying of his body,
in heaven. God did not induce death, death was not in his purpose;

but *veluti medium opportunum, quo vas confractum rursus fingere-*
tur, As a means, whereby a broken vessell might be made up againe,
God tooke death, and made it serve for that purpose, That men by
³⁷⁰ the grave might be translated to heaven.

So then, to the resurrection of the body, there is an ordinary way,
The grave; To the resurrection of the soule, there is an ordinary way
too, The Church. In the grave, the body that must be there prepared
for the last resurrection, hath wormes that eat upon it: In the Church,
the soule that comes to this first resurrection, must have wormes,
The worme, the sting, the remorse, the compunction of Conscience;
In those that have no part in this first resurrection, the worme of
conscience shall never die, but gnaw on, to desperation; but those
that have not this worme of conscience, this remorse, this compunc-
³⁸⁰ tion, shall never live. In the grave, which is the furnace, which ripens
the body for the last resurrection, there is a putrefaction of the body,
and an ill savour: In the Church, the wombe where my soule must
be mellowed for this first resurrection, my soul, which hath the savour
of death in it, as it is leavened throughout with sin, must stink in
my nostrils, and I come to a detestation of all those sins, which have
putrified her. And I must not be afraid to accuse my selfe, to condemne my selfe, to humble my selfe, lest I become a scorne to men;

Nemo me derideat ab eo medico ægrum sanari, à quo sibi præstitum
est ne ægrotaret; Let no man despise me, or wonder at me, that I am
³⁹⁰ so humbled under the hand of God, or that I fly to God as to my
Physitian when I am sick, since the same God that hath recovered
me as my Physitian when I was sick, hath been his Physitian too,
and kept him from being sick, who, but for that Physitian, had been
as ill as I was: At least he must be his Physitian, if ever he come to
be sick, and come to know that he is sick, and come to a right desire

to be well. Spirituall death was before bodily; sinne before the wages of sin; God hath provided a resurrection for both deaths, but first for the first; This is the first resurrection, Reconciliation to God, and the returning of the soule of our soule, Grace, in his Church, by his
400 Word, and his seales there.

Now every repentance is not a resurrection; It is rather a waking out of a dreame, then a rising to a new life: Nay it is rather a startling in our sleep, then any awaking at all, to have a sudden remorse, a sudden flash, and no constant perseverance. *Awake thou that sleep-est,* sayes the Apostle, out of the Prophet: First *awake,* come to a sense of thy state; and then *arise from the dead,* sayes he, from the practise of dead works; and then, *Christ shall give thee light:* life, and strength to walk in new wayes. It is a long work, and hath many steps; *Awake, arise,* and *walke,* and therefore set out betimes; At the
410 last day, in those, which shall be found alive upon the earth, we say there shall be a sudden death, and a sudden resurrection, *In raptu, in transitu, in ictu oculi,* In an instant, in the twinckling of an eye; but do not thou trust to have this first Resurrection *In raptu, in transitu, in ictu oculi,* In thy last passage upon thy death-bed, when the twinckling of the eye, must be the closing of thine eyes: But as we assign to glorified bodies after the last Resurrection, certain *Dotes,* (as we call them in the Schoole) certaine Endowments, so labour thou to finde those endowments, in thy soule here, if thou beest come to this first Resurrection.

Ephes. 5.14
Esay 60.1

420 Amongst those Endowments we assigne *Subtilitatem, Agilitatem;* The glorified bodie is become more subtile, more nimble, not en-cumbred, not disable for any motion, that it would make; So hath that soule, which is come to this first Resurrection, by grace, a spir-ituall agility, a holy nimblenesse in it, that it can slide by tentations, and passe through tentations, and never be polluted; follow a call-ing, without taking infection, by the ordinary tentations of that call-ing. So have those glorified bodies *Claritatem,* a brightnesse upon them, from the face of God; and so have these soules, which are come to this first resurrection, a sun in themselves, an inherent light,
430 by which they can presently distinguish betweene action and action; what must, what may, what must not bee done. But of all the endow-ments of the glorified body, we consider most, *Impassibilitatem,* That

that body shall suffer nothing; and is sure that it shall suffer nothing. And that which answers that endowment of the body most in this soule, that is come to this first resurrection, is as the Apostle speaks,

Rom. 8.[35]

That neither persecution, sicknesse, nor death, shall separate her from Christ Iesus. In Heaven we doe not say, that our bodies shall devest their mortality, so, as that naturally they could not dye; for they shall have a composition still; and every compounded thing may perish: 440 but they shal be so assured, and with such a preservation, as they shall alwaies know they shall never dye. S. *Augustine* saies well,

Aug.

Assit motio, absit fatigatio, assit potestas vescendi, absit necessitas esuriendi; They have in their nature a mortality, and yet be immortall; a possibility and an impossibility of dying, with those two divers relations, one to nature, the other to preservation, will consist together. So in this soule, that hath this first Resurrection from sin, by grace, a conscience of her owne infirmity, that she may relapse, and yet a testimony of the powerfulnesse of Gods Spirit, that easily she shall not relapse, may consist well together. But the last seale of this 450 holy confidence is reserved for that, which is the third acceptation of this first Resurrection; not from persecutions in this world, nor from sin in this world, but from all possibility of falling back into sin, in the world to come; and to this, have divers Expositors referred these words, this first resurrection. *Blessed and holy is he, that hath part in this first Resurrection.*

3 Part

Now, a Resurrection of the soule, seemes an improper, an impertinent, an improbable, an impossible forme of speech; for, Resurrection implies death, and the soule does not dye in her passage to Heaven. And therefore *Damascen* makes account, that he hath

De ortho. fid. l. 4. c. ult.

460 sufficiently proved the Resurrection of the body (which seems so incredible) if he could prove any Resurrection; if there be any Resurrection at all, saies he, it must be of the body, for the soule cannot dye, therefore not rise. Yet have not those Fathers, nor those Expositors, who have in this text, acknowledged a Resurrection of the soule, mistaken nor miscalled the matter. Take *Damascens* owne definition of Resurrection: *Resurrectio est ejus quod cecidit secunda surrectio:* A Resurrection is a second rising to that state, from which any thing is formerly fallen. Now though by death, the soule do not fall into any such state, as that it can complaine, (for what can that

⁴⁷⁰ lack, which God fils?) yet by death, the soule fals from that, for which it was infused, and poured into man at first; that is, to be the forme of that body, the King of that Kingdome; and therefore, when in the generall Resurrection, the soule returnes to that state, for which it was created, and to which it hath had an affection, and a desire, even in the fulnesse of the Joyes of Heaven, then, when the soule returnes to her office, to make up the man, because the whole man hath, therefore the soule hath a Resurrection; not from death, but from a deprivation of her former state; that state, which she was made for, and is ever enclined to.

⁴⁸⁰ But that is the last Resurrection; and so the soule hath part even in that last Resurrection; But we are in hand with the first Resurrection of the soule; and that is, when that soule, which was at first breath'd from God, and hath long suffered a banishment, a close imprisonment in this body, returnes to God againe; The returning of the soule to him, from whom it proceeded at first, is a Resurrection of the soule. Here then especially, I feele the straitnesse of time; two considerations open themselves together, of such a largenesse, as all the time from *Moses* his *In principio,* when time began, to the Angels *Affidavit,* in this booke, *That shall say and sweare, that time* [Apoc. 10.6]
⁴⁹⁰ *shall be no more,* were too narrow to contemplate these two Hemispheares of Man, this Evening, and Morning of Mans everlasting day; The miseries of man, in this banishment, in this emprisonment, in this grave of the soule, the body, And the glory, and exaltation of that soule in her Resurrection to Heaven. That soule, which being borne free, is made a slave to this body, by comming to it; It must act, but what this body will give it leave to act, according to the Organs, which this body affords it; and if the body be lame in any limme, the soule must be lame in her operation, in that limme too; It must doe, but what the body will have it doe, and then it must
⁵⁰⁰ suffer, whatsoever that body puts it to, or whatsoever any others will put that body to: If the body oppresse it selfe with Melancholy, the soule must be sad; and if other men oppresse the body with injury, the soule must be sad too; Consider, (it is too immense a thing to consider it) reflect but one thought, but upon this one thing in the soule, here, and hereafter, In her grave, the body, and in her Resurrection in Heaven; That is the knowledge of the soule.

Here saies S. *Augustine,* when the soule considers the things of this world, *Non veritate certior, sed consuetudine securior;* She rests upon such things as she is not sure are true, but such as she sees, are
510 ordinarily received and accepted for truths: so that the end of her knowledge is not Truth, but opinion, and the way, not Inquisition, but ease: But saies he, when she proceeds in this life, to search into heavenly things, *Verberatur luce veritatis,* The beames of that light are too strong for her, and they sink her, and cast her downe, *Et ad familiaritatem tenebrarum suarum, non electione sed fatigatione convertitur;* and so she returnes to her owne darknesse, because she is most familiar, and best acquainted with it; *Non electione,* not because she loves ignorance, but because she is weary of the trouble of seeking out the truth, and so swallowes even any Religion to escape
520 the paine of debating, and disputing; and in this lazinesse she sleeps out her lease, her terme of life, in this death, in this grave, in this body.

But then in her Resurrection, her measure is enlarged, and filled at once; There she reads without spelling, and knowes without thinking, and concludes without arguing; she is at the end of her race, without running; In her triumph, without fighting; In her Haven, without sayling: A free-man, without any prentiship; at full yeares, without any wardship; and a Doctor, without any proceeding: She knowes truly, and easily, and immediately, and entirely, and ever-
530 lastingly; Nothing left out at first, nothing worne out at last, that conduces to her happinesse. What a death is this life? what a resurrection is this death? For though this world be a sea, yet (which is most strange) our Harbour is larger then the sea; Heaven infinitely larger then this world. For, though that be not true, which *Origen* is said to say, That at last all shall be saved, nor that evident, which *Cyril* of Alexandria saies, That without doubt the number of them that are saved, is far greater then of them that perish, yet surely the number of them, with whom we shall have communion in Heaven, is greater then ever lived at once upon the face of the earth: And of
540 those who lived in our time, how few did we know? and of those whom we did know, how few did we care much for? In Heaven we
Aug.   shall have Communion of Joy and Glory with all, alwaies; *Vbi non intrat inimicus, nec amicus exit,* Where never any man shall come in that loves us not, nor go from us that does.

Beloved, I thinke you could be content to heare, I could be content to speake of this Resurrection, our glorious state, by the low way of the grave, till God by that gate of earth, let us in at the other of precious Stones. And blessed and holy is he, who in a rectified conscience desires that resurrection now. But we shall not depart far
550 from this consideration, by departing into our last branch, or conclusion, That this first Resurrection may also be understood to be the first riser Christ Jesus; and *Blessed and holy is he that hath part in that first Resurrection.*

This first Resurrection is then without any detorting, any violence, very appliable to Christ himself, who was *Primitiæ dormientium,* in that, that action, *That he rose again, he is become* (sayes the Apostle) *the first fruits of them that sleep:* He did rise, and rise first; others rose with him, none before him: for S. *Hierome* taking the words as he finds them in that Euangelist, makes this note, That
560 though the graves were opened, at the instant of Christs death, (death was overcome, the City opened the gates) yet the bodies did not rise till after Christs Resurrection. For, for such Resurrections as are spoken of, *That women received their dead raised to life again,* and such as are recorded in the old and new Testament, they were all unperfect and temporary resurrections, such, as S. *Hierome* sayes of them all, *Resurgebant iterum morituri;* They were but reprieved, not pardoned; They had a Resurrection to life, but yet a Resurrection to another death. Christ is the first Resurrection; others were raised; but he only rose; they by a forraine, and extrinsique, he by his
570 owne power.

But we call him not the first, in that respect onely; for so he was not onely the first, but the onely; he alone rose by his owne power; but with relation to all our future Resurrections, he is the first Resurrection. First, *If Christ be not raised, your faith is in vaine,* saies the Apostle; You have a vaine faith if you beleeve in a dead man. He might be true Man, though he remained in death; but it concernes you to beleeve, that he was the Son of God too; *And he was declared to be the Son of God, by the Resurrection from the dead.* That was the declaration of himselfe, his Justification; he was justified by the
580 Spirit, when he was proved to be God, by raising himselfe. But thus our Justification is also in his Resurrection. For, *He was raised from*

4 Part

I Cor. 15.20

Hier. in
Mat.
27.52

Heb. 11.35

Hier.

I Cor. 15.17

Rom. 1. 4

Rom. 4. ult.

the dead, for our Iustification: how for ours? *That we should be also in the likenesse of his Resurrection.* What is that? that he hath told us before; *Our Resurrection in Christ is, that we should walke in new-nesse of life.*

Rom. 6.4

So that then Christ is the first Resurrection, first, Efficiently, the onely cause of his owne Resurrection; First, Meritoriously, the onely cause of our Resurrection; first, Exemplarily, the onely patterne, how we should rise, and how we should walke, when we are up; and
590 therefore, Blessed and happy are we, if we referre all our resurrections to this first Resurrection Christ Jesus. For as *Iob* said of Comforters, so miserable Resurrections are they all without him.

If therefore thou need and seeke this first Resurrection, in the first acceptation, a Resurrection from persecutions, and calamities, as they oppresse thee here, have thy recourse to him, to Christ. Remember that at the death of Christ, there were earthquakes; the whole earth trembled; There were rendings of the Temple; Schismes, Convulsions, distractions in the Church will be: But then, the graves opened in the midst of those commotions; Then when thou thinkest thy selfe
600 swallowed, and buried in affliction, as the Angell did his, Christ Jesus shall remove thy grave stone, and give thee a resurrection; but if thou thinke to remove it by thine owne wit, thine owne power, or the favour of potent Friends, *Digitus Dei non est hic,* The hand of God is not in all this, and the stone shall lye still upon thee, till thou putrifie into desperation, and thou shalt have no part in this first Resurrection.

If thou need, and seek this first resurrection, in the second acceptation, from the fearfull death of hainous sin, have thy recourse to him, to Christ Jesus, and remember the waight of the sins that lay upon
610 him: All thy sins, and all thy Fathers, and all thy childrens sins, all those sins that did induce the first flood, and shall induce the last fire upon this world; All those sins, which that we might take example by them to scape them, are recorded, and which, lest we should take example by them, to imitate them, are left unrecorded; all sins, of all ages, all sexes, all places, al times, all callings, sins heavy in their substance, sins aggravated by their circumstances, all kinds of sins, and all particular sins of every kind, were upon him, upon Christ Jesus; and yet he raised his holy Head, his royall Head, though under

thornes, yet crowned with those thornes, and triumphed in this first
620 Resurrection: and his body was not left in the Grave, nor his soule
in Hell. Christs first tongue was a tongue that might be heard, He
spoke to the Shepheards by Angels; His second tongue was a Star,
a tongue which might be seene; He spoke to the Wisemen of the
East by that. Hearken after him these two waies; As he speakes to
thine eare, (and to thy soul, by it) in the preaching of his Word, as
he speakes to thine eye, (and so to thy soule by that) in the exhibit-
ing of his Sacraments: And thou shalt have thy part in this first
Resurrection. But if thou thinke to overcome this death, this sense
of sin, by diversions, by worldly delights, by mirth, and musique, and
630 society, or by good works, with a confidence of merit in them, or
with a relation to God himselfe, but not as God hath manifested
himselfe to thee, not in Christ Jesus, The stone shall lye still upon
thee, till thou putrifie into desperation, and then hast thou no part in
this first Resurrection.

If thou desire this first Resurrection in the third acceptation, as
S. *Paul* did, To be dissolved, and to be with Christ, go Christs way
to that also. He desired that glory that thou doest; and he could have
laid down his soul when he would; but he staid his houre, sayes the
Gospel. He could have ascended immediatly, immediatly in time,
640 yet he staid to descend into hell first; and he could have ascended
immediatly of himself, by going up, yet he staid till he was taken up.
Thou hast no such power of thine own soul and life, not for the time,
not for the means of comming to this first Resurrection by death; Stay
therefore patiently, stay chearfully Gods leasure till he call; but not
so over-chearfully, as to be loath to go when he cals. Reliefe in persecution by power, reconciliation in sin by grace, dissolution, and
transmigration to heaven by death, are all within this first Resurrection: But that which is before them all, is Christ Jesus.

And therefore, as all that the naturall man promises himself with-
650 out God, is impious, so all that we promise our selves, though by God,
without Christ, is frivolous. God, who hath spoken to us by his Son,
works upon us by his Son too; He was our Creation, he was our Redemption, he is our Resurrection. And that man trades in the world
without money, and goes out of the world without recommendation,
that leaves out Christ Jesus. To be a good Morall man, and refer all

to the law of Nature in our hearts, is but *Diluculum,* The dawning
of the day; To be a godly man, and refer all to God, is but *Crepus-*
culum, A twylight; But the Meridionall brightnesse, the glorious
noon, and heighth, is to be a Christian, to pretend to no spirituall, no
660 temporall blessing, but for, and by, and through, and in our only
Lord and Saviour Christ Jesus; for he is this first Resurrection, and
Blessed and holy is he, that hath part in this first Resurrection.

Number 3.

Preached at Saint Dunstans
Aprill 11. 1624.

The first Sermon in that Church, as Vicar thereof.

DEUT. 25.5. *IF BRETHREN DWELL TOGETHER, AND ONE OF THEM DIE, AND HAVE NO CHILDE, THE WIFE OF THE DEAD SHALL NOT MARY WITHOUT, UNTO A STRANGER; HER HUSBANDS BROTHER SHALL GOE IN UNTO HER, AND TAKE HER TO HIM TO WIFE, AND PERFORME THE DUTY OF AN HUSBANDS BROTHER UNTO HER.*

FROM THE beginning God intimated a detestation, a dislike of *singularity;* of beeing *Alone.* The first time that God himselfe is named in the Bible, in the first verse of *Genesis,* hee is named *Plurally, Creavit Dii, Gods,* Gods in the plurall, Created Heaven and Earth. God, which is but *one,* would not appeare, nor bee presented so *alone,* but that hee would also manifest more persons. As the *Creator* was not *Singular,* so neither were the *creatures;* First, he created *heaven and earth;* both together; which were to be the generall parents, and out of which were to bee produced all other creatures; and then, he made all those other creatures plurally too; *Male, and Female created hee them;* And when he came to make *him,* for whose sake (next to his own glory) he made the whole world, *Adam,* he left not *Adam alone,* but joyned an *Eve* to him; Now, when they were *maried,* we know, but wee know not when they were *divorced;* we heare when *Eve* was made, but not when shee *dyed;* The husbands

81

death is recorded at last, the wives is not at all. So much detestation hath God himselfe, and so little memory would hee have kept of any singularity, of being alone. The union of Christ to the whole Church is not expressed by any metaphore, by any figure, so oft in the Scrip-
²⁰ ture, as by this of *Mariage:* and there in that union with Christ to the whole Church, neither husband, nor wife can ever die; Christ is immortall as hee is *himselfe,* and immortall, as hee is the *head* of the Church, the *Husband* of that wife: for that wife, the Church is immortall too; for as a Prince is the same Prince, when he fights a battaile, and when hee triumphs after the victory: so the militant, and the triumphant Church is the same Church. There can bee no *Widower,* There can bee no *Dowager,* in that case; *Hee* cannot, *shee* cannot die. But then this Metaphore, this spirituall Mariage, holds not onely betweene Christ and the whole Church, in which case there
³⁰ can be no Widow, but in the union between Christs *particular Ministers,* and *particular Churches;* and there, in that case, the husband of that wife may die; The present Minister may die, and so that Church be a Widow; And in that case, and for provision of such Widows, wee consider the accommodation of this Law, *If brethren dwell together, and one of them die, and have no childe, the wife of the dead shall not mary without, unto a stranger, &c.*

This law was but a *permissive* law; rather a *dispensation,* then a *law:* as the permitting of *usury* to bee taken of strangers, and the permitting of *divorces* in so many cases, were. At most it was but a
⁴⁰ *Iudiciall* law, and therefore layes no obligation, upon any other nation, then *them,* to whom it was given, the *Iews.* And therefore wee enquire not the *reasons* of that law, (the *reasons* were determined in that *people*) wee examine not the *conveniences* of the law; (the *conveniences* were determined in those *times*) wee lay hold onely upon the *Typique signification,* and appliablenesse of the law, as that *secular Mariage* there spoken of, may be appliable to this *spirituall Mariage,* the Mariage of the Minister to the Church: *If Brethren dwell together, &c.*

Divisio   From these words then, wee shall make our approaches, and ap-
⁵⁰ plication, to the present occasion, by these steps; First, there is a mariage, in the case. The taking, and leaving of a Church, is not an indifferent, an arbitrary thing; It is a *Mariage,* and Mariage implies,

Honour: It is an honourable estate, and that implies *Charge,* it is a burdensome state; There is *Honos,* and *Onus,* Honour, and labour, in Mariage; You must bee content to afford the *honour,* wee must bee content to endure the *labour.* And so in that point, as our *Incumbencie* upon a Church, is our *Mariage* to that Church, wee shall as farre, as the occasion admits, see what mariage includes, and what it excludes; what it requires, what it forbids. It is a mariage, and a

⁶⁰ mariage after the death of another: *If one dye,* sayes the Text; Howsoever the *Romane Church* in the exercise of their *Tyranny,* have forbidden Church-men to mary, then when they have *Orders,* and forbidden *Orders* to bee given to any, who have formerly beene maried, if they maried *Widowes,* God is pleased here, to afford us, some intimation, some adumbration, a *Typicall* and exemplar knowledge of the lawfulnesse of such mariages, hee maries after the death of a former husband; and then farther, a brother maries the wife of his deceased brother. Now into the *reasons* of the law, literally given, and literally accepted, wee looke not; It is enough, that *God* hath a

⁷⁰ care of the preservation of *names* and *families* and *inheritances* in those distinctions, and in those *Tribes,* where hee layd them then; but for the accommodation of the law to our present application, it must bee a *brother, a spirituall brother, a professor* of the *same faith,* that succeeds in this mariage, in this possession, and this government of that widow Church. It must be a brother, and *Frater cohabitans,* says our Text, a brother that dwelt together, with the former husband; he must be of *the same houshold of the faithfull,* as well as professe the same faith; he must dwell in the house of God, not *separate* himselfe, or encourage others to doe so, for matter of *Ceremonies,* and *disci-*

⁸⁰ *pline; Idolaters* must not, *Separatists* must not be admitted to these mariages, to these widow Churches. And then it is a surrendring to a brother *dead without Children:* In this *spirituall procreation* of children, we all dye without children *of our own;* Though by our labours, when God blesses them, you become children, yet you are *Gods children,* not ours; we *nurse* you by his word, but his *Spirit begets you by the same word;* we must not challenge to *us,* that which God onely can doe. And then being thus maried to this widow, taking the charge of this Church, he must, says our text, *performe the duty of a husbands brother. He must,* it is a *personall* service, not to

[Gal. 6.10]

⁹⁰ be done always by *Proxy*, and *Delegates; He must;* and he must *performe;* not *begin* well, and not *persist, commence* and not *consummate*, but *performe* the worke; and performe the worke, as it is a
duty; It is a meer *mercy* in God, to send us to you, but it is a *duty* in
us, to doe that which we are sent for, by his *Word*, and his *Sacraments,*
to establish you in his holy obedience, and his rich, and honourable
service. And then our duty consists in both these, that we behave our
selves, *as your husband,* which implies a *power,* an *authority;* but a
power and authority rooted in *love,* and exercised with love; and then
that we doe all as *brothers to the former husband,* that as one inten-
¹⁰⁰ tion of this law was, that *inheritances,* and *temporall proprieties*
might be preserved, so our care might be through predecessor, and
successor, and all, that all rights might be preserved to all men, that
nothing not due, or due onely in rigor, be extorted from the people,
nothing that is in truth, or in equity due, be with-held from the
Minister; but that the true *right* of *people,* and *Pastor,* and *Patron*
be preserved, to the preservation of love, and peace, and good opinion
of one another.

*Matri-
monium*

First then, that which we take upon us, is a *Mariage.* Amongst the
Jews, it was almost an ignominious, an infamous thing, to die un-
¹¹⁰ maried, at least to die without children, being maried. Amongst the
Gentiles it was so too, all well governed States ever enlarged themselves, in giving places of command and profit, to *maried men.* Indeed
such men are most properly said to keep *this world* in reparations,
that provide a succession of children; and for the *next world,* though
all that are borne into this world, doe not enter into the number of
Gods Saints, in heaven, yet the Saints of heaven can be made out of
no other materialls, but men borne into this world. Every stone in
the quarry is not sure to be imployed in the building of the Church,
but the Church must be built out of those stones; and therefore they
¹²⁰ keep this world, they keep heaven it selfe in reparation, that *mary*
in the feare of God, and in the same feare bring up the children of
such a mariage. But I presse not this too literally, nor over perswa-

[Acts
10:34]

sively, that every man is bound to *mary; God is no accepter of persons,* nor of *conditions.* But being to use these words in their figurative
application, I say, every man is bound to marry himselfe to a profession, to a calling: God hath brought him from being *nothing,* by

creating him, but he resolves himselfe into nothing againe, if he take no calling upon him. In our *Baptisme* we make our contract with *God,* that we will believe all those *Articles* there recited; there's our
130 contract with *him;* and then, pursuing this contract, in the *other Sacrament,* when we take his body and his blood, we are *maried* to him. So at the same time, at our *Baptisme,* we make a contract in the presence of God, and his congregation, with the *world;* that we wil forsake the covetous desires of the world, that is, the covetous proprieting of all things to our selves, the covetous living onely for our selves, there's our contract with the world, that we will mutually assist, and serve our brethren in the world; and then, when we take *particular callings,* by which we are enabled to perform that former contract, then we are maried to the world; so every man is duly *con-*
140 *tracted* to the world, in *Baptisme,* and lawfully *maried* to the world in accepting a *profession.* And so this service of ours to the Church is our mariage.

Now in a Matrimoniall state, there is *Onus* and *Honos,* a burden to be born, an *Honour* to be received. The burden of the sinnes of the *whole world,* was a burden onely for *Christs* shoulders; but the sinnes of *this Parish,* will ly upon my shoulders, if I be *silent,* or if I be *indulgent,* and denounce not Gods Judgement upon those sinnes. It will be a burden to us, if we doe not, and God knowes it is a burden to us, when we do denounce those Judgements. *Esay* felt, and groned
150 under this burden, when he cried *Onus Babylonis, Onus Moab,* and *Onus Damasci, O the burden of Babylon,* and the *burden of Damascus,* and so the other Prophets grone often under this burden, in contemplation of other places: It burdened, it troubled, it grieved the holy Prophets of God, that they must denounce Gods judgements, though upon Gods enemies. We reade of a compassionate *Generall,* that looking upon his great Army, from a hill, fell into a bitter weeping, upon this consideration, that in fiftie or sixtie yeares hence, there will not be a man of these that fight now, alive upon the earth. What Sea could furnish mine eyes with teares enough, to poure out, if I
160 should think, that of all this Congregation, which lookes me in the face now, I should not meet one, at the Resurrection, at the right hand of God! And for so much as concerns me, it is all one, if none of you be saved, as if none of you be saved by *my help,* my means,

Onus

my assistance, my preaching. If I put you upon miraculous wayes, to
be saved without hearing, or upon extraordinary wayes to be saved
by *hearing others,* this shall aggravate my condemnation, though you
be saved: How much more heavy must my burden be, if by my negligence both I and you perish too? So then this calling, this marriage,
is a burden every way. When at any midnight I heare a bell toll from
170 this steeple, must not I say to my selfe, what have I done at any time
for the instructing or rectifying of that mans Conscience, who lieth
there now ready to deliver up his own account, and my account to
Almighty God? If he be not able to make a good account, he and I
are in danger, because I have not enabled him; and though he be for
himself able, that delivers not me, if I have been no instrument for
the doing of it. Many, many burdens lie upon this calling, upon this
marriage; but our *recompense* is, that marriage is as well an honourable as a painefull calling.

Honos.   *If I be a Father, where is mine Honour?* saith God: If you can
Malac. 1.6 180 answer God, *Why, you have it in your Prophets, They have it,* that
satisfieth him, that dischargeth you. For, *he that receiveth them, receiveth him:* But if Christ, who repeats that complaint, in every one
of the foure Evangelists, finde it repeated in every one of his *Prophets*
[Joh. 4.44] too, in every one of *us,* That *a Prophet hath no honour in his own
Countrie,* that a *Pastor* is least respected of his *own flock,* you have
not your *Quietus est,* for the honour due to God; God never discharges the honour due to him, if it be not paid into their hands,
whom he sendeth for it, to them upon whom he hath directed it.
Would the King believe that man, to honour him, that violateth his
190 *Image,* or that calumniateth his *Ambassadour?* Every man is the
Image of God; every *Creature* is the *Ambassadour* of God; *The
[Psa. 19.1] Heavens,* (and as well as the Heavens, the Earth) *declare the glory
of God;* but the *Civill Magistrate,* and the *Spirituall Pastor,* who have
married the *two Daughters of God,* The *State* and the *Church,* are
the *Images* and *Ambassadours of God,* in a higher and more peculiar
sense, and for that marriage are to be honoured. And then Honour
implieth *that,* by which Honour subsisteth, *maintenance;* and they
which withdraw *that injuriously,* or with-hold *that contentiously,* dishonour God, in the dishonour of his servants, and so make this mar-
200 riage, this calling onely burdensome and not honourable.

So then the interest of your *particular Minister,* and the particular Church, being such as between *Man* and *Wife, a marriage,* we consider the uses of marriage in Gods first intention, and apply them to this marriage. Gods first intentions in marriage were two. *In adjutorium,* for mutuall helpers, and *in prolem,* for procreation, and education of Children. For both these are we made Husbands of Churches; *In prolem,* to assist in the *regeneration of Children,* for the inheritance of Heaven; and *in adjutorium,* to be helpers to one another. And therefore if the husband, the Pastor, put the wife, his flock in a

210 *Circumcision,* to pare themselves to the quick, to take from their necessary means to sustain their families, to satisfie him; the wife will say as *Zipporah* said to *Moses, Sponsus sanguinum, a bloudy husband art thou,* that exactest and extortest more then is due. In that case the Husband is no *helper.* But if we be always ready to help your children over the threshold, (as Saint *Augustine* calls Baptisme, *Limen Ecclesiæ*) always ready to *Baptize* the Children; if we be always ready to help you in all your *spirituall diseases,* to that *Cordiall,* that *Balsamum,* the *body and bloud of Christ Jesus;* If we be always ready to help you in all your *bodily distresses,* ready even at your last gasp to

220 open your eyes then, when your best friends are ready to close them; ready to deliver your souls into the hands of God, when all the rest about you are ready to receive into their hands, that which you leave behinde you, and then ready to lay up the *garments* of your *soules,* your bodies, in the *wardrobe* the *grave,* till you call for them, and put them on again, in the resurrection, then are we truely *helpers,* true husbands; and then if the Wife will say, as *Jobs* wife to the husband, *Curse God and die,* be sorry, that thou hast taken this *Profession* upon thee, and live in penury, and die in povertie; In a word, if he presse too much, if she withdraw too much, this frustrates Gods purpose in

230 making that a marriage; they are not mutuall helpers to one another. These were Gods two principall intentions in marriage, *in adjutorium, in prolem.* But then mans fall induced a third, *in remedium,* That for a remedy against burning, and to avoid fornication, every man should have his own wife, every woman her own husband. And so *in remedium,* for a remedy against *spirituall fornication,* of running after *other men* in other places, out of disaffection to their own Pastor, or over affecting another, God hath given every wife, her own hus-

[Exod. 4.25]

[Job 2.9]

band, Every Church her own Pastor. And to all these purposes, our
function is a marriage.

Defuncti   ²⁴⁰   It is a marriage, it deserves the honour, it undertakes the burden of
Levit. 21.14   that state; and then it is a marriage *of a widow, of a Church left in*
widow-hood by the death of her former husband. In the Law literally
God forbad the *High Priest* to *marry a widdow.* The Romane Church
continues that literally, and more; they extend it; that which was in
figure, enjoined to the *High Priest* onely, they in *fact* extend to all
Priests; no man that ever married a widow, may be a priest, though
she be dead, when he desires orders. There is no question but there is
a more *exemplary sanctity* required in the Priest, then in other persons, and more in those, who are in high places in the Church, then
²⁵⁰ in those of inferiour Jurisdictions, and the name and title of *Virginity,*
hath ever been exhibited as an Embleme, as a Type of especiall
2 Cor. 11.2   Sanctity. And as such the Apostle uses it when he saith, *That he would*
present the Church of Corinth, as a chaste Virgine to Christ; That is,
as chaste as a Virgin, though married, for so he saith in the words
immediately before, *That he had espoused them to a husband:* As
[Heb. 13.4]   marriage is an honourable state, though in poverty, so is the *bed*
undefiled with strange lust, a chaste bed even in marriage. And in the
accommodation of the *Figure* to the present occasion, our marriage
to severall Churches, if we might marry no *widowes,* (no Churches,
²⁶⁰ which had been wives to former husbands) we should finde few
Virgins, that is, Churches newly erected for us. But when the wife of
a former husband is left a widow, *Nubat in Domino,* saith the Apostle,
1 Cor. 7.39   *In Gods name let her marry.*

But the former husband must be *dead:* The husbands *absence*
makes not the wife a widow; nor doth the necessary, and lawfull
absence of the Pastor, make the Church *vacant.* The *sicknesse* of the
husband makes not a widow; The *bodily weaknesse nay the spirituall*
weaknes of the Pastor in case that his parts and abilities, and faculties,
be grown but weak, do not make his Church vacant. If the Pastor be
²⁷⁰ *suspended,* or otherwise censured, this is but as a separation, or as a
divorce; and as the wife is not a widow, upon a divorce, so neither is
the Church vacant, upon such censures. And therefore for them that
take advantages upon the weaknesses, or upon the *disgrace,* or upon
the *povertie* of any such *incumbent,* and so insinuate themselves into

his Church, this is *intrusion,* this is *spirituall adultery,* for the husband
is not *dead,* though he be sick. Nay if they would remove him by way
of *preferment,* yet that is a *supplantation;* when *Jacob* had *Esau* by the   Gen. 25.26
heel, whether he kept him in, till he might be strong enough to goe out
before him, or whether he pushed him out, before he would have gone,
²⁸⁰ *Jacob* was a supplanter. Some few cases are put when a wife becomes
as a widow, her husband living; but regularly it is by death. In some
few cases, Churches may otherwise be vacant, but regularly it is by
death. And then *Esto vidua in Domo Patris,* saith *Judah* to *Thamar,*   Gen. 38.11
Remain a widow at thy fathers house: Then the Church remaineth in
the house, in the hands of her *Father,* the *Bishop* of that *Dioces,* till a
new husband be lawfully tendred unto her: And till that time, as our
Saviour Christ recommended his most blessed Mother, to Saint *John,*
but not as a wife, so that Bishop delivers that Church, to the care and
administration of some other during her widowhood, till by due
²⁹⁰ course she become the wife of another.

    Thus our calling is a mariage; It should have *honour;* It must have   *Fratris*
labour; and it is a lawfull mariage upon a just and equitable *vacancy*
of the place, without any supplantation; upon death; And then it is
upon death of a *brother; If brethren dwell together, and one of them
die, and have no childe, the wife, &c.* Aswell Saint *Gregory,* as Saint   Gregor.
Augustine before, interpret this of our elder, our eldest brother *Christ*   Aug.
Iesus. That *hee* being dead, we mary his wife, the Church, and become
husbands to her. But Christ, in that capacity, as he is head of the
Church, cannot die. That to which, the application of this law, leads
³⁰⁰ us, is, That *predecessor,* and *successor,* bee brethren of the same faith,
and the same profession of faith. The Sadduces put a case to Christ of
a woman maried successively to *seven* men; let seven signifie infinite;
still those seven were *brethren.* How often soever any wife change her
husband, any Church, her Pastor, God sends us still a succession of
brethren, sincere, and unfeigned *Preachers* of the same truth, sonnes
of the same father; Who is that father? God is our Father; *Have we*   Mal. 2.10
not all one Father, says the Prophet? Yes, we have, and so a worme,
and we, are brethren, by the same father, and mother, the same God,
the same Earth. *Hath not the raine a father?* The raine hath; and the   Iob 38.28
³¹⁰ same that wee have. More narrowly, and yet very largely, Christ is our
father; One of his names is, *The everlasting Father;* And then after   Esa. 9.6

I Sam. 24.11

Bellarmin.

Ier. 2.27
Iob 17.14

Cohabitans

I Chron.
25.7

these, after God, after Christ, the *King* is our father; *See, my father, the skirt of thy robe, in my hand,* says *David* to his King *Saul;* Now if any husband should be offered to any widow, any Pastor to any vacant Church, who were not our *brother by all* these *fathers,* in a right beliefe in *God,* the Father of all *men,* in a right profession of *Christ Iesus,* the Father of all *Christians,* in a right affection, and allegiance to the *King,* the Father of all *Subjects,* Any that should incline to a forain father, an imaginary universall father, he of whom ³²⁰ his *Vice-fathers,* his Junior fathers, the *Iesuites* (for all the Jesuits are *Fathers*) says, That the Fathers of the Church are but sons, and not fathers, to *him;* They that say to a stock, to the Image of the beast, *Thou art my father,* who, (not in a sense of humiliation, as *Iob* speaks the words) but of pride, say to *corruption, Thou art my father,* that is, that prostrate themselves to all the corruptions of a prostitute Church: If any so inclined of himself, or so inclinable if occasion should invite him, or rather tempt him, be offered for a husband to any widow, for a Pastor to any vacant Church, he is not within the accommodation of this law, hee is not our *brother,* by the *whole bloud,* ³³⁰ who hath not a brotherhood rooted in the same *religion,* and in the *allegiance* to the same Soveraign.

He must be a brother, and *Frater Cohabitans, a brother dwelling with the former brother.* As he is a brother, we consider the *unity of faith:* As he dwels in the same house, we consider the *unity of discipline;* That as he beleeves, and professes the same articles of faith, so by his own obedience, and by his instructing of others, hee establish the same government; A *Schismatique* is no more a brother to this purpose, then an *Heretique.* If we look well, we shall see, that Christ provided better for his garments, then for his flesh; he suffered his ³⁴⁰ flesh to be torn, but not his seamlesse garment. There may bee, in many cases, more mischief, in disobeying the uniformity of the discipline of the Church, then in mistaking in opinion, some doctrine of the Church. Wee see in Gods institution of his first Church, whom he called *brethren:* Those who were instructed, and *cunning in the songs of the Church,* they are called *brethren;* To oppose the orders of the Church solemnly ordained, or customarily admitted, for the advancement of Gods glory, and the devotion of the Congregation, forfeits this brotherhood, or at least discontinues the purpose and use of it; for,

howsoever they may bee in a kinde, *brothers,* if they succeed in the
³⁵⁰ profession of the same faith, yet wee see where the blessednesse is
settled, *Blessed are they that dwell in thy house;* And we see, where the
goodnesse, and the pleasantnesse is settled, *Behold, how good, and
how pleasant a thing it is, for brethren to dwell together in unity:* So
that, if they be not *brothers* in the *same faith,* and brothers in the
same houshold of the faithfull, and brothers in the same *allegiance,*
If they advance not the *truth* of the Church, and the *peace* of the
Church, and the *head* of the Church, fomentors of *Error,* and of
Schisme, and *Sedition,* are not husbands for these widows, Pastors for
these Churches.

Psal. 84.4
[Psal.] 133.1

³⁶⁰   Hee must bee a brother; A brother dwelling in the same house of
Christ, and then brother to one dead *without children,* as *Tertullian*
expresses it in his particular elegancy *Illiberis;* that is, content to be his
brother, in that sense, in that capacity, to claime no children, no
spirituall children of his own begetting; not to attribute to *himself*
that holy generation of the Saints of God, as though his learning, or
his wit, or his labour, had saved them; but to content himselfe to have
been the *foster father,* and to have nursed those children, whom the
Spirit of God, by over-shadowing the Church, hath begot upon her,
for, though it be with the word of truth, in our preaching, yet of *his*
³⁷⁰ *own will begot he us,* though *by the word,* says the Apostle. Saint *Paul*
might say to the *Corinthians, Though you have tenne thousand instructors in Christ, yet have yee not many fathers, for in Christ Jesus I
have begotten you through the Gospel;* And hee might say of his
spirituall sonne *Onesimus, That he begot him in his bonds;* Those, to
whom *he first of any* presented the Gospel, That had not heard of a
Christ, nor a *holy Ghost,* before, They, into whom, he infused a new
religion, new to *them,* might well enough bee called his children, and
hee their father; But *we* have *no new* doctrine to present, no new
opinion to infuse, or *miracles* to amaze, as in the Romane Church,
³⁸⁰ they are full of all these: wee have no children to beget of our own:
*Paul was not crucified for you, nor were you baptized in the name of
Paul,* sayes *Paul* himself; as he sayes again, *who is Paul? but a Minister
by whom ye beleeved,* and that also not by him, but *as the Lord gave to
every man;* Not as *Paul* preached to every man, for he preached alike
to every man; but as the Lord gave to every man; *I have planted,* says

Sine liberis

Iam. 1.18

1 [Cor.]
4.15

Phil. 10

1 Cor.
1.13
3.5

he, it is true, but *he that planteth is nothing,* says he also; Only they that proceed, as they proceed in the Romane Church *Ex opere operato,* to tye the grace of God, to the action of the man, will venter to call Gods children, *their* children in that sense. My prayer shal be against

Hose. 9.14   390 that commination, That God will not *give us a miscarrying womb,* nor *dry breasts;* that you may always suck pure milk from us, and then not cast it up, but digest it, to your spirituall growth; And I shall call upon God with a holy passion, as vehement as *Rachels* to *Jacob,*

Gen. 30.1   *Da mihi liberos, give me children, or I die:* That God would give *me* children, but *his* children; that *he* by his Spirit, may give you an *inward regeneration,* as *I,* by his ordinance shall present to you, the *outward means,* that so being begot by himselfe, the father of life, and of light, you may be *nursed,* and brought up, in his service by *me.* That so, not attributing the work to *any man,* but to Gods Ordinances,

400 you doe not tye the power of God, nor the breath of life, to any one mans lips, as though there were no regeneration, no begetting, but by *him;* but acknowledging the other to be but an *instrument,* and the weakest to be *that,* you may remember also, That though a man can cut deeper with an Axe, then with a knife, with a heavy, then with a lighter instrument; yet God can pierce as far into a conscience, by a plain, as by an exquisite speaker.

Ille   Now this widow being thus maried, This Church thus undertaken, *He must perform the duty of a husbands brother:* First, it is a *personall office,* he must doe it *himself.* When Christ shall say, at the Judgement,

Mat. 25.43   410 *I was naked, and ye cloathed me not, sick, and ye visited me not,* it shall be no excuse to say, *When saw we thee naked, when saw we thee sick?* for wee might have seen it, wee should have seen it. When we shall come to our accompt, and see *them,* whose salvation was committed to *us,* perish, because they were uninstructed, and ignorant, dare we say then, *we never saw them* show their ignorance, wee never heard of it? That is the greatest part of our fault, the heaviest weight upon our condemnation, that we saw so little, heard so little, conversed so little amongst them, because we were made watchmen, and bound to see, and bound to hear, and bound to be heard; not by *others,* but

420 by our *selves;* My sheep may be saved by others; but *I* save them not, that are saved so, nor shall *I* my self be saved by *their* labour, where *mine* was necessarily required.

The office is *personall, I* must doe it, and it is *perpetuall,* I must   *Perpetuall*
perform it, sayes the text, goe through with it. *Lots* wife looked backe,
and God never gave her leave to look forward again. *That man who*   Luke 9.62
hath put his hand to the plow, and looks back, Christ disables him for
the kingdome of God. The *Galatians* who had begun in the spirit, and   [Gal.] 3.3
then *relapsed,* before *whose eyes Christ Iesus had been evidently set*
forth, as the Apostle speaks, fall under that reproach of the Apostle,
430 to bee called, and called againe, *fooles,* and *men bewitched.* If I be-
ginne to preach amongst you, and proceed not, I shall fall under that
heavy increpation from my God, *you beganne,* that you might for
your owne glory, shew that you were in some measure, able to serve
the Church, and when you had done enough for your *own glory,* you
gave over *my glory,* and the salvation of their souls, to whom I sent
you. God hath set our eyes in our foreheads, to look forward, not
backward, not to be proud of that which we have done, but diligent in
that which we are to doe. In the Creation, if God had given over his
worke, the third, or fift day, where had man been? If I give over my
440 prayers, due to the Church of God, as long as God enables me to doe
it service, I lose my thanks, nay, I lose the testimony of mine own
conscience for all. My office is *personall,* and it is *perpetuall,* and then
it is *a duty. He must perform the duty of a husbands brother unto her.*

It is not of *curtesie,* that we preach, but it is a *duty,* it is not a *bounty*   *Duty*
given, but it is a *debt* paid: for, *though I preach the Gospel, I have*
nothing to glory of, for a necessity is laid upon me, sayes Saint *Paul*   1 Cor. 9.16
himself. It is true, that as there is a *Væ si non, Wo be unto mee, if I doe*
not preach the Gospel, so there is an *Euge bone serve, Well done, good,*   Mat. 25.21
and faithfull servant, to them that doe. But the *Væ,* is of *Justice,* the
450 *Euge* is of *Mercy;* If I doe it *not,* I deserve *condemnation* from God;
but if I *doe it,* I deserve not *thanks* from him. Nay, it is a debt, not
onely to God, but to *Gods people,* to *you:* and indeed there is more
due to you, then you can claime, or can take knowledge of. For the
people can claime but according to the *laws* of that State, and the
Canons of that Church, in which God hath placed them; such preaching, as those Laws, and those Canons enjoyn, is a debt which they
can call for: but the Pastor himself hath another Court, another Barre
in himselfe, by which hee tries himselfe, and must condemne himselfe, if hee pay not this debt, performe not this duty, as often, as him-
460 self, knowes himself, to bee fit, and able to doe it.

Mariti
1 Cor. 11.3

2 Tim. 4.2

[Eph. 5.25]
[Col. 3.19]

[Gen. 24.67]

1 Sam. 1.5

Fratris

It is a duty, and it is the *duty of an husbands brother*. Now the husband hath *power,* and *authority* over the wife. *The head of the woman is the Man;* and when the office of this spirituall husband is particularly expressed, thus, *Reprove, Rebuke, Exhort,* you see, for one word of familiarity, that is, *Exhort,* there are two of authority, *Reprove,* and *Rebuke*. But yet, all the authority of the husband, secular, or ecclesiasticall, temporall, or spirituall husband, is grounded, rooted in *love:* for, the Apostle seemes to delight himself, in the repeating of that Commandement, to the *Ephesians,* and to the *Colossians, Hus-*
470 *bands love your wives. Moses* extends himselfe no farther, in express-ing all the happinesses, that *Isaak* and *Rebecca* enjoyed in one another, but this, *shee became his wife, and he loved her*. If shee had not beene his wife, *Moses* would never have proposed that love for an example; for so it is also betweene *Elkanah,* and his wife *Hannah,* 1 Sam. 1.5. *Vnto Hannah he gave a double portion, for* (sayes the Text) *hee loved Hannah*. If the Pastor *love,* there will bee a *double labour;* if the People *love,* there will bee double respect. But being so, hee thought hee said all, when he said *they loved one another;* For where the Congregation loves the Pastor, hee will forbeare bitter reproofes, and
480 wounding increpations, and where the Pastor loves his Congregation, his *Rebukes,* because they proceed out of *love,* will bee acceptable, and well interpreted by them.

It is a *duty,* and *personall,* and *perpetuall;* a duty, of *a husband,* and lastly, of *a husband that is brother to the former husband;* In which last circumstance, we have time to mark but this one note, that the *reason* of that law, which drew the brother to this *mariage,* was the *preservation* of the *temporall inheritance,* in that family. Even in our spirituall mariages to widow Churches, we must have a care to pre-serve the *temporall rights* of all persons; That the Parish be not op-
490 pressed with heavy *extortions,* nor the *Pastor* defrauded with unjust *substraction,* nor the Patron damnified by *usurpations,* nor the *Ordi-nary* neglected by *disobediences;* but that people, and Pastor, and Patron, and Ordinary, continuing in possession of their severall rights, *love* being the *root* of all, the *fruit* of all may be peace, *love* being the *soul* of all, the *body* of all may be unity; which the Lord of unity, and concord, grant to us all, for his Sonne Christ Jesus sake, *Amen*.

Number 4.

The second Sermon Preached by the Author
after he came to St. Dunstanes,
25 Apr. 1624

PSAL. 34.11. *COME YE CHILDREN, HEARKEN UNTO ME, I WILL TEACH YOU THE FEAR OF THE LORD.*

THE TEXT does not call *children* simply, literally, but such men, and women, as are willing to come in the *simplicity* of children; such children, as *Christ* spoke of, *Except ye become as little children, ye shall not enter into the Kingdome of heaven; Come ye children;* come *such* children. Nor does the Text call such as come, and would fain be gone again; it is *Come* and *Hearken;* not such as wish *themselves away,* nor such as wish *another man here;* but such as value Gods ordinance of *Preaching,* though it be, as the Apostle says, but *the foolishnesse of Preaching,* and such, as consider the *office,* and
10 not the *person,* how meane soever; *Come ye children;* And, when ye are come, *Hearken,* And, though it be but *I, Hearken unto me; And, I will teach you the feare of the Lord;* the most noble, the most couragious, the most magnanimous, not *affection,* but *vertue,* in the world; *Come ye children, Hearken unto me, and I will teach you the feare of the Lord.*

To every Minister and Dispenser of the word of God, and to every Congregation belong these words; And therefore we will divide the Text between us; To you one, to us appertains the other part. You must *come,* and you must *hearken;* we must *teach,* and teach to *edifica-*
20 *tion;* There is the *Meum & Tuum,* your part, and our part. From each Part, these branches flow out naturally; In yours, first, the *capacity,* as *children;* Then the *action,* you *Come;* Then your *Disposition* here,

Mat. 18.3

1 Cor. 1.21

Divisio

95

you *hearken;* And lastly, your *submission* to Gods Ordinance, you *hearken* even *unto me,* unto *any* Minister of *his* sending. In our Part, there is first a *Teaching;* for, else, why should you *come,* or *hearken unto me,* or *any?* It is a *Teaching,* it is not onely a *Praying;* And then, there is a *Catholique* doctrine, a *circular* doctrine, that walks the round, and goes the *compasse* of our whole lives, from our first, to our *last childhood,* when *age* hath made us children again, and it is ³⁰ the *Art of Arts,* the root, and fruit of all true wisdome, *The true feare of the Lord. Come ye children, hearken unto mee, and I will teach you the feare of the Lord.*

I Part

First then, the word, in which, in the first branch of the first part, your *capacity* is expressed, *filii, pueri, children,* is, from the *Originall,* which is *Banim,* often accepted in three notions, and so rendred; Three ways, men are called children, out of that word *Banim,* in the Scriptures. Either it is *servi, servants;* for, they are *filii familiares;* as the Master is *Pater familias,* Father of the family, (and that he is, though there be no naturall children in the family) the servants are ⁴⁰ children of the family, and are very often in Scriptures called so, *Pueri, children;* Or it is *Alumni, Nurse-children, foster-children, filii mammillares,* children of the breasts; whether wee minister to them, *temporall* or *spirituall nourishment,* they are children; Or else it is *filii viscerales,* children of our bowels, our *naturall children.* And in all these three capacities, as *servants,* as *sucking children,* as *sons,* are you called upon in this appellation, in this compellation, *children.*

Servi

First, as you are *servants,* you are *children;* for, without distinction of *age,* servants are called so, frequently, ordinarily, in the Scriptures,

1 Sam. 21.5   *Pueri.* The Priest asks *David,* before he would give him the holy ⁵⁰ bread, *An vasa puerorum sancta, Whether those children,* (speaking of *Davids* followers) *were clean from women;* Here were children that were able to get children. Nay, *Davids* Soldiers are often called so,

1 King 20.15   *pueri,* children. In the first of the Kings, he takes a Muster, *recenset pueros;* Here were children that were able to kill men. You are his children, (of what *age* soever) as you are his servants; and in that

[Luke 17.10]   capacity he cals you. You are *unprofitable servants;* but it is not an *unprofitable service,* to serve God; He can get nothing by you, but you can have nothing without him. The Centurions servants *came,* when he said, *Come;* and was *their wages* like *yours?* Had they their

⁶⁰ *beeing,* their ever-lasting *well-beeing* for their service? You will scarce
receive a servant, that is come from another man, without testimony;
If you put your selves out of Gods service, whither will ye goe? *In his
service,* and his onely, *is perfect freedome.* And therefore as you love
freedome, and liberty, bee his servants; and call the freedome of the
Gospel, the best freedome, and come to the Preaching of that.

He cals you *children,* as you are *servants,* (*filii familiares*) and he   *Alumni*
cals you children, as you are *Alumni, nurse-children, filii mammillares,*
as he requires the humility, and simplicity of little children in you.
For, *Cum simplicibus sermocinatio ejus,* (as the vulgat reads that   Prov. 3.32
⁷⁰ place) *Gods secret discourse is with the single heart.* The first that
ever came to Christ, (so as he came to us, in *blood*) they that came to
him so, before he came so *to us,* that died for *him,* before *he* died for
them, were such *sucking children,* those whom *Herod* slew. As Christ
thought himself bound to thank his Father, for that way of proceeding,
I thank thee, O Father, Lord of heaven and earth, that thou hast re-   Mat. 11.25
vealed these things unto babes; so Christ himself pursues the same
way, *Suffer little children, and forbid them not, to come unto me, for*   19.14
of such is the Kingdome of heaven. Of *such;* not onely of those who
were truly, literally children, (children in *age*) but of *such* as those,
⁸⁰ (*Talium est regnum cœlorum*) such as come in such a disposition, in
the humility, in the simplicity, in the singlenesse of heart, as children
do. An habituall sinner is always in *minority,* always an *Infant;* an
Infant to this purpose, all his *acts,* all the *bands* of an Infant, are void;
all the *outward* religious actions, even the band and contract of *Baptism* in an habituall sinner is void, and ineffectuall. He that is in the
house, and favour of God, though he be a *child,* (a child to this purpose, simple, supple, tractable, single-hearted) is, as *Adam* was in the
state of Innocency, a *man* the first minute, able to stand upright in the
sight of God. And out of one place of *Esay, our* Expositors have drawn,   Esay 65.20
⁹⁰ conveniently enough, both these conclusions; *A child shall die* 100
years old, says the Prophet; that is, (say some) a sinner though he live
100 years, yet he dies a child, in *ignorance;* And then, (say others, and
both truly) He that comes willingly, when God cals, though he die a
child in age, he hath the *wisdome* of 100 years upon him. There is not
a graver thing, then to be such a child; to conform his will to the will
of God. Whether you consider temporall or spirituall things, you are

Gods children. For, for *temporall,* if God should take off his hand, withdraw his hand of *sustentation,* all those things, which assist us temporally, would relapse to the first feeble, and childish estate, and
100 come to their first *nothing.* Armies would be but Hospitals, without all strength; Councell-tables but Bedlams, without all sense; and Schools and Universities, but the wrangling of children, if God, and his Spirit did not inanimate our Schools, and Armies, and Councels. His adoption makes us *men,* therefore, because it makes us his *children.* But we are his children in this consideration especially, as we are his *spirituall children,* as he hath nursed us, fed us with his *word.* In which sense, the Apostle speaks of those who had embraced the true

Heb. 2.13 Religion, (in the same words that the Prophet had spoken before) *Behold, I, and the children that God hath given me;* And in the same
110 sense, the same Prophet, in the same place, says of them who had

Esay 2.6 fallen away from the true Religion, *They please themselves in the children of strangers,* In those men, who have derived their *Orders,* and their *Doctrine* from a *forein* Jurisdiction. In that State where *Adoptions* were so frequent, (in old *Rome*) a *Plebeian* could not adopt a *Patrician,* a *Yeoman* could not adopt a *Gentleman,* nor a *young* man could not adopt an *old.* In the new *Rome,* that endevours to adopt *all,* in an imaginary *filiation,* you that have the perfect freedome of Gods service, be not adopted into the slavery, and bondage of *mens traditions;* you that are in possession of the ancient Religion, of Christ, and
120 his Apostles, be not adopted into a yonger Religion. *Religio à religando;* That is Religion, that *binds; that* binds, that is necessary to salvation. That which *we* affirm, our adversaries deny not; that which *we* professe, they confesse was always necessary to salvation. They will not say, that all that they say *now,* was *always* necessary; That a man could not be saved without beleeving the Articles of the *Councell of Trent,* a week before that Councell shut up. You are his children, as

Malach.
[1.6] children are *servants;* and, *If he be your Lord, where is his fear?* you are his children, as he hath *nursed* you, with the milk of his word; and *if he be your Father so, (your foster Father) where is his love?*
130 But he is your Father otherwise; you are not onely *Filii familiares,* children because *servants,* nor onely *Filii mammillares,* children because *noursed* by him, but you are also *Filii viscerales,* children of his bowells. For, we are otherwise allied to *Christ,* then we can be to any

of his *instruments,* though *Angels* of the Church, *Prophets,* or Apostles; and yet, his Apostle says, of one whom he loved, of *Onesimus,*   Phil. *v.* 12
Receive him, that is mine owne bowells; my Sonne, says he, *whom I*
have begotten in my bands. How much more art thou bound to receive
and refresh those bowells from which thou art derived, *Christ Jesus*
himselfe; *Receive* him, *Refresh* him. Carry that, which the wiseman
¹⁴⁰ hath said, *Miserere animæ tuæ,* bee mercifull to thine owne soule,   [Ecclus.
higher then so; and *Miserere salvatoris tui,* have mercy upon thine   30.23]
owne Saviour, *put on the bowells of mercy,* and put them on even   Colos. 3.12
towards *Christ Jesus* himselfe, who needs thy mercy, by beeing so
torne, and mangled, and embowelled, by blasphemous oaths, and
execrations. For, beloved, it is not so absurd a prayer, as it is conceived, if *Luther* did say upon his death bed, *Oremus pro Domino*
nostro Jesu Christo, Let us pray for our Lord and Saviour Jesus Christ.
Had we not need pray for him? If he complaine that *Saul* persecutes
him, had we not need pray for him? It is a seditious affection in civill
¹⁵⁰ things, to divide the *King* and the *kingdome;* to *pray,* to *fight* for the
one, and leave out the other, is seditiously done. If the *kingdome* of
Christ need thy prayers, and thy assistance, *Christ* needs it; If the
Body need it, the *Head* needs it; If thou must pray for his *Gospell,*
thou must pray for *him;* Nay, thou canst not pray for *thy selfe,* but
thou must pray for *him,* for, thou art *his bowells;* when thou in thy
forefathers, the first *Christians* in the *Primitive Church,* wast persecuted, Christ cryed out, *why persecutest thou me?* Christ made *thy*   [Acts 9.4]
case *his,* because thou wast of his bowells. When Christ is disseised,
and dispossest, his truth profligated, and thrown out of a nation, that
¹⁶⁰ professed it before, when Christ is wounded by the *blasphemies* of
others, and crucified by thee, in thy *relapses to repented sinnes,* wilt
thou not say to *Them,* to *Thy selfe,* in the behalfe of Christ, *why per-*
secute yee me? Wilt thou not make *Christs* case *thine,* as hee made
thine his? Art not thou the bowells of Christ? If not, (and thou art
not, if thou have not this *sense* of his *suffering*) thou hast no interest
in his *death,* by thy *Baptisme,* nor in his *Resurrection,* by thy feeble
halfe repentances. But in the *duty* of a child, as thou art a servant, in
the simplicity of a child, as thou hast sucked from him, in the *interest*
and *inheritance* of a child, as thou art the Son of his bowells, in all

¹⁷⁰ these capacities, (and with all these we have done) God calls thee, *come ye children;* and that is our next step, the Action, *Come.*

Venite

Passing thus from the Persons to the action, *Venite, Come,* we must aske first, *what* this *comming* is? The whole mystery of our redemp-

1 Tim. 1.15

tion is expressed by the Apostle in this word, *venit, that Christ Jesus is come into the world.* All that thou hast to do, is to *come* to, and to meet him. Where is he? At home; in his own house, in the *Church.* Which is his house, *which is* his Church? That to *thee,* in which he hath given *thee* thy *Baptisme,* if *that* do still afford thee, as much as is necessary for thy salvation. Come thither, to the participation of his
¹⁸⁰ ordinances, to the exercises of Religion there. The gates of heaven

[Mat. 25.34]

shall be opened to you, at last in that word, *Venite benedicti, come ye blessed,* the *way* to those gates is opened to you now, in the same word, *Venite filii,* come ye children, *come.* Christ can come, and does often, into thy *bed-chamber,* in the visitation of his private Spirit, but, here, he calls *thee* out into the congregation, into the communion of Saints. And then the Church celebrates Christs coming in the flesh, a moneth before he comes, in *four Sundays of Advent,* before *Christmas.* When thou comest to meet him in the Congregation, come not occasionally, come not casually, not indifferently, not collaterally; come not as to
¹⁹⁰ an entertainment, a show, a spectacle, or company, come solemnly, with preparation, with meditation. He shall have the lesse profit, by the prayer of the Congregation, that hath not been at his private prayer before he came. Much of the mystery of our Religion lay in the *venturus,* that Christ was to come, all that the law and Prophets undertooke for, was *that venturus,* that Christ was to come; but the consummation of all, the end of the law and the Prophets, is in the *venit,* he *is come.* Do not clogge thy coming with future conditions, and contingencies, thou wilt come, *if thou canst wake, if thou canst rise, if thou canst be ready,* if thou *like the company,* the *weather,* the

Matt. 9.2

²⁰⁰ *man.* We finde one man who was brought in his *bed* to Christ; but it was but one. *Come,* come actually, come earnestly, come early, come often; and come to meet him, Christ Jesus and no body else. *Christ is come into the world;* and therefore thou needest not goe out of the world to meet him; He doth not call thee from thy *Calling,* but

Gen. 8.11

in thy Calling. The Dove went up and down, from the Arke, and to the Arke, and yet was not disappointed of her Olive leafe, Thou

maiest come to this place at due times, and maiest doe the businesses
of the world, in other places too, and still keep thy *Olive*, thy peace
of Conscience. If no *Hereticall recusancy*, (thou dost like the *Doc-*
210 *trine*) no *schismaticall recusancy*, (thou dost like the *Discipline*) no
lasie recusancy, (thou forbearest not because thou canst not sit at thine
ease) no *proud recusancie*, (that the company is not good enough for
thee) if none of these detain thee, thou maist be *here*, even when
thou art *not here;* God may accept thy desire; as, in many cases, thou
maist be *away*, when thou art *here;* as, in *particular* thou art, if being
here, thou do not *hearken* to that which is said here; for that is added
to the *coming*, and follows in a third consideration, after the capacity,
Children, and the Action, *Come*, The disposition, *Hearken: Come
ye children and hearken.*

220   Upon those words of *David, Conturbata sunt ossa mea*, St. *Basil*
saith well, *Habet & anima ossa sua, The soul hath bones as well as
the body.* And in this Anatomy, and dissection of the soul, as the
bones of the soul, are the constant and strong resolutions thereof, and
as the *seeing* of the soul is *understanding* (*The eyes of your understanding being opened*) so the *Hearing* of the *soul* is *hearkning;* in
these religious exercises, we doe not *hear*, except we *hearken;* for
hearkning is the *hearing* of the soul. Some men draw some reasons,
out of some stories of some credit, to imprint a belief of *extasie*, and
raptures; That the body remaining upon the floore, or in the bed, the
230 soul may be gone out to the contemplation of heavenly things. But
it were a strange and a perverse extasie, that the body being here,
at a religious exercise, and in a religious posture, the soul should be
gone out to the contemplation, and pursuit of the pleasures or profits
of this world. You come hither but to your own funeralls, if you
bring nothing hither but your bodies; you come but to be *enterred*,
to be *laid in the earth*, if the ends of your comming be *earthly respects*, prayse, and opinion, and observation of men; you come to be
Canonized, to grow *Saints*, if your souls be here, and by grace here
alwayes diffused, grow up to *a sanctification. Bonus es Domine animæ*
240 *quærenti te,* Thou art good, O Lord, to that soul that seeks thee; It
is St. *Augustines* note, that it is put in the singular, *Animæ*, to *that
soul:* Though many come, few come to him. A man may thread Sermons by half dozens a day, and place his merit in the number, a man

Audite
Psalm. 6.3.
[Vulg.
numb.]

Ephes. 1.18

[2 Cor.
2.16]

may have been all day in the perfume and incense of preaching, and
yet have receivd none of the *savor of life unto life*. Some things an
Ape can do as wel as a Man; some things an Hypocrite as wel as a
Saint. We cannot see *now*, whether thy soul be here *now*, or no; but,
to *morrow*, *hereafter*, in the course of thy life, they which are near
thee, and know whether thy former faults be mended, or no, know

[Rom.
10.17]

²⁵⁰ whether thy soul use to be at Sermons, as well as thy body uses to go
to Sermons. *Faith comes by hearing*, saith the Apostle; but it is by
that hearing of the soul, *Hearkning, Considering*. And then, as the
soul is infused by God, but diffused over the whole body, and so
there is a *Man*, so *Faith* is infused from God, but diffused into our
works, and so there is a *Saint*. Practise is the *Incarnation of Faith*,
Faith is incorporated and manifested in a body, by works; and the
way to both, is that *Hearing*, which amounts to this *Hearkning*, to
a diligent, to a considerate, to a profitable *Hearing*. In which, one
essentiall circumstance is, that we be not over affectionately trans-
²⁶⁰ ported with an opinion of any *one person*, but apply our selves to the
Ordinance, Come, and *hearken* unto *me*, To *any* whom God sends
with the Seale and *Character* of his Minister, which is our fourth and
last branch in your part.

Me

    David doth not determine this in his own person, that you should
hearken to *him*, and *none but him*, but that you should hearken to
him in that capacity and qualification, which is common to *him* with
others, as we are sent by God upon that Ministery; that you say to all

[Psa.
118.26]

such, *Blessed art thou that comest in the Name of the Lord*. St. *Augustine*, and not he alone, interprets this whole Psalme of Christ, that
²⁷⁰ it is a *thankesgiving of Christ* to his *Father*, upon some deliverance
received in some of his Agonies, some of his persecutions; and that
Christ calleth us to hearken unto *him;* To *him*, so, as he is present
with *us*, in the Ministery of his Church. He is a perverse servant, that
will receive no commandment, except he have it immediately from
his Masters mouth; so *is he too*, that pretendeth to rest so wholly in
the *Word of God*, the *Scriptures*, as that he seeks *no interpretation,
no exposition, no preaching*, All is in the *Scriptures*, but all the *Scriptures* are not alwaies evident to all understandings. He also is a perverse servant, that wil receive no commandment by any *Officer* of
²⁸⁰ his Masters, except he like the *man*, or, if his Master might, in his

opinion, have chosen a *fitter man,* to serve in that place. And such a perversnesse is in those hearers who more respect the *man,* then the *Ministery,* and his *manner* of delivering it, then the *message* that he delivers. *Let a man so account of us, as of the Ministers of Christ, and Stewards of the mysteries of God.* That is our *Classis,* our rank, our station, what names soever we brought into the world by our extraction from this or that family, what name soever we took in our *baptisme,* and contract between God and us, that name, in which we come to you, is *that, The Ministers of Christ, The Stewards of the* ²⁹⁰ *Mysteries of God, And so let men account of us,* says the Apostle. *Invention,* and *Disposition,* and *Art,* and *Eloquence,* and *Expression,* and *Elocution,* and *reading,* and *writing,* and *printing,* are secondary things, accessory things, auxiliary, subsidiary things; men may account us, and make account of us, as of *Orators* in the pulpit, and of *Authors,* in the shop; but if they account of us as *of Ministers and Stewards,* they give us our due; that's our name to you. All the Evangelists mention *John Baptist* and his *preaching;* but two of the foure say never a word of his *austerity of life,* his *Locusts,* nor his *Camels haire;* and those two that do, *Matthew* and *Marke,* they insist, *first,* ³⁰⁰ upon his *calling,* and *then* upon his *actuall preaching,* how he pursued that Calling, And *then* upon the *Doctrine* that he preached, *Repentance,* and *Sanctification,* and *after that,* they come to these secondary and subsidiary things, which added to his estimation, and assisted the passage of his Doctrine, His good life. Learning, and other good parts, and an exemplar life fall into second places; They have a first place, in *their* consideration who are to call them, but in *you,* to whom they are sent, but a second; fixe you, in the first place, upon the *Calling.* This Calling circumcised *Moses* uncircumcised lips; This made *Jeremy* able to speak, though he called himself a ³¹⁰ childe; This is *Esays coale from the Altar, which takes away even his sinne, and his iniquity.* Be therefore content to passe over some infirmities, and rest your selves upon the *Calling.* And when you have thus taken the simplicity of *Children,* (they are the *persons,* which was our first step) and are *come* to the *Congregation,* (that is your *Action,* and was our second) and have conformed your selves to *hearken,* (that also is the *Disposition* here, which was our third) And all this with a reverence to the *Calling* before an affection to the

1 Cor. 4.1

Exod. 6.12
Ier. 1.6
Esa. 6.6

man, (that is your submission to Gods Ordinance, and was our fourth and last step) you have then built up our first part in your selves, and
320 laid together all those peeces which constitute *your Duty, Come ye Children, and hearken unto me;* And from hence we passe, to *our duty, I will teach you the fear of the Lord.*

2 Part

Docebo

In this second part, we made two steps; first, The manner, *Docebo, I will teach;* And then the *Matter, Timorem Domini, I will teach you the feare of the Lord.* Upon the first, we will stay no longer, but to confesse, That we are bound to *teach,* and that this *teaching* is to *preach;* And *Væ si non, Wo be unto us,* if we do *not preach.* Wo to *them,* who out of *ease,* or *state, silence themselves;* And woe to *them* too, who by their *distemper,* and *Schismaticall* and seditious *manner*
330 of preaching, occasion and force *others to silence them;* and think, (and think it out of a profitable, and manifold experience) That as forbidden books sell best, so silenced Ministers thrive best. It is a Duty, *Docendum,* we must teach, *Preach;* but a duty that excludes not *Catechizing;* for catechizing seems especially to be intended here, where he calls upon *them* who are to be taught, by that name, *Children.* It is a duty that excludes not *Praying;* but Praying excludes not *it* neither. Prayer and Preaching may consist, nay they must meet in the Church of God. Now, he that will teach, must have *learnt* before, many yeers before; And he that will preach, must have *thought* of
340 it before, many days before. *Extemporall Ministers,* that resolve in a day what they will *be, Extemporall Preachers,* that resolve in a minute, what they will *say,* out-go Gods Spirit, and make too much hast. It was Christs way; He tooke first Disciples to learne, and then, out of them, he tooke *Apostles* to teach; and those Apostles made more Disciples. Though *your* first consideration be upon the *Calling,* yet *our* consideration must be for our *fitnesse* to that Calling. Our Prophet

Psal. 71.17

David hath put them both together, well, *O God, thou hast taught me from my youth;* (you see what was his *Vniversity; Moses* was his *Aristotle;* he had studied *Divinity* from his *youth*) *And hitherto have*
350 *I declared thy wondrous works,* says he there. *Hitherto?* How long was that? It follows in the next verse, *Now am I old, and gray headed,* and yet *he* gave not over. Then Gods work goes well forward, when they whom God hath taught, teach others. He that can say with *David, Docuisti me, O God thou hast taught me,* may say with him

too, *Docebo vos, I will teach you.* But what? that remains only, *I will teach you the fear of the Lord.*

Timor Naturalis

There is a fear, which needs no teaching, a fear that is *naturally* imprinted in us. We need not teach men to bee *sad,* when a mischiefe is upon them, nor to *feare* when it is coming towards them; for, fear ³⁶⁰ respects the *future,* so as sadnesse does the *present;* fear looks upon *Danger,* and sadnesse upon *Detriment;* fear upon a *sick* friend, and sadnesse upon a *dead.* And as these need not bee *taught* us, because they are *naturall,* so, because they are naturall, they need not be *untaught* us, they need not be forbidden, nor disswaded. Our Saviour Christ had them both, fear, and sadnesse; and that man lacks *Christian wisedom,* who is without a provident fear of future dangers, and without *Christian charity,* who is without a compassionate sadnesse in present calamities. Now this fear, though but imprinted in nature, is *Timor Domini,* The fear of the Lord, because the Lord is the Lord ³⁷⁰ of *Nature,* He is the *Nature of Nature,* Lord of all endowments and impressions in Nature. And therefore, though for this naturall feare, you goe no farther then *Nature,* (for it is born with you, and it lives in you) yet the *right use* even of this naturall fear, is *from Grace,* though in the *root* it be a feare of *nature,* yet in the *government* thereof, in the degrees, and *practise* thereof, it is the *feare of the Lord;* Not onely as hee is *Lord of Nature,* (for so, you have the feare it selfe from the Lord) but as this naturall fear produces good or bad *effects,* as it is regulated and ordered, or as it is deserted, and abandoned, by the Spirit of the Lord; And therefore you are called hither, *Come,* ³⁸⁰ that you may learne the fear of the Lord, that is, the *right use of naturall fear,* and *naturall affections, from the Law of God;* For, as it is a wretched condition, to be *without naturall affections,* so is it a dangerous dereliction, if our naturall affections be left to themselves, and not regulated, not inanimated by the Spirit of God; for *then* my sadnesse will sinke into *Desperation,* and my *fear will betray the succours which reason offereth.* This I gain by letting *in* the fear of the Lord, into my naturall fear; that whereas the naturall object of my naturall fear is *malum,* something that I apprehend *sub ratione mali,* as it is *ill,* ill for *me,* (for, if I did not conceive it to be *ill,* I would ³⁹⁰ not fear it) yet when I come to thaw this Ice, when I come to discusse this cloud, and attenuate this damp, by the light and heat of

Sap. 17.12

Grace, and the illustration of the Spirit of God, breathing in his word, I change my *object,* or at least, I look upon it in *another line,* in *another angle,* I look not upon that evill which my naturall fear presented me, of an affliction, or a calamity, but I look upon the glory that God receives by my Christian constancy in that affliction, and I look upon that everlasting blessednes, which I should have lost, if God had not laid that affliction upon me. So that though fear look upon evill, (for affliction is *malum pœnæ,* evill as it hath the nature
400 of *punishment*) yet when the feare of the Lord is entred into my naturall feare, my feare is more conversant, more exercised upon the contemplation of *Good,* then *Evill,* more upon the glory of God, and the joys of heaven, then upon the afflictions of this life, how malignant, how manifold soever. And therefore, that this feare, and all your *naturall affections,* (which seem weaknesses in man, and are so indeed, if they bee left to themselves, now in our corrupt and depraved estate) may advance your *salvation,* (which is the end *why* God hath planted them in you) *Come and learn the fear of the Lord,* Learn from the Word of God, explicated by his Minister, in his Or-
410 dinance upon occasions leading him thereunto, the *limits* of this naturall fear, and where it may become sin, if it be not regulated, and inanimated by a better fear, then it self.

Timor semi-naturalis   There is a fear, which grows out of a second nature, *Custome,* and so is *half-naturall,* to those men that have it. The custome of the *place* we live in, or of the *times* we live in, or of the *company* we live in. *Topical* customes of such a place, *Chronical* customes of such an Age, *Personal* customes of such a company. The time, or the place, or the persons in power have advanced, and drawn into fashion and reputation, some *vices,* and such men as depend upon *them,* are afraid,
420 not to concur with them in their vices; for, amongst *persons,* and in *times,* and *places,* that are *vicious,* an honest man is a *rebel;* he goes against *that* State, and *that* Government, which is the *kingdom of sin.* Amongst drunkards, a sober man is a *spy* upon them; Amongst blasphemers, a prayer is a *libell* against them; And amongst dissolute and luxurious persons, a chast man is a *Bridewell,* his person, his presence is a *house of Correction.* In vicious times and companies, a good man is unacceptable, and cannot prosper. And, because as amongst *Merchants,* men trade halfe upon *stock,* and halfe upon

credit, so, in all other courses, because men rise according to the
⁴³⁰ *opinion* and *estimation* which persons in power have of them, as well
as by *reall goodnesse,* therefore to build up, or to keep up this opinion
and estimation in *them* upon whom they depend, they are afraid to
crosse the vices of the Time, so far, as by being vertuous in their owne
particular. They are afraid it will be called a *singularity,* and a *schismaticall* and *seditious* disposition, and taken for a *Reproach,* and a
Rebuke laid upon their *betters,* if they be not content to be as *ill,* as
those their *betters* are. Now, the fear of the Lord brings the *Quo
Warranto* against all these priviledged sins, and priviledged places,
and persons, and overthrows all these Customes, and Prescriptions.
⁴⁴⁰ The fear of the Lord is not a Topicall, not a Chronicall, not a Personall, but a *Catholique,* a *Canonicall,* a *Circular,* an *Vniversall* fear;
It goes through all, and over all; and when this *halfe-naturall* feare,
this feare grown out of *Custome,* suggests to me, That if I be thus
tender-conscienced, if I startle at an *Oath,* if I be sick at a *Health,* if I
cannot conform my selfe to the vices of my betters, I shall lose my
Master, my Patron, my Benefactor, This feare of the Lord enters, and
presents the infallible losse of a farre greater Master, and Patron, and
Benefactor, if I comply with the other. And therefore as you were
called hither, (that is to the explication of the Word of God) to learn
⁴⁵⁰ how to regulate the *naturall* fear, that *that* fear doe not deject you
into a *diffidence* of Gods mercy, so come hither to learne the fear of
God, against this *half-naturall* fear, that is, bee guided by the Word
of God, how far you are to serve the turnes of those persons, upon
whom ye depend, and when to leave their commandements un-
performed.

   Well; what will this feare of the Lord teach us? *Valour,* fortitude;   *Fortitudo*
feare teach valour? yes; And nothing but feare; True feare. As *Moses*
his Serpents devoured the false serpents, so doth true fear all false fear.
There is nothing so contrary to God, as false fear; neither in his own
⁴⁶⁰ nature, nor in his love to *us.* Therefore Gods first Name in the Bible,
and the Name which he sticks to, in all the worke of the Creation, is
his Name of Power, *Elohim; El,* is *fortis Deus,* The God of Power;
and it is that Name in the plurall, multiplied power, All Power; And
what can he feare? God descends to many other humane affections;
you shall read that God was Angry, and sory, and weary; But *non*

timuit Deus, God was never afraid. Neither would God that man should be. So his first blessing upon man, was to fill the earth, and to *subdue the creatures,* and to *rule over them,* and to eat what he would upon the earth; All Acts of Power, and of Confidence. As soon as ⁴⁷⁰ hee had offended God, the first impotency that he found in himself,

Gen. 3.10
was *fear: I heard thy voice, and I was afraid,* says he. He had heard the voice of Lions, and was not afraid. There is not a greater com-

Ps. 53.5
mination of a curse, then that, *They shall be in a great fear, where no fear is;* Which is more vehemently expressed in another place, *I*

Lev. 26.17
will set my face against you, and you shall flye, when none pursues

36
you; I will send a faintnesse into their hearts, and the sound of a shaken leafe, shall chase them, as a sword. False feare is a fearfull curse. To feare that all favours, and all preferments, will goe the wrong way, and that therefore I must clap on a byasse, and goe that ⁴⁸⁰ way too, this inordinate fear is the curse of God. *Davids* last counsail

I Reg. 2.2
to *Solomon,* (but reflecting upon us all) was, *Be thou strong there-*

Gregor.
fore, and show thy selfe a man. E Culmine corruens, ad gyrum laboris venit, The Devill fell from his place in heaven, and now is put to *compasse* the earth. The fearfull man that fals from his morall and his Christian constancy, from the fundamentall rules of his religion, fals into labyrinths, of incertitudes, and impertinencies, and ambigui-

Iob 7.1
ties, and anxieties, and irresolutions. *Militia, vita;* our whole life is a warfare; God would not chuse *Cowards;* hee had rather we were valiant in the fighting of his battels; for battels, and exercise of valour, ⁴⁹⁰ we are sure to have. God sent a *Cain* into the world before an *Abel;*

Gregor.
An Enemy, before a Champion. *Abel non suspicor qui non habet Cain;* we never heare of an *Abel,* but there is a *Cain* too. And there-

I Pet. 4.12
fore *think it not strange, concerning the fiery triall, as though some strange thing happened unto you;* Make account that this world is your Scene, your Theater, and that God himself sits to see the com-

Chrysost.
bat, the wrestling. *Vetuit Deus mortem Job; Job* was Gods Champion, and God forbad Satan the taking away of *Jobs* life; for, if he die, (sayes God in the mouth of that Father) *Theatrum nobis non amplius plaudetur,* My Theater will ring with no more *Plaudites,* I shall bee ⁵⁰⁰ no more glorified in the valour and constancy of my Saints, my Cham-pions. God delights in the constant and valiant man, and therefore a various, a timorous man frustrates, disappoints God.

My errand then is to teach you *valour;* and must my way be to intimidate you, to teach you feare? yes, still there is no other fortitude, but the fear of the Lord. We told you before, sadnesse and fear differ but in the present, and future. And as for the present, *Nihil aliud triste quàm Deum offendere,* There is no just cause of sadnesse, but to have sinned against God, (for, sudden sadnesse arising in a good Conscience, is a sparke of fire in the Sea, it must goe out;) so
510 there is no just cause of fear, but in Gods displeasure. *Mens in timore Domini constituta, non invenit extra quod metuat.* God is *all;* and if I be established in him, what thing can I fear, when there is nothing without him? nothing simply, at least nothing that can hurt me; *Quæ sunt in mundo non nocent iis qui extra mundum sunt,* This world cannot hurt him that made it, nor them that are laid up in him. *Jonas* did but change his vessell, his ship, when he entred the Whale, he was not shipwracked, God was his Pilot there, as well as in the ship, and therefore he as confident there. It is meant of Christ, which is spoken in the person of Wisdome, *Who so hearkneth unto*
520 *me, shall dwell safely, and be quiet from the feare of evill.* And therefore, *when you heare of warres and commotions, be not terrified; these things must come to passe, but the end is not by and by;* Imaginations, and tentations, and alienations, and tribulations must come: But this is not the end; the end that God lookes for, is, that by the benefit of his *fear we should* stand out all *these.*

So then to teach you the fear of the Lord, is to teach you what it *doth,* that you may *love* it, and what it *is,* that you may *know* it. That which it doth, is, that it makes you a constant, a confident, a valiant man, That which God, who is alwayes the same, loves. How doth
530 it that? Thus. As he that is falne into the Kings hand for debt to *him,* is safe from other creditors, so is *he,* that fears the Lord, from other fears. He that loves the Lord, loves him with all his love; he that fears the Lord, fears him with all his fear too; God takes no half affections. Upon those words, *Be not high-minded, but fear, Clement* of *Alexandria,* hath another reading; *super-time, over-feare;* that is, carry thy fear to the highest place; place thy fear *there,* where it may be above all other fears. *In the multitude of dreams, there are divers vanities, but feare thou the Lord.* All fearfull things passe away as dreams, as vanities, to him that fears the Lord; They offer at him, but in vain,

Chrysost.

Gregor.

Chrysost.

Prov. 1.33

Luc. 21.9

Quid operatur

Rom. 11.20

Eccles. 5.7

⁵⁴⁰ if he be established with that fear. In Christ there was no bone bro-
ken; In him that feares the Lord, no constant purpose is ever shaken.

Iob 1.1

Of *Job* it is said, that he was *perfect and upright;* That is a rare wonder, but the wonder is qualified in the addition, *He feared God.* So

Luke 2.25

are they put together in *Simeon, Justus & timoratus, he was a just
man;* how should he be otherwise? *He feared God.* Consider your
enemies, and be not deceived with an imagination of their power,
but see whether they be worthy of your feare, if you feare God. The

Iohn 16.33

World is your enemy; *sed vici mundum, be of good cheare, for I have
overcome the world,* saith Christ. If it were not so, yet we are none

15.19

⁵⁵⁰ of it; *Ye are not of the world, for I have chosen you out of the world.*
Howsoever, the world would doe us no harm, the world would be
good enough of it self, but that the Prince of the world, the *Devill,* is
anima mundi, the soul of this lower world, he inanimates, he actuates,
he exalts, the malignity of the world against us; and he is our second
enemy. It was not the Apple, but the Serpent that tempted; *Eve,* no
doubt, had looked upon the fruit before, and yet did not long. But
even this enemy is not so dangerous, as he is conceived. In the life
of St. *Basil,* we have a story, that the Devil appeared to a penitent
sinner at his prayers, and told him, *If you will let me alone, I will let*
⁵⁶⁰ *you alone, meddle not with me, and I will not meddle with you;* He
found that by this good souls prayers to God, God had weakned his
power, not onely upon that man that prayed, but upon others too;
and therefore he was content, to come to a cessation of armes with
him, that he might turn his forces another way. Truely he might say
to many of us, in a worse sense, *Let me alone, and I will let you alone;
tempt not me, and I will not tempt you:* Our idlenes, our high diet,
our wanton discours, our exposing our selves to occasion of sin, provoke and call in the Devill, when he seeks not us. The Devill possesses the world, and we possesse the Devill. But then, if the fear of
⁵⁷⁰ the Lord possesse us, our owne *Concupiscencies,* (though they be
indeed our greatest enemies, because the warre that they maintain is
a civill warre) shall doe us no harm, for as the *Septuagint* in their
Translation, diminish the power of the Devill, in that name *Myrme-
coleon,* (a disproportioned Creature, made up of a *Lion* and an *Ant,*
because as St. *Gregory* saith upon that place) *formicis Leo est, vola-
tilibus formica,* The Devill is a Lion to Ants, dasheth whole hills *of*

them with his paw, that creep under him, but he is but an Ant to birds; they prey upon him, that flie above him. If wee feare the Lord, our concupiscencies, our carnall affections, our selves, may prove our
580 best friends, because, as the fire in the furnace did not burn the men, but it burnt off those bands, that fettered and manacled them, (for they were loose, and walked in the furnace) so our *concupiscencies,* if we resist them, shall burn off themselves, and file *off* their own rust, and our salvation shall be surer by occasion of temptations. We may prevent *mortem mortificatione,* everlasting death, by a discipli-nary life. *Mori, ne moriamur,* is *his* rule, too, To die to the fires of lust here, lest wee die in unquenchable fires hereafter; to *die daily,* (as S. *Paul* speaks of himself) lest we die at the last day. To end this, this is the working of the fear of the Lord, it devours all other fears;
590 God will have no *half-affections,* God will have no partners; He that fears God fears nothing else.

This then is the operation of the feare of the Lord, this is his work-ing; remaines onely to consider what this feare of the Lord is: And, beloved in him, be not afraid of it; for, this *fear* of God, is the *love* of God. And, howsoever there may be some amongst us, whom the heighth of birth, or of place, or of spirit hath kept from *fear,* They never feared any thing, yet, I think, there is none, that never *loved* any thing. Obligations of *Matrimony,* or of *friendship,* or of *blood,* or of *alliance,* or of *conversation,* hath given every one of us, no doubt,
600 some sense in our selves, what it is to *love,* and to enjoy that which we doe love; And the *fear* of God, is the *love* of God. *The love of the Lord passeth all things,* saith the Wise man: The love, what is that to fear? It follows, *The fear of the Lord, is the beginning of his love.* As they that build Arches, place centers under the Arch, to beare up the work, till it bee dried, and setled, but, after, all is Arch, and there is no more center, no more support; so to lie at the Lords feet a while, delivers us into his arms, to accustome our selves to his fear, estab-lishes us in his love. Be content to stop a little, even at the lowest fear, the *fear of hell.* When *Saul* was upon an expedition, and did not
610 finde himself well followed, he took a yoke of Oxen, and hewed them in pieces, and proclaimed, that whosoever came not to the supply, all his Oxen should be so served; and upon this, (says the Text there) *The fear of the Lord fell upon all the people, and they came out, as*

Dan. 3.25

August.

[1 Cor. 15.31]

Quid iste Timor

Ecclus. 25.11

1 Sam. 11.7

one man, three hundred and thirty thousand. If *Sauls* threatning of their *worldly goods,* wrought so; let Gods threatning of thy selfe, thine inwardest self, thy soul, with *hell,* make thee to stop even upon thy fear of the Lord, the fear of *Torment.* Stop upon the second fear too, the fear of *privation,* and losse of the sight of God in heaven; That when all wee have disputed, with a modest boldnesse, and wondred 620 with a holy wonder, what kinde of sight of God we shall have in heaven, then when thou shouldst come to an end, and to an answer of all these doubts, in an experimentall triall, how he shall be seen, ·(seen thus) thou shalt see then that thou shalt never see him. After thou hast used to hear, all thy life, blessednesse summed up into that one act, *We shall see God,* thou shalt never come nearer to that knowledge, thou shalt never see him; fear the Lord therefore in this second fear, fear of *privation.* And fear him in a third fear, the fear of the *losse of his grace* here in this world, though thou have it now. S. *Chrysostome* serves himself and us, with an ordinary comparison, 630 A Tyler is upon the top of the house, but he looks to his footing, he is afraid of falling. A righteous man is in a high place in Gods favour, but hee may lose that place. Who is higher then *Adam,* higher then the *Angels?* and whither fell they? Make not thou then thy assurance of standing, out of their arguments, that say it is *impossible* for the righteous to fall, The sins of the righteous are *no sins* in the sight of God; but build thy assurance upon the testimony of a good conscience, that thou usest all diligence, and holy industry, that thou maist continue in Gods favour, and fearest to lose it; for, hee that hath no fear of losing, hath no care of keeping. Accustome thy self to these fears, 640 and these fears will flow into a love. As *love,* and *jealousie* may bee the same thing, so the *feare* and *love* of God will be all one; for, jealousie is but a fear of losing. *Brevissima differentia Testamentorum, Timor & Amor;* This distinguishes the two Testaments, The Old is a Testament of *fear,* the New of *love;* yet in this they grow all one, That we determine the Old Testament, in the New, and that we prove the New Testament by the Old; for, but by the Old, we should not know, that there was to bee a New, nor, but for the New, that there was an Old; so the two Testaments grow *one Bible;* so in these two Affections, if there were not a *jealousie,* a fear of losing God, we 650 could not love him; nor can we fear to lose him, except we doe love

August.

him. Place the affection, (by what name soever) upon the right object, God, and I have, in some measure, done that which this Text directed, (*Taught you the fear of the Lord*) if I send you away in either disposition, *Timorous,* or *amorous;* possessed with either, the fear, or the love of God; for, this fear is inchoative love, and this love is consummative fear; The love of God begins in fear, and the fear of God ends in love; and that love can never end, for God is love.

Number 5.

Preached upon Whitsunday
[Conjecturally assigned to 1624]

I COR. 12.3. *ALSO NO MAN CAN SAY, THAT IESUS IS THE LORD, BUT BY THE HOLY GHOST.*

Iudg. 20.16

W E READ that in the Tribe of *Benjamin,* which is, by interpretation *Filius dextræ, The Son of the right hand,* there
were seven hundred left-handed Men, that could sling
stones at a haires breadth, and not faile. S. *Paul* was of that Tribe; and
though he were from the beginning, in the purpose of God, *Filius
dextræ,* A man ordained to be a dextrous Instrument of his glory, yet
he was for a time a left-handed man, and tooke sinister wayes, and
in those wayes, a good mark-man, a laborious and exquisite persecutor of Gods Church; And therefore it is, that *Tertullian* sayes of him,
10 *Paulum mihi etiam Genesis olim repromisit,* I had a promise of *Paul*
in *Moses;* Then, when *Moses* said, *Iacob blessed Benjamin thus, Benjamin shall ravin as a Wolfe, In the morning he shall devoure the
prey, and at night he shall divide the spoile,* that is, At the beginning
Paul shall scatter the flocke of Christ, but at last, he shall gather, and
re-unite the Nations to his service: As he had *breathed threatnings,
and slaughter against the Disciples of the Lord,* so he became *Os orbi
sufficiens,* A mouth loud enough for all the world to heare: And as
he had drawne and sucked the blood of Christs mysticall body, the
Church, so, in that proportion that God enabled him to, he recom-
20 pensed that damage, by effusion of his owne blood, *He fulfilled the
sufferings of Christ, in his flesh,* as himselfe saies, to the *Colossians;*
And then he bequeathed to all posterity these Epistles, which are, as
S. *Augustine* cals them, *Vbera Ecclesiæ,* The Paps, the Breasts, the
Udders of the Church, And which are, as that cluster of Grapes of

Gen 49.[27]

Acts 9.1
Chrysost.

Colos. 1.24

Numb. 13.23

114

the Land of Canaan, which was borne by two; for here, every couple,
every paire, may have their load, Jew and Gentile, Learned and Ignorant, Man and Wife, Master and Servant, Father and Children,
Prince and People, Counsaile and Client, how distinct soever they
thinke their callings to be towards the world, yet here every paire
30 must equally submit their necks to this sweet and easie yoake, of confessing Jesus to be the Lord, and acknowledging that Confession to
proceed from the working of the Holy Ghost, for *No man can say,
that Iesus is the Lord, without the Holy Ghost.*

In which words, these shall be the three things, that we will con-   *Divisio*
sider now; first, The generall impotency of man, in spirituall duties,
Nemo potest, no man can do this, no man can doe any thing; secondly, How, and what those spirituall duties are expressed to be, It is
a profession of Jesus to be the Lord, to say it, to declare it; And
thirdly, the meanes of repairing this naturall impotency, and rectify-
40 ing this naturall obliquity in man, That man by the Holy Ghost may
be enabled to do this spirituall duty, to professe sincerely Jesus to be
the Lord. In the first we shall see first, the universality of this flood,
the generality of our losse in *Adam, Nemo,* none, not one, hath any,
any power; which notes their blasphemy, that exempt any person
from the infection of sin: And secondly, we shall see the impotency,
the infirmity where it lies, It is *in homine,* no man; which notes their
blasphemy, that say, Man may be saved by his naturall faculties, as
he is man: And thirdly, by just occasion of that word, *Potest,* he can,
he is able, we shall see also the lazinesse of man, which, though he
50 can doe nothing effectually and primarily, yet he does not so much
as he might doe; And in those three, we shall determine our first
part. In the second, what this spirituall duty, wherein we are all so
impotent, is, It is first, an outward act, a profession; not that an outward act is enough, but that the inward affection alone is not enough
neither; To thinke it, to beleeve it, is not enough, but we must say
it, professe it: And what? why, first, That Jesus is; not only assent
to the history, and matter of fact, that Jesus was, and did all that is
reported, and recorded of him, but that he is still that which he pretended to be; *Cæsar* is not *Cæsar* still, nor *Alexander, Alexander;* But
60 Jesus is Jesus still, and shall be for ever. This we must professe, That
he is; And then, That he is the Lord; He was not sent hither as the

greatest of the Prophets, nor as the greatest of the Priests; His worke consists not only in having preached to us, and instructed us, nor in having sacrificed himselfe, thereby to be an example to us, to walk in those wayes after him; but he is Lord, he purchased a Dominion, he bought us with his Blood, He is Lord; And lastly, he is The Lord, not only the Lord Paramount, the highest Lord, but The Lord, the only Lord, no other hath a Lordship in our soules, no other hath any part in the saving of them, but he: And so far we must necessarily enlarge
70 our second consideration. And in the third part, which is, That this cannot be done but by the holy Ghost, we shall see, that in that *But,* is first implyed an exclusion of all means but one; And therefore that one must necessarily be hard to be compassed, The knowledge and discerning of the holy Ghost, is a difficult thing; And yet, as this *But* hath an exclusion of all meanes but one, so it hath an inclusion, an admission, an allowance of that one, It is a necessary duty; nothing can effect it, but the having of the holy Ghost, and therefore the holy Ghost may be had: And in those two points, The hardnesse of it, And the possibility of it, will our last consideration be employed.

I. Part 80   For the first branch of the first part, The generality, that reaches to
Generalitas us all, and to us all over; to all our persons, and to all our faculties; *Perdidimus per peccatum, bonum possibilitatis,* sayes S. *Augustine,* We have lost our possession, and our possibility of recovering, by *Adams* sin. *Adam* at his best had but a possibility of standing; we are fallen from that, and from all possibility of rising by any power derived from him: We have not only by this fall broke our armes, or our legs, but our necks; not our selves, not any other man can raise us; Every thing hath in it, as Physitians use to call it, *Naturale Balsamum,* A naturall Balsamum, which, if any wound or hurt which that creature
90 hath received, be kept clean from extrinsique putrefaction, will heale of it self. We are so far from that naturall Balsamum, as that we have a naturall poyson in us, Originall sin: for that, originall sin, (as it hath relation to God, as all sin is a violating of God) God being the God of mercy, and the God of life, because it deprives us of both those, of mercy, and of life, in opposition to mercy, it is called anger and wrath
Ephes. 2.3 (*We are all by nature the children of wrath*) And in opposition to life,
Rom. 5.12 it is called death, *Death enters by sin, and death is gone over all men;* And as originall sin hath relation to our souls, It is called that indeleble

foulnesse, and uncleannesse which God discovers in us all, (*Though* Jer. 2.22
¹⁰⁰ *thou wash thee with nitre, and take thee much sope, yet thine iniquity*
is marked before me, saith the Lord) And which every man findes in
himself, as *Iob* did, *If I wash my self in Snow-water, and purge my* Job 9.[30]
hands never so cleane, yet mine own clothes shall make me filthy. As
it hath relation to our bodies, so it is not only called *Lex carnis,* A law
which the flesh cannot disobey, And *Lex in membris,* A law written
and imprinted naturally in our bodies, and inseparably inherent there,
but it is a law that hath got *Posse comitatus,* All our strength, and
munition into her own hands, all our powers, and faculties to execute
her purposes against us, and (as the Apostle expresses it fully) *Hath* Rom. 7.5
¹¹⁰ *force in our members, to bring forth fruits unto death.*

Consider our originall weaknesse, as God lookes upon it, so it is
inexcusable sin; consider it, as our soules suffer by it, so it is an indeleble foulnesse; consider it as our bodies contribute to it, and harbour
it, and retain it, and so it is an unquenchable fire, and a brand of hell it
self; It hath banished me out of my self, *It is no more I that do any*
thing, but sin that dwelleth in me: It doth not only *dwell,* but *reign*
in these mortall bodies; not only *reign,* but *tyrannize,* and *lead us* Ver. 23
captives under the law of sin, which is in our members. So that we
have utterly lost *Bonum possibilitatis,* for as men, we are out of all
¹²⁰ possibility, not only of that victorious, and triumphant gratulation and
acclamation to our selves, as for a delivery, *I thank God through Iesus* Ver. ult.
Christ, but we cannot come to that sense of our misery, as to cry out
in the Apostles words, immediately preceding, *O wretched man that*
I am, who shall deliver me from the body of this death?

Now as this death hath invaded every part and faculty of man, understanding, and will, and all, (for though originall sin seem to be
contracted without our will, yet *Sicut omnium natura, ita omnium*
voluntates fuere originaliter in Adam, sayes S. *Augustine,* As the
whole nature of mankinde, and so of every particular man, was in
¹³⁰ *Adam,* so also were the faculties, and so the will of every particular
man in him) so this death hath invaded every particular man; Death
went over all men, for as much as all men had sinned. And therefore
they that do blasphemously exempt some persons from sin, they set
them not above the Law, but without the Law: They out-law them,
in taking from them the benefit of the new Law, the Gospel, and of

the author of that Law, Christ Jesus, who came a Physitian to the sick, and was sent only to save sinners; for them that are none, it is well that they need no Redeemer, for if they did, they could have no part in ours, for he came only to redeem sinners, and they are none. God brought his Son out of Ægypt, not out of Goshen in Ægypt; not out of a priviledged place in Ægypt, but out of Ægypt; God brought his Son Christ Jesus out of the Virgin *Mary* without sin, but he brought not her so, out of her mother. If they might be beleeved that the blessed Virgin, and *Iohn Baptist,* and the Prophet *Ieremy* were without all sin, they would goe about at last to make us beleeve, that *Ignatius* were so too. For us, in the highest of our sanctification, still let us presse with that, *Dimitte nobis debita nostra, O Lord forgive us our trespasses,* and confesse that we needed forgivenesse, even for the sins which we have not done; *Dimissa fateor, & quæ mea sponte* ¹⁵⁰ *feci, & quæ te duce, non feci,* sayes S. *Augustine,* I confesse I need thy mercy, both for the sins which I have done, and for those, which if thy grace had not restrained me, I should have done. And therefore if another think he hath scaped those sins that I have committed, *Non me derideat ab eo medico ægrum sanari, à quo ei præstitum ne ægrotaret;* Let him not despise me, who am recovered, since it is the same physitian who hath wrought upon us both, though by a diverse method, for he hath preserved him, and he hath recovered me: for, for himselfe, we say still with the same Father, *Perdiderat bonum possibilitatis,* As well he as I, had lost all possibility of standing, or rising ¹⁶⁰ after our fall.

This was our first branch, The universall impotency; And our second is, That this is *In homine,* In man, no man (as man) can make this profession, *That Iesus is the Lord:* and therefore, we consider first, wherein, and how far man is disabled. In every Age, some men have attributed to the power of nature, more then a naturall man can doe, and yet no man doth so much as a naturall man might doe. For the over-valuing of nature, and her power, there are impressions in the Fathers themselves, which (whether mis-understood by the Readers, or by the Authors) have led and prevailed much. When *Iustin* ¹⁷⁰ *Martyr* sayes, *Ratio pro fide Græcis & Barbaris,* That rectified reason did the same office in the Gentiles, as faith did in the Christians; when *Clement* sayes, *Philosophia per sese justificavit Græcos,* That the

August.

Quid homo potest

Gentiles to whom the Law and Gospell was not communicated, were justified by their Philosophy; when *Chrysostome* sayes, *Satis fuit Gentibus abstinuisse ab Idololatria,* It was sufficient for the Gentiles, if they did not worship false gods, though they understood not the true; when S. *Augustine* sayes, *Rectè facis, nihil quærere ampliùs, quàm quod docet ratio,* He doth well that seeks no farther, then his reason leads them, these impressions in the Fathers have transported 180 later men farther; so far, as that *Andradius* in the Romane Church, saves all honest Philosophers, that lived morally well without Christ: And *Tostatus* takes all impediments out of their way, That originall sin is absolutely remitted to them, *In prima bona operatione in chari-tate,* In their first good morall work that they do. So that they are in an easier way then we, who are but Christians; for in the opinion of *Tostatus* himselfe, and that whole Church, we cannot be delivered from originall sin, but by baptisme; nothing lesse then a Sacrament would deliver us from originall sin, and any good worke shall deliver any of the Gentiles so disposed.

190   In all ages, in all Churches, there have been men, who have been *Ingrati gratiæ,* as S. *Augustine* calls them, that have been unthankfull to the grace of God, and attributed that to nature, which belonged to grace. But we have an universall conclusion, *God hath made of one blood all mankinde,* And no man can adopt himselfe into the family of God; man is excluded, and all power in man, and all assistance from man; neither your owne reason, nor the reason of your Masters, whom you relie upon, can raise you to this knowledge: for *Ægyptus homo, non Deus, The Egyptians are men, and not Gods, and their horses are flesh, and not spirit; and when the Lord shall stretch out his hand,* 200 *the helper shall fall, and he that is holpen shall fall, and they shall fall together.* The Atheist and all his Philosophy, Helper and hee that is Holpen, Horse and Man, Nature and Art, Reason mounted and advanced upon Learning, shall never be able to leap over, or breake thorough this wall, No man, no naturall man can doe any thing towards a supernaturall work.

This was our second Branch, That too much is ordinarily attributed by man to man, And our third is, That too little is done by any man, and that is worse then the other. When *Nebuchadnezzar* had made his Image of gold of sixtie Cubits, it had been a madnesse in him, not

Act. 17.26

Esay 31.3

Quid homo facit

²¹⁰ to have celebrated the Dedication thereof, with all the pomp, and
solemnity that he did: To have gone so farre, and not to have made it
serve his farther uses, had been a strange impertinence. So is it a
strange contemplation, to see a man set up a golden Image, to attribute
even Divinity to our nature, and to imagine it to be able to doe, whatsoever the grace of God can doe, and yet with this Angelicall nature,
with this celestiall soule, to contribute lesse to the glory of God, then
an Ant, or a plant, or a stone. As the counsell of the Philosopher
Epictetus directs thee, if thou take any new action in hand, consider
what *Socrates* would doe in that case; that is, dispose thy selfe therein,
²²⁰ according to the example, and precedent of some wise man: So if
thou wilt take this new action in hand, (that which is new, but should
be ordinary unto thee) if thou wilt take a view of thy sins that are
past, doe but consider, if ever thou didst any sin, which *Socrates,* or
Seneca would not have forborne. And whatsoever thou seest another
can doe, by the power of that reason, and that perswasion which thou
art able to minister, who are not able to infuse faith, nor inspire grace
into him, but must work by thy reason, and upon his reason, why
shouldest not thou be as powerfull upon thy selfe, and as strong in
thine owne behalfe, and obey that counsell from thy selfe, which thou
²³⁰ thinkest another man mad, if he doe not obey, when thou givest it?
Why shouldest thou pretend Reason, why another should forbeare
any particular sin, and not present that Reason to thy selfe, or not obey
it? To love the Scriptures of God better then any other booke; to love
the house of God better then any other Court; to love the Communion
of Saints better then any other Conversation; to study to know the
revealed will of God, rather then the secrets of any Princes; to consider the direct purposes of God against his enemies, rather then the
sinister supplantations of pretenders to places in Court; briefly to
Reade, to Heare, to Beleeve the Bible, is a worke within the ability of
²⁴⁰ nature, within the power of a morall man.

He that attributes more to nature, he that allowes her any ability of
disposing her selfe before hand, without prevention of grace, or concurrence and co-operation after, without continuall assistance of particular graces, he sets up an Idoll, and magnifies nature beyond that
which appertaines unto her. But he that goes not so farre as this, That
the reason of man, and his naturall faculties, are the Instruments and

Organs that God works in by his grace, howsoever he may in discourse
and in argument exalt nature, howsoever he may so give too much to
her, yet he does not so much with her, as he might doe: He hath
250 made her a Giant, and then, as though he were afraid of her, hee
runs away from her: He will not doe that which is in his power, and
yet he thinks it is in his power to repent when he lists, and when he
lists to apply the merits of Christ to himselfe, and to doe all those duties
which are implyed in our next Part, *To say that Iesus is the Lord.*

In this, our first duty is an outward act, *Dicere,* to professe Christ
Jesus. *Non erubesco,* sayes S. *Paul, I am not ashamed of the Gospel of
Christ Iesus, for it is the power of God unto salvation:* And, *Qui
erubuerit,* sayes Christ, *Whosoever shall be ashamed of me, and of my
word, of him shall the Son of Man be ashamed, when he shall come in*
260 *glory.* This is a necessary duty, but is it the duty of this place? for here
it is not *non vult,* but *non potest;* not that he is loath to professe Jesus,
but that he is not able to doe it. We see that some could say that, and
say it aloud, preach it, and yet without the Holy Ghost; *Some* (sayes
the Apostle) *preach Christ through envy and strife, supposing to adde
more afflictions unto my bands.* Which may well be, that some Jews
and Gentiles, to exasperate the State against *Paul,* fained themselves
also to be converted to his religion, because when they had made him
odious by drawing off others, they who pretended to have been drawn
by him, could alwayes save themselves with recanting, and renouncing
270 their new profession: So they could say *Dominum Iesum, That Iesus
was the Lord,* and never meane it. And of those twelve whom Christ
chose to preach, *Iudas* was one, of whom Christ sayes, *Have I not
chosen you twelve, and one of you is a devill?* So that this devill *Iudas,*
and that devill that made him a devill, the devill himself, could say
as much as this, *Iesus I know, and Paul I know;* They said it, they
cryed it, *Thou art the Christ, the Son of God,* and that incessantly,
*Till Iesus rebuked them, and suffered them not to say, That they
knew him to be The Christ.*

But besides that, even this confessing of Christ, is not *Sine omni
280 impulsu Spiritus sancti,* Altogether without any motion of the holy
Ghost (for the holy Ghost, even in these cases, had a purpose to draw
testimonies for Christ, out of the mouthes of his adversaries) this is
not the professing required here; When *Tiberius* had a purpose to

2. Part
Dicere
Rom. 1.16
Luke 9.26

Phil. 1.15

John 6.70

Acts 19.15
Luke 4.41

canonize Christ Jesus, and to admit him into the number of the Romane Gods, and to make him beholden to him for that honour, he therefore proposed it to the Senate, that so that honour, which Jesus should have, might bee derived from him, And when the Senate had an inclination of themselves to have done Christ that honour, but yet forbore it, because the intimation came not from themselves, but 290 from the Emperour, who still wrought and gained upon their priviledges, neither of these, though they meant collaterally and obliquely to doe Christ an honour, neither of them did say *Iesum Dominum,* that is, professe Jesus, so as is intended here, for they had their owne ends, and their own honors principally in Contemplation.

There is first an open profession of the tongue required; And therefore the Holy Ghost descended in fiery tongues, *Et lingua propria Spiritui Sancto,* sayes S. *Gregory,* The tongue is the fittest Instrument for the Holy Ghost to worke upon, and to worke by, *Qui magnam habet cognationem cum Verbo,* sayes he, The Son of God is the Word, 300 and the Holy Ghost proceeds from him, And because that faith that unites us to God, is expressed in the tongue, howsoever the heart be the center in which the Holy Ghost rests, the tongue is the Spheare, in which he moves: And therefore, sayes S. *Cyril,* as God set the Cherubim with a fiery sword, to keep us out of Paradise, so he hath set the Holy Ghost in fiery tongues to let us in againe. As long as *Iohn Baptist* was unborne, *Zachary* was dumbe; when hee was borne, *Zachary* spoke; Christ is not borne in us, we are not regenerate in him, if we delight not to speake of his wondrous mercyes, and infinite goodnesse to the sons of men; as soone as he is borne in us, his Spirit 310 speakes in us, and by us; in which, our first profession is *Iesum esse,* That Jesus is, That there is a Jesus.

Iesus   This is to professe with *Esay,* That he is *Germen Iehovæ,* The Bud
Esay 4.2   of the Lord, The Blossome of God himselfe; for this Profession is a two-edged sword; for it wounds the Arians on one side, That Jesus is Jehovah, (because that is the name that signifies the very essence of God) And then it wounds the Jews on the other side, because if Jesus be *Germen Iehovæ,* The Bud, the Blossome, the Off-spring of God, then there is a plurality of Persons, Father and Son in the God-head. So that it is a Compendiary and Summary Abridgement, and Cate-320 chisme of all our Religion, to professe that Jesus is, for that is a profes-

sion of his everlasting Essence, that is, his God-head. It hath been denied that he was such as he was pretended to be, that is, borne of a Virgin; for the first Heretiques of all, *Cerinthus,* and *Ebion,* who occasioned S. *Iohns* Gospel, affirmed him to be a meere man, made by ordinary generation, between *Ioseph* and *Mary.* It hath been denied, that he was such a man, as those Heretiques allowed him to bee, for *Apelles* his Heresie was, That he made himselfe a Body out of the Elements, as hee came downe from Heaven, through them. It hath been denied, that he had any Body at all; *Cerdon* and *Marcion* said,
330 That he lived and dyed, but *in Phantasmate,* in apparance, and onely in a forme and shape of a Body assumed; but, in truth, no Body, that did live or dye, but did onely appeare, and vanish. It hath beene denied that that Body which hee had, though a true and a naturall Body did suffer, for *Basilides* said, That when he was led to Execution, and that on the way, the Crosse was laid upon *Simon* of *Cyren,* Christ cast a mist before their eyes, by which they tooke *Simon* for him, and crucified *Simon,* Christ having withdrawne himselfe invisibly from them, as at other times he had done. It hath been denied, (though he had a true Body, and suffered truly therein) that he hath any Body
340 now in Heaven, or shall returne with any, for hee that said hee made his Body of the Elements as hee came downe from Heaven, sayes also that hee resolved that Body into those Elements againe, at his returne. It hath beene denied, That hee was, That he is, That he shall be; but this Profession, that Jesus is, includes all, for, He of whom that is alwayes true, *Est,* He is, He is Eternall, and He that is Eternall, is God: This is therefore a Profession of the God-head of Christ Jesus.

Now, in the next, as we professe him to be *Dominus, A Lord,* we professe him to be God and man, we behold him as he is a mixt person, and so made fit to be the Messias, the Anointed high Priest, King of
350 that Church, which he hath purchased with his blood, And the anointed King of that Kingdome which he hath conquered with his Crosse. As he is *Germen Iehovæ,* The off-spring of Jehovah, so he must necessarily be Jehovah; and that is the name, which is evermore translated The Lord; So also as he is Jehovah, which is the fountaine of all Essence and of all Beeing, so he is Lord, by his interest, and his concurrence, in our Creation; It is a devoute exercise of the soule, to consider, how absolute a Lord he is, by this Title of Creation; If the

Dominus.
A Lord

King give a man a Creation by a new Title, the King found before
in that man, some vertuous and fit disposition, some preparation, some
360 object, some subject of his favour. The King gives Creations to men,
whom the Universities, or other Societies had prepared; They Created
persons whom other lower Schooles had prepared; At lowest, he that
deales upon him first, finds a man, begotten and prepared by Parents,
upon whom he may worke. But remember thy Creator, that called
thee, when thou wast not, as though thou hadst beene, and brought
thee out of nothing; which is a condition (if we may call it a condition,
to be nothing, not to be) farther removed from Heaven, then hell it
selfe: Who is the Lord of life, and breathed this life into thee, and
sweares by that eternall life, which he is, that he would have this life

[Ezek.
33.11]
370 of thine immortall, *As I live, saith the Lord, I would not the death
of a sinner.*

This Contemplation of Jesus, as a Lord, by Creating us, is a devout,
and an humble Contemplation; but to contemplate him as Lord by
Redeeming us, and breeding us in a Church, where that Redemption
is applied to us, this is a devout, and a glorious Contemplation. As he
is Lord over that which his Father gave him, (his Father gave him
all power in Heaven and in earth, and *Omne Iudicium,* His Father
put all Judgement into his hands, all judiciary and all military power
was his; He was Lord Judge, and Lord of Hosts) As he is Lord over

Acts 20.28   380 his owne purchase, *Quod acquisivit sanguine, That Church which he
purchased with his owne blood:* So he is more then the Heretiques of
our time have made him, That he was but sent as a principall Prophet
to explaine the Law, and make that cleare to us in a Gospel; Or as a
Priest, to sacrifice himselfe, but not for a Ransome, not for a Satisfaction, but onely for a lively example, thereby to incline us to suffer for
Gods glory, and for the edification of one another. If we call him
Dominum, A Lord, we call him *Messiam, Vnctum, Regem,* anointed
with the oyle of gladnesse by the Holy Ghost, to bee a cheerefull con-
querour of the world, and the grave, and sin, and hell, and anointed in
390 his owne blood, to be a Lord in the administration of that Church,
which he hath so purchased. This is to say that Jesus is a Lord; To
professe that he is a person so qualified, in his being composed of
God and Man, that he was able to give sufficient for the whole world,
and did give it, and so is Lord of it.

When we say *Iesus est,* That Jesus is, There we confesse his eternity, and therein, his Godhead: when we say *Iesus Dominus,* that he is a Lord, therein we confesse a dominion which he hath purchased; And when we say *Iesum Dominum,* so, as that we professe him to be the Lord, Then we confesse a vigilancy, a superintendency, a residence, ⁴⁰⁰ and a permanency of Christ, in his Dominion, in his Church, to the worlds end. If he be the Lord, in his Church, there is no other that rules with him, there is no other that rules for him. The temporall Magistrate is not so Lord, as that Christ and he are Collegues, or fellow-Consuls, that if he command against Christ, he should be as soone obeyed as Christ; for a Magistrate is a Lord, and Christ is the Lord, a Magistrate is a Lord to us, but Christ is the Lord to him, and to us, and to all, None rules with him, none rules for him; Christ needs no Vicar, he is no non-resident; He is nearer to all particular Churches at Gods right hand, then the Bishop of Rome, at his left. Direct lines, ⁴¹⁰ direct beames doe alwaies warme better, and produce their effects more powerfully, then oblique beames doe; The influence of Christ Jesus directly from Heaven upon the Church, hath a truer operation, then the oblique and collaterall reflections from Rome: Christ is not so far off, by being above the Clouds, as the Bishop of Rome is, by being beyond the Hils. *Dicimus Dominum Iesum,* we say that Jesus is the Lord, and we refuse all power upon earth, that will be Lord with him, as though he needed a Coadjutor, or Lord for him, as though he were absent from us.

To conclude this second part, *To say that Iesus is the Lord,* is to con- ⁴²⁰ fesse him to bee God from everlasting, and to have beene made man in the fulnesse of time, and to governe still that Church, which he hath purchased with his blood, and that therefore hee lookes that we direct all our particular actions to his glory. For this voice, wherein thou saiest *Dominus Iesus, The Lord Iesus,* must be, as the voyce of the Seraphim in *Esay,* thrice repeated, *Sanctus, sanctus, sanctus,* Holy, holy, holy; our hearts must say it, and our tongue, and our hands too, or else we have not said it. For when a man will make Jesus his companion, and be sometimes with him, and sometimes with the world, and not direct all things principally towards him; when he will make ⁴³⁰ Jesus his servant, that is, proceed in all things, upon the strength of his outward profession, upon the colour, and pretence, and advantage

Dominus.
The Lord

Esay 6.3

of Religion, and devotion, would this man be thought to have said

Luke 6.46

Iesum Dominum, That Iesus is the Lord? Why call ye me Lord, Lord, and doe not the things I speake to you? saies Christ; Christ places a tongue in the hands; Actions speake; and *Omni tuba clarior per opera Demonstratio,* sayes S. *Chrysostome,* There is not onely a tongue, but a Trumpet, in every good worke. When Christ sees a disposition in his hearers, to doe according unto their professing, then only he gives

Iohn 13.13

allowance to that that they say, *Dicitis me Dominum, & bene dicitis,*
440 You call me Lord, and you doe well in doing so, doe ye therefore, as I have done to you. To call him Lord, is to contemplate his Kingdome of power, to feele his Kingdome of grace, to wish his Kingdome of glory. It is not a *Domine usque quò,* Lord how long before the Consummation come, as though we were weary of our warfare: It [is] not

Iohn 11.21

a *Domine si fuisses, Lord if thou hadst beene here, our brother had not died,* as *Martha* said of *Lazarus,* as though, as soon as we suffer any worldly calamity, we should thinke Christ to be absent from us, in his

Luke 9.54

power, or in his care of us; It is not a *Domine vis mandemus, Lord wilt thou that we command fire from Heaven to consume these*
450 *Samaritans,* as though we would serve the Lord no longer, then he would revenge his owne and our quarrel; for, (that we may come to our last part) to that fiery question of the Apostles, Christ answered, *You know not of what spirit you are;* It is not the Spirit of God, it is not the Holy Ghost, which makes you call Jesus the Lord onely to serve your own ends, and purposes; and *No man can say, that Iesus is the Lord, but by the Holy Ghost.*

3 Part
Difficultas

For this Part, we proposed onely two Considerations, first that this *But,* excluding all meanes but one, that one must therefore necessarily be difficult, and secondly that that *But,* admitting one meanes, that one
460 must therefore necessarily be possible; so that there is a difficulty, but yet a possibility in having this working by the Holy Ghost. For the first, of those hereticall words of *Faustus* the *Manichæan,* That in the Trinity, the Father dwelt *In illa luce inaccessibili,* In that light which none can attaine to, And the Son of God dwelt in this created light, whose fountaine and roote is the Planet of the Sun, And the Holy Ghost dwelt in the Aire, and other parts illumined by the Sun, we may make this good use, that for the knowledge of the Holy Ghost, wee have not so present, so evident light in reason, as for the knowledge

of the other blessed Persons of the glorious Trinity. For, for the Son,
470 because he assumed our nature, and lived and dyed with us, we conceive certaine bodily impressions, and notions of him; and then
naturally, and necessarily, as soon as we heare of a Son, we conceive
a Father too. But the knowledge of the Holy Ghost is not so evident,
neither doe we bend our thoughts upon the consideration of the Holy
Ghost, so much as we ought to doe. The Arians enwrapped him in
double clouds of darknesse, when they called him *Creaturam Creaturæ;* That Christ himselfe, from whom (say they) the Holy Ghost
had his Creation, was but a Creature, and not God, and so the Holy
Ghost, the Creature of a Creature. And *Maximus ille Gigas,* (as Saint
480 *Bernard* cals *Plato*) That Giant in all kinde of Learning, *Plato,* never
stopped at any knowledge, till he came to consider the holy Ghost:
Vnum inveni, quod cuncta operatur, I have (saies *Plato*) found One,
who made all things; *Et unum per quod cuncta efficiuntur,* And I
have found another, by whom all things were made; *Tertium autem
non potui invenire,* A Third, besides those two, I could never finde.

Though all the mysteries of the Trinity be things equally easie to
faith, when God infuses that, yet to our reason, (even as reason serves
faith, and presents things to that) things are not so equall, but that
S. *Basil* himselfe saw, that the eternall generation of the Son, was too
490 hard for Reason; but yet it is in the proceeding of the Holy Ghost, that
he clearely professes his ignorance: *Si cuncta putarem nostra cogita-
tione posse comprehendi, vererer fortè ignorantiam profiteri,* If I
thought that all things might bee knowne by man, I should bee as
much afraid, and ashamed, as another man, to be ignorant; but, saies
he, since we all see, that there are many things whereof we are ignorant,
Cur non de Spiritu sancto, absque rubore, ignorantiam faterer? Why
should I be ashamed to confesse mine ignorance in many things concerning the Holy Ghost?

There is then a difficulty, no lesse then an impossibility, in searching   *Possibilitas*
500 after the Holy Ghost, but it is in those things which appertain not to
us; But in others, there is a possibility, a facility and easinesse. For,
there are two processions of the holy Ghost, *Æterna,* and *Temporaria,*
his proceeding from the Father, and the Son, and his proceeding into
us. The first we shall never understand, if we reade all the books of
the world, The other we shall not choose but understand, if we study

our own consciences. In the first, the darknesse, and difficulty is rec-
ompenced in this, That though it be hard to finde any thing, yet it is
but little that we are to seek; It is only to finde that there is a holy
Ghost, proceeding from Father, and Son; for in searching farther,
⁵¹⁰ the danger is noted by S. *Basil,* to be thus great, *Qui quomodo inter-*
rogas, & ubi ut in loco, & quando ut in tempore, interrogabis; If thou
give thy curiosity the liberty to ask How the holy Ghost proceeded,
thou wilt ask where it was done, as though there were severall roomes,
and distinct places, in that which is infinite, And thou wilt ask when
it was done, as though there were pieces of time, in that which is
eternall: *Et quæres, non ut fidem, sed ut infidelitatem invenias,*
(which is excellently added by that Father) The end of thy enquir-
ing will not be, that thou mightest finde any thing to establish thy
beliefe, but to finde something that might excuse thine unbeliefe; All
⁵²⁰ thy curious questions are not in hope that thou shalt receive satisfaction, but in hope that the weaknesse of the answer may justifie thy
infidelity.

Thus it is, if we will be over curious in the first, the eternall proceeding of the Holy Ghost. In the other, the proceeding of the holy
Ghost into us, we are to consider, that as in our naturall persons, the
body and soul do not make a perfect man, except they be united, except our spirits (which are the active part of the blood) do fit this
body, and soule for one anothers working; So, though the body of
our religion may seem to be determined in these two, our Creation,
which is commonly attributed to the Father, *Tanquam fonti Deitatis,*
As the fountaine of the Godhead, (for Christ is God of God) And
⁵³⁰ our Redemption, which belongs to the Son, yet for this body there
is a spirit, that is, the holy Ghost, that takes this man, upon whom
the Father hath wrought by Creation, and the Son included within
his Redemption, and he works in him a Vocation, a Justification, and
a sanctification, and leads him from that *Esse,* which the Father gave
him in the Creation, And that *Bene esse* which he hath in being admitted into the body of his Son, the visible Church, and Congregation, to an *Optimè esse,* to that perfection, which is an assurance of
the inhabitation of this Spirit in him, and an inchoation of eternall
blessednesse here, by a heavenly and sanctified conversation, without
⁵⁴⁰ which Spirit *No man can say, that Iesus is the Lord,* because he is

not otherwise in a perfect obedience to him, if he embrace not the means ordained by him in his Church.

So that this Spirit disposes, and dispenses, distributes, and disperses, and orders all the power of the Father, and all the wisdome of the Son, and all the graces of God. It is a Center to all; So S. *Bernard* sayes upon those words of the Apostle, *We approve our selves as the Ministers of God;* But by what? *By watching, by fasting, by suffering, by the holy Ghost, by love unfained. Vide, tanquam omnia ordinantem, quomodo in medio virtutum, sicut cor in medio corporis,*
550 *constituit Spiritum Sanctum:* As the heart is in the midst of the body, so between these vertues of fasting and suffering before, and love unfained after, the Apostle places the holy Ghost, who only gives life and soule to all Morall, and all Theologicall vertues. And as S. *Bernard* observes that in particular men, so doth S. *Augustine* of the whole Church; *Quod in corpore nostro anima, id in corpore Christi, Ecclesia, Spiritus Sanctus;* That office which the soule performes to our body, the holy Ghost performes in the body of Christ, which is the Church.

And therefore since the holy Ghost is thus necessary, and thus neare,
560 as at the Creation the whole Trinity was intimated in that plurall word, *Elohim, creavit Dii,* but no person of the Trinity is distinctly named in the Creation, but the holy Ghost, *The Spirit of God moved upon the waters,* As the holy Ghost was first conveyed to our knowledge in the Creation, so in our Regeneration, by which we are new creatures, though our Creation, and our Redemption be religious subjects of our continuall meditation, yet let us be sure to hold this that is nearest us, to keep a neare, a familiar, and daily acquaintance, and conversation with the holy Ghost, and to be watchfull to cherish his light, and working in us. *Homines docent quærere, solus ipse, qui*
570 *docet invenire, habere, frui;* Men can teach us wayes how to finde some things; The Pilot how to finde a Lande, The Astronomer how to finde a Star; Men can teach us wayes how to finde God, The naturall man in the book of creatures, The Morall man in an exemplar life, The Jew in the Law, The Christian in generall in the Gospell, But *Solus ipse, qui docet invenire, habere, frui,* Only the holy Ghost enables us to finde God so, as to make him ours, and to enjoy him. First you must get more light then nature gives, for, *The naturall man per-*

[2 Cor. 6.4]

Bernard.

I Cor. 2.14

ceiveth not the things of the Spirit: When that light is so mended, that you have some sparkes of faith, you must also leave the works

Iud. 19 580 of the flesh, For, *Fleshly men have not the Spirit:* When the Spirit offers it self in approaches, *Resist it not,* as *Stephen* accuses them to have done, *Act. 7.* When it hath prevailed, and sealed you to God,

Ephes. 4.30 *Grieve not the holy Spirit, by whom ye are sealed unto Redemption.* For this preventing the Spirit, by trusting to nature, and morality, this infecting the Spirit, by living ill in a good profession, this grieving of the Spirit, by neglecting his operations, induces the last desperate

I Thes. 5.[19] work of *Quenching the Spirit,* which is a smothering, a suffocating of that light, by a finall obduration.

Iohn 3.8 *Spiritus ubi vult spirat,* sayes our Saviour Christ; which S. *Augus-* 590 *tine,* (and indeed most of the Fathers) interpret of the holy Ghost, and not of the winde, though it may also properly enough admit that interpretation too. But *The holy Ghost,* sayes he, *breathes where it pleases him; Et vocem ejus audis,* sayes Christ, *You heare the voice of the holy Ghost;* for, (sayes S. *Augustine* upon those words of Christ) *Sonat psalmus, vox est Spiritus sancti,* When you heare a Psalme sung, you heare the voice of the holy Ghost; *Sonat Euangelium, sonat sermo Divinus,* You heare the Gospell read, you heare a Sermon preached, still you heare the voice of the holy Ghost; And yet, as Christ sayes in that place, *Nescis unde venit, Thou knowest not from* 600 *whence that voice comes,* Thou canst finde nothing in thy self, why the holy Ghost should delight to entertain thee, and hold discourse with thee, in so familiar, and so frequent, and so importunate a speaking to thee; *Nescis unde venit,* Thou knowest not from whence all this goodnesse comes, but meerly from his goodness; So also, as Christ adds there, *Nescis quò vadat, Thou knowest not whither it goes,* how long it will last and goe with thee. If thou carry him to darke and foule corners, if thou carry him back to those sins, of which, since he began to speake to thee, at this time, thou hast felt some remorse, some detestation, he will not goe with thee, he will give thee 610 over. But as long as he, The Spirit of God, by your cherishing of him, staies with you, when Jesus shall say to you, (in your consciences)

[Mat. 16.15] *Quid vos dicitis? Whom doe you say that I am?* You can say *Iesus Dominus,* We say, we professe, *That thou art Iesus, and that Iesus is*

[Mal. 1.6] *the Lord:* If he proceed, *Si Dominus, ubi timor? If I be Lord, where*

is my feare? You shall shew your feare of him, even in your confidence in him, *In timore Domini, fiducia fortitudinis, In the feare of the Lord, is an assured strength:* You shall not only say *Iesum Dominum,* professe Jesus to be the Lord, but *Veni Domine Iesu,* You shall invite, and solicite Jesus to a speedy judgement, and be able, in his right, to

620 stand upright in that judgement. This you have, if you have this Spirit; and you may have this Spirit, if you resist it not, now; For, *As when Peter spake, the holy Ghost fell upon all that heard,* So in the Ministery of his weaker instruments, he conveyes, and diffuses, and seales his gifts upon all, which come well disposed to the receiving of him, in his Ordinance.

[Prov. 14.26]

Acts 10.[44]

Number 6.

Preached at S. Dunstans
upon Trinity-Sunday. 1624.

MAT. 3.17. *AND LO, A VOYCE CAME FROM*
HEAVEN, SAYING, THIS IS MY BELOVED
SONNE, IN WHOM I AM WELL PLEASED.

IT HATH been the custome of the Christian Church to appropriate
certaine Scriptures to certaine Dayes, for the celebrating of certaine Mysteries of God, or the commemorating of certaine benefits from God: They who consider the age of the Christian Church,
too high or too low, too soone or too late, either in the cradle, as it is
exhibited in the Acts of the Apostles, or bed-rid in the corruptions of
Rome, either before it was come to any growth, when Persecutions
nipped it, or when it was so over-growne, as that prosperity and outward splendor swelled it, They that consider the Church so, will
10 never finde a good measure to direct our religious worship of God by,
for the outward Liturgies, and Ceremonies of the Church. But as
soon as the Christian Church had a constant establishment under
Christian Emperours, and before the Church had her tympany of
worldly prosperity under usurping Bishops, in this outward service
of God, there were particular Scriptures appropriated to particular
dayes. Particular men have not liked this that it should be so: And
yet that Church which they use to take for their patterne, (I meane
Geneva) as soone as it came to have any convenient establishment
by the labours of that Reverend man, who did so much in the rectify-
20 ing thereof, admitted this custome of celebrating certaine times, by the
reading of certaine Scriptures. So that in the pure times of the Church,
without any question, and in the corrupter times of the Church, without any infection, and in the Reformed times of the Church, without
any suspition of back-sliding, this custome hath beene retained, which

our Church hath retained; and according to which custome, these
words have been appropriated to this day, for the celebrating thereof,
And lo, A voice came, &c.

In which words we have pregnant and just occasion to consider,
first, the necessity of the Doctrine of the Trinity; Secondly, the way
³⁰ and meanes by which we are to receive our knowledge and under-
standing of this mystery; And thirdly, the measure of this knowledge,
How much we are to know, or to inquire, in that unsearchable mystery: The *Quid,* what it is; the *Quomodo,* How we are to learne it;
and the *Quantum,* How farre we are to search into it, will be our
three Parts. We consider the first of these, the necessity of that knowledge to a Christian, by occasion of the first Particle, in the Text, *And;*
A Particle of Connexion, and Dependance; and we see by this Connexion, and Dependance, that this revealing, this manifestation of
the Trinity, in the text, was made presently after the Baptisme of
⁴⁰ Christ; and that intimates, and inferres, That the first, and principall
duty of him, who hath ingrafted himself into the body of the Christian Church, by Baptisme, is to informe himself of the Trinity, in
whose name he is Baptized. Secondly, in the meanes, by which this
knowledge of the Trinity is to be derived to us, in those words, (*Lo,
a voyce came from heaven, saying*) we note the first word, to be a
word of Correction, and of Direction; *Ecce, Behold,* leave your blindnesse, look up, shake off your stupidity, look one way or another; A
Christian must not goe on implicitely, inconsiderately, indifferently,
he must look up, he must intend a calling: And then, *Ecce* againe,
⁵⁰ *Behold,* that is, Behold the true way; A Christian must not thinke he
hath done enough, if he have been studious, and diligent in finding
the mysteries of Religion, if he have not sought them the right way:
First, there is an *Ecce corrigentis,* we are chidden, if we be lazy; And
then, there is an *Ecce dirigentis,* we are guided if we be doubtfull.
And from this, we fall into the way it selfe; which is, first, *A voyce,*
There must be something heard; for, take the largest Spheare, and
compasse of all other kinds of proofes, for the mysteries of Religion,
which can be proposed, Take it first, at the first, and weakest kinde
of proofe, at the book of creatures, (which is but a faint knowledge
⁶⁰ of God, in respect of that knowledge, with which we must know
him) And then, continue this first way of knowledge, to the last, and

powerfullest proofe of all, which is the power of miracles, not this
weake beginning, not this powerfull end, not this *Alpha* of Creatures,
not this *Omega* of miracles, can imprint in us that knowledge, which
is our saving knowledge, nor any other meanes then a voyce; for this
[Rom.
10.14]
knowing is beleeving, And, *how should they beleeve, except they
heare?* sayes the Apostle. It must be *Vox, A voyce,* And *Vox de cœlis,
A voyce from heaven:* For, we have had *voces de terra,* voyces of men,
who have indeed but diminished the dignity of the Doctrine of the
70 Trinity, by going about to prove it by humane reason, or to illustrate
it by weak and low comparisons; And we have had *voces de Inferis,*
voyces from the Devill himselfe, in the mouthes of many Heretiques,
blasphemously impugning this Doctrine; Wee have had *voces de profundis,* voyces fetched from the depth of the malice of the Devill,
Heretiques; And *voces de medio,* voyces taken from the ordinary
strength of Morall men, Philosophers; But this is *vox de Excelsis,*
onely that voyce that comes from Heaven, belongs to us in this mystery: And then lastly, it is *vox dicens, a voyce saying,* speaking, which
is proper to man, for nothing speaks but man; It is Gods voyce, but
80 presented to us in the ministery of man; And this is our way; To
behold, that is, to depart from our own blindnesse, and to behold a
way, that is shewed us; but shewed us in the word, and in the word
of God, and in that word of God, preached by man. And after all this,
we shall consider the measure of this knowledge, in those last words,
This is my beloved Son, in whom I am well pleased; For, in that
word, *Meus, My,* there is the Person of the Father; In the *Filius,* there
is the Person of the Son; and in the *Hic est, This is,* there is the Person of the Holy Ghost, for that is the action of the Holy Ghost, in
that word, He is pointed at, who was newly baptized, and upon whom
90 the Holy Ghost, in the Dove, was descended, and had tarried. But
we shall take those words in their order, when we come to them.

I Part
First then, we noted the necessity of knowing the Trinity, to be
pregnantly intimated in the first word, *Et, And:* This connects it to
the former part of the history, which is Christs Baptisme, and presently upon that Baptisme, this manifestation of the holy Trinity. Consider a man, as a Christian, his first element is Baptisme, and his next
is Catechisme; and in his Catechisme, the first is, to beleeve a Father,
Son, and holy Ghost. There are in this man, this Christian, *Tres*

nativitates, sayes S. *Gregory,* three births; one, *Per generationem,* so
100 we are borne of our naturall mother; one *Per regenerationem,* so we
are borne of our spirituall Mother, the Church, by Baptisme; and a
third, *Per Resurrectionem,* and so we are borne of the generall Mother
of us all, when the earth shall be delivered, not of twins, but of millions, when she shall empty her selfe of all her children, in the Resurrection. And these three Nativities our Saviour Christ Jesus had; Of
which three, *Hodie alter salvatoris natalis,* sayes S. *Augustine,* This
day is the day of Christs second birth, that is, of his Baptisme. Not that
Christ needed any Regeneration; but that it was his abundant goodnesse, to sanctifie in his person, and in his exemplar action, that
110 Element, which should be an instrument of our Regeneration in Baptisme, the water, for ever. Even in Christ himselfe, *Honoratior se-*
cunda, sayes that Father, The second birth, which he had at his
Baptisme, was the more honourable birth; for, *Ab illa se, Pater qui*
putabatur, Ioseph excusat, At his first birth, *Ioseph,* his reputed
Father, did not avow him for his Son; *In hac se, Pater qui non puta-*
batur, insinuat, At this his second birth, God, who was not known to
be his Father before, declares that now: *Ibi laborat suspicionibus*
Mater, quia professioni deerat Pater, There the Mothers honour was
in question, because *Ioseph* could not professe himselfe the Father
120 of the childe; *Hic honoratur genetrix, quia filium Divinitas protesta-*
tur, Here her honour is repaired, and magnified, because the God-
head it selfe, proclaimes it selfe to be the Father.

If then, Christ himselfe chose to admit an addition of dignity at
his Baptisme, who had an eternall generation in heaven, and an innocent conception without sin, upon earth, let not us undervalue that
dignity, which is afforded us by Baptisme, though our children be
borne within the Covenant, by being borne of Christian Parents; for
the Covenant gives them *Ius ad rem,* a right to Baptisme; children
of Christian parents may claime Baptisme, which aliens to Christ
130 cannot doe; but yet they may not leave out Baptisme: A man may
be within a generall pardon, and yet have no benefit by it, if he sue
it not out, if he plead it not; a childe may have right to Baptisme, and
yet be without the benefit of it, if it be neglected.

Christ began at Baptisme; Naturall things he did before; He fled
into Ægypt, to preserve his life from *Herods* Persecution, before: And

a miraculous thing he did before; He overcame in disputation, the Doctors in the Temple, at twelve yeares old; but yet, neither of these neither, before his Circumcision, which was equivalent to Baptisme, to this purpose; but before he accepted, or instituted Baptisme, he
140 did some naturall, and some miraculous things. But his ordinary work which he came for, his preaching the Gospel, and thereby raising the frame for our salvation, in his Church, he began not, but after his Baptisme: And then, after that, it is expresly, and immediatly recorded, That when he came out of the waters, *he prayed;* and then, the next thing in the history is, that he *fasted,* and upon that, *his tentation in the wildernesse.* I meane no more in this, but this, That no man hath any interest in God, to direct a prayer unto him, how devoutly soever, no man hath any assurance of any effect of his endeavours in a good life, how morally holy soever, but in relation to
150 his Baptisme, in that seale of the Covenant, by which he is a Christian: Christ took this Sacrament, his Baptisme, before he did any other thing; and he took this, three yeares before the institution of the other Sacrament of his body and blood: So that the Anabaptists obtrude a false necessity upon us, that we may not take the first Sacrament, Baptisme, till we be capable of the other Sacrament too; for, first in nature, *Priùs nascimur, quàm pascimur,* we are borne before we are fed; and so, in Religion, we are first borne into the Church, (which is done by Baptisme) before we are ready for that other food, which is not indeed milk for babes, but solid meat for stronger
160 digestions.

They that have told us, that the Baptisme, that Christ took of *Iohn,* was not the same Baptisme, which we Christians take in the Church,
John 1.6 speak impertinently; for *Iohn* was sent by God to baptize; and there is but one Baptisme in him. It is true, that S. *Augustine* calls *Iohns* Baptisme, *Præcursorium ministerium,* as he was a fore-runner of Christ, his Baptisme was a fore-running Baptisme; It is true, that *Iustin Martyr* calls *Iohns* Baptisme, *Euangelicæ gratiæ præludium,* A Prologue to the grace of the Gospel; It is true, that more of the Fathers have more phrases of expressing a difference between the
170 Baptisme of *Iohn,* and the Baptisme of Christ: But all this is not *De essentia,* but *De modo,* Not of the substance of the Sacrament, which is the washing of our soules in the blood of Christ, but the difference

was in the relation; *Iohn* baptized *In Christum moriturum,* Into
Christ, who was to dye, and we are baptized *In Christum mortuum,*
Into Christ who is already dead for us. *Damascen* expresses it fully,
Christus baptizatur suo Baptismo: Christ was baptized with his own
Baptisme; It was *Iohns* Baptisme, and yet it was Christs too. And so
we are baptized with his Baptisme, and there neither is, nor was any
other; And that Baptisme is to us, *Ianua Ecclesiæ,* as S. *Augustine*
¹⁸⁰ cals it, The Doore of the Church, at that we enter, And *Investitura*
Christianismi, The investing of Christianity, as S. *Bernard* cals it,
There we put on Christ Jesus; And, (as he, whom wee may be bold
to match with these two floods of spirituall eloquence, for his Eloquence, that is *Luther,* expresses it) *Puerpera regni Cœlorum,* The
Church in Baptisme, is as a Woman delivered of child, and her child
is the Kingdome of Heaven, and that kingdome she delivers into his
armes who is truly Baptized. This Sacrament makes us Christians;
this denominates us, both Civilly, and Spiritually; there we receive
our particular names, which distinguish us from one another, and
¹⁹⁰ there we receive that name, which shall distinguish us from the Na-
tions, in the next World; at Baptisme wee receive the name of Christians, and there we receive our Christian names.

　　When the Disciples of Christ, in generall, came to be called *Chris-*   Act. 11.26
tians, wee finde, it was a name given upon great deliberation; *Bar-*
nabas had Preached there, who was a good Man, and full of the Holy
Ghost, and of faith, himselfe. But he went to fetch *Paul* too, a Man
of great gifts, and power in Preaching; and both they continued a
yeare Preaching in *Antioch,* and there, first of all, *the Disciples were*
called Christians: Before they were called *Fideles,* and *Fratres,* and
²⁰⁰ *Discipuli;* The Faithfull, and the Brethren, and the Disciples, and
(as S. *Chrysostome* sayes) *De via,* Men that were in the way; for, all
the World besides, were beside him, who was *The Way, the Truth,*
and the Life. But, (by the way) we may wonder, what gave S. *Chrys-*
ostome occasion of that opinion or that conjecture, since in the Ec-
clesiastique Story (I thinke) there is no mention of that name,
attributed to the Christians: And in the Acts of the Apostles, it is
named but once; when *Saul* desired Letters to Damascus, to punish   Acts 9.2
them, whom he found to be of *That way.* Where we may note also,
the zeale of S. *Paul,* (though then, in a wrong cause) against them,

²¹⁰ who were of *That way,* that is, That way inclined; And our stupidity, who startle not at those men, who are not onely inclined another way, a crosse way, but labour pestilently to incline others, and hope confidently to see all incline that way againe. Here then at Antioch, they began to be called Christians; not onely out of Custome, but, as it may seeme, out of decree. For, if there belong any credit to that Councell, which the Apostles are said to have held at Antioch, (of which Councell there was a Copy, whether true or false, in *Origens* Library, within two hundred yeares after Christ) one Canon in that

Lorinus in   Councell is, *Vt credentes in Iesum, quos tunc vocabant Galilæos,*
Act. 11.20   ²²⁰ *vocarentur Christiani,* That the followers of Christ, who, till then, were called Galileans, should then be called Christians. There, in generall, we were all called Christians; but, in particular, I am called a Christian, because I have put on Christ, in Baptisme.

Now, in considering the infinite treasure which we receive in Baptisme, insinuated before the text, *That the Heavens opened,* that is, The mysteries of Religion are made accessible to us, we may attaine to them; And then, *The Holy Ghost descends,* (And he is a Comforter, whilest we are in Ignorance, and he is a Schoolemaster to teach us all truths) And he comes as a *Dove,* that is, Brings peace of con-
²³⁰ science with him, and he rests upon us as a *Dove,* that is, Requires simplicity, and an humble disposition in us, That not onely as *Elias* opened and shut Heaven, *Vt pluviam aut emitteret, aut teneret,* That he might poure out or withhold the raine; but (as that Father, S. *Chrysostome* pursues it) *Ita apertum, ut ipse conscendas, & alios, si velles, tecum levares,* Heaven is so opened to us in baptisme, as that we our selves may enter into it, and by our good life, lead others into it too; As we consider, I say, what we have received in Baptisme, so, if we be not onely *Dealbati Christiani,* (as S. *Augustine* speaks) White-lim'd Christians, Christians on the out-side, we must consider
²⁴⁰ what we are to doe upon all this. We are baptized, *In plena & adulta Trinitate,* sayes S. *Cyprian,* not in a Father without a Son, nor in either, or both, without a Holy Ghost, but in the fulnesse of the Trinity: And this mystery of the Trinity, is *Regula fidei,* sayes S. *Hierom,* It is the Rule of our faith, this onely regulates our faith, That we beleeve aright of the Trinity; It is *Dogma nostræ Religionis,* sayes S. *Basil,* As though there were but this one Article; It is, sayes he, the

foundation, the summe, it is all the Christian Religion, to beleeve aright of the Trinity. By this wee are distinguished from the Jews, who accept no plurality of Persons; And by this we are distinguished 250 from the Gentiles, who make as many severall persons, as there are severall powers, and attributes belonging to God. Our Religion, our holy Philosophy, our learning, as it is rooted in Christ, so it is not limited, not determined in Christ alone; wee are not baptized in his name alone, but our study must be the whole Trinity; for, he that beleeves not in the Holy Ghost, as well as in Christ, is no Christian: And, as that is true which S. *Augustine* sayes, *Nec laboriosius aliquid quæritur, nec periculosius alicubi erratur,* As there is not so steepy a place to clamber up, nor so slippery a place to fall upon, as the doc- trine of the Trinity; so is that also true which he addes, *Nec fructuo-* 260 *sius invenitur.* There is not so fulfilling, so accomplishing, so abundant an Article as that of the Trinity, for it is all Christianity. And there- fore let us keepe our selves to that way, of the manifestation of the Trinity, which is revealed in this text; and that way is our second part.

We must necessarily passe faster through the branches of this part, then the Dignity of the subject, or the fecundity of the words will well admit; but the clearenesse of the order must recompence the speed and dispatch. First then, in this way here is an *Ecce,* An awak- ing, an Alarum, a calling us up, *Ecce, Behold.* First, an *Ecce correc-* 270 *tionis,* A voyce of chiding, of rebuking. If thou lye still in thy first bed, as thou art meerely a Creature, and thinkest with thy selfe, that since the Lilly labours not, nor spins, and yet is gloriously cloathed, since the Fowles of the Heavens sow not, nor reape, and yet are plen- tifully fed, thou mayest do so, and thou shalt bee so; *Ecce animam,* Behold thou hast an immortall soule, which must have spirituall food, the Bread of life, and a more durable garment, the garment of right- eousnesse, and cannot be emprisoned and captivated to the compari- son of a Lilly that spins not, or of a Bird that sowes not. If thou thinke thy soule sufficiently fed, and sufficiently cloathed at first, in thy bap- 280 tisme, That that Manna, and those cloathes shall last thee all thy pilgrimage, all thy life, That since thou art once Baptized, thou art well enough, *Ecce fermentum,* take heed of that *leaven of the Phari- sees,* Take heed of them that put their confidence in the very act and

2 Part

Ecce Correctionis

[Mat. 16.6]

character of the Sacrament, and trust to that: for there is a Confirmation belongs to every mans Baptisme; not any such Confirmation as should intimate an impotency, or insufficiency in the Sacrament, but out of an obligation, that that Sacrament layes upon thee, That thou art bound to live according to that stipulation and contract, made in thy behalfe, at thy receiving of that Sacrament, there belongs a Con-
²⁹⁰ firmation to that Sacrament, a holy life, to make sure that salvation, sealed to thee at first. So also, if thou thinke thy selfe safe, because thou hast left that leaven, that is, Traditions of men, and livest in a Reformed, and Orthodox Church, yet, *Ecce Paradisum,* Behold Paradise it selfe, even in Paradise, the bed of all ease, yet there was labour required; so is there required diligence, and a laborious holinesse, in the right Church, and in the true Religion. If thou thinke thou knowest all, because thou understandest all the Articles of faith already, and all the duties of a Christian life already, yet *Ecce scalam,* Behold the life of a Christian is a *Iacobs* Ladder, and till we come up to God,
³⁰⁰ still there are more steps to be made, more ways to bee gone. Briefly, to the most learned, to him that knowes most, To the most sanctified, to him that lives best, here is an *Ecce correctionis,* there is a farther degree of knowledge, a farther degree of goodnesse, proposed to him, then he is yet attained unto.

So it is an *Ecce correctionis,* an *Ecce instar stimuli,* God by calling us up to Behold, rebukes us because wee did not so, and provokes us to doe so now: It is also an *Ecce directionis,* an *Ecce instar lucernæ,* God by calling us up to Behold, gives us a light whereby wee may doe so, and may discerne our way: whomsoever God cals, to him hee
³¹⁰ affords so much light, as that, if he proceed not by that light, hee himselfe hath winked at that light, or blown out that light, or suffered that light to wast, and goe out, by his long negligence. God does not call man with an *Ecce,* To behold him, and then hide himselfe from him; he does not bid him looke, and then strike him blinde. We are all borne blinde at first; In Baptisme God gives us that *Collyrium,* that eye-salve, by which we may see, and actually by the power of that medicine, we do all see, more then the Gentiles do. But yet, *Ecce*
Mat. 7.4   *trabs in oculis,* sayes *Christ;* Behold there is *a beame* in our *eye,* that is, Naturall infirmities. But for all this beame, when Christ bids us
³²⁰ behold, we are able to see, by Christs light, our owne imperfections;

though we have that beame, yet we are able to see that we have it. And when this light which Christ gives us, (which is his first grace) brings us to that, then Christ proceeds to that which followes there, *Projice trabem, Cast out the beame that is in thine eye,* and so we become able by that succeeding grace, to overcome our former impediments: If Christ bid us behold, he gives us light, if he bid us cast out the beame, he gives us strength. There is an *Ecce mutus,* cast upon *Zachary, Behold thou shalt be dumbe,* God punished *Zacharies* incredulity with dumbnesse; But there is never an *Ecce cæcus,* Behold

330 thou shalt be blinde, That God should call man to see, and then blow out the candle, or not shew him a candle, if he were in utter darknesse; for this is an *Ecce directionis,* an *Ecce lucernæ,* God cals, and he directs, and lightens our paths; never reproach God so impiously as to suspect, that when he cals, he does not meane that we should come.

    Well then, with what doth he enlighten thee? Why, *Ecce vox, Behold a voyce, saying.* Now, for this *voyce* in the Text, by whom it was heard, as also by whom the *Dove* that descended was seen, is sometimes disputed, and with some perplexity amongst the Fathers. Some

340 thinke it was to Christ alone, because two of the Euangelists, *Mark* and *Luke,* record the words in that phrase, *Tu es filius,* not as we reade it in our Text, *This is,* but, *Thou art my beloved Sonne:* But so, there had been no use, neither of the *Dove,* nor of the *voyce;* for Christ himselfe lacked no testimony, that he was that Sonne. Some thinke it was to Christ, and *Iohn Baptist,* and not to the company; Because, say they, The mysterie of the Trinity was not to be presented to them, till a farther and maturer preparation; And therefore they observe, that the next manifestation of Christ, and so of the Trinity, by a like voyce, was almost three years after this, in his Transfigura-

350 tion, after he had manifested this doctrine by a long preaching amongst them; And yet, even then, it was but to his Apostles, and but to a few of them neither, and those few forbidden to publish too; and how long? Till his resurrection; when by that resurrection he had confirmed them, then it was time to acquaint them with the Doctrine of the Trinity. But for the Doctrine of the Trinity, as mysterious as it is, it is insinuated and conveyed unto us, even in the first verse of the Bible, in that extraordinary phrase, *Creavit Dii, Gods,*

Luke 1.20

Vox

[Mark 1.11
Luke 3.22]

Mat. 17.[5]

Gods in the plurall, *created heaven and earth;* There is an unity in
the action, it is but *Creavit,* in the singular, and yet there is a plurality
360 in the persons, it is not *Deus, God,* but *Dij, Gods:* The Doctrine of
the Trinity, is the first foundation of our Religion, and no time is too
early for our faith, The simplest may beleeve it; and all time is too
early for our reason, The wisest cannot understand it. And therefore,
as *Chrysostome* is well followed in his opinion, so he is well worthy
to be followed, That both the *Dove* was seen, and the *voyce* was heard
by all the company: for, neither was necessary to Christ himselfe;
And the voyce was not necessary to *Iohn Baptist,* because the signe

[Joh. 1.33]   which was to governe him, was the *Dove; He that sent me, said, upon
whom thou shalt see the Spirit come down, and tarry still, it is he*
370 *that baptizeth with the Holy Ghost.* But to the company, both voyce
and Dove were necessary: for, if the voyce had come alone, they might
have thought, that that testimony had been given of *Iohn,* of whom
they had, as yet, a far more reverend opinion, then of Christ; And
therefore, God first points out the person, and by the Dove declares
him to all, which was He, and then, by that voyce declares farther to
them all, what He was. This benefit they had by being in that company, they saw, and they heard things conducing to their salvation;
for, though God worke more effectually upon those particular persons in the Congregation, who, by a good use of his former graces,
380 are better disposed then others, yet to the most gracelesse man that
is, if he be in the Congregation, God vouchsafes to speake, and would
be heard.

Via   They that differ in the persons, who heard it, agree in the Reason;
Creaturæ   All they heard it, in all their opinions, to whom it was necessary to
heare it; And it is necessary to all us, to have this meanes of understanding and beleeving, to heare. Therefore God gives to all that shall
be saved, *vocem,* his voyce. We consider two other wayes of imprinting the knowledge of God in man; first in a darke and weake way,
the way of Nature, and the book of Creatures; and secondly, in that
390 powerfull way, the way of Miracles. But these, and all between these,
are uneffectuall without the Word. When *David* sayes of the Crea-

Psal. 19.3   tures, *There is no speech nor language, where their voyce is not heard,*
(the voyce of the Creature is heard over all) S. *Paul* commenting

Rom. 10.18   upon those words, says, *They have heard, All the world hath heard;*

but what? The voyce of the Creature; now that is true, so much all the world had heard then, and does heare still: But the *hearing* that S. *Paul* intends there, is such a hearing as begets *faith,* and that the voyce of Creature reaches not to. The voyce of the Creature alone, is but a faint voyce, a low voyce; nor any voyce, till the voyce of the
400 Word inanimate it; for then when the Word of God hath taught us any mystery of our Religion, then the booke of Creatures illustrates, and establishes, and cherishes that which we have received by faith, in hearing the Word: As a stick bears up, and succours a vine, or any plant, more precious then it selfe, but yet gave it not life at first, nor gives any nourishment to the root now: so the assistance of reason, and the voyce of the Creature, in the preaching of Nature, works upon our faith, but the roote, and the life is in the faith it selfe; The light of nature gives a glimmering before, and it gives a reflexion after faith, but the meridianall noone is in faith.

410 Now, if we consider the other way, the way of power, Miracles, no man may ground his beliefe upon that, which seems a Miracle to him. *Moses* wrought Miracles, and *Pharaohs* instruments wrought the like: we know, theirs were no true Miracles, and we know *Moses* were; but how do we know this? By another voyce, by the Word of God, who cannot lie: for, for those upon whom those Miracles were to worke on both sides, *Moses,* and they too, seemed to the beholders, diversly disposed to do Miracles. One Rule in discerning, and judging a Miracle, is, to consider whether it be done in confirmation of a necessary Truth: otherwise it is rather to be suspected for an Illusion,
420 then accepted for a Miracle. The Rule is intimated in *Deuteronomy,* where, though a Prophets prophecy do come to passe, yet, if his end be, to draw to other gods, he must be slaine. What Miracles soever are pretended, in confirmation of the inventions of Men, are to be neglected. God hath not carried us so low for our knowledge, as to Creatures, to Nature, nor so high, as to Miracles, but by a middle way, By a *voyce.*

But it is *Vox de Cœlis, A voyce from heaven.* S. *Basil* applying (indeed with some wresting and detorting) those words in the 29 Psalme, vers. 3. (*The voyce of the Lord is upon the waters, the God*
430 *of glory maketh it to thunder*) to this Baptisme of Christ, he sayes, *Vox super aquas Ioannes,* The words of *Iohn* at Christs Baptisme,

*Via miracu-
lorum*

Deut. 13

De Cœlis

were this voyce that *David* intends; And then that manifestation
which God gave of the Trinity, (whatsoever it were) altogether, that
was the Thunder of his Majesty: so this Thunder then, was *vox de
Cœlis,* A voyce from heaven; And in this voyce the person of the
Father was manifested, as he was in the same voyce at his Transfiguration. Since this voyce then is from Heaven, and is the Fathers
voyce, we must looke for all our knowledge of the Trinity from
thence. For, (to speake of one of those persons, of Christ) *no man*

Mat. 11.27
440 *knoweth the Sonne, but the Father;* Who then, but he, can make us
know him? If any knew it, yet it is an unexpressible mystery, no man

Mat. 16.17
could reveale it; *Flesh and blood hath not revealed it unto thee, but
my Father which is in heaven;* If any could reveale it to us, yet none

Iohn 6.44
could draw us to beleeve it; *No man can come to me, except the
Father draw him:* So that all our voyce of Direction must be from
thence, *De Cœlis, from Heaven.*

De Inferis
We have had *Voces de Inferis,* voyces from Hell, in the blasphemies
of Heretiques; That the Trinity was but *Cera extensa,* but as a Rolle
of Wax spread, or a Dough Cake rolled out, and so divided into per-
450 sons: That the Trinity was but a nest of Boxes, a lesser in a greater,
and not equall to one another; And then, that the Trinity was not
onely three persons, but three Gods too; So far from the truth, and
so far from one another have Heretiques gone, in the matter of the
Trinity; and *Cerinthus* so far, in that one person, in Christ, as to say,
That Jesus, and Christ, were two distinct persons; and that into Jesus,
who, sayes he, was the sonne of *Ioseph,* Christ, who was the Spirit of
God, descended here at his Baptisme, and was not in him before, and
withdrew himselfe from him againe, at the time of his Passion, and
was not in him then; so that he was not borne Christ, nor suffered
460 not being Christ; but was onely Christ in his preaching, and in his
Miracles; and in all the rest, he was but Jesus, sayes *Cerinthus.*

De Medio
We have had *Voces de Inferis, de profundis,* from the depth of
hell, in the malice of Heretiques, And we have had *Voces de medio,*
voyces from amongst us, Inventions of men, to expresse, and to make
us understand the Trinity, in pictures, and in Comparisons: All which
(to contract this point) are apt to fall into that abuse, which we will
onely note in one; At first, they used ordinarily to expresse the Trinity
in foure letters, which had no ill purpose in it at first, but was a re-

ligious ease for their memories, in Catechismes: The letters were Π
470 and Y, and Λ, and Π; The Π was Πατὴρ, and the Υ was Υιὸς, and
the two last belonged to the last person, for Λ was Ἅγιον, and Π was
Πνεῦμα, and so there was Father, Sonne, and Holy Ghost, as if we
should expresse it in *F,* and *S,* and *H,* and *G.* But this came quickly
thus far into abuse, as that they thought, there could belong but three
letters, in that picture, to the three persons; and therefore allowing
so many to Father, Sonne, and Holy Ghost, they tooke the last letter
P, for *Petrus,* and so made *Peter* head of the Church, and equall to the
Trinity. So that for our knowledge, in this mysterious doctrine of the
Trinity, let us evermore rest, *in voce de cœlis,* in that voyce which
480 came from heaven.

But yet it is *Vox dicens, A voice saying,* speaking, A voice that man   *Dicens*
is capable of, and may be benefited by. It is not such a voice as that was,
(which came from heaven too) when Christ prayed to God *to glorifie*   Iohn 12.28
his name, That the people should say, some, that it was a *Thunder,*
some that it was an *Angel that spake.* They are the sons of Thunder,
and they are the Ministeriall Angels of the Church, from whom we
must heare this voice of heaven: Nothing can speak, but man: No voice
is understood by man, but the voice of man; It is not *Vox dicens,* That
voyce sayes nothing to me, that speaks not; And therefore howsoever
490 the voice in the Text were miraculously formed by God, to give this
glory, and dignity to this first manifestation of the Trinity in the person of Christ, yet because he hath left it for a permanent Doctrine
necessary to Salvation, he hath left ordinary means for the conveying
of it; that is, The same voice from heaven, the same word of God, but
speaking in the ministery of man. And therefore for our measure of
this knowledge, (which is our third and last Part) we are to see, how
Christian men, whose office it hath been to interpret Scriptures, that is,
how the Catholike Church hath understood these words, *Hic est*
Filius, This is my beloved Son, in whom I am well pleased.

500 How we are to receive the knowledge of the Trinity, *Athanasius*   3 Part
hath expressed as far as we can goe; Whosoever will be saved, hee
must beleeve it; but the manner of it is not exposed so far as to his
beliefe. That question of the Prophet, *Quis enarrabit?* who shall de-   [Isa. 53.8]
clare this? carries the answer with it, *Nemo enarrabit,* No man shall
declare it. But a manifestation of the Beeing of the Trinity, they have

always apprehended in these words, *Hic est Filius, This is my beloved Son.* To that purpose therefore, we take, first, the words to be expressed by this Euangelist S. *Matthew,* as the voyce delivered them, rather then as they are expressed by S. *Marke,* and S. *Luke;* both
510 which have it thus, *Tu es, Thou art my beloved Son,* and not *Hic est, This is;* They two being onely carefull of the sense, and not of the words, as it fals out often amongst the Euangelists, who differ oftentimes in recording the words of Christ, and of other persons. But where the same voice spake the same words againe, in the Transfiguration, there all the Euangelists expresse it so, *Hic est, This is,* and not
Tu es, Thou art my beloved Son; And so it is, where S. *Peter* makes

2 Pet. 1.17   use by application of that history, it is *Hic est,* and not *Tu es.* So that this *Hic est,* This man, designs him who hath that marke upon him, that the holy Ghost was descended upon him, and tarried upon him;
520 for so far went the signe of distinction given to *Iohn,* The holy Ghost was to descend and tarry: *Manet,* sayes S. *Hierome,* The holy Ghost tarryes upon him, because he never departs from him, *sed operatur quando Christus vult, & quomodo vult,* The holy Ghost works in Christ, when Christ will, and as Christ will; and so the holy Ghost tarryed not upon any of the Prophets; They spoke what hee would, but he wrought not when they would. S. *Gregory* objects to himselfe, that there was a perpetuall residence of the holy Ghost upon the faith-

[Ioh. 14.16]   full, out of those words of Christ, *The Comforter shall abide with you for ever;* But as S. *Gregory* answers himselfe, This is not a plenary
530 abiding, and *secundùm omnia dona,* in a full operation, according to all his gifts, as he tarried upon Christ: Neither indeed is that promise of Christs to particular persons, but to the whole body of the Church.

Now this residence of the holy Ghost upon Christ, was his unction; properly it was that, by which he was the Messias, That he was anointed above his fellowes; And therefore S. *Hierome* makes account, that Christ received his unction, and so his office of Messias, at this his Baptisme, and this descending of the holy Ghost upon him: And he thinks it therefore, because presently after Baptisme, he went to preach in the Synagogue, and he took for his Text those words of

Esay 61.1   540 the Prophet *Esay, The Spirit of the Lord is upon me, because he hath anointed me, that I should preach the Gospel to the poore.* And when

[Luke 4.21]   he had read the Text, he began his Sermon thus, *This day is this*

Scripture fulfilled in your eares. But we may be bold to say, that this is mistaken by S. *Hierome;* for the unction of Christ by the holy Ghost, by which he was anointed, and sealed into the office of Messias, was in the over-shadowing of the holy Ghost in his conception, in his assuming our nature: This Descending now at his baptisme, and this Residence, were onely to declare, That there was a holy Ghost, and that holy Ghost dwelt upon this person.

550 It is *Hic,* This person; And it is *Hic est,* This is my Son; It is not onely *Fuit,* He was my Son, when he was in my bosome, Nor onely *Erit,* He shall be so, when he shall return to my right hand againe; God does not onely take knowledge of him in Glory; But *Est,* He is so now; now in the exinanition of his person, now in the evacuation of his Glory, now that he is preparing himselfe to suffer scorne, and scourges, and thornes, and nailes, in the ignominious death of the Crosse, now he is the Son of the glorious God; Christ is not the lesse the Son of God for this eclipse.

Est

Hic est, This is he, who for all this lownesse is still as high as ever
560 he was, and that height is, *Est Filius,* He is the Son. He is not *Servus,* The Servant of God; or not that onely, for he is that also. *Behold my servant,* (sayes God of him, in the Prophet) *I will stay upon him, mine elect, in whom my soule delighteth; I have put my Spirit upon him, and he shall bring forth judgement to the Gentiles.* But Christ is this Servant, and a Son too: And not a Son onely; for so we observe divers filiations in the Schoole; *Filiationem vestigii,* That by which all creatures, even in their very being, are the sons of God, as *Iob* cals God *Pluviæ patrem, The father of the raine;* And so there are other filiations, other wayes of being the sons of God. But *Hic est,* This
570 person is, as the force of the Article expresses it, and presses it, *Ille Filius,* The Son, That Son, which no son else is, neither can any else declare how he is that which he is.

Filius

Esay 42.1

This person then is still The Son, And *Meus Filius,* sayes God, *My Son.* He is the sonne of *Abraham,* and so within the Covenant; as well provided by that inheritance, as the son of man can be naturally. He is the Son of a Virgin, conceived without generation, and therefore ordained for some great use. He is the son of *David,* and therefore royally descended; But his dignity is in the *Filius meus,* that God avows him to be his Son; for, *Vnto which of the Angels said he at any*

Meus

Heb. 1.5

[Isa. 43.1]   580 *time, Thou art my sonne?* But to Christ he sayes in the Prophet, *I have called thee by thy name:* And what is his name? *Meus es tu, Thou art mine. Quem à me non separat Deitas,* sayes *Leo, non dividit potestas, non discernit æternitas:* Mine so, as that mine infinitenesse gives me no roome nor space beyond him, hee reaches as far as I, though I be infinite; My Almightinesse gives me no power above him, he hath as much power as I, though I have all; My eternity gives me no being before him, though I were before all: In mine Omnipotence, in mine Omnipresence, in mine Omniessence, he is equall partner with me, and hath all that is mine, or that is my selfe, and so he is *mine.*

Dilectus   590   *My Son,* And *My beloved Son;* but so we are all, who are his sons,
?rov. 8.31   *Deliciæ ejus,* sayes *Solomon,* His delight, and his contentment is to be with the sons of men. But here the Article is extraordinarily repeated againe, *Ille dilectus,* That beloved Son, by whom, those, who were neither beloved, nor Sons, became the beloved Sons of God; For, there is so much more added, in the last phrase, *In quo complacui, In whom I am well pleased.*

In quo   Now, these words are diversly read. S. *Augustine* sayes, some Copies that he had seen, read them thus, *Ego hodie genui te, This is my beloved Son, this day have I begotten him:* And with such Copies, it 600 seemes, both *Iustin Martyr,* and *Irenæus* met, for they reade these words so, and interpret them accordingly: But these words are misplaced, and mis-transferred out of the second Psalme, where they are. And as they change the words, and in stead of *In quo complacui, In whom I am well pleased,* reade, *This day have I begotten thee;* S. *Cyprian* addes other words, to the end of these, which are, *Hunc audite, Heare him:* Which words, when these words were repeated at the Transfiguration, were spoken, but here, at the Baptisme, they were not, what Copy soever misled S. *Cyprian,* or whether it were the failing of his own memory. But S. *Chrysostome* gives an expresse 610 reason, why those words were spoken at the Transfiguration, and not here: Because, saies he, Here was onely a purpose of a Manifestation of the Trinity, so farre, as to declare their persons, who they were, and no more: At the Trans-figuration, where *Moses* and *Elias* appeared with Christ, there God had a purpose to preferre the Gospel above the Law, and the Prophets, and therefore in that place he addes that,
[Mat. 17.5]   *Hunc audite, Heare him,* who first fulfills all the Law, and the

Prophets, and then preaches the Gospel. He was so well pleased in him, as that he was content *to give all them, that received him, power* *to become the Sons of God,* too; as the Apostle sayes, *By his grace, he* ⁶²⁰ *hath made us accepted in his beloved.*

    Beloved, That you may be so, Come up from your Baptisme, as it is said that Christ did; Rise, and ascend to that growth, which your Baptisme prepared you to: And the heavens shall open, as then, even *Cataractæ cæli,* All the windowes of heaven shall open, and raine downe blessings of all kindes, in abundance; And the Holy Ghost shall descend upon you, as a Dove, in his peacefull comming, in your simple, and sincere receiving him; And he shall rest upon you, to effect and accomplish his purposes in you. If he rebuke you, (as Christ, when he promises the Holy Ghost, though he call him *a Comforter,* ⁶³⁰ sayes, That *he shall rebuke the world* of divers things) yet he shall dwell upon you as a Dove, *Quæ si mordet, osculando mordet,* sayes S. *Augustine:* If the Dove bite, it bites with kissing, if the Holy Ghost rebuke, he rebukes with comforting. And so baptized, and so pursuing the contract of your Baptisme, and so crowned with the residence of his blessed Spirit, in your holy conversation, hee shall breathe a soule into your soule, by that voyce of eternall life, *You are my beloved Sonnes, in whom I am well pleased.*

[Ioh. 1.12]
Eph. 1.6

[Gen. 7.11]

John 16.7

Number 7.

Preached to the Earl of Exeter, and his company, in his Chappell at Saint Johns; 13. Jun. 1624.

Apoc. 7.9. *AFTER THIS, I BEHELD, AND LOE, A GREAT MULTITUDE, WHICH NO MAN COULD NUMBER, OF ALL NATIONS, AND KINDREDS, AND PEOPLE, AND TONGUES, STOOD BEFORE THE THRONE, AND BEFORE THE LAMBE, CLOTHED WITH WHITE ROBES, AND PALMES IN THEIR HANDS.*

WE SHALL have occasion by and by, to say something of the danger of *Curiosity*, and something of the danger of the *broad way*, in which, too many walk: we will not therefore fall into either of these faults, at first, we will not be over curious, nor we will not stray, nor cast our selves into that broad, and boundlesse way, by entring into those various, and manifold senses, which Expositors have multiplyed, in the handling of this place, and this part of this book; but we take the plainest way, and that in which, the best meet, and concur, that these words are spoken of the *Ioyes,* and *Glory,* reserved for them, who overcome the *fraud,* and the *fury,* the *allurements,* and the *violences* of *Antichrist;* in whom, in that name, and person of *Antichrist,* we consider all *supplanters,* and all *seducers,* all opposers of the kingdome of Christ, in us; for, as every man hath *spontaneum dæmonem,* (as S. *Chrysostome* speakes) a devill of his own making, (which is, some *customary,* and *habituall sin* in him) so every man hath *spontaneum Antichristum,* an *Antichrist* of his own making, some objections in the weaknesse of his

150

faith, some oppositions in the perverseness of his *manners,* against the
kingdome of Christ in himself; and as, if God would *suspend* the devill,
²⁰ or *slumber* the devill a day, I am afraid we should be as ill that day,
as if the devill were awake, and in action, so if those disputed, and
problematical *Antichrists, Eastern* and *Western* Antichrist, Antichrist
of *Rome,* and Antichrist of *Constantinople, Turk* and *Pope,* were removed out of the world, we should not for all that be delivered of
Antichrist, that is, of that opposition to the kingdome of Christ, which
is in our selvs. This part of the book of the *Revelation,* is literally, and
primarily, the glorious victory of them, who, in the later end of the
world, having stood out the persecutions of the *Antichrist,* enter into
the triumph of heaven: And it extends it self to all, by way of fair
³⁰ accommodation, who after a battel with their own *Antichrists,* and
victory over their owne enemies, are also made partakers of those
triumphs, those joyes, those glories, of which S. *Iohn,* in this *propheticall glasse,* in this *perspective of visions,* saw *A great multitude, which
no man could number, of all nations &c.*

    We are then upon the contemplation of the joyes of heaven, which *Divisio*
are everlasting, and must we wring them into the discourse of an
houre? of the glory of heaven which is intire, and must we divide it
into *parts?* we must; we will; we doe; into two parts; first, the
number, the great number of those that shall be saved; And then, the
⁴⁰ glorious *qualities,* which shall be imprinted on them, who are saved:
first, that salvation is a more extensive thing, and more communicable,
then sullen cloystrall, that have walled salvation in a monastery, or in
an ermitage, take it to be; or then the over-valuers of their own
purity, and righteousnesse, which have determined salvation in themselves, take it to be; for, *It is a great multitude, which no man can
number, of all nations &c.* And then, in the second place, salvation is
the possession of such endowments, as *naturally* invite all, to the
prosecution of that, which is exposed and offered to all; that we all
labour here, that we may all stand hereafter, *before the Throne, and
⁵⁰ before the Lambe, clothed in white robes &c.*

    In the first of these, we shall passe by these steps; first, we shall
consider the *sociablenesse,* the *communicablenesse* of God himself,
who gives us the *earth,* and offers us *heaven,* and desires to have his
kingdome well peopled; he would have *many,* he would have *all,* he

would have *every one* of them have all. And then, the first word of
the text, (*After this*) will carry us to the consideration of that which
was done before; which was, first, that they which were of this number, *were sealed,* and then they which were so sealed before, were a
great number, *one hundred forty four thousand;* but they who were
⁶⁰ made partakers of all this after, were innumerable, *After this I beheld
a great multitude, which no man could number;* And therefore we
shall shut up that first part with this consideration, what sense, what
[Mat. 7.14]   interpretation, may belong unto those places, where Christ says, *that
the way to heaven is narrow, and the gate straight:* of these peeces we
shall make up our first part; And for the particulars belonging to the
second, we shall fitliest open them, then, when we come to the
handling of them.

I Part   Our first step then in this first part, is, the *sociablenesse,* the *communicablenesse* of God; He loves holy meetings, he loves the *com-
⁷⁰ munion of Saints,* the *houshold of the faithfull: Deliciæ ejus,* says
[Prov. 8.31]   *Solomon, his delight is to be with the Sons of men,* and that the Sons
of men should be with him: Religion is not a *melancholy;* the spirit
of God is not a *dampe;* the Church is not a *grave:* it is a *fold,* it is an
Arke, it is a *net,* it is a *city,* it is a *kingdome,* not onely a house, but a
house that hath *many mansions* in it: still it is a *plurall* thing, con-
sisting of *many:* and very good *grammarians* amongst the *Hebrews,*
have thought, and said, that that *name,* by which God notifies himself
to the world, in the very beginning of *Genesis,* which is *Elohim,* as it
is a *plurall word* there, so it hath no *singular:* they say we cannot name
⁸⁰ God, but *plurally:* so sociable, so communicable, so extensive, so deriva-
tive of himself, is God, and so manifold are the beames, and the
emanations that flow out from him.

Deus unus   It is a garden worthy of your walking in it: Come into it, but by
the gate of *nature:* The naturall man had much to do, to conceive
God: a God that should be but *one God:* and therefore scattered his
thoughts upon a multiplicity of Gods: and he found it, (as he thought)
reasonable, to think, that there should be a God of *Justice,* a God of
Wisedome, a God of *Power,* and so made the severall *Attributes* of
God, severall *Gods,* and thought that one God might have enough to
⁹⁰ do, with the matters of *Justice,* another with the causes that belonged
to *power,* and so also, with the courts of *Wisedome:* the naturall man,

as he cannot conceive a *vacuity*, that any thing should be empty, so he cannot conceive that any one thing, though that be a *God*, should fill all things: and therefore strays upon a *pluralty* of Gods, upon many Gods, though, in truth, (as *Athanasius* expresses it) *ex multitudine numinum, nullitas numinum*, he that constitutes many Gods destroys all God; for no God can be God, if he be not *all-sufficient;* yet naturally, (I mean in such nature, as our nature is) a man does not easily conceive God to be *alone*, to be but *one;* he thinks there should 100 be company in the Godhead.

Bring it farther then so. A man that lies in the dregs of obscured, and vitiated nature, does not easily discern, *unicum Deum*, a God that should be *alone*, a God that should be but one God. Reason rectified, (rectified by the word of God) can discern this, this one God. But when by that means of the *Scripture*, he does apprehend *Deum unicum, one God*, does he finde that God *alone?* are there not three *Persons*, though there be but *one God?* 'Tis true the *Romans* mis-took infinitely, in making 300 *Iupiters; Varro* mis-took infinitely, in making *Deos terrestres*, and *Deos cœlestes, sub-lunary*, and *super-lunary*, 110 heavenly, and earthly Gods, and *Deos marinos*, and *fluviatiles, Sea Gods*, and *River Gods, salt*, and *fresh-water Gods*, and *Deos mares*, and *fœminas*, he *Gods*, and she *Gods*, and (that he might be sure to take in all) *Deos certos & incertos*, Gods, which they were sure were Gods, and Gods which might be Gods, for any thing they knew to the contrary. There is but one God; but yet was that one God ever *alone?* There were more *generations* (infinitely infinite) before the world was made, then there have been *minutes*, since it was made: all that while, there were no *creatures;* but yet was God alone, any one minute of al this? was there not alwais a *Father* and a *Son*, and a *holy* 120 *Ghost?* And had not they, always an acquiescence in one another, an exercise of *Affection*, (as we may so say) a love, a delight, and a complacency towards one another? So, as that the Father could not be without the *Son* and the *holy Ghost*, so as neither *Sonne*, nor *holy Ghost* could be without the *Father*, nor without one another; God was from all eternity collected into *one God*, yet from all eternity he derived himselfe into *three persons:* God could not be so alone, but that there have been three persons, as long as there hath been one God.

Had God company enough of himselfe; was he satisfied in the *three*

3 Personæ

Creatio

Persons? We see he proceeded further; he came to a *Creation;* And
¹³⁰ as soon as he had made *light,* (which was his first Creature) he took
a pleasure in it; he said *it was good;* he was glad of it; glad of the *Sea,*
glad of the *Earth,* glad of the *Sunne,* and *Moone,* and *Starres,* and he
said of every one, *It is good;* But when he had made *All,* peopled the
whole world, brought all creatures together, then he was *very glad,*
and then he said, not onely, that *it was good,* but that *it was very good:*
God was so far from being *alone,* as that he found not the fulnesse of
being well, till *all* was made, till all Creatures met together, in *an Host,*
as *Moses* calls it; then the *good* was extended into *very good.*

Angeli

Did God satisfie himselfe with this *visible* and discernible world;
¹⁴⁰ with all on earth, and all between that, and him? were those *foure
Monarchies,* the *foure Elements,* and all the subjects of those foure
Monarchies, (if all the foure Elements have Creatures) company
enough for God? was that *Heptarchie,* the *seven kingdomes* of the
seven Planets, conversation enough for him? Let every Starre in the
firmament, be (so some take them to be) a severall world, was all this
enough? we see, God drew persons nearer to him, then Sunne, or
Moon, or Starres, or any thing, which is *visible,* and discernible to us,
he created *Angels;* How many, how great? Arithmetique lacks *numbers* to expresse them, proportion lacks *Dimensions* to figure them;
¹⁵⁰ so far was God from being *alone.*

Homines

And yet God had not shed himselfe far enough; he had the *Leviathan,* the Whale in the Sea, and *Behemoth* and the *Elephant* upon the
land; and all these great *heavenly bodies* in the way, and *Angels* in
their infinite numbers, and manifold offices, in heaven; But, because
Angels could not propagate, nor make more *Angels,* he enlarged his
love, in making *man,* that so he might enjoy all natures at once, and
have the nature of *Angels,* and the nature of *earthly Creatures,* in one
Person. God would not be without man, nor he would not come single,
not alone to the making of man; but it is *Faciamus hominem, Let us,*
¹⁶⁰ *us, make man;* God, in his whole counsail, in his whole Colledge, in
his whole society, in the whole Trinity, makes man, in whom the
whole nature of all the world should meet.

[Gen. 1.26]

Christus

And still our large, and our Communicable God, affected this asso-
ciation so, as that having *three Persons* in himselfe, and having
Creatures of divers natures, and having collected all natures in *man,*

who consisted of a spirituall nature, as well as a bodily, he would have one liker himselfe, then man was; And therefore he made *Christ,* God and Man, in one person, Creature and Creator together; One greater then the *Seraphim,* and yet lesse then a worme; Soveraigne to
170 all *nature,* and yet subject to *naturall* infirmities; Lord of *life, life* it selfe, and yet prisoner to *Death;* Before, and beyond all measures of *Time,* and yet *Born* at so many *moneths, Circumcised* at so many *days, Crucified* at so many *years, Rose* againe at so many *Houres;* How sure did God make himselfe of a companion in Christ, who united himselfe, in his godhead, so inseparably to him, as that that godhead left not that body, then when it lay dead in the grave, but staid with it then, as closely, as when he wrought his greatest miracles.

Beyond all this, God having thus maried soule and body in one man, and man and God, in one Christ, he maries this Christ to the
180 Church. Now, consider this Church in the *Type* and figure of the Church, *the Arke;* in the Arke there were more of every sort of cleane Creatures reserved, then of the uncleane; *seven* of those, for *two* of these: why should we feare, but that in the Church, there are more reserved for salvation then for destruction? And into *that* room (which was not a Type of the Church, but the very Church it selfe) in which they all met upon *whitsunday,* the *holy Ghost* came so as that they were enabled, by the *gift of tongues,* to convay, and propagate, and derive God, (as they did) *to every nation under heaven:* so much does God delight in man, so much does God desire to unite and asso-
190 ciate man unto him; and then, what shall disappoint, or frustrate Gods desires and intentions so farre, as that they should come to him, but singly, *one by one,* whom he *cals,* and *wooes,* and *drawes* by thousands, and by whole Congregations?

Be pleased to carry your considerations, upon another testimony of Gods love to the society of man, which is, his dispatch in making this match, his *speed* in gathering and establishing this Church; for, for-wardnesse is the best argument of love, and dilatory interruptions by the way, argue no great desire to the end; *disguises* before, are shrewd *prophecies* of jealousies after: But God made hast to the consumma-
200 tion of this Marriage, between Christ and the Church. Such words as those to the *Colossians,* (and such words, that is, words to such pur-pose, there are divers) *The Gospell is come unto you, as it is into all*

Ecclesia

Gen. 7.2

Act. 2.[4]

Quàm citò

1.6

the world; And againe; *It bringeth forth fruit, as it doth in you also;*

[Col. 1.] 23 And so likewise, *The Gospell which is preached to every creature which is under heaven;* such words, I say, a very great part of the *Antients* have taken so literally, as thereupon to conclude, That in the life of the *Apostles* themselves, the Gospell was preached, and the Church established over all the world.

Quæ Instrumenta

Now will you consider also, *who* did this, what persons? cunning 210 and crafty persons are not the best *instruments* in great businesses, if those businesses be *good,* as well as great. Here God imployed such persons, as would not have perswaded a man, that *grasse* was green, that *blood* was red, if it had been denyed unto them: Persons that could not have bound up your understanding, with a *Syllogisme,* nor have entendred, or mollified it with a *verse:* Persons that had nothing

[1 Cor. 1.21] but that which God himselfe calls *the foolishnesse of preaching,* to bring *Philosophers* that argued, *Heretiques* that wrangled, *Lucians,* and *Julians,* men that whet their *tongues,* and men that whet their *swords* against God, to God.

Quæ Doctrina

220 Unbend not this *bowe,* slacken not these holy thoughts, till you have considered, as well as *how soone,* and by *what persons,* so to *what Doctrine,* God brought them. Wee aske but St. *Augustins* question, *Quis tantam multitudinem, ad legem, carni & sanguini contrariam, induceret, nisi Deus? Who but God himselfe, would have drawn the world to a Religion so contrary to flesh and blood?* Take but one piece of the Christian Religion, but *one article* of our *faith,* in the same Fathers mouth; *Res incredibilis resurrectio;* That this body should be eaten by *fishes* in the sea, and then those fishes eaten by other *men,* or that one man should be eaten by another man, and so become *both* 230 *one man,* and then that for all this assimilation, and union, there should arise two men, at the resurrection, *Res incredibilis,* sayes he, this resurrection is an incredible thing, *Sed magis incredibile, totum mundum credidisse rem tam incredibilem, That all the world should so soone believe a thing so incredible, is more incredible, then the thing it selfe.* That any should believe *any,* is strange, but more that *all* such believe *all,* that appertains to Christianity. The *Valentinians,* and the *Marcionites,* pestilent Heretiques, grew to a great number, *Sed vix duo vel tres, de iisdem, eadem docebant,* says *Irenæus,* scarce any two or three amongst them, were of one opinion. The *Acatians,*

²⁴⁰ the *Eunomians,* and the *Macedonians, omnes Arium parentem ag-*
noscunt, sayes the same Father, they all call themselves *Arians,* but   Irenæus
they had as many opinions, not onely as *names,* but as *persons.* And
that one Sect of *Mahomet,* was quickly divided, and sub-divided into
70 sects. But *so God loved the world,* the society and company of good   [Joh. 3.16]
soules, *ut quasi una Domus Mundus,* the whole world was as one well
governed house; *similiter credunt quasi una anima,* all beleeved the
same things, as though they had all but one soule; *Constanter præ-*
dicabant, quasi unum os, At the same houre there was a Sermon at
Jerusalem, and a Sermon at *Rome,* and both so like, for *fundamentall*
²⁵⁰ things, as if they had been preached out of one mouth.

And as this Doctrine, so *incredible* in reason, was *thus soone,* and   *Durat adhuc*
by *these persons,* thus uniformely preached over all the world, so shall
it, as it doth, continue to the worlds end; which is another argument
of Gods love to our company, and of his loathnesse to lose us. All
Heresies, and the very names of the *Heretiques,* are so utterly perished
in the world, as that, if their memories were not preserved in those
Fathers which have written against them, we could finde their names
no where. *Irenæus,* about *one hundred and eighty* yeers after Christ,
may reckon about *twenty* heresies; *Tertullian, twenty* or *thirty* yeares
²⁶⁰ after *him,* perchance *twenty seven;* and *Epiphanius,* some *a hundred*
and fifty after him, *sixty;* and *fifty* yeare after that, St. *Augustine* some
ninety: yet after all these, (and but a very few yeares, after *Augustine*)
Theodoret sayes, that in his time there was no one man alive, that held
any of those heresies: That all those heresies should rot, being upheld
by the sword, and that onely the Christian Religion should grow up,
being mowed down by the sword, That one graine of Corne should
be cast away, and many eares grow out of that, (as *Leo* makes the
comparison) That one man should be executed, because he was a
Christian, and all that saw him executed, and the *Executioner* himself,
²⁷⁰ should thereupon become *Christians,* (a case that fell out more then
once, in the *primitive Church*) That as the flood threw down the
Courts of Princes, and lifted up the Arke of God, so the effusion of
Christian blood, should destroy *heresies,* and advance *Christianity* it
self; this is argument abundantly enough, that God had a love to man,
and a desire to draw man to his society, and in great numbers to bring
them to salvation.

Reformatio
    I will not dismisse you from this consideration, till you have brought it thus much nearer, as to remember a later testimony of Gods love to our company, in the *reformation of Religion;* A miracle scarce lesse, ²⁸⁰ then the first propagation thereof, in the primitive Church. In how few yeares, did God make the number of *learned Writers,* the number of persons of all qualities, the number of *Kings,* in whose Dominions the reformed Religion was exercised, equall to the number of them, who adhered to the Roman Church?

Tu ipse
    And yet, thou must not depart from this contemplation, till thou have made *thy self* an argument of all this; till thou have concluded out of this, that God hath made love to thy soule, thy weake soule, thy sick, and foule, and sinfull soule, That he hath *written* to thee, in all his *Scriptures,* sent *Ambassage* to thee, in all his *preachers, presented* ²⁹⁰ thee, in all his *temporall,* and *spirituall* blessings, That he hath come to thee, even in actions of *uncleannesse,* in actions of *unfaithfulnesse* towards men, in actions of *distrustfulnesse* towards God, and hath checked thy conscience, and delivered thee from some sins, even then when thou wast ready to commit them, as all the rest, (That that God, who is but one in himselfe, is yet *three persons,* That those three, who were *all-sufficient* to themselves, would yet make more, make *Angels,* make *man,* make a *Christ,* make him a *Spouse,* a *Church,* and first propagate that, by so *weake men,* in so *hard a doctrine,* and in so *short a space,* over all *the world,* and then *reforme* that Church againe, so ³⁰⁰ soone, to such a heighth) as these, I say, are to all the world, so be thou thy *self,* and Gods exceeding goodnesse to thee, an argument, That that God who hath shewed himself so loath to lose *thee,* is certainly loath to lose *any other* soule; but as he communicates himself to us all here, so he would have us all partake of his joy, and glory hereafter; he that fils his *Militant* Church thus, would not have his *Triumphant* Church empty.

Sigillati
    So far we consider the accessiblenesse, the communicablenesse, the conversation of our good, and gracious *God* to us, in the generall. There is a more speciall manner intimated, even in the first word of ³¹⁰ our Text, *After this;* After what? After he had seene the servants of God *sealed;* sealed: This seale seales the contract betweene God and Man: And then consider how generall this seale is: First, God sealed us, in imprinting his *Image* in our soules, and in the powers thereof,

at our *creation;* and so, every man hath this seale, and he hath it, as soone as he hath a soule: The *wax,* the *matter,* is in his *conception;* the *seale,* the forme, is in his quickning, in his *inanimation;* as, in *Adam,* the waxe was that *red earth,* which he was made of, the *seale* was that *soule,* that *breath* of *life,* which God breathed into him. Where the Organs of the body are so indisposed, as that this soule cannot exercise
320 her faculties, in that man, (as in *naturall Idiots,* or otherwise) there, there is a *curtaine* drawn over this Image, but yet there this Image is, the Image of God, is in the most *naturall Idiot,* as well as in the wisest of men: worldly men draw *other pictures* over this picture, other images over this image: The *wanton* man may paint *beauty,* the *ambitious* may paint *honour,* the *covetous wealth,* and so deface this image, but yet there this image is, and even *in hell* it selfe it will be, in him that goes down into hell: *uri potest in gehenna, non exuri,* sayes St. *Bernard,* The Image of God may burne in hell, but as long as the soule remaines, that image remaines there too; And then, thou who
330 wouldest not burne their picture, that loved thee, wilt thou betray the picture of thy Maker, thy Saviour, thy Sanctifier, to the torments of hell? Amongst the manifold and perpetuall interpretations of that article, *He descended into hell,* this is a new one, that thou sentest him to hell in thy soule: Christ had his *Consummatum est,* from the *Jewes;* he was able to say at last, *All is finished,* concerning *them;* shall he never have a *Consummatum est* from thee; never be at an end with thee? Never, if his Image must burne eternally in thy soule, when thou art dead, for everlasting generations.   [Joh. 19.30]

Thus then we were *sealed;* all sealed; all had his *image* in our *crea-*
340 *tion,* in the faculties of our soules: But then we were all sealed againe, sealed in our *very flesh,* our mortall flesh, when the image of the invisible God, *Christ Jesus,* the onely Sonne of God, tooke our nature: for, as the *Tyrant* wished, that all mankinde were but one body, that he might behead all mankinde at a blow, so God tooke into his mercie, all mankinde in one person: As intirely, as all mankinde was in *Adam,* all mankinde was in *Christ;* and as the *seale of the Serpent* is in all, by *originall sinne,* so the *seale* of God, *Christ Jesus,* is on us *all,* by his assuming our *nature.* Christ Jesus tooke our souls, and our bodies, our whole nature; and as no Leper, no person, how infec-
350 tiously soever he be diseased in his body, can say, surely Christ never   *In Christo*

tooke this body, this Leprosie, this pestilence, this rottennesse, so no Leprous soule must say, Christ never tooke this pride, this adultery, this murder upon himself; he sealed us all in *soule* and *body,* when he tooke *both,* and though both dye, the *soule in sin* daily, the *body in sicknesse,* perchance this day, yet he shall afford a resurrection to both, to the *soule* here, to the *body* hereafter, for his seale is upon both.

In Baptismo   These two seales then hath God set upon us all, his *Image* in our soules, at our *making,* his *Image,* that is his *Sonne,* upon our bodies and soules, in his *incarnation;* And both these seales he hath set upon 360 us, then when neither we our selves, nor any body else knew of it: He sets another seale upon us, when, though *we* know not of it, yet the *world,* the *congregation* does, in the Sacrament of *Baptisme,* when the seale of his *Crosse,* is a testimony, not that Christ was *borne,* (as the former seale was) but that also he *dyed* for us; there we receive that seale upon the *forehead,* that we should conforme our selves to him, who is so sealed to us. And after all these seales, he offers us

Cant. 8.6   another, and another seale, *Set me as a seale upon thy heart, and as a seale upon thine arme,* says Christ to all us, in the person of the spouse; in the *Heart,* by a constant *faith,* in the *Arme,* by *declaratory* 370 *works;* for then are we sealed, and *delivered,* and *witnessed;* that's our full evidence, then have we *made sure our salvation,* when the works of a holy life, doe daily refresh the contract made with God there, at our *Baptisme,* and testifie to the Church, that we doe carefully remember, what the *Church* promised in our behalfe, at that time: for, otherwise, beloved, without this *seale upon the arme,* that is, a stedfast proceeding in the *works* of a holy life, we may have received many

Eph. 4.30   of the other seales, and yet deface them all. *Grieve not the holy Ghost, whereby you are sealed, unto the day of Redemption,* says the Apostle: they were sealed, and yet might *resist* the Spirit, and *grieve* the Spirit, 380 and *quench* the Spirit, if by a continuall watchfulnesse over their particular actions, they did not refresh those seales (formerly received in their *Creation,* in Christs *incarnation,* in their *Baptisme,* and in their beginnings of *faith*) to themselves, and plead them to the Church, and to the world, by such a declaration of a holy life. But these seales being so many, and so universall, that argues still, that which we especially seek to establish, that is, the *Accessiblenesse,* the communicablenesse, the sociablenesse, the *affection*, (shall I say) the *Ambition*, that God hath, to have us all.

Now how is this extensivenesse declared here, in our text? It is
390 declared in the great *number* of those who were *sealed*, both before, and after; to the consideration of both which, we are invited, by this phrase, which beginnes the text, *After this:* for, before that *John* saw this, there were *one hundred forty foure thousand sealed;* Is that then, (that *one hundred forty foure thousand*) intended for a small number? If it had been so, it would rather have been said, *of such a Tribe but twelve thousand, and but twelve thousand of such a Tribe;* but God as expressing a joy, that there were so many, repeats his number of *twelve thousand, twelve times over, of Juda twelve thousand, of Levi twelve thousand,* and *twelve thousand of every Tribe.* So that then,
400 we may justly take this number of *twelve* and *twelve thousand,* for an indefinite, and uncertain number; and as Saint *Augustine* does, wheresoever he finds that number of *twelve,* (as the *twelve Thrones,* where the *Saints shall judge the world,* and divers such) we may take that number of *twelve,* and *twelve, pro universitate salvandorum,* that that number signifies, all those who shall be saved. If we should take the number to be a certaine and exact number, so many, and no more, yet this number hath relation to the *Jews* onely; And of the *Jews,* it is true, that there is so long a time of their exclusion, so few of them doe come in, since Christ came into the world, as that we may, with Saint
410 *Augustine,* interpret that place of *Genesis,* where *Abrahams* seed is

compared both to the *Starres of heaven,* and to the *dust of the earth,* that the Stars of heaven signifie those that shall be saved in heaven, and the dust of the earth, those that perish; and the dust of the earth may be more then the Stars of heaven; though (by the way) there are an infinite number of *Stars* more then we can distinguish, and so, by Gods grace, there may be an infinite number of soules saved, more then those, of whose salvation, we discerne the *ways,* and the *meanes.* Let us embrace the way which God hath given us, which is, the knowledge of his Sonne, *Christ Jesus:* what other way God may take with
420 others, how he wrought upon *Iob,* and *Naaman,* and such others as were not in the *Covenant,* let us not inquire too curiously, determine too peremptorily, pronounce too uncharitably: God be blessed, for his declaring his good-wil towards *us,* and *his will be done* his way upon

others. Truly, even those places, which are ordinarily understood of the *paucity of the Jews,* that shall be saved, will receive a charitable

3.14   interpretation, and extension. God says, in *Ieremy, I will take you, one out of a City, and two out of a family;* yet he says, he wil do this therefore, *because he is married to them;* so that this seems to be an act of his love; And therefore, I had rather take it, that God would take

⁴³⁰ a particular care of them, *one by one,* then that he would take in but

27.12 *one and one:* As it is in that place of *Esay, In that day ye shall be gathered one by one, o yee children of Israel;* that is, in the day of Christ, of his comming to and toward Judgement; Howsoever they come in but thinly yet, by the way, yet the Apostle pleads in their

Rom. 11.1 behalfe thus, *Hath God cast away his people? God forbid. At this*

5   *present,* says he, *there is a Remnant;* then when they had newly crucified Christ, God had a care of them. *God hath given them the*

8   *spirit of slumber,* says he also; it is but a slumber, not a death, not a dead sleep. *Have they stumbled that they should fall?* Fall utterly?

⁴⁴⁰ God forbid. But says he, *as concerning the Gospell, they are enemies, for your sakes;* (that is, that room might be made for you the *Gentiles*) but, as touching election, they are beloved for their *Fathers sakes;* that is, they have interest by an ancient title, which God will never disannull. And therefore a great part, of the *ancient,* and *later* men too, doe interpret divers passages of Saint *Paul,* of a generall salvation of the *Jews,* that *all* shall be effectually wrought upon, to salvation, before the second comming of Christ. I end this, concerning the *Jews,* with this note, that in all these Tribes, which yeelded to this sealing, *twelve thousand* a peece, the *Tribe of Dan* is left out, it is not

⁴⁵⁰ said, that any were sealed of the Tribe of *Dan;* many have enquired the reason, and satisfied themselves over easily with this, that because *Antichrist* was to come of that Tribe, that Tribe is forsaken. It is true, that very many of the Fathers, *Irenæus, Ambrose, Augustine, Gregory,* (and more then these) have thought so, that *Antichrist* must be of that Tribe; but yet, for all that profession, which they make in the *Roman*

Tostat. *Church,* of adhering to the *Fathers,* one amongst them, says, *Incertum,* be the Fathers as clear, and as unanimous as they will in it, it is a very

Oleast. uncertain, a very disputable thing; and another says, *fabulosum est,* be the Fathers as earnest, as they will, it is but a poeticall and a fabulous

⁴⁶⁰ thing, that Antichrist must come of the Tribe of *Dan.* But he that hath

most of the *markes* of Antichrist upon him, of any person in the world now, is thus far of the Tribe of *Dan; Dan* signifies *Iudgement;* And he will needs be the Judge of all *faith,* and of all *actions* too; and so severe a Judge, as to give an irrevocable Judgement of *Damnation,* upon all that agree not with them, in all points. Certainly, this Tribe of *Dan,* that is, of such uncharitable Judges of all other men, that will afford no salvation to any but *themselves,* are in the greatest danger to be left out, at this generall seale; nothing hinders our own salvation more, then to deny salvation, to all but our selves.

470   This then which was done *before,* though it concerne but the *Jews,* was in a great number, and was a great argument, of Gods sociable application of himselfe to man, but that which was *after,* was more, *A great multitude, which no man could number, of all nations &c.* Gods mercy was not confined, nor determined upon the *Iews; Other sheep have I, which are not of this fold,* says *Christ, them also I must bring in: I must;* it is expressed, not onely as an act of his *good will,* but of that *eternall decree,* to which, he had, at the making thereof, submitted himself: *I must bring them;* who are they? *Many shall come from the east, and from the west, and shall sit downe with* 480 *Abraham, Isaac and Iacob, in the kingdom of heaven;* from the *Eastern* Church, and from the *Western* Church too, from the *Greek* Church, and from the *Latine* too, and, (by Gods grace) from them that *pray not in Latine too,* from *every Church,* (so it be truly, and fundamentally a Church) *Many shall come;* How many? *a multitude that no man can number:* For, *the new Ierusalem,* in the Revelation, (which is heaven) hath *twelve gates,* three to every corner of the world; so that no place can be a stranger, or lacke accesse to it: Nay, it hath (says that Text) *twelve foundations, Other foundation can no man lay, then that which is layd, Christ Iesus:* But that *first founda-* 490 *tion-stone* being kept, though it be not hewed, nor layd alike in every place, though Christ be not preached, nor presented in the same manner, for outward *Ceremonies,* or for *problematicall opinions,* yet the *foundation* may remaine *one,* though it be, in such a sort, varied; and men may come in at any of the *twelve gates,* and rest upon any of the *twelve foundations,* for they are all *gates,* and *foundations* of one and the same *Ierusalem;* and they that enter, are a *multitude that no man can number.*

Christiani

[Joh. 10.16]

Mat. 8.11

21.12

[1 Cor. 3.11]

Via angusta

Mat. 7.13

Psal. 119.96

Mat. 18.9

Esai. 60.11

Apoc. 3.[20]

If then there be this sociable, this applyable nature in God, this large and open entrance for man, why does Christ call it a *straite gate,* and 500 a *narrow way?* Not that it is strait in it self, but that we think it so, and, indeed, we make it so. *Christ is the gate,* and every wound of his admits the whole world. The *Church is the gate;* And *in omnem terram,* says *David,* she hath opened her mouth, and her voice is gone over all the world. His *word* is the *gate;* And, *thy Commandement is exceeding broad,* says *David* too; His word and his light reaches to all cases, and all distresses. *Lata porta Diabolus;* saith Saint Chrysostome, *The Devill is a broad gate;* but he tells us how he came to be so, *Non magnitudine potestatis extensus, sed superbiæ licentia dilatatus;* not that God put such a power into his hands, at first, as that we might 510 not have resisted him, but that he hath usurp'd upon us, and we have given way to his usurpations: so, says that Father, *Angusta porta Christus,* Christ is a narrow gate, but he tels us also *wherein,* and in what respect, *Non parvitate potestatis exiguus, sed humilitatis ratione collectus;* Christ is not a narrow gate, so as that the *greatest man* may not come in, but called narrow, because he fits himselfe to the *least child,* to the simplest soule, that will come in: not so strait, as that all may not enter, but so strait as that there can come in but *one at once,* for *he that will not forsake Father and Mother, and wife, and children for him, cannot enter in.* Therefore we call the Devils way broad, be- 520 cause men walke in that, with all their equipage, all their sumpters, all their state, all their sinnes; and therefore we call Christs way strait, because a man must strippe himselfe of all inordinate affections, of all desires of ill getting, and of all possessions that are ill gotten. In a word, it is not strait to a mans selfe, but if a man will carry his sinfull company, his sinfull affections with him, and his sinfull possessions, it is strait, for then he hath made himselfe a *Camel,* and to a Camel Heaven gate is as a *needles eye: But it is better comming into heaven with one eye, then into hell with two;* Better comming into heaven without Master, or Mistresse, then into hell for over-humouring of 530 either. There, *The gates are not shut all day;* says the Prophet, and, *there is no night there;* And here, if we shut the doore, yet Christ *stands at the doore and knocks;* Be but content to open thy doore, be but content to let *him* open it, and he will enter, and be but thou content to enter into *his,* content to be led in by his preaching, content

to be drawn in by his benefits, content to be forced in by his corrections, and he will open *his:* since thy God would have dyed for thee,
if there had been no man born but thou, never imagine, that he who
lets in multitudes, *which no man can number, of all Nations, &c.*
would ever shut out *thee,* but labour to enter there; *ubi non intrat*   August.
540 *inimicus, ubi non exit amicus,* where never any that hates thee, shall
get to thee, nor any that loves thee, part from thee.

    We have but ended our first part, The assurance which we have   2 Part
from Gods manner of proceeding, that Religion is not a *sullen,* but a
cheerfull Philosophy, and salvation not cast into a corner, but dis-
played as the Sunne, over all. That which we called at first, our second
part, must not be a *Part,* admit it for a *Conclusion;* It is that, and
beyond that; It is beyond our *Conclusion,* for it is our everlasting
endowment in heaven: and if I had kept minutes enough for it, who
should have given me *words* for it? I will but paraphrase the words of
550 the Text, and so leave you in that, which, I hope, is your *gallery* to
heaven, your own *meditations:* The words are, *You shall stand before
the Throne, and before the Lamb, clothed with white Robes, and
palms in their hands.*

    First, *stabitis,* you *shall stand;* which is not, that you shall not *sit,*   *Stabunt*
for the Saints shal *sit and judg the world;* and they shall sit *at the*   [1 Cor. 6.2]
right hand of God; It is not, that you shall not *sit,* nor that you shall
not *lie,* for you shall *lye in Abrahams bosom:* But yet you shal *stand,*
that is, you shall *stand sure,* you shall never *fall,* you shall *stand,* but
yet you shall but *stand,* that is, remaine in a continuall disposition and
560 readinesse to serve God, and to minister to him. And therefore account
no abundance, no height, no birth, no place here, to exempt you from
standing and labouring in the service of God, since even your glorious
state in heaven is but a *station,* but a standing in readinesse to doe his
will, and not a posture of idlenesse: you shall stand, that is, stand *sure,*
but you shall but stand, that is, still be bound to the service of God.

    Stabitis ante Thronum; you shall stand, and *stand before the*   *Ante*
Thronum; Here in the *militant Church,* you stand, but you stand in the   *Thronum*
porch, there, in the *triumphant,* you shall stand *in Sancto sanctorum,*
in the *Quire,* and the *Altar.* Here you stand, but you stand upon Ice,
570 perchance in *high* and therefore in *slippery places;* And at the judgement you shall stand, but stand at the *barre;* But when *you stand*

Ante
Agnum

before the Throne, you stand, (as it is also added in this place) *before the Lamb:* who having not opened his mouth, to save his owne *fleece,* when he was in the shearers hand, nor to save his own *life,* when he was in the slaughterers hand, will much lesse open his mouth to any repentant sinners condemnation, or upbrayd you with your former crucifyings of him, in this world, after he hath nailed those sinnes to that crosse, to which those sinnes nayled him.

Stolis

[2 Sam.
10.4]

You shall stand *amicti stolis,* (for so it follows) *covered with Robes,* 580 that is, covered *all over:* not with *Adams* fragmentary raggs of *fig-leafes,* nor with the *halfe-garments of Davids servants:* Though you have often offered God *halfe-confessions,* and *halfe-repentances,* yet if you come at last, to stand before *the Lambe,* his fleece covers all; hee shall not cover the sinnes of your youth, and leave the sinnes of your age open to his justice, nor cover your sinfull actions, and leave your sinfull words and thoughts open to justice, nor cover your own personall sinnes, and leave the sinnes of your Fathers before you, or the sinnes of others, whose sins your tentations produced and begot, open to justice; but as he hath enwrapped the whole world in one garment, 590 the *firmament,* and so cloathed that part of the earth, which is under our feet, as gloriously as this, which we live, and build upon: so those sinnes which we have hidden from the world, and from our own consciences, and utterly forgotten, either his *grace* shall enable us, to recollect, and to *repent in particular,* or (we having used that holy diligence, to examine our consciences so) he shall wrap up even those sinnes, which we have forgot, and cover all, with that garment of his own righteousnesse, which leaves no foulnesse, no nakednesse open.

Albis

Esa. 63.2

You shall be covered with Robes, All over; and with *white Robes;* That as the Angels wondred at Christ coming into heaven, in his 600 Ascension, *Wherefore art thou red in thine Apparell, and thy garments like him that treadeth the wine fat?* They wondred how innocence it selfe should become red, so shall those Angels wonder at thy coming thither, and say, *Wherefore art thou white in thine apparell?* they shall wonder how sinne it selfe shall be clothed in innocence.

Palma

Exod. 15.23

And in thy *hand shall be a palm,* which is the last of the endowments specifyed here. After the *waters of bitternesse,* they came to seventy (to innumerable) *palmes;* even the bitter waters were sweetned, with another wood cast in: The wood of the *Crosse* of Christ Jesus, refreshes

all teares, and sweetens all bitternesse, even in this life: but after these
610 bitter waters, *which God shall wipe from all our eies,* we come, to the
seventy, to the seventy thousand palms; infinite seales, infinite testimonies, infinite extensions, infinite durations of infinite glory: Go in,
beloved, and raise your own contemplations, to a height worthy of
this glory; and chide me for so lame an expressing of so perfect a
state, and when the abundant spirit of God hath given you some
measure, of conceiving that glory here, Almighty God give you, and
me, and all, a reall expressing of it, by making us actuall possessors of
that Kingdome, which his Sonne, our Saviour Christ Jesus hath purchased for us, with the inestimable price of his incorruptible blood.
620 *Amen.*

Number 8.

Preached at Pauls, upon Christmas Day, in the Evening. 1624.

ESAIAH 7.14. PART OF THE FIRST LESSON, THAT EVENING. *THEREFORE THE LORD SHALL GIVE YOU A SIGNE; BEHOLD, A VIRGIN SHALL CONCEIVE, AND BEARE A SON, AND SHALL CALL HIS NAME IMMANUEL.*

SAINT *Bernard* spent his consideration upon three remarkable conjunctions, this Day. First, a Conjunction of God, and Man in one person, Christ Jesus; Then a conjunction of the incompatible Titles, Maid and Mother, in one blessed woman, the blessed Virgin *Mary:* And thirdly a conjunction of Faith, and the Reason of man, that so beleeves, and comprehends those two conjunctions. Let us accompany these three with another strange conjunction, in the first word of this Text, *Propterea, Therefore;* for that joynes the anger of God, and his mercy together. God chides and rebukes the King

10 *Achaz* by the Prophet, he is angry with him, and *Therefore,* sayes the Text, because he is angry he will give him a signe, a seale of mercy, *Therefore the Lord shall give you a signe, Behold, a Virgin, &c.* This

Divisio   *Therefore,* shall therefore be a first part of this Exercise, That God takes any occasion to shew mercy; And a second shall be, The particular way of his mercy, declared here, *The Lord shall give you a signe;* And then a third and last, what this signe was, *Behold, a Virgin, &c.*

In these three parts, we shall walk by these steps; Having made our entrance into the first, with that generall consideration, that Gods

20 mercy is alwaies in season, upon that station, upon that height we shall

look into the particular occasions of Gods mercy here, what this King *Achaz* had done to alien God, and to avert his mercy, and in those two branches we shall determine that part. In the second, we shall also first make this generall entrance, That God persists in his own waies, goes forward with his own purposes, And then what his way, and his purpose here was, he would give them a signe: and farther we shall not extend that second part. In the third we have more steps to make; First, what this sign is in generall, it is, that there is a Redeemer given. And then how, thus; First, *Virgo concipiet, a Virgin shall conceive,*
30 she shall be a Virgin then; And *Virgo pariet, a Virgin shall bring forth,* she shall be a Virgin then; And *Pariet filium, she shall beare a Son,* and therefore he is of her substance, not only man, but man of her; And this Virgin shall call this Son *Immanuel, God with us,* that is, God and Man in one person. Though the Angel at the Conception tell *Ioseph,* That he shall call his name Jesus, and tell *Mary* her selfe, that she shall call his name Jesus, yet the blessed Virgin her selfe shall have a further reach, a clearer illustration, *She shall call his name Immanuel, God with us:* Others were called *Iesus, Iosuah* was so, divers others were so; but, in the Scriptures there was never any but
40 Christ called *Immanuel.* Though *Iesus* signifie a Saviour, *Ioseph* was able to call this childe *Iesus,* upon a more peculiar reason, and way of salvation then others who had that name, because they had saved the people from present calamities, and imminent dangers; for, the Angel told *Ioseph,* that he should therefore be called *Iesus,* because *he should save the people from their sins;* and so, no *Iosuah,* no other *Iesus* was a *Iesus.* But the blessed Virgin saw more then this; not only that he should be such a *Iesus* as should save them from their sins, but she saw the manner how, that he should be *Immanuel, God with us,* God and man in one person; That so, being Man, he might suffer, and
50 being God, that should give an infinite value to his sufferings, according to the contract passed between the Father and him; and so he should be *Iesus,* a Saviour, a Saviour from sin, and this by this way and meanes. And then that all this should be established, and declared by an infallible signe, with this *Ecce, Behold;* That whosoever can call upon God by that name *Immanuel,* that is, confesse Christ to bee come in the flesh, that Man shall have an *Ecce,* a light, a sign, a token, an assurance that this *Immanuel,* this Jesus, this Saviour belongs unto

Mat. 1.21
Luc. 1.31

[Luke 2.30]   him, and he shall be able to say, *Ecce, Behold, mine eyes have seen thy*
                     salvation.

I Part   60   We begin with that which is elder then our beginning, and shall
Psal. 101.1   over-live our end, The mercy of God. *I will sing of thy mercy and*
                     judgement, sayes *David;* when we fixe our selves upon the meditation
                     and modulation of the mercy of God, even his judgements cannot put
                     us out of tune, but we shall sing, and be chearefull, even in them. As
                     God made grasse for beasts, before he made beasts, and beasts for man,
                     before he made man: As in that first generation, the Creation, so in
                     the regeneration, our re-creating, he begins with that which was neces-
                     sary for that which followes, Mercy before Judgement. Nay, to say
                     that mercy was first, is but to post-date mercy; to preferre mercy but so,
                70   is to diminish mercy; The names of first or last derogate from it, for
                     first and last are but ragges of time, and his mercy hath no relation to
                     time, no limitation in time, it is not first, nor last, but eternall, ever-
                     lasting; Let the Devill make me so far desperate as to conceive a time
                     when there was no mercy, and he hath made me so far an Atheist,
                     as to conceive a time when there was no God; if I despoile him of his
                     mercy, any one minute, and say, now God hath no mercy, for that
                     minute I discontinue his very Godhead, and his beeing. Later Gram-
                     marians have wrung the name of mercy out of misery; *Misericordia*
                     præsumit miseriam, say these, there could be no subsequent mercy, if
                80   there were no precedent misery; But the true roote of the word mercy,
                     through all the Prophets, is *Racham,* and *Racham* is *diligere,* to love;
[1 Joh. 4.16]   as long as there hath been love (and *God is love*) there hath been
                     mercy: And mercy considered externally, and in the practise and in
                     the effect, began not at the helping of man, when man was fallen and
                     become miserable, but at the making of man, when man was nothing.
                     So then, here we consider not mercy as it is radically in God, and an
                     essentiall attribute of his, but productively in us, as it is an action, a
                     working upon us, and that more especially, as God takes all occasions
                     to exercise that action, and to shed that mercy upon us: for particular
                90   mercies are feathers of his wings, and that prayer, *Lord let thy mercy*
                     lighten upon us, as our trust is in thee, is our birdlime; particular
                     mercies are that cloud of Quailes which hovered over the host of
                     Israel, and that prayer, *Lord let thy mercy lighten upon us,* is our net
                     to catch, our Gomer to fill of those Quailes. The aire is not so full of

Moats, of Atomes, as the Church is of Mercies; and as we can suck in
no part of aire, but we take in those Moats, those Atomes; so here in
the Congregation we cannot suck in a word from the preacher, we
cannot speak, we cannot sigh a prayer to God, but that that whole
breath and aire is made of mercy. But we call not upon you from this
100 Text, to consider Gods ordinary mercy, that which he exhibites to all
in the ministery of his Church; nor his miraculous mercy, his extraordinary deliverances of States and Churches; but we call upon particular Consciences, by occasion of this Text, to call to minde Gods
occasionall mercies to them; such mercies as a regenerate man will
call mercies, though a naturall man would call them accidents, or
occurrences, or contingencies; A man wakes at midnight full of unclean thoughts, and he heares a passing Bell; this is an occasionall
mercy, if he call that his own knell, and consider how unfit he was to
be called out of the world then, how unready to receive that voice,
110 *Foole, this night they shall fetch away thy soule.* The adulterer, whose
eye waites for the twy-light, goes forth, and casts his eyes upon forbidden houses, and would enter, and sees a *Lord have mercy upon us*
upon the doore; this is an occasionall mercy, if this bring him to know
that they who lie sick of the plague within, passe through a furnace,
but by Gods grace, to heaven; and hee without, carries his own furnace
to hell, his lustfull loines to everlasting perdition. What an occasionall
mercy had *Balaam,* when his Asse Catechized him? What an occasionall mercy had one Theefe, when the other catechized him so, *Art
thou not afraid being under the same condemnation?* What an occa-
120 sionall mercy had all they that saw that, when the Devil himself fought
for the name of Jesus, and wounded the sons of *Sceva* for exorcising
in the name of Jesus, with that indignation, with that increpation,
Iesus we know, and Paul we know, but who are ye? If I should declare
what God hath done (done occasionally) for my soule, where he
instructed me for feare of falling, where he raised me when I was
fallen, perchance you would rather fixe your thoughts upon my ill-
nesse, and wonder at that, then at Gods goodnesse, and glorifie him
in that; rather wonder at my sins, then at his mercies, rather consider
how ill a man I was, then how good a God he is. If I should inquire
130 upon what occasion God elected me, and writ my name in the book
of Life, I should sooner be afraid that it were not so, then finde a reason

[Luke
12.20]

[Luke
23.40]

Act. 19.15

why it should be so. God made Sun and Moon to distinguish seasons, and day, and night, and we cannot have the fruits of the earth but in their seasons: But God hath made no decree to distinguish the seasons of his mercies; In paradise, the fruits were ripe, the first minute, and in heaven it is alwaies Autumne, his mercies are ever in their maturity. We ask *panem quotidianum,* our daily bread, and God never sayes you should have come yesterday, he never sayes you must againe to morrow, but *to day if you will heare his voice,* to day he will heare you. If some King of the earth have so large an extent of Dominion, in North, and South, as that he hath Winter and Summer together in his Dominions, so large an extent East and West, as that he hath day and night together in his Dominions, much more hath God mercy and judgement together: He brought light out of darknesse, not out of a lesser light; he can bring thy Summer out of Winter, though thou have no Spring; though in the wayes of fortune, or understanding, or conscience, thou have been benighted till now, wintred and frozen, clouded and eclypsed, damped and benummed, smothered and stupified till now, now God comes to thee, not as in the dawning of the day, not as in the bud of the spring, but as the Sun at noon to illustrate all shadowes, as the sheaves in harvest, to fill all penuries, all occasions invite his mercies, and all times are his seasons.

If it were not thus in generall, it would never have been so in this particular, in our case, in the Text, in King *Achaz;* If God did not seeke occasion to doe good to all, he would never have found occasion to doe good to King *Achaz.* Subjects are to look upon the faults of Princes, with the spectacles of obedience, and reverence, to their place, and persons; little and dark spectacles, and so their faults, and errors are to appeare little, and excusable to them; Gods perspective glasse, his spectacle is the whole world; he looks not upon the Sun, in his spheare onely, but as he works upon the whole earth: And he looks upon Kings, not onely what harme they doe at home, but what harme they occasion abroad; and through that spectacle, the faults of Princes, in Gods eye, are multiplyed, farre above those of private men. *Achaz* had such faults, and yet God sought occasion of Mercy. *Iotham,* his Father, is called *a good King,* and yet all Idolatry was not removed in his time, and he was a good King, for all that. *Achaz* is called *ill,* both because himselfe sacrificed Idolatrously, (And the King was a com-

[Psa. 95.7]

140

150

Achaz case

160

manding person) And because he made the Priest *Vriah* to doe so,
¹⁷⁰ (And the Priest was an exemplar person) And because he made his
Son commit the abominations of the heathen; (And the actions of the
Kings Son pierce far in leading others.) *Achaz* had these faults, and
yet God sought occasion of mercy. *If the evening skie be red, you*   Mat. 16.2
promise your selves a faire day, sayes Christ; you would not doe so if
the evening were black and cloudy: when you *see the fields white with*   Joh. 4.35
corne, you say harvest is ready; you would not doe so if they were
white with frost. *If ye consent, and obey, you shall eat the good things*   Esay 1.19
of the Land, sayes God in the Prophet; shall ye doe so if you refuse,
and rebell? *Achaz* did, and yet God sought occasion of mercy. There
¹⁸⁰ arise diseases for which there is no *probatum est,* in all the bookes of
Physitians; There is scarce any sin of which we have not had experi-
ments of Gods mercies; He concludes with no sin, excludes no occasion, precludes no person: And so we have done with our first part,
Gods generall disposition, for the Rule, declared in *Achaz* case for
the example.

Our second part consists of a Rule, and an Example too: The Rule,   2 Part
That God goes forward in his own wayes, proceeds, as he begun, in
mercy; The Example, what his proceeding, what his subsequent
mercy to *Achaz* was. One of the most convenient Hieroglyphicks of
¹⁹⁰ God, is a Circle; and a Circle is endlesse; whom God loves, hee loves
to the end: and not onely to their own end, to their death, but to his
end, and his end is, that he might love them still. His hailestones, and
his thunder-bolts, and his showres of bloud (emblemes and instruments of his Judgements) fall downe in a direct line, and affect and
strike some one person, or place: His Sun, and Moone, and Starres,
(Emblemes and Instruments of his Blessings) move circularly, and
communicate themselves to all. His Church is his chariot; in that, he
moves more gloriously, then in the Sun; as much more, as his begotten
Son exceeds his created Sun, and his Son of glory, and of his right
²⁰⁰ hand, the Sun of the firmament; and this Church, his chariot, moves
in that communicable motion, circularly; It began in the East, it came
to us, and is passing now, shining out now, in the farthest West. As
the Sun does not set to any Nation, but withdraw it selfe, and returne
againe; God, in the exercise of his mercy, does not set to thy soule,
though he benight it with an affliction. Remember that our Saviour

Christ himselfe, in many actions and passions of our humane nature, and infirmities, smothered that Divinity, and suffered it not to worke, but yet it was alwayes in him, and wrought most powerfully in the deepest danger; when he was absolutely dead, it raised him again: If
210 Christ slumbred the God-head in himselfe, The mercy of God may be slumbred, it may be hidden from his servants, but it cannot be taken away, and in the greatest necessities, it shall break out. The Blessed Virgin was overshadowed, but it was with the Holy Ghost that over-shadowed her: Thine understanding, thy conscience may be so too, and yet it may be the work of the Holy Ghost, who moves in thy dark-nesse, and will bring light even out of that, knowledge out of thine ignorance, clearnesse out of thy scruples, and consolation out of thy Dejection of Spirit. *God is thy portion,* sayes *David; David* does not speak so narrowly, so penuriously, as to say, God hath given thee thy
220 portion, and thou must look for no more; but, *God is thy portion,* and as long as he is God, he hath more to give, and as long as thou art his, thou hast more to receive. Thou canst not have so good a Title, to a subsequent blessing, as a former blessing; where thou art an ancient tenant, thou wilt look to be preferred before a stranger; and that is thy title to Gods future mercies, if thou have been formerly accustomed to them. The Sun is not weary with sixe thousand yeares shining; God cannot be weary of doing good; And therefore never say, God hath given me these and these temporall things, and I have scattered them wastfully, surely he will give me no more; These and these spirituall
230 graces, and I have neglected them, abused them, surely he will give me no more; For, for things created, we have instruments to measure them; we know the compasse of a Meridian, and the depth of a Di-ameter of the Earth, and we know this, even of the uppermost spheare in the heavens: But when we come to the Throne of God himselfe, the Orbe of the Saints, and Angels that see his face, and the vertues, and powers that flow from thence, we have no balance to weigh them, no instruments to measure them, no hearts to conceive them: So, for temporall things, we know the most that man can have; for we know all the world; but for Gods mercy, and his spirituall graces, as that
240 language in which God spake, the Hebrew, hath no superlative, so, that which he promises, in all that he hath spoken, his mercy hath no superlative; he shewes no mercy, which you can call his Greatest

Mercy, his Mercy is never at the highest; whatsoever he hath done for thy soule, or for any other, in applying himselfe to it, he can exceed that. Onely he can raise a Tower, whose top shall reach to heaven: The Basis of the highest building is but the Earth; But though thou be but a Tabernacle of Earth, God shall raise thee peece by peece, into a spirituall building; And after one Story of Creation, and another of Vocation, and another of Sanctification, he shall bring
²⁵⁰ thee up, to meet thy selfe, in the bosome of thy God, where thou wast at first, in an eternall election: God is a circle himselfe, and he will make thee one; Goe not thou about to square eyther circle, to bring that which is equall in it selfe, to Angles, and Corners, into dark and sad suspicions of God, or of thy selfe, that God can give, or that thou canst receive no more Mercy, then thou hast had already.

This then is the course of Gods mercy, He proceeds as he begun, which was the first branch of this second part; It is always in motion, and always moving towards *All,* alwaies perpendicular, right over every one of us, and always circular, always communicable to
²⁶⁰ all; And then the particular beame of this Mercy, shed upon *Achaz* here in our Text, is, *Dabit signum, The Lord shall give you a signe.* It is a great Degree of Mercy, that he affords us signes. A naturall man is not made of Reason alone, but of Reason, and Sense: A Regenerate man is not made of Faith alone, but of Faith and Reason; and Signes, externall things, assist us all.

Signum

In the Creation, it was part of the office of the Sunne and Moone, to be significative; he created them for signes, as well as for seasons: hee directed the Jews to Christ, by signes, by sacrifices, and Sacraments, and ceremonies; and he entertaines us with Christ, by the
²⁷⁰ same meanes to; we know where to finde Christ; In his House, in his Church; And we know at what signe he dwels; where the Word is rightly Preached, and the Sacraments duly administred. It is truly, and wisely said, *Sic habenda fides verbo Dei, ut subsidia minimè contemnamus;* We must so farre satisfie our selves, with the word of God, as that we despise not those other subsidiary helps, which God in his Church hath afforded us: which is true (as of Sacraments especially) so of other Sacramentall, and Rituall, and Ceremoniall things, which assist the working of the Sacraments, though they infuse no power into the Sacraments. For, therefore does the Prophet say, when

Calvin

V. 13 ²⁸⁰ *Achaz* refused a signe, *Is it a small thing to weary* (or disobey) *men, but that you will weary* (disobey) *God himselfe?* He disobeyes God, in the way of contumacy, who refuses his signes, his outward assistances, his ceremonies which are induced by his authority, derived from him, upon men, in his Church, and so made a part, or a help, of his ordinary service, as Sacraments and Sacramentall things are.

There are signes of another sort, not fixed by Gods Ordinance, but signes which particular men, have sometimes desired at Gods hand, for a farther manifestation of Gods will, in which, it is not, otherwise, already fully manifested, and revealed. For, to seeke such signes, in ²⁹⁰ things which are sufficiently declared by God, or to seeke them, with a resolution, That I will leave a duty undone, except I receive a signe, this is to tempt God, and to seeke a way to excuse my selfe, for not doing that, which I was bound to doe, by the strength of an old commandement, and ought not to look for a new signe. But the greatest fault in this kinde, is, that if God, of his abundant goodnesse, doe give me a signe, for my clearer directions, and I resist that signe, I dispute against that signe, I turne it another way, upon nature, upon fortune, upon mistaking, that so I may goe mine owne way, and not be bound, by beleeving that signe to be from God, to goe that way, ³⁰⁰ to which God by that signe calls me. And this was *Achaz* case; God

V. 11 spoke unto him, and said, *Aske a signe* (that he would deliver him, from the enemy, that besieged Jerusalem) and he said, *I will not aske a signe, nor tempt God;* For, though St. *Augustine,* and some with him, ascribe this refusall of *Achaz,* to a religious modesty, yet St. *Hierome,* and with him, the greatest party, justly impute this, for a fault to *Achaz:* both because the signe was offered him from God, and not sought by himselfe, (which is the case that is most subject to errour) And because the Prophet, who understood Gods minde, and the Kings minde to, takes knowledge of it, as of a great fault, *In this,* ³¹⁰ *thou hast contemned, and wearyed, not Man but God.* For, though there be but a few cases, in which we may put God to give a signe,

Mat. 12.39 (for Christ calls the Pharisees *an evill, and an adulterous generation,*
Exod. 4 therefore, because they *sought a signe*) yet God gave *Moses* a signe, of a Rod changed into a Serpent, and a signe of good flesh changed
Gen. 15.8 into leprous, and leprous into good, unasked: And after, *Abraham* askes a signe, whereby shall I know, that I shall inherit the land?

and God gave him a signe. So *Gideon,* in a modest timorousnesse
askes a signe, and presses God to a second signe: First, he would
have all the dew upon the fleece, and then, none of the dew upon the
320 fleece. God does give signes, and when he does so, he gives also irradi-
ations, illustrations of the understanding, that they may be discerned
to be his signes; and when they are so, it is but a pretended modesty,
to say, we will not tempt God to ask a sign, we will not trouble God
to tell us whether this be a sign or no, but against all significations
from God, goe on, as though all were but naturall accidents.

God gives signes *rectè petentibus,* to them that aske them upon due
grounds, (so to *Abraham,* so to *Gideon*) And it is too long for this
time, to put cases, when a man may or may not put God to a signe;
He gives signes also *Non petentibus,* without being asked, to illustrate
330 the case, and to confirme the person, and so he did to *Moses.* Both
these are high expressions of his mercy; for what binds God, to begin
with man, and give him a signe before he aske; or to waite upon man,
and give it him, when he askes? But the highest of all, is, to persever
in his mercy so far, as to give a signe, though upon the offer thereof,
it be refused; And that is *Achaz* case: *Aske ye,* says God, And, *I will
not,* says *Achaz,* and then, It is not *Quamvis,* for all that, though thou
refuse, but it is *Propterea, Therefore,* because thou refusest, *The Lord
himselfe shall give thee a signe.* His fault is carried thus high: Because he had treasure to pay an army, because he had contracted with
340 the Assyrians to assist him with men, therefore he refuses the assistance offerd by the Prophet from God, and would faine goe his owne
wayes, and yet would have a religious pretext, *He will not tempt God.*
Nay his fault is carried thus much higher, That which we read, *Non
tentabo, I will not tempt,* is in the Originall, *Nasas;* and *Nasas* is *non
Extollam, non glorificabo,* I will not glorifie God so much, that is, I
will not be beholden to God for this victory, I will not take him into
the league for this action, I will do it of my selfe: And yet, (and then,
who shall doubt of the largenesse of Gods mercy?) God proceeds in
his purpose: *Aske a signe,* will ye not? *Therefore the Lord shall give
350 you a signe:* Because you will doe nothing for your selfe, the Lord shall
doe all; which is so transcendent a mercy, as that, howsoever God
afforded it to *Achaz* here, we can promise it to no man hereafter.

We are come to our third part, which is more peculiar to this Day: 3. Part

It is, first, what the signe is in generall, And then, some more particular circumstances, *Behold a Virgin shall conceive, &c.* In generall then, the signe that God gives *Achaz* and his company, is, That there shall bee a Messias, a Redeemer given. Now, how is this future thing, (There shall be a Messias) a signe of their present deliverance from that siege? First, In the notion of the Prophet, it was not a future thing; for, as in Gods owne sight, so in their sight, to whom he opens himselfe, future things are present. So this Prophet says, *Puer datus, filius natus, unto us a child is borne, unto us a Son is given:* He was not given, he was not borne in six hundred yeares after that; but such is the clearenesse of a Prophets sight, such is the infallibility of Gods declared purpose. So then, if the Prophet could have made the King beleeve, with such an assurednesse, as if he had seene it done, that God would give a deliverance, to all mankinde, by a Messias, that had beene signe enough, evidence enough to have argued thereupon, That God who had done so much a greater worke, would also give him a deliverance from that enemy, that pressed him then: If I can fixe my selfe, with the strength of faith, upon that which God hath done for man, I cannot doubt of his mercy, in any distresse: If I lacke a signe, I seeke no other but this, That God was made man for me; which the Church and Church-writers, have well expressed by the word Incarnation, for that acknowledges, and denotes, that God was made my flesh: It were not so strange, that he who is spirit, should be made my spirit, my soule, but he was made my flesh: Therefore have the Fathers delighted themselves, in the variation of that word; so far, as that *Hilarie* cals it *Corporationem,* That God assumed my Body; And *Damascen* cals it *Inhumanationem,* That God became this man, soule and body; And *Irenæus* cals it *Adunationem,* and *Nysen Contemperationem,* A mingling, says one, an uniting, saies the other, of two, of God and man, in one person. Shall I aske, what needs all this? what needed God to have put himselfe to this? I may say with S. *Augustine, Alio modo poterat Deus nos liberare, sed si aliter faceret, similiter vestræ stultitiæ displiceret:* What other way soever God had taken for our salvation, our curiosity would no more have beene satisfied in that way, than in this: But God having chosen the way of Redemption, which was the way of Justice, God could do no otherwise: *Si homo non vicisset inimicum hominis, non justè victus*

Esay 9.6

360

370

380

390

esset inimicus, saies *Irenæus;* As, if a man should get a battaile by the power of the Devill, without fighting, this were not a just victory; so, if God, in mans behalfe, had conquered the devill, without man, without dying, it had not beene a just conquest. I must not aske why God tooke this way, to Incarnate his Son; And shall I aske how this was done? I doe not aske how *Rheubarb,* or how *Aloes* came by this, or this vertue, to purge this, or this humour in my body: *In talibus* August. *rebus, tota ratio facti, est potentia facientis:* Even in naturall things, all the reason of all that is done, is the power, and the will of him, 400 who infused that vertue into that creature. And therefore much more, when we come to these supernaturall points, such as this birth of Christ, we embrace S. *Basils* modesty, and abstinence, *Nativitas ista silentio honoretur,* This mysterie is not so well celebrated, with our words, and discourse, as with a holy silence, and meditation: *Immo potius ne cogitationibus permittatur,* Nay, (saies that Father) there may be danger in giving our selves leave, to thinke or study too much of it. *Ne dixeris quando,* saies he, *præteri hanc interrogationem:* Aske not thy selfe overcuriously, when this mystery was accomplished; be not over-vehement, over-peremptory, (so far, as to the perplexing of 410 thine owne reason and understanding, or so far, as to the despising of the reasons of other men) in calculating the time, the day or houre of this nativity: *Præteri hanc interrogationem,* pass over this question, in good time, and with convenient satisfaction, *Quando,* when Christ was borne; But *noli inquirere Quomodo,* (saies S. *Basil* still) never come to that question, how it was done, *cum ad hoc nihil sit quod responderi possit,* for God hath given us no faculties to comprehend it, no way to answer it. That's enough, which we have in S. *Iohn,* *Every spirit, that confesses, that Iesus is come in the flesh, is of God:* I Ioh. 4.2 for, since it was a comming of Iesus, Iesus was before; so he was God; 420 and since he came in the flesh, hee is now made man; And, that God and Man, are so met, is a signe to mee, that God, and I, shall never bee parted.

This is the signe in generall; That God hath had such a care of all *Virgo* men, is a signe to me, That he hath a care of me: But then there are signes of this signe; Divers; All these; *A Virgin shall conceive,* A Virgin shall *bring forth,* Bring forth *a Son, And* (whatsoever have been prophesied before) *she shall call his name Immanuel.*

First, a Virgin shall be a mother, which is a very particular signe, and was seene but once. That which *Gellius,* and *Plinie* say, that a Virgin ⁴³⁰ had a child, almost 200. yeares before Christ, that which *Genebrard* saies, that the like fell out in France, in his time, are not within our faith, and they are without our reason; our faith stoopes not downe to them, and our Reason reaches not up to them; of this Virgin in our text, If that be true, which *Aquinas* cites out of the Roman story, that in the times of *Constantine* and *Irene,* upon a dead body found in a sepulchre, there was found this inscription, in a plate of gold, *Christus nascetur ex Virgine, & ego credo in eum,* Christ shall be borne of a Virgin, and I beleeve in that Christ, with this addition, in that inscription, *O Sol, sub Irenæ, & Constantini temporibus, iterum me* ⁴⁴⁰ *videbis,* Though I be now buried from the sight of the sun, yet in *Constantines* time, the sun shall see me againe; If this be true, yet our ground is not upon such testimonie; If God had not said it, I would never have beleeved it. And therefore I must have leave to doubt of that which some of the Roman Casuists have delivered, That a Virgin may continue a virgin upon earth, and receive the particular dignity of a Virgin in Heaven, and yet have a child, by the insinuation and practise of the Devill; so that there shall be a father, and a mother, and yet both they Virgins. That this Mother, in our text, was a Virgin, is a peculiar, a singular signe, given, as such, by God; never done but ⁴⁵⁰ then; and it is a singular testimony, how acceptable to God, that state of virginity is; Hee does not dishonour physick, that magnifies health; nor does hee dishonour marriage, that praises Virginity; let them embrace that state, that can; and certainly, many more might doe it, then do, if they would try whether they could, or no; and if they would follow S. *Cyprians* way, *Virgo non tantum esse, sed & intelligi esse debet, & credi:* It is not enough for a virgin to bee a virgin in her owne knowledge, but she must governe her selfe so, as that others may see, that she is one, and see, that shee hath a desire, and a disposition, to continue so still; *Ita, ut nemo, cum virginem viderit, dubitet an sit* ⁴⁶⁰ *virgo,* saies that Father, She must appeare in such garments, in such language, and in such motions, (for, as a wife may weare other clothes, so she may speake other words, then a virgin may do) as they that see her, may not question, nor dispute, whether she be a maid or no. The word in the Text, is derived *à latendo,* from retiring, from pri-

vatenesse: And *Tertullian,* who makes the note, notes withall, that *Ipsa concupiscentia non latendi, non est pudica,* The very concupiscence of conversation, and visits, is not chaste: *Studium placendi, publicatione sui, periclitatur,* saies the same Author: Curious dressings are for publique eyes; and the Virgin that desires to publish her
470 selfe, is weary of that state: It is usefully added by him, *Dum percutitur oculis alienis, frons duratur, & pudor teritur,* the eyes of others, that strike upon her, (if she be willing to stand out that battery) dry up that blood, that should blush, and weare out that chastity, which should be preserved. So precious is virginity in Gods eye, as that hee lookes upon that, with a more jealous eye, than upon other states.

This blessed Mother of God, in our text, was a Virgin: when? *Concepit* *Virgo concipiet,* saies our Text, *A Virgin shall conceive,* when she conceived, she was a Virgin. There are three Heresies, all noted by S. *Augustine,* that impeach the virginity of this most blessed Woman:
480 The Cerinthians said she conceived by ordinary generation; *Iovinian* said, she was delivered by ordinary meanes; And *Helvidius* said, she had children after: All against all the world besides themselves, and against one another. For the first, that is enough which S. *Basil* sayes, that if the word Virgin in our text signified no more but *adolescentulam,* a yong woman (as they pretend) it had been an impertinent, an absurd thing for the Prophet to have made that a sign, and a wonder, that a yong woman should have a childe. This is enough; but that is abundantly enough, that S. *Matthew,* who spoke with the same spirit that *Esay* did, sayes in a word, which can admit no mis-interpre-
490 tation, That that was fulfilled which *Esay* had said, *A Virgin shall* Mat. 1.23 *conceive;* S. *Matthews* word without question, is a Virgin, and not a yong woman, and S. *Matthew* took *Esaies* word to be so too; and S. *Matthew* (at least he that spake in S. *Matthew*) did not, could not mistake, and mistake himself, for it was one and the same Holy Ghost Ps. 22.[6] that spake both. Christ sayes therefore of himself, *vermis sum,* I am a [22 : 21 F worm, but sayes S. *Ambrose, vermis de Manna,* a worm out of a pure as in *Vulg.*] substance, a holy Man, from a blessed Virgin; *Virgo concepit,* she was a Virgin then, then when she had conceived.

She was so to, *In partu,* then when she was delivered; *Iovinian* *In partu*
500 denied that: A better then he (*Tertullian*) denied it: *Virgo quantum à viro, non quantum à partu,* says he, she was such a Virgin as knew

no man, not such a Virgin as needed no midwife: *Virgo concepit,* sayes he, *in partu nupsit,* a Virgin in her conception, but a wife in the deliverance of her Son. Let that be wrapped up amongst *Tertullians* errors, he had many; The text cleares it, *A virgin shall conceive, a virgin shall beare a Son:* The Apostles Creed cleares it, sayes S. *Augustine,* when it sayes, *Born of the Virgin Mary;* and S. *Ambrose* cleares it, when hee says, with such indignation, *De via iniquitatis produntur dicere, virgo concepit, sed non virgo generavit,* It is said,

510 that there are some men so impious, as to deny that she remained a Virgin at the birth of her Son: S. *Ambrose* wondred there should be, scarce beleeved it to be any other then a rumour, or a slander, that there could be any so impious, as to deny that: And yet there have

Cramerus beene some so impious, as to charge *Calvin,* with that impiety, with denying her to be a Virgin then; It is true, he makes it not a matter of faith, to defend her perpetuall virginity; but that's not this case, of her Virginity in her Deliverance: And even of that, (of her perpetuall virginity) he saies thus, *Nemo unquam quæstionem movebit, nisi curiosus, nemo pertinaciter insistet, nisi contentiosus rixator;* He

520 is over-curious, that will make any doubt of it; but no man will persist in the denyall of it, but a contentious wrangler; And in that very point, S. *Basil* saies fully as much, as *Calvin.* But, at his birth, and after his birth, there is evidence enough in this text, *A Virgin shall conceive, A Virgin shall bring forth, A Virgin shall call him Immanuel,* In all those future, and subsequent Acts, still it is the same person, and in the same condition.

Filium   *Pariet, & pariet filium, She shall bring forth a Son;* If a Son, then of the substance of his Mother; that the Anabaptists deny; But had it not beene so, Christ had not beene true Man, and then, man were

530 yet unredeemed. He is her Son, but not her ward; his Father cannot dye: Her Son, but yet he asked her no leave, to stay at Jerusalem, nor to dispute with the Doctors, nor to goe about his Fathers worke: His setling of Religion, his governing the Church, his dispensing of his graces, is not by warrant from her: They that call upon the Bishop of Rome, in that voyce, *Impera Regibus,* command Kings and Emperors, admit of that voyce, *Impera filio,* to her, that she should command her Sonne. The naturall obedience of children to Parents, holds not in such civill things, as are publique; A woman may be a Queen-

Dowager, and yet a subject; The blessed Virgin *Mary* may be in a high
540 ranke, and yet no Soveraigne; *Blessed art thou amongst women,* saies
the Angell to her; Amongst women, above women; but not above
any person of the Trinity, that she should command her Son. *Luther*
was awake, and risen, but he was not readie; Hee had seene light,
and looked toward it, but yet saw not so clearely by it, then, when
he said, That the blessed Virgin was of a middle condition, betweene
Christ, and man; that man hath his conception, and his quickning
(by the infusion of the soule) in originall sin; that Christ had it in
neither, no sin in his conception, none in his inanimation, in the
infusion of his soule; But, saies *Luther,* howsoever it were at the con-
550 ception, certainly at the inanimation, at the quickning, she was preserved from originall sin. Now, what needs this? may I not say, that
I had rather be redeemed by Christ Jesus then bee innocent? rather
be beholden to Christs death, for my salvation, then to *Adams* standing in his innocencie? *Epiphanius* said enough, *Par detrimentum
afferunt religioni,* they hurt Religion as much, that ascribe too little, to
the blessed Virgin, as they who ascribe too much; much is due to her,
and this amongst the rest, That she had so cleare notions, above all
others, what kind of person, her Son was, that as *Adam* gave names,
according to natures, so the Prophet here leaves it to her, to name her
560 Son, according to his office, *She shall call his name Immanuel.*

Wee told you at first, that both *Ioseph* and *Mary,* were told by the
Angel, that his name was to be Jesus, and we told you also, that others,
besides him, had beene called by that name of Jesus: but, as, though
others were called Jesus, (for *Iosuah* is called so, *Heb.* 4.8. *If Iesus had
given them rest;* that is, If *Iosuah* had &c. And the son of *Iosedech*
is called so, throughout the Prophet *Aggai*) yet there is observed a difference in the pointing, and sounding of those names, from this our
Jesus: so though other women were called *Mary,* as well as the blessed
Virgin, yet the Euangelists, evermore make a difference, betweene
570 her name, and the other *Maries;* for Her they call *Mariam,* and the
rest *Maria.* Now this Jesus, in this person, is a reall, an actuall Saviour,
he that hath already really, and actually accomplished our salvation;
But the blessed Virgin had a clearer illustration, then all that; for she
onely knew, or she knew best, the capacity, in which he could be a
Saviour, that is, as he is *Immanuel, God with us;* for she, and she

Luke [1.28]

Immanuel

onely knew, that he was the Sonne of God, and not of naturall generation by man. How much is enwrapped in this name *Immanuel,*
and how little time to unfold it? I am afraid none at all; A minute
will serve to repeate that which S. *Bernard* saies, and a day, a life will
580 not serve to comprehend it; (for to comprehend is not to know a
thing, as far as I can know it, but to know it as far, as that thing can
be knowne; and so onely God, can comprehend God.) *Immanuel est*
verbum infans, saies the Father; He is the ancient of daies, and yet in
minority; he is the Word it selfe, and yet speechlesse; he that is All,
that all the Prophets spoke of, cannot speake: He addes more, He is
Puer sapiens, but a child, and yet wiser then the elders, wiser in the
Cradle, then they in the Chaire: Hee is more, *Deus lactens,* God, at
whose breasts all creatures suck, sucking at his Mothers breast, and
such a Mother, as is a maid. *Immanuel* is God with us; it is not we
590 with God: God seeks us, comes to us, before wee to him: And it is
God with us, in that notion, in that termination, *El,* which is *Deus*
fortis, The powerfull God; not onely in infirmity, as when hee died
in our nature, but as he is *Deus fortis,* able and ready to assist, and
deliver us, in all encumbrances; so he is with us; And with us, *usque*
ad consummationem, till the end of the world, in his Word, and in
Cornelius   the Sacraments: for, though I may not say, as some have said, That
by the word of Consecration, in the administration of the Sacrament,
Christ is so infallibly produced, as that, if Christ had never been incarnate before, yet, at the pronouncing of those words of consecra-
600 tion, he must necessarily be incarnate then, yet I may say, that God
is as effectually present, with every worthy receiver, as that hee is not
more effectually present with the Saints in Heaven.

Ecce   And this is that, which is intimated in that word, which we seposed
at first, for the last of all, *Ecce, Behold; Behold, a Virgin shall con-*
ceive, &c. God does not furnish a roome, and leave it darke; he sets
up lights in it; his first care was, that his benefits should be seene; he
made light first, and then creatures, to be seene by that light: He
sheds himselfe from my mouth, upon the whole auditory here; he
[Rom.   powres himselfe from my hand, to all the Communicants at the table;
16.20]   610 I can say to you all here, *The grace of our Lord Iesus Christ be with*
you, and remaine with you all; I can say to them all there, *The Body*
of our Lord Iesus Christ which was given for you, preserve you to

everlasting life: I can bring it so neare; but onely the worthy hearer, and the worthy receiver, can call this Lord, this Jesus, this Christ, *Immanuel, God with us;* onely that Virgin soule, devirginated in the blood of *Adam,* but restored in the blood of the Lambe, hath this *Ecce,* this testimony, this assurance, that God is with him; they that have this *Ecce,* this testimony, in a rectified conscience, are Godfathers to this child Jesus, and may call him *Immanuel, God with us;* for, as no man can deceive God, so God can deceive no man; God cannot live in the darke himselfe, neither can he leave those, who are his, in the darke: If he be with thee, he will make thee see, that he is with thee; and never goe out of thy sight, till he have brought thee, where thou canst never goe out of his.

Number 9.

A Sermon Preached at Saint Dunstan's upon New-Years-day, 1624. [*1624/5*]

GEN. 17.24. *ABRAHAM HIMSELFE WAS NINETY NINE YEARES OLD, WHEN THE FORESKIN OF HIS FLESH WAS CIRCUMCISED.*

THIS IS the place where *Circumcision* began, and this is the *Day*, when *Circumcision* ended; in this Scripture it was Instituted, in the person of *Abraham;* and upon this *Day* it was perfected and consummated in the person of *Christ Jesus:* for, though Circumcision were admitted in a few cases, in the *Apostles* time, *after* Christ, yet that was, *as dead herbs* are re-admitted into *medicines* in the *winter,* when fresh and green herbs cannot be had of that kind: So Circumcision was sometimes admitted for *peace,* and to avoid *scandall,* and the better to propagate the Church, after the vertue thereof was

Divisio 10 extinguished in Christ. In the *Institution* thereof in this Text, we will consider *Abrahams* ready, and exact obedience: In the *Consummation* thereof, in the person of *Christ,* we will consider *that,* to which, this Circumcision had relation, that is, the *spirituall Circumcision* of our hearts. It is a *Text* well handled, and it is a *Day* well spent, if the *Text* teach us to obey God readily, and immediately, what inconveniences soever present themselves in the way, and if the celebration

[Rom. 2.29] of the *Day,* teach us to come this Day, to *that* which is the true Circumcision, the *Circumcision* of *the Heart*. In the first, in *Abraham's* example, we shall passe by these steps: First, that though there be

[1 Thess. 5.21] 20 allowed to us an *Omnia probate,* a *Triall of all things,* and a spirit to *discerne spirits;* yet when once it appeares to us, to be a commandement of God, there's *a fine leavied,* all Titles concluded, no more claime to be made by our *understanding,* our *reason,* but a present, and an exact obedience must be given to it. Secondly, that in par-

ticular Men, and in particular cases, there may arise tentations, objections, reasons, why a Man might forbeare altogether, or at least
defer the execution of such a commandement, as there may have done
in *Abraham's* case, as we shall see anon. Thirdly, that though such
tentations doe arise in us out of our infirmities, yet God gives his
30 Children strength to overcome those difficulties, and to oppose stronger
reasons against those reasons, and so to come to a willing obedience to
his will. And then lastly, the *triumph* that belongs to this *victory;*
which we shall find, in considering what *benefit Abraham* received
by this obedience in his Circumcision: And these will be the branches
of our first part, rising out of the *Institution* of Circumcision, in the
person of *Abraham* at that great age, First, that Gods *manifest will*
must not be disputed, nor reasoned upon: Secondly, that Mans *corrupt
nature* will offer reasons against it: Thirdly, that God will give the
issue with the tentation, reason above that reason: And lastly, he will
40 accompany that victory, with other blessings too.

First then, for our *exact obedience* to that which God exacts of us, it
is well said by *Luther, Depuerascendum est, cum agitur de obedientia
Dei:* when the question is, whether this, or this be commanded by
God or no, when *traditions* and additions of *men,* are imposed upon
us, as commandements of *God,* here's no *Depuerascendum* in this
case, this is no Childs-play; then, *viriliter agendum,* (as the Apostle
speaks) we must *quit our selves like men,* we must *dispute* like Men,
(like *learned* men) *preach* like Men, (like *Zealous* Men) *pray* like
men (like *devout* Men) *resist* like Men, (like *valiant* Men) or at least,
50 (in cases where we may not resist) *suffer* like Men, (like *constant*
Christian Men.) But when the question is, *De obedientia Dei,* that
this is agreed to be the will of God, and all the question is, whether
God might not be content to accept an obedience to some part of it,
or to all of that hereafter, but not now, whether God would not forgive
the debt, or at least give day for the payment of it; either when we are
old, or by legacies to *pious uses,* when we die, when this is the question,
Depuerascendum est, we must grow *Children* again; we must not
onely, not argue, not dispute against it (which are acts of *men,* of
strong and able understandings) but we must return to the first weak-
60 nesse of Children, to be *speechlesse,* to be *thoughtlesse;* we must not
utter a word, not conceive a thought against it *Periculosa & pestilens*

1 Part
*Obedien-
dum*

[1 Cor.
16.13]

quæstio, Quare; saies *Luther* also, It is a Dangerous and Infectious *Monosillable, How* or *Why:* If I will aske a *reason,* why God commands such a thing; first, *Periculosum est,* It is Dangerous; for, I have nothing to answer me, but mine owne *reason,* and that affords not Lead enough, nor Line enough, to sound the depth of Gods proceedings, nor length enough, nor strength enough to reach so farre, and therefore I may mistake the reason, and goe upon false grounds. So, *Periculosum est,* It is a Dangerous question, and a lost question, be-
70 cause I can have no certaine answer; and it is an *infectious* question too, for here is one coale of the Devils fire, of his pride, kindled in me;
[Isa. 14.14] as the Devil said, *Similis ero Altissimo, I will be like the Highest,* and see whether I may not stand by my selfe, without any Influence from God, without any Dependance upon God: so, in our case, I will be so farre equall to God, as that I will measure his actions by my reason, and not doe his Commandements till I know *why* he commanded them: And then, when the infection is got into a House, who can say, it shall end here in this Person, and kill no more; or it shall end this weeke, and last no longer? So if that *infectious inquisition,* that *Quare,*
80 (*Why* should God command this or this particular?) be entred into me, all my *Humilitie* is presently infected, and I shall looke for a reason, why God made a world, or why he made a world no sooner then 6000. yeares agoe, and why he saves *some,* and why *but* some, and I shall examine God upon all the *Interrogatories* that I can frame, upon the *Creed* (why I should believe a Sonne of a Virgin without a Man, or believe the Sonne of God to descend into Hell) Or frame upon the *Pater Noster,* (why I should worship such a God, that must be prayed to, *not to leade me into tentation*) Or frame upon the *Ten Commandements,* why after all is done and heapt, for any sinfull
90 action, yet I should be guilty of all, for coveting in my heart another mans horse or house. And therfore *Luther* pursues it farther, with words of more vehemence, *Odiosa & exitialis vocula, Quare,* It is an Execrable and Damnable Monosillable, *Why;* it exasperates God, it ruines us: For, when we come to aske a reason of his actions, either we doubt of the *goodnesse* of God, that he is not so carefull of us, as we would be; or of his *power,* that he cannot provide for us, so well as we could doe; or of his *wisdome,* that he hath not grounded his Commandements so well as we could have advised him: whereas Saint

Augustine saies justly, *Qui rationem quærit voluntatis Dei, aliquid*
¹⁰⁰ *majus Deo quærit,* He that seekes a reason of the will of God, seekes
for something greater then God. It was the Devill that opened our
eies in Paradise, it is our parts to shut them so farre, as not to gaze
upon Gods secret purposes. God guided his Children as well by a
Pillar of Cloud, as by a *Pillar of Fire,* and both, Cloud and Fire, were   [Exod.
equally Pillars: There is as much strength in, and as safe relying upon   13.21]
some ignorances, as some knowledges; for God provided for his peo-
ple, as well in *this,* that he *hid Moses body* from them, as that he re-   [Deut. 34.6]
vealed other Mysteries to them, by him. All is well summ'd and
collected by Saint *Augustine, Dominus cur jusserit, viderit; faciendum*
¹¹⁰ *est à serviente, quod jusserit: Why* God commands any thing, God
himselfe knowes; our part is, not to enquire *why,* but to doe *what* he
commands.

This is the Rule: 'Tis true, there should not be: but yet is there not   *Tamen*
sometimes, in the minds and mouths of good and godly men, a *Quare,*   *tentamur*
a reasoning, a disputing against *that* which God hath commanded or
done? The murmuring of the Children in the Desert, had still this
Quare, Quare eduxisti, Wherefore have you brought us hither to die   Num.
here, in this miserable place, *where there is no Seed, no Figges, no*   20.[5]
Vines, no Pomegranates, no Water? Saul had this *Quare,* this rebel-
¹²⁰ lious inquisition, upon that Commandement of God against the
Amalekites, Slay both Man and Woman, Infant and Suckling, Oxe   1 Sam.
and Sheep, Camell and Asse: And from this *Quare,* from this disputa-   15.[3]
tion of his, arose that conclusion, That it were better to spare some for
Sacrifice, then to destroy all: But though his pretence had a religious
colour, *that* would not justifie a slacknesse in obeying the manifested
will of God; for, for *this,* God repented that he made him *King,* and
told him that he had more pleasure in *Obedience,* then in *Sacrifice.*
But, to come to better men then the *Israelites* in the Wildernesse, or
Saul in his Government, *Job,* though *he,* and his Friends held out
¹³⁰ long, (*They sate upon the ground seven daies and seven nights, and*   [Job 2.13]
none spoke a word) yet at last fell into these *Quares, Why did I not*
die in the birth? or, why sucked I the breast? Peter himselfe had this
reluctation; and though that were out of piety, yet he was chidden for
it, *Quare lavas,* saies he, *Lord, doest thou wash my feet? thou shalt*   Joh. 13.[6]

never wash my feet: till Christ was faine to say, *If I wash thee not, thou shalt have no part with me.*

Upon this common infirmitie, inherent in the best men that may (and not unlikely) be, that when God commanded *Abraham,* at that great age to circumcise himselfe, there might arise such *Quares,* such
140 scruples and doubts, as there, in *Abrahams* minde, (for, as Saint *Paul* saies of himselfe, *If any man thinke he hath whereof to trust in the*

Phil. 3.[4   *flesh, much more I, Circumcised, an Hebrew, an Israelite, a Pharisee,*
and 5]   *a Zealous Servant in the persecution, and in righteousnesse unblameable*) So if any man might have taken this libertie to have disputed with God, upon his precepts, *Abraham* might have done it; for, when

Gen. 15.[5]   God called him out to *number the Starres,* (which was, even to *Art,* impossible) and promised him, that his seed should equall them,

[6]   (which was, in *Nature,* incredible) for all this *Incredibilitie* and *Impossibilitie, Abraham believed, and this was accounted to him for*
150 *Righteousnesse:* And *Abraham* had declared his easie, and forward, and *implicit faith* in God, when God called him, and he went out, not

Heb. 11.[8]   knowing whither he went: And therefore when God offered him a new seale, *Circumcision, Abraham* might have said, *Quare sigillum?* What needs a seale betweene thee and me? I have used to take thy word before, and thou hast tried me before: But *Abraham* knew that *Obedience* was better then *wit* or *disputation;* for, though *Obedience* and good *works,* do not *beget faith,* yet they *nurse* it; *Per ea augescit fidei, & pinguescit,* saies *Luther,* Our faith grows into a better state, and into a better liking, by our good works.

160   Againe, when *Abraham* considered, that it was, *Mandatum in re turpi,* That this Circumcision, in it selfe, was too frivolous a thing; and, in that part of the Bodie, too obscene a thing, to be brought into the fancy of so many Women, so many young Men, so many Strangers to other Nations, as might bring the Promise and Covenant it selfe into scorne, and into suspicion, that should require such a seale to it as that was, he might have come to this, *Quare tam turpe, quare tam sordidum?* why does God command me so base and uncleane a thing, so scornfull and mis-interpretable a thing, as Circumcision, and Circumcision in that part? Againe, when he considered, that to Circum-
170 cise *all his family in one day,* (as by the Commandement he must) which could not be (in likelyhood) of lesse then 400. (for he went out

before, to the rescue of *Lot,* with 318. borne and brought up in his Gen. 14.[14]
House) he must make his House a *Spittle* of so many impotent Persons, unable to helpe one another for many daies, (for such was the
effect of Circumcision, as we see in their Story, when *Simeon* and *Levi* Gen. 34.[25]
came upon the *Sichemites* three daies after they had beene, by their
perswasion, circumcised, the *Sichemites* were unable to resist or defend themselves, and so were slaine: Yea the sorenesse and incom-
modity upon Circumcision was so great, as that the very Commande-
¹⁸⁰ ment it selfe of Circumcision, was forborne in the Wildernesse, because they were then put to suddaine removes, which presently after
a Circumcision, they could not have perform'd) Might not *Abraham*
have come to his *Quare tam molestum?* Why will God command me
so troublesome and incommodious a thing as this? And (to contract
this) when he considered, That one principall reason of the Commandement of Circumcision, was, that that marke might be alwaies a
remembrance to them against *intemperance* and *incontinency,* Might
not *Abraham* have come to his *Quare mihi?* What use is there of this,
in my Body, which is now dried up and withered by 99. yeares? What
¹⁹⁰ *Quares,* what reluctations *Abraham* had, or whether he had any or no,
is not expressed; but very religious and good men, sometimes, out of
humane infirmities, have them: But then, God brings them quickly
about to Christ's *Veruntamen, Yet not my will, but thine be done;* and [Luke
he delivers them from the tentation, and brings them to an intire 22.42]
obedience to his will, which is that which we proposed for the next
Branch in this part.

    Tu qui vas figuli, sayes the Apostle; whensoever any disputation *Liberat*
against a commandement of God, arises in Gods children, the Spirit of *Deus*
God smothers that spirit of Rebellion with that, *Tu qui vas figuli,* wilt
²⁰⁰ thou who art but the vessell, dispute with the potter, that fashioned
thee? If *Abraham* had any such doubts, of a *frivolousnesse* in so base
a seale, of an *obscenity* in so foule a seale, of an *incommodiousnesse* in
so troublesome a seale, of a *needlesnesse* in so impertinent a seale; if
he had these doubts, no doubt but his forwardnesse in obeying God,
did quickly oppose these reasons to those, and overcome them: That
that part of the body is the most rebellious part; and that therefore,
onely that part *Adam* covered, out of shame, for all the other parts he
could rule: *Ad hominis inobedientiam redarguendam, suâ inobedi-* *August.*

entiâ quodammodo caro testimonium perhibet, to reproach Mans re-
210 bellion to *God, God* hath left one part of Mans body, to rebell against
him; for though the seeds of this rebellion be dispersed through all
the body, yet, *In illa parte magis regnat additamentum Leviathan,*
sayes Saint *Bernard,* the spawns of *Leviathan,* the seed of sinne, the
leven of the Devil, abounds and reignes most in that part of the body;
it is *sentiva peccati,* saies the same Father, the *Sewar* of all sinne; not
onely because all sinne is deriv'd upon us, by *generation,* and so implyed, and involv'd in *originall sinne;* but because, almost all other
sinnes have relation to *this:* for, *Gluttony* is a preparation to this sinne
in our selves; *Pride* and *excesse* is a preparation to it, in others, whom
220 we would enveigle and allure, by our bravery; *Anger* and malice inclines us to pursue this sinfull and inordinate love, quarrelsomly, so,
as, that *then,* we doe not quarrell for wayes, and walls in the street, but
we quarrell for our way to the Devil; and when we cannot go fast
enough to the Devil, by wantonnesse in the chamber, we will quarrell
with him, who hinders us of our Damnation, and find a way, to go
faster in the field, by *Duells,* and unchristian *Murder,* in so foule a
cause, as unlawfull lust. In this rebellious part, is the root of all sinne,
and therefore did that part need this stigmaticall marke of Circumcision, to be imprinted upon it. Besides, (for the Jewes in particular)
230 they were a Nation prone to *Idolatry,* and most, upon this occasion, if
they mingled themselves with Women of other Nations: And therefore, *Dedit est signum, ut admoverentur de generatione pura,* saies
Saint *Chrysostome, God* would be at the cost even of a *Sacrament,*
(which is the greatest thing that passes between *God* and *Man* next to
his *Word*) to defend them thereby against dangerous alliances, which
might turne their hearts from *God; God* imprinted a marke in that
part, to keep them still in mind of that law, which forbade them
Theodor.　　*foraigne Marriages,* or any company of *strange Women: Custodia*
pietati servandæ, ne macularent paternam Nobilitatem, lest they
240 should degenerate from the Nobility of their race, *God* would have
them carry this memoriall about them, in their flesh. And *God* fore-
saw that extreme Idolatry, that grosse Idolatry, which that Nation
would come to, and did come to, when *Maachah* the Mother of *Asa*
1 Reg. 15.13　　worshipped that Idol, which Saint *Hierome* calls *Belphegor,* and is not
fit to be nam'd by us; and therefore, in foresight of that Idolatry, *God*

gave this marke, and this mutilation upon this part. If *Abraham* were surprized with any suggestions, any *half-reasons* against this commandement, he might quickly recollect himself, and see, that Circumcision was first, *Signum memorativum, & monimentum isti fœderis,*
250 it was a signe of the *Covenant* between *God* and *Abraham;* the *Covenant* was the *Messias,* who being to come, by a carnall continuance of *Abrahams* race, the signe and seale was conveniently placed in that part. And that was, secondly, *Signum representativum,* it represented *Baptisme, In Christ you are circumcised,* saies the Apostle, *in that you are buried with him, through Baptisme:* And then, that was *Signum Distinctivum;* for, besides that it kept them from *Idolatry,* as the Greeks called all Nations, whom they despised, *Barbares, Barbarians,* so did the Jewes, *Incircumcisos, Uncircumcised:* And that was a great threatning in the Prophet, *Thou shalt die the death of the*
260 *Uncircumcised;* that is, without any part in the everlasting promise, and Covenant. But yet, the principall dignity of this Circumcision, was, that it was *Signum figurativum,* it prefigured, it directed to that Circumcision of the heart; *Circumcise the foreskin of your heart, for the Lord your God is God of Gods, and Lord of Lords.* And for all the other reasons that could be assigned, of *Remembrance,* of *Representation,* of *Distinction, Caret ubique ratione Judaica carnis Circumcisio,* (sayes *Lactantius*) *Nisi quod est Circumcisionis figura, quæ est Cor Mundum:* The Jewish Circumcision were an absurd and unreasonable thing, if it did not intimate and figure the Circumcision of the
270 heart: And that is our Second part of this Exercise: But before we come to that, we are to say a word of the fourth branch of this part, That as there is no *Quare* to be made nor admitted against God, (which was our first part) If Man, out of his infirmity, doe fall into *that,* (which was our Second) God provides and furnishes them with Reasons against those Reasons, (which was our third.) And then, *God* rewards their fighting of that battaile, (which is his owne worke) with victories, and crownes, and blessings here; (which must be our fourth branch.)

Of Examples of this, the Booke of *God* is full: but we contract our-
280 selves onely to *that,* which *God* did to *Abraham* at this time, in contemplation of this obedience. We consider *Abraham* at the end of one Age, he was almost *one hundred, ninety nine when he was*

Gen. 17.[10]

Colos. 2.[11 and 12]

Ezek. 28.[10]

Deut. 10.[16]

Retributio

Circumcised; and now was entring into another age, (for he liv'd
seventy five yeares after this:) this therefore was as the Eve of his
New years-day, and *God* presents him thus many *New-years-gifts:*
First, he gives him a *new Name;* in which change of his Name, from
Abram, to *Abraham,* (besides that he was chang'd from *Pater Mag-*
nus, to *Pater Multitudinis,* from the Father of a *great possession* and
family, to the Father of *a great succession* and *posterity,* for that dimin-
²⁹⁰ ishes any Greatnesse, to have no posterity to leave that to) this also
arises to be noted, that *Gods* Name *Jehovah,* having in that two Letters of one kind, two *HH, God* divides with his Servant, *God* affords
one of those letters to the dignifying of *Abrahams* name, he adds an
H of his owne Name to his: *Jehovah* is his *essentiall name;* and in
communicating any beame of that Essence, any letter of that Name,
we become *semen Dei,* the seed of God; and *filii Dei,* the Sonnes of

[2 Pet. 1.4]   God; and *participes divinæ naturæ,* Partakers of the Divine nature;
and *idem spiritus cum Domino,* the same spirit with the Lord; and

[Psa. 82.6]   Hearers of that voice; *Ego dixi Dii estis,* I have said you are Gods:
³⁰⁰ If we were carefull to answer our old name, the name of *Christians,*
in our conformity to Christ, and performance of Christianly duties,
that were well, and other Names needed not, as remembrancers unto
us: But God does give us *new Names* and *additions* of *Offices,* and
Titles in *Schoole,* or *Court,* or *Common-wealth,* as new testimonies
of his love, and *rebukes* of our former negligences, and *Remem-*
brancers of our present Duties in those places, and Encouragers to a
more carefull proceeding in them. Secondly, God gave *Abraham* a
new Wife: in which, the blessing was, that he tooke not from him
that virtuous and obedient Wife which he had before, *Sara,* but now
³¹⁰ he made her *a Wife* unto him, and he supplied *that* onely defect
which was in her, *Barrennesse,* and so made her fully a Wife, *a*
Mother. Thirdly, he gave him a *new Sonne;* for, God who purposed
to blesse all Nations in *Abraham's* seed, would not onely repaire and
furnish his *old house,* (that is, blesse *Ismael* with temporall blessings) but he would build him a *new house,* raise him up a new Sonne,
Isaac: He would not onely fulfill that petition of *Abrahams, Oh that*
Ismael might live in thy sight! not onely preserve *Ismael,* which signifies, *Exauditionem Domini,* that the Lord had heard that prayer, in
the behalf of *Ismael;* but he would give him an *Isaac,* which signi-

³²⁰ fies, *Risum, lætitiam,* that is, he would give him a new, and true occasion of *joy.* Fourthly, he gave him a *new promise;* that as in *Adam* he had promised a *Messias, in semine mulieris, in the seed of the Woman;* now he contracts that promise to *Abraham, in semine tuo, in thy seed shall all Nations be blessed;* and so makes *Abraham,* not onely a *Partner* with his other Children, in the Salvation of that *Messias,* but he makes *Abraham a meanes* to derive that Salvation upon others also, *In semine tuo, thou* shalt not onely be blessed *in the Seed of the Woman,* but all Nations shall be blessed in *thy seed.* And lastly, he gives him a *new seale;* not onely *that* seale, under which he was
³³⁰ wont to deale with him, not onely an *inward* seale in his *heart,* but he gives him a new seale, a *visible* seale, the seale of *Circumcision.* This being then the Dignity of Gods precepts, that they require a present, and an exact obedience, without any counter-disputing; this being the infirmity of mans nature, that he is ever ready to object and oppose reasons, according to flesh and blood, against Gods precepts; this being the overflowing measure of Gods mercy to his Children, to give them the issue with the tentation; Reason above that Reason, victory at last, and alacrity in the performance of that precept; and this being his infinite bounty, to give us such rewards and retribu-
³⁴⁰ butions for those victories, of which, onely his goodnesse, and his strength, was the Author in us, when we doe performe those duties, (all which we have seen in *Abrahams* obedience to a fleshly Circumcision) *that* Circumcision being come to an end in the Circumcision of *Christ,* performed this day: Let us come to *this* Circumcision, of which, that was but a *Figure,* a *Spirituall Circumcision,* the *Circumcision of the heart,* and God shall give us *new Names* (new Demonstrations, that our names are written in the Booke of life) and *new Marriages* (refresh his promise in the Prophet, that *he will marry himselfe to us for ever*) and *new Sonnes,* new *Isaacks* (assurance of [Hos. 2.19]
³⁵⁰ *new Joyes, Essentiall* and *Accidentall,* in the Kingdome of Heaven, and *inchoative* here in the way) and *new promises,* and *new seales* (new obligations of his Blessed Spirit) that that *Infallibility* of salvation which we have conceived, is well grounded.

We have done with our first part, with that which was occasioned by the *Institution* of Circumcision in *Abraham;* we passe to that, which is occasioned by the celebrating of this Day, in which this legall 2 Part

Circumcision taking an end, in the Person of Christ, we come aptly to consider *Spirituall Circumcision,* by which onely we can be made

Divisio conformable to our patterne and example, *Christ Jesus:* In which, 360 we will charge your memory but with these two considerations; First, *Quid sit, what* this spirituall Circumcision is, (for in that is implyed the *Quomodo, how* this Circumcision is to be wrought and effected) And Secondly, the *Ubi, what part* of a Man is to be circumcised in this Circumcision, for that implyes *Integritatem,* that it is the whole Man in every part.

Quid Briefly then, Spirituall Circumcision is to *walke in the spirit; for*
Gal. 5.[16] *then,* saies the Apostle, *ye shall not fulfill the lusts of the flesh;* no Circumcision can bring us to this, that we shall not *have* them, for they are borne in us, and they will live in us, whilst we live; but this 370 is this Circumcision, not to *fulfill* them. Neither was *Abraham's* race, which was to be circumcised, more numerous, more plentifull, more manifold, then is this issue of the flesh, *Sinne:* How suddaine, and how large a pedigree! A Child, at the first minute, when the soule enters, is *as good a Sinner,* that is, as absolute a Sinner, and hath as good title to Damnation, by being conceived in sinne, as the eldest man; nay, he is *as old a Sinner* as the eldest man that *is;* nay, as the eldest man that *ever was;* for, he sinn'd in *Adam,* and, though conceived but this night, sinn'd 6000 yeares agoe. In young Men, vanity begets excesse; excesse, licentiousnesse; licentiousnesse, envy, hatred, 380 quarrels, murders; so that here is generation upon generation, here are risen *Grandfather* and *Great-grandfather-sinnes* quickly, a forward generation: And then they grow suddainly to be *habits,* and they come to prescribe in us: *Prescription* is, when there is no memory to the contrary; and we cannot remember when that sinfull custome begun in us: yea, our sinnes come to be reverenced in us, and by us; our sinnes contract a majestie, and a state, and they grow *sacred* to us; we dare not trouble a sinne, we dare not displace it, nor displease it; we dare not dispute the prerogative of our sinne, but we come to thinke it a kinde of sedition, a kinde of innovation, and a troubling 390 of the state, if we begin to question our Conscience, or change that security of sinne which we sleepe in, and we thinke it an easier Reformation to repent a sinne once a yeare, at *Easter,* when we must needs Receive, then to watch a sinne every Day.

There is scarce any sinne, but that in that place of the Apostle to the *Galatians,* it comes within the name of *workes of the flesh;* for, though he names divers sinnes, which are litterally and properly workes of the flesh, (*as Adultery, fornication, uncleannesse, wantonnesse*) yet those sinnes that are against a mans owne selfe, (as *Gluttony* and *Drunkennesse*) those that are against other men, (as
400 *Contentions* and *Murders*) those that are directed upon *new Gods* (as *Idolatry*) those that are Contracts with the *Devil* (as *Witchcraft*) those that are offences to the *Church* ·(as *Heresy*) are all called by Saint *Paul* in that place, *workes of the flesh:* So that the object of this *Spirituall Circumcision* is all that concernes the *flesh,* the *world,* the *Devil,* or *God,* or *man,* or the *Church;* in every one of these we may finde somewhat to circumcise. But because abundance and superfluity begets these workes of the flesh, (for though we carry the *Serpent* about us, yet he does not sting, nor hisse, till he be *warme:* As long as poverty and wretchednesse freezes our *Concupiscences,* they
410 are not so violent) therefore spirituall Circumcision is well expressed by Saint *Bernard, Moralis Circumcisio est, victum & vestitum habentem, esse contentum;* A cutting off of these superfluities, is this morall, that is, this spirituall Circumcision.

Now for some understanding of these superfluities, we must consider, that sometimes a poore man, that hath no superfluity in his *estate,* is yet wastfull in his *minde,* and puts himselfe to superfluous expences, in his diet, in his apparell, and in all things of outward shew and ostentation: And on the other side, a covetous man, that hath a superfluous estate, yet starves himselfe, and denies himselfe
420 all conveniences for this life: Here's a *superfluous confidence* in the one, that he cannot want, though he throw away money; and here's a *superfluous feare* in the other, that he shall want, if he give himselfe bread; and here's worke for this spirituall Circumcision on both sides: But then the Circumcision is not necessarily to be applied to the riches of the rich man, so as that every rich man must necessarily cast away his riches (a Godly man may be rich) nor necessarily applied so to all outward expences of the free and liberall minded man, as that he should shut up dores, and weare ragges; for, a Godly man may fare in his diet, and appeare in his garments, according to that
430 *Degree* which he holds in that state: But the *superfluity* is, and (con-

Modus

sequently the *Circumcision* is to be) in the *Affection,* in our *Confidence,* that whatsoever we wast, by one meanes or other, we shall have more; or in our *diffidence,* that if we lay not up *all,* we shall never have *enough.* These be the inordinate affections that must be Circumcised: But how? for that's intended in this part. We need enquire no farther, for the meanes of this spirituall Circumcision, then to the very word which the Holy Ghost hath chosen for *Circumcision* here, which is *Mul* and *Namal;* for that word hath in other places of Scripture, *three* significations, that expresse much of the *manner,* how this Cir-
440 cumcision is to be wrought: It signifies, *Purgare,* to purge, to discharge the *Conscience:* (and that is, by *Confession* of our sinnes) It signifies, *Mundare,* to cleanse and purify the Conscience: (and that is, by *Contrition* and *Detestation* of that sinne) And it signifies, *Succidere,* to cut downe, to weed and root out whatsoever remaines in our possession, that is unjustly got (and that is) by *Restitution.*

Purgare   Now for the first of these, the *purging;* the proper use and working of *purging Physick,* is, not that that Medicine pierces into those parts of the Body, where the peccant humour lies, and from which parts, Nature, of her selfe, is not able to expell it: the substance of the
450 Medicine does not goe thither, but the Physick lies still, and draws those peccant humours together; and being then so come to an unsupportable Masse, and burden, Nature her selfe, and their owne waight expels them out. Now, that which *Nature* does in a naturall body, *Grace* does in a regenerate soule, for *Grace* is the *nature* and the *life* of a regenerate man. As therefore the bodily Physick goes not to that part of the body that is affected; we must not stay till our *Spirituall Physick* (the *Judgements* of God) worke upon that particular sinne, that transports us: That God should weaken me with a *violent sicknesse,* before I will purge my selfe of my *licentiousnesse;*
460 Or strike me with poverty, and losse of my stocke, before I will purge my selfe of my usury; or lay me flat with disgraces and dis-favours of great Persons, before I will purge my selfe of my *Ambition;* or evict my land from me, by some *false title,* that God, in his just Judgement, may give way to, to punish my sinnes, before I will purge my selfe of my *oppression,* and racking of Tenants: But before these violent Medicines come, if thou canst take Gods ordinary Physick, administred in the Word and Sacraments; if thou canst but endure that

qualme of calling thy selfe to an *account,* and an *examination;* if thou
canst draw all thy sinnes together, and present them to thine owne
470 Conscience, *then* their owne waight will finde a vent, and thou wilt
utter them in a full and free *Confession* to thy God, and that is *Circumcision;* as Circumcision consists in the *purging* of the Conscience,
to be mov'd upon hearing the *Word preached,* and the denouncing
of his *Judgements* in his Ordinance, before those Judgements surprize
thee, to recollect thy sinnes in thine owne *memory,* and poure them
out in a true *Confession.*

    The next step in this Circumcision, (as they are intimated in that   *Mundare*
word, which the Holy Ghost uses here) is *Mundare,* to cleanse; and
this is a *Contrition* for those sinnes, and a *Detestation* of those sinnes,
480 which I have thus gathered in my Memory, and poured out in my
Confession. A house is not clean, though all the Dust be swept together, if it lie still in a corner, within Dores; A Conscience is not
clean, by having recollected all her sinnes in the *Memory,* for they
may fester there, and *Gangreen* even to *Desperation,* till she have
emptied them in the bottomlesse Sea of the bloud of Christ Jesus,
and the mercy of his Father, by *this* way of *Confession.* But a house
is not clean neither, though the Dust be thrown out, if there hang
Cobwebs about the Walls, in how dark corners soever. A Conscience
is not clean, though the sins, brought to our memory by this Exami-
490 nation, be cast upon Gods mercy, and the merits of his Sonne, by
Confession, if there remaine in me, but a *Cobweb,* a little, but a sinfull delight in the *Memory* of those sins, which I had formerly committed. How many men sinne over the sinnes of their youth again,
in their age, by a sinfull *Delight* in remembring those sinnes, and a
sinfull *Desire,* that their Bodies were not past them? How many men
sin over some sins, but *imaginarily,* (and yet *Damnably*) a hundred
times, which they *never sinned actually* at all, by filling their *Imaginations,* with such thoughts as these, How would I be revenged of
such an Enemy, if I were in such a place of Authority? How easily
500 could I overthrow such a wastfull young Man, and compasse his Land,
if I had but Money, to feed his humours? Those sinnes which we
have never been able to doe *actually,* to the harme of others, we doe
as hurtfully to our owne Souls, by a sinfull *Desire* of them, and a
sinfull *Delight* in them. Therefore is there a *cleansing* required in

this Circumcision; such a cleansing as God promises, *I will cleanse*
their bloud, that is, the fountaine, the work of all corrupt *Desires,*
and sinfull *Delights.* Now there is no clensing of *our* bloud, but by *his*
bloud; and the infusion, and application of his bloud, is in the seale
of the *Sacrament;* so that that soule onely is so clensed, as is required
510 in this spirituall circumcision, that preserves it selfe alwayes, or returnes speedily, to a disposition of a worthy receiving of that holy and
blessed Sacrament: He that is now in that disposition, as that, in a
rectified Conscience, he durst meet his Saviour at that *Table,* and receive him there, (which cannot be done without *Contrition,* and
Detestation of former sins) hath admitted this spirituall Circumcision, so far, as is intended in the second signification of this word,
which is, *To clense.*

Succidere   But then there is a third action, which is, *succidere,* to *cut up,* to
root out all, from whence this sinne may grow up againe, as the word
[Verse 16]   520 is used in *Job* 18. *His root shall be dryed beneath, and all his branches*
shall be cut downe. In this Circumcision, we must cut the *root,* the
mother-sinne, that nourishes all our sinnes, and the *branches* too, that
if one sinne have begot another, there be a fall of all our woods, of
our *timber* wood, (our growne and *habituall* sinnes) and of our *under-*
woods, (those *lesser* sinnes which grow out of them.) It is a *cutting*
downe, and a *stubbing up,* which is not done, till we have shak'd off
all, that we have gotten by those Sinnes: It is not the Circumcision
of an *Excessive* use of that sinne, that will serve our turne, but such
a Circumcision, as amounts to an *Excession,* a cutting off the *root,* and
530 *branch,* the *sinne,* and the *fruits,* the *profits* of that sinne. I must not
think to *bribe* God, by giving him some of the profit of my sinne, to
let me enjoy the rest: for, was God a *venturer* with me in my sinne?
Or did God set me to Sea, that is, put me into this world, to see what
I could get by *Usury,* by *Oppression,* by *Extortion,* and then give him
a part to *charitable uses?* As this word signifies *Excedere,* to cut off
all that is grown out of sinne, so from this word *Namal,* comes
Nemâla, which is *Formica, an Ant,* which the *Hebrewes* derive from
this word, out of this reason, That as an Ant doth gnaw all the Corne
it layes up, upon one side, so that it may never grow againe, so this
540 spirituall Circumcision must provide, that that sinne take no new
roote: but as long as thou makest profit, or takest pleasure in any

Joel 3.[21]

thing sinfully gotten, thy sinne growes; so that this Circumcision is
not perfected but by *restitution* and *satisfaction* of all formerly damnified. These then be all the waies that are presented in these significations and use of this word, which the *holy Ghost* hath chosen here,
purging by *Consideration* and *Confessing*, clensing by *Contrition* and
Detesting, preventing of future growth by *Satisfaction* in *Restoring*.
A little remains to be said (though it be also implyed in that which
hath been said) of the *Ubi*, the place where this Circumcision is to
550 be applyed. The Scripture speaks of *uncircumcised hearts*, and *uncircumcised lips*, and *uncircumcised eares;* And our *eyes* in looking,
and coveting, and our *hands* in reaching to *that* which is not *ours*,
are as farre *uncircumcised* as *eares*, or *lips*, or *hearts:* Therefore we
are to carry this Circumcision all over; we must Circumcise, sayes
Saint *Bernard, In carne, peccatum*, the flesh, the body, the substance
of the sinne, *in cute, operimentum*, in the skin, all covers, and pallia-
tions, and disguises, and extenuations of the sinne; and, *in sanguine
incentivum*, in the blood all fomentations and provocations to that
sinne: the sinne it self, the *circumstances* of the sinne, the *relapses* to
560 or towards that sin must be circumcised: *Judæus ut parvulus, con-
gruum accepit mandatum, exiguæ Circumcisionis*, saies the same
Father, The Jew was but in an infancy, in a minority, and God did
not looke for so strong a proceeding from the *Jew*, as from *us*, but
led him by the armes, by the helpe of *Ceremonies* and *Figures*, and
accordingly required but a *Circumcision* in *one* part of the body: but
God lookes for more, at the hands of *Christians*, to whom he hath
fully manifested and applied himselfe. As Christ said to the Jewes,
Except your righteousnesse exceed the righteousnesse of the Scribes
and Pharisees, it is nothing: So except *our* righteousnesse exceed
570 them that exceeded the Scribes, it is nothing; and therefore, *Toto
corpore baptizamur* (saies *Bernard*) *quia totius hominis integra Circumcisio;* to shew, that it is the whole man that is to be circumcised,
we are baptized, we are washed all over, (for *so long, even to Ber-
nards time*, it seemes, that *manner of Baptizing*, by *Immersion* of the
whole body, and not by *Aspersion* upon the face onely, continued in
the generall practice of the Church.) So that if it be not an *entire*
Circumcision of the *whole* man, that will fall upon us, which God
threatens in the Prophet, *I will visit all them which are circumcised*,

Ubi

[Mat. 5.20]

Jer. 9.25

with them which are not circumcised; If we circumcise in part, leave
580 some sinnes, and cleave to others, we shall be, in the sight of God,
altogether uncircumcised; *Adam* was not the lesse naked in Gods
sight, for his *Figge-leafe; halfe-repentances* are no repentances; either
we are in a *privation,* or in a *habit;* covered over with righteousnesse,
or naked.

When therefore the Lord and his Spirit cals thee to this spirituall
Circumcision, remember that *Abraham* did not say when he was
call'd, Lord, I have followed thy voyce, in leaving my Country; Lord,
I have built thee an Altar, what needs more demonstration of my
obedience? Say not thou, Lord, I have built an *Hospitall;* Lord, I
590 have *fed the poore* at *Christmas;* Lord, I have made peace amongst
thy people at home; I have endowed an *Almes-house;* but persevere
in doing good *still,* for, God takes not the Tree, where it *growes,* but
where it *fals;* for the most part, the death of a man is such, as his life
was; but certainly the life of a man, that is, his everlasting life, is such
as his death is. Againe, *Abraham* did not say of this, that it was a
Commandement in a slight, and frivolous, and uncivill matter; doe
not thou say, that it is an impertinent thing in this spirituall Circumcision, to watch thy eating and drinking, and all such *indifferent
actions,* and to see that all they be done to the glory of God; for, as
[1 Cor.
1.25] 600 the Apostle saies, *That the foolishnesse of God is wiser then the wisdome of man;* so we may piously say, that the *levity* of God is graver
then the *gravity* of all the Philosophers and Doctors of the world; as
we may see in all his *Ceremoniall Lawes,* where the *matter* seemes
very light in many places, but yet the *signification* very important;
and therefore apply this Circumcision, even in thy least, and most
familiar action. So also *Abraham* was not diverted from obeying God,
by the inconvenience of having *all* his family diseas'd at *once;* he did
not say, I am content to circumcise my Sonne, but would spare my
Servants yet, for necessary uses; doe not thou say, thou art content
610 to circumcise thine eldest Sonne, to abate somewhat of that sinne
which thou beganst with in thy youth, but wouldst faine spare some
serviceable and profitable sinnes for a time, and circumcise them
hereafter. To pursue this example, *Abraham* did not say, *Cras Domine,* Lord, I will doe all this to morrow; but, as the Commandement
was given in that phrase of expedition, *Circumcidendo circumcides,*

In Circumcising thou shalt circumcise; which denoted a diligent and a present dispatch; so *Abraham* did dispatch it diligently and presently that day. Doe not thou say, *Cras Domine,* to morrow, some other day, in the day of mine *age,* or of my *Death,* or of *affliction* and
620 *tribulation,* I will circumcise all; for age, and sicknesse, and tribulations, are Circumcisions of themselves; a *Feaver* circumcises thee then, or an *Apoplexy,* and not thy *Devotion;* and *incapacity* of sinning is not *sanctification:* If any man put off his Repentance till death, *Fateor non negamus quod petit,* saies Saint *Augustine,* I dare not deny that man, whatsoever God may be pleased to grant him; *Sed non præsumimus, quod bene erit;* I dare not presume to say, that that man died well, *Non præsumo, non vos fallo, non præsumo,* saies that Father, with some vehemency, I dare not warrant him, let me not deceive you with saying that I dare, for I dare not: And, Beloved,
630 that is but a suspicious state in any man, in which another Christian hath just reason to doubt of his salvation, as Saint *Augustine* doth shrewdly doubt of these late Repenters, *Sicut ejus damnatio incerta, ita remissio dubia;* As I am not sure he is damned, so I am not sure he is saved, no more sure of one then of the other. It is true, we have the example of the *Crucified Thiefe,* but it is but a hard case, when a *Thiefe* must guide us and be our Example; we suspect *wills* that are made of temporall goods in that state, at the last gaspe, and shall we think a Man to be *compos mentis,* of a perfect understanding for the bequeathing of his Soule at his last gaspe? *non præsumo, non vos*
640 *fallo, non præsumo,* I should deceive you, if I should say it, I dare not say it, sayes that Father. Come therefore to this Circumcision betimes, come to it, *this Day,* come *this Minute:* This Day thy Saviour was Circumcised in the flesh, for thee; this Day Circumcise thy heart to him, and all thy *senses,* and all thy *affections.* It is not an utter *destroying* of thy senses, and of thy affections, that is enjoyned thee; but, as when a Man had taken a beautifull Woman captive in the warres, he was not bound to kill her, but he must *shave her head, and pare her nailes, and change her garments,* before he might marry her; so captivate, subdue, change thy affections, and that's the Destruction
650 which makes up this Circumcision: change thy *choler* into *Zeale,* change thy *amorousnesse* into *devotion,* change thy *wastfulnesse* into *Almes* to the poore, and then thou hast circumcised thy *affections,* and

Deut. 21.11

mayest retaine them, and mayest confidently say with the Apostle,

Phil. 3.3
we are the Circumcision, which worship God in the spirit, and re-joyce in Christ Jesus, and have no confidence in the flesh. Doe this to day; as God this day gives thee a *New yeare,* and hath not surpriz'd thee, nor taken thee away in the sinnes of last yeare; as he gives thee a new yeare, doe thou give him a *New-years-gift, Cor novum,* a new and a Circumcised heart, and *Canticum novum,* a new Song, a de-
660 light to magnifie his name, and speak of his glory, and declare his wondrous works to the Sonnes of men, and be assured that whether *I,* or any other of the same Ministry, shall speake to you from this place, this day twelve-month, and shall aske your consciences then, whether those things which you heard now, have brought you to this Circum-cision, and made you better this yeare than you were the last, and find you under the same uncircumcision still, be assured that God will not, God cannot be mocked, but as he wil receive us, with an

[Mat. 25.21]
Euge bone serve, Well done my good and faithfull Servant; so he will say to you, *Perditio tua ex te, Your destruction is from your selves:*
670 Enough hath been done for you by me, enough hath been said to you

[Ezek. 18.31]
by my Servants, *Quare moriemini, Why will you die ô house of Israel?* And after a long despising of his graces, he will come to a finall sepa-

[Luke 19.14]
ration; you shall come to say, *Nolumus hunc regnare,* we will not have Christ Jesus to reigne over us; and Christ Jesus shall come to

[Psa. 95.7]
say, *Nescio vos,* I know you not, nor whence you are. *Hodie si vocem*

[Luke 23.43]
ejus, If you wil heare his voice this day, *Hodie eritis, This day you shall be with him in Paradise,* and dwell in it all the yeare, and all the yeares of an Everlasting life, and of infinite generations. *Amen.*

Number 10.

*Preached at S. Pauls, The Sunday after
the Conversion of S. Paul.* [*1624/5*]

ACTS 9.4. *AND HE FELL TO THE EARTH, AND
HEARD A VOYCE, SAYING, SAUL, SAUL, WHY
PERSECUTEST THOU ME?*

LET US NOW *praise famous Men, and our Fathers that begat us,* (saies   Ecclus. 44.1
the Wiseman) that is, that assisted our second generation, our
spirituall Regeneration; Let us praise them, commemorate
them. *The Lord hath wrought great glory by them, through his power*   Ver. 2
from the beginning, saies he there, that is, It hath alwaies beene the
Lords way to glorifie himselfe in the conversion of Men, by the ministery of Men. For he adds, *They were leaders of the people by their*   Ver. 4
counsaile, and by their knowledge and learning meet for the people,
wise and eloquent men in their instructions; and that is, That God
10 who gives these gifts for this purpose, looks for the employment of
these gifts, to the edification of others, to his glory. *There be of them,*   Ver. 8
that have left a name behinde them, (as it is also added in that place)
that is, That though God can amply reward his servants in the next
world, yet he does it sometimes in this world; and, though not with
temporall happinesses, in their life, yet with honor, and commemora-
tions, and celebrations of them, after they are gone out of this life,
they leave a name behind them. And amongst them, in a high place,
shines our blessed and glorious Apostle S. *Paul,* whose Conversion the
Church celebrates now, and for the celebration thereof, hath appointed
20 this part of Scripture from whence this text arises, to be the Epistle of
the Day, *And he fell to the earth, and heard a voyce, saying, Saul, Saul,*
why persecutest thou me?

There are words in the text, that will reach to all the Story of S.   *Divisio*
Pauls Conversion, embrace all, involve and enwrap all; we must con-

205

tract them; into lesse then three parts, we cannot well; those will be
these; first, The Person, *Saul,* He, *He fell to the earth;* and then, his
humiliation, his exinanition of himselfe, his devesting, putting off of
himselfe, *He fell to the earth;* and lastly, his investing of Christ, his
putting on of Christ, his rising againe by the power of a new inanima-
30 tion, a new soule breathed into him from Christ, *He heard a voyce,*
saying, Saul, Saul, why persecutest thou me? Now, a re-distribution,
a sub-division of these parts, into their branches, we shall present to
you anon, more opportunely, as we shall come in due order to the
handling of the parts themselves. In the first, the branches will be but
these; *Sauls* indisposition when Christ tooke him in hand, and Christs
worke upon him; what he found him, what he left him, will determine
our first part, The person.

1 Part
Quid ante

First then, what he was at that time, the Holy Ghost gives evidence
enough against him, and he gives enough against himselfe. Of that
40 which the Holy Ghost gives, you may see a great many heavy pieces,
a great many appliable circumstances, if at any time, at home, you do
but paraphrase, and spread to your selves the former part of this
Chapter, to this text. Take a little preparation from me; *Adhuc spirans,*
saies the first verse, *Saul yet breathing threatnings and slaughter,* Then
when he was in the height of his fury, Christ laid hold upon him. It

Mat. 8.24

was, for the most part, Christs method of curing. Then when the Sea
was in a tempestuous rage, when the waters covered the ship, and the
storme shaked even that which could remove mountaines, the faith
of the Disciples, then Christ rebukes the winde, and commands a
50 calme. Then when the Sun was gone out to run his race as a Giant,
(as *David* speaks) then God by the mouth of another, of *Ioshuah,* bids
the Sun stand still. Then when that uncleane spirit foam'd, and fum'd,
and tore, and rent the possessed persons, then Christ commanded them
to go out. Let the fever alone, say our Physitians, till some fits be
passed, and then we shall see farther, and discerne better. The note is
S. *Chrysostomes,* and he applies it to Christs proceeding with *Saul;*
Non expectavit ut fatigatus debacchando mansuesceret, says he,
Christ staid not till *Saul* being made drunke with blood, were cast into
a slumber, as satisfied with the blood of Christians; *Sed in media in-*
60 *sania superavit,* but in the midst of his fit, he gave him physick, in the
midst of his madnesse, he reclaimes him. So is it also part of the

evidence that the Holy Ghost gives against him, *Quod petiit Epistolas,* that he sued to the State for a Commission to persecute Christians. When the State will put men to some kinde of necessity of concurring to the endamaging or endangering of the cause of Christ, and will be displeased with them, if they doe not, men make to themselves, and to their consciences some faint colour of excuse: But when they themselves set actions on foote, which are not required at their hands, where is their evasion? Then when *Saul* sued out this Commission, *That if*
70 *he found any of that way,* (that is, Christians) (for he had so scattered them before, that he was not sure to finde any, They did not appeare in any whole body, dangerous, or suspicious to the State) but, If hee found any, *Any man or woman,* That he might have the Power of the State, so as that he need not feare men, That hee might have the impartiality, and the inflexibility of the State, so as that he need not pity women, Then when his glory was *to bring them bound to Ierusalem,* that he might magnifie his triumph and greatnesse in the eye of the world, Then, then sayes Christ, to this tempest, Be calme, to this uncleane spirit, Come out, to this Sun, in his own estimation, Go no
80 farther.

Thus much evidence the Holy Ghost gives against him; and thus much more himselfe, *I persecuted this way unto the death; I bound and delivered into prison, both men and women;* And after, more then this, *I punished them,* and that oft, and, *in every Synagogue,* and, *compelled them to blaspheme,* and, *was exceedingly mad against them, and persecuted them even unto strange Cities.* What could he say more against himselfe? And then, sayes Christ, to this tempest, *Quiesce,* Be still, to this glaring Sunne, *Siste,* stand still, to this uncleane spirit, *Veni foras,* come forth. In this sense especially doth S. *Paul* call him-
90 selfe *Abortivum,* a person borne out of season, That whereas Christs other Disciples and Apostles, had a breeding under him, and came first *ad Discipulatum,* and then *ad Apostolatum,* first to be Disciples, and after to be Apostles; S. *Paul* was borne a man, an Apostle, not carved out, as the rest in time; but a fusil Apostle, an Apostle powred out, and cast in a Mold; As *Adam* was a perfect man in an instant, so was S. *Paul* an Apostle, as soone as Christ tooke him in hand.

Now, Beloved, wilt thou make this perverse use of this proceeding, God is rich in Mercy, Therefore I cannot misse Mercy? Wouldest thou

Act. 22.4

Act. 26.11

I Cor. 15.8

say, and not be thought mad for saying so, God hath created a West
100 Indies, therefore I cannot want Gold? Wilt thou be so ill a Logician to
thy selfe, and to thine own damnation, as to conclude so, God is
alwayes the same in himselfe, therefore he must be alwayes the same
to me? So ill a Musician as to say, God is all Concord, therefore He
and I can never disagree? So ill a Historian as to say, God hath called
Saul, a Persecutor, then when he breathed threatnings and slaughter,
then when he sued to the State for a Commission to persecute Christ,
God hath called a theife, then when he was at the last gaspe; And
therefore if he have a minde to me, he will deale so with me too, and, if
he have no such minde, no man can imprint, or infuse a new minde in
110 God? God forbid. It is not safe concluding out of single Instances. It
is true, that if a soure, and heavy, and severe man, will adde to the dis-
comforts of a disconsolate soule, and in that souls sadnesse, and dejection of spirit, will heap up examples, that God hath still suffered
high-minded sinners to proceed and to perish in their irreligious wayes,
and tell that poore soule, (as *Iobs* company did him) It is true, you take
God aright, God never pardons such as you, in these cases, these
singular, these individuall examples, That God hath done otherwise
once, have their use. One instance to the contrary destroys any per-
emptory Rule, no man must say, God never doth it; He did it to *Saul*
120 here, He did it to the Theife upon the Crosse. But to that presumptu-
ous sinner, who sins on, because God shewed mercy to One at last, we
must say, a miserable Comforter is that Rule, that affords but one
example. Nay, is there one example? The Conversion of *Saul* a Perse-
Gregor.   cutor, and of the Theife upon the Crosse, is become *Proverbium pec-*
catorum, The sinners proverb, and serves him, and satisfies him in all
cases. But is there any such thing? Such a story there is, and it is as
true as Gospel, it is the truth of Gospel it selfe; But was this a late
Repentance? Answer S. *Cyril, Rogo te frater,* Tell me, Beloved, Thou
that deferrest thy Repentance, doest thou do it upon confidence of
130 these examples? *Non in fine, sed in principio conversus latro,* Thou
deludest thine owne soule; The Theife was not converted at last, but
at first; As soone as God afforded him any Call, he came; And at how
many lights hast thou winked? And to how many Cals hast thou
[Luke   stopped thine eares, that deferrest thy repentance? Christ said to him,
23.43]   *Hodie mecum eris, This day thou shalt be with me in paradise;* when

thou canst finde such another day, looke for such another mercy; A day that cleft the grave-stones of dead men; A day that cleft the Temple it selfe; A day that the Sunne durst not see; A day that saw the soule of God (may we not say so, since that Man was God too)
140 depart from Man; There shall be no more such dayes; and therefore presume not of that voyce, *Hodie,* This day thou shalt be with me, if thou make thy last minute that day, though Christ, to magnifie his mercy, and his glory, and to take away all occasion of absolute despera-tion, did here, under so many disadvantages call, and draw S. *Paul* to him.

But we say no more of that, of the danger of sinning by precedent, and presuming of mercy by example; we passe from our first Con-sideration, From what, to the other, To what, Christ brought this persecutor, this *Saul.* He brought him to that remarkable height, as
150 that the Church celebrates the Conversion of no man but this. Many bloody Executioners were converted to Christ, even in the act of that bloody Execution; Then when they tooke a delight in tearing the bowels of Christians, they were received into the bowels of Christ Jesus, and became Christians. Men that road to Market, and saw an Execution upon the way; Men that opened a window to take ayre, and saw an Execution in the street; The Ecclesiasticall Story abounds with examples of occasionall Convertits, and upon strange occasions; but yet the Church celebrates no Conversion, but this. The Church doth not consider the Martyrs as borne till they die; till the world see
160 how they persevered to the end, shee takes no knowledge of them; Therefore shee cals the dayes of their deaths, *Natalitia,* their birth-dayes; Then she makes account they are borne, when they die. But of S. *Paul* the Church makes her selfe assured the first minute; and there-fore celebrates his Conversion, and none but his. Here was a true Transubstantiation, and a new Sacrament. These few words, *Saul, Saul, why persecutest thou me,* are words of Consecration; After these words, *Saul* was no longer *Saul,* but he was Christ: *Vivit in me Christus,* sayes he, *It is not I that live,* not I that do any thing, *but Christ in me.* It is but a little way that S. *Chrysostome* goes, when he
170 speaks of an inferior Transubstantiation, of a change of affections, and sayes *Agnus ex Lupo,* that here is another manner of Lycanthropy, then when a man is made a Wolfe; for here a Wolfe is made a Lambe,

Quid factus

[Gal. 2.20]

Ex lupo Agnus. Ex vepribus racemus, sayes that Father, A bramble is
made a vine; *Ex zizaniis frumentum,* Cockle and tares become wheat;
Ex pirata gubernator, A Pirat becomes a safe Pilot; *Ex novissimo
primus,* The lees are come to swim on the top, and the last is growne
first; and *ex abortivo perfectus,* He that was borne out of time, hath
not onely the perfection, but the excellency of all his lineaments. S.
Chrysostome goes farther then this, *Ex blasphemo, Os Christi, & lyra*
¹⁸⁰ *spiritus,* He that was the mouth of blasphemy, is become the mouth of
Christ, He that was the instrument of Satan, is now the organ of the
Holy Ghost. He goes very far, when he sayes, *In Cælis homo, in terris
Angelus,* Being yet but upon earth, he is an Angel, and being yet but a
man, he is already in Heaven. Yet S. *Paul* was another manner of
Sacrament, and had another manner of Transubstantiation, then all
this; As he was made *Idem spiritus cum Domino,* The same spirit
with the Lord, so in his very body, he had *Stigmata,* the very marks of

Gal. 6.17

the Lord Jesus. From such a lownesse, raysed to such a height, as that
Origen sayes, many did beleeve, that S. *Paul* had been that Holy Ghost,
¹⁹⁰ which Christ had promised to the world, after his departing from it.

It is but a little way that S. *Ierome* hath carried his commendation
neither, when he cals him *Rugitum leonis,* The roaring of a Lion, if
we consider in how little a forest the roaring of a Lion is determined;
but that he calls him *Rugitum Leonis nostri,* The roaring of our Lion,
of the Lion of the Tribe of *Iuda,* That as far as Christ is heard, S. *Paul*

Idem

is heard too; *Quem quoties lego, non verba mihi videor audire, sed
tonitrua,* Wheresoever I open S. *Pauls* Epistles, I meet not words, but
thunder, and universall thunder, thunder that passes through all the

Theodor.

world. For, *Ejus excæcatio totius orbis illuminatio,* That that was done
²⁰⁰ upon him, wrought upon all the world; he was struck blind, and all
the world saw the better for that. So universall a Priest, (sayes S.
Chrysostome, who loves to be speaking of S. *Paul*) as that he sacrificed,
not sheep and goats, *sed seipsum,* but himselfe; and not onely that,
sed totum mundum, He prepared the whole world, as a sacrifice to
God. He built an Arke, that is, established a Church; and to this day,
receives, not eight, but all into that Arke: And whereas in *Noahs* Ark,
Quem corvum recepit, corvum emisit, If he came in a Raven, he went
out a Raven; S. *Paul,* in his Arke, *Ex milvis facit columbas,* as himself
was, so he transubstantiates all them, and makes them Doves of

²¹⁰ Ravens. Nay, so over-absolutely did he sacrifice himselfe, and his state in this world, for this world, as that he sacrificed his reversion, his future state, the glory and joy of heaven, for his brethren, and chose rather to be *Anathema,* separated from Christ, then they should. I love thee, sayes S. *Chrysostome* to Rome, for many excellencies, many great-nesses; But I love thee so well, sayes he, therefore because S. *Paul* loved thee so well. *Qualem Rosam Roma Christo,* (as he pursues this con-templation) What a fragrant rose shall Rome present Christ with, when he comes to Judgement, in re-delivering to him the body of S. *Paul?* And though he joyne them both together, *Iugati boves Ecclesiæ,*
²²⁰ That S. *Peter* and S. *Paul* were that yoak of oxen that ploughed the whole Church, Though he say of both, *Quot carceres sanctificastis?* How many Prisons have you two consecrated, and made Prisons Churches? *Quot catenas illustrastis?* How many fetters and chains of iron have you two changed into chaines of gold? Yet we may observe a difference in S. *Chrysostomes* expressing of persons so equall to one another, *Quid Petro majus?* sayes he, But, *Quid Paulo par fuit?* What can exceed *Peter,* or what can equall *Paul?* Still be all this far from occasioning any man to presume upon God, because he afforded so abundant mercy to a Persecuter: but still from this, let every faint
²³⁰ soule establish it selfe in a confidence in God; God that would find nothing to except, nothing to quarrell at, in S. *Paul,* will not lie heavy upon thy soule, though thou must say, as he did, *Quorum ego maxi-mus,* That thou art a greater sinner then thou knowest any other man to be.

[1 Tim. 1.15]

We are, in our order proposed at first, devolved now to our second Part; from the person, and in that, what he was found, A vehement persecuter, And then, what he was made, A laborious Apostle, To the Manner, to his Humiliation, *Cecidit super terram, He fell,* and *he fell to the ground,* and *he fell blind,* as by the history, and context appeares.
²⁴⁰ We use to call every declination, of any kind, and in any subject, a falling; for, for our bodies, we say a man is falne sick, And for his state, falne poore, And for his mind, falne mad, And for his conscience, falne desperate; we are borne low, and yet we fall every way lower, so universall is our falling sicknesse. Sin it selfe is but a falling; The irremediable sin of the Angels, The undeterminable sinne of *Adam,* is called but so, *The fall of Adam, The fall of Angels.* And therefore the

2 Part

effectuall visitation of the holy Ghost to man, is called a falling too; we are fallen so low, as that when the holy Ghost is pleased to fetch us againe, and to infuse his grace, he is still said *to fall upon us*. But
250 the fall which we consider in the Text, is not a figurative falling, not into a decay of estate, nor decay of health, nor a spirituall falling into sin, a decay of grace; but it is a medicinall falling, a falling under Gods hand, but such a falling under his hand, as that he takes not off his hand from him that is falne, but throwes him downe therefore that he may raise him. To this posture he brings *Paul,* now, when he was to re-inanimate him with his spirit; rather, to pre-inanimate him; for, indeed, no man hath a soule till he have grace.

Christ, who in his humane nature hath received from the Father all Judgement, and power, and dominion over this world, hath received
260 all this, upon that condition that he shall governe in this manner,
Aske of me, and I shall give thee the Heathen for thine inheritance, sayes the Father; How is he to use them, when he hath them? Thus, *Thou shalt breake them with a rod of iron, and dash them in pieces like a potters vessell.* Now, God meant well to the Nations, in this bruising and breaking of them; God intended not an annihilation of the Nations, but a reformation; for Christ askes the Nations for an Inheritance, not for a triumph; therefore it is intended of his way of governing them; and his way is to bruise and beat them; that is, first to cast them downe, before he can raise them up, first to breake them
270 before he can make them in his fashion. *Novit Dominus vulnerare ad amorem;* The Lord, and onely the Lord knowes how to wound us, out of love; more then that, how to wound us into love; more then all that, to wound us into love, not onely with him that wounds us, but into love with the wound it selfe, with the very affliction that he inflicts upon us; The Lord knowes how to strike us so, as that we shall lay hold upon that hand that strikes us, and kisse that hand that wounds us. *Ad vitam interficit, ad exaltationem prosternit,* sayes the same Father; No man kills his enemy therefore, that his enemy might have a better life in heaven; that is not his end in killing him: It is Gods end; Therefore
280 he brings us to death, that by that gate he might lead us into life everlasting; And he hath not discovered, but made that Northerne passage, to passe by the frozen Sea of calamity, and tribulation, to Paradise, to the heavenly Jerusalem. There are fruits that ripen not, but by frost;

Psal. 2.8

August.

There are natures, (there are scarce any other) that dispose not themselves to God, but by affliction. And as Nature lookes for the season
for ripening, and does not all before, so Grace lookes for the assent of
the soule, and does not perfect the whole worke, till that come. It is
Nature that brings the season, and it is Grace that brings the assent;
but till the season for the fruit, till the assent of the soule come, all is
²⁹⁰ not done.

Therefore God begun in this way with *Saul,* and in this way he led
him all his life. *Tot pertulit mortes, quot vixit dies,* He dyed as many
deaths, as he lived dayes; for so himselfe sayes, *Quotidie morior, I die
daily;* God gave him sucke in blood, and his owne blood was his daily
drink; He catechized him with calamities at first, and calamities were
his daily Sermons, and meditations after; and to authorize the hands
of others upon him, and to accustome him to submit himself to the
hands of others without murmuring, Christ himself strikes the first
blow, and with that, *Cecidit, he fell,* (which was our first considera-
³⁰⁰ tion, in his humiliation) and then, *Cecidit in terram, He fell to the
ground,* which is our next.

I take no farther occasion from this Circumstance, but to arme you
with consolation, how low soever God be pleased to cast you, Though
it be to the earth, yet he does not so much cast you downe, in doing
that, as bring you home. Death is not a banishing of you out of this
world; but it is a visitation of your kindred that lie in the earth; neither
are any nearer of kin to you, then the earth it selfe, and the wormes of
the earth. You heap earth upon your soules, and encumber them with
more and more flesh, by a superfluous and luxuriant diet; You adde
³¹⁰ earth to earth in new purchases, and measure not by Acres, but by
Manors, nor by Manors, but by Shires; And there is a little Quillet, a
little Close, worth all these, A quiet Grave. And therefore, when thou
readest, That God makes thy bed in thy sicknesse, rejoyce in this, not
onely that he makes that bed, where thou dost lie, but that bed where
thou shalt lie; That that God, that made the whole earth, is now
making thy bed in the earth, a quiet grave, where thou shalt sleep in
peace, till the Angels Trumpet wake thee at the Resurrection, to that
Judgement where thy peace shall be made before thou commest, and
writ, and sealed, in the blood of the Lamb.
³²⁰ *Saul* falls to the earth; So farre; But he falls no lower. God brings his
servants to a great lownesse here; but he brings upon no man a per-

Chrysost.
[1 Cor.
15.31]

In terram

verse sense, or a distrustfull suspition of falling lower hereafter; His hand strikes us to the earth, by way of humiliation; But it is not his hand, that strikes us into hell, by way of desperation. Will you tell me, that you have observed and studied Gods way upon you all your life, and out of that can conclude what God meanes to doe with you after this life? That God took away your Parents in your infancy, and left you Orphanes then, That he hath crossed you in all your labours in your calling, ever since, That he hath opened you to dishonours, and
330 calumnies, and mis-interpretations, in things well intended by you, That he hath multiplied sicknesses upon you, and given you thereby an assurance of a miserable, and a short life, of few, and evill dayes, nay, That he hath suffered you to fall into sins, that you your selves have hated, To continue in sins, that you your selves have been weary of, To relapse into sins, that you your selves have repented; And will you conclude out of this, that God had no good purpose upon you, that if ever he had meant to doe you good, he would never have gone thus farre, in heaping of evills upon you? Upon what doest thou ground this? upon thy selfe? Because thou shouldest not deal thus with any
340 man, whom thou mean'st well to? How poore, how narrow, how impious a measure of God, is this, that he must doe, as thou wouldest doe, if thou wert God! God hath not made a week without a Sabbath; no tentation, without an issue; God inflicts no calamity, no cloud, no eclipse, without light, to see ease in it, if the patient will look upon that which God hath done to him, in other cases, or to that which God hath done to others, at other times. *Saul fell to the ground,* but he fell no lower; God brings us to humiliation, but not to desperation.

Cæcus
Iohn 9.39   *He fell; he fell to the ground,* And *he fell blinde;* for so it is evident in the story. Christ had said to the Pharisees, *I came into the world, that*
350 *they which see, might be made blinde;* And the Pharisees ask him, *Have you been able to doe so upon us? Are we blinde?* Here Christ gives them an example; a reall, a literall, an actuall example; *Saul,* a Pharisee, is made blinde. He that will fill a vessell with wine, must take out the water; He that will fill a covetous mans hand with gold, must take out the silver that was there before, sayes S. *Chrysostome.* Christ, who is about to infuse new light into *Saul,* withdrawes that light that was in him before; That light, by which *Saul* thought he saw all before, and thought himselfe a competent Judge, which was the onely

true Religion, and that all others were to be persecuted, even to death,
360 that were not of his way. *Stultus factus est omnis homo à scientia,* sayes
God in the Prophet, Every man that trusts in his owne wit, is a foole.
But *let him become a foole, that he may be wise,* sayes the Apostle;
Let him be so, in his own eyes, and God will give him better eyes,
better light, better understanding. *Saul* was struck blinde, but it was
a blindnesse contracted from light; It was a light that struck him
blinde, as you see in his story. This blindnesse which we speak of,
which is a sober and temperate abstinence from the immoderate study,
and curious knowledges of this world, this holy simplicity of the
soule, is not a darknesse, a dimnesse, a stupidity in the understanding,
370 contracted by living in a corner, it is not an idle retiring into a Monastery, or into a Village, or a Country solitude, it is not a lazy affectation
of ignorance; not darknesse, but a greater light, must make us blinde.

    The sight, and the Contemplation of God, and our present benefits by
him, and our future interest in him, must make us blinde to the world
so, as that we look upon no face, no pleasure, no knowledge, with such
an Affection, such an Ambition, such a Devotion, as upon God, and
the wayes to him. *Saul* had such a blindnesse, as came from light; we
must affect no other simplicity, then arises from the knowledge of
God, and his Religion. And then, *Saul* had such a blindnesse, as that
380 he fell with it. There are birds, that when their eyes are cieled, still
soare up, and up, till they have spent all their strength. Men blinded
with the lights of this world, soare still into higher places, or higher
knowledges, or higher opinions; but the light of heaven humbles us,
and layes flat that soule, which the leaven of this world had puffed and
swelled up. That powerfull light felled *Saul;* but after he was fallen, his
owne sight was restored to him againe; *Ananias* saies to him, *Brother
Saul, receive thy sight.* To those men, who imploy their naturall faculties to the glory of God, and their owne, and others edification, God
shall afford an exaltation of those naturall faculties; In those, who use
390 their learning, or their wealth, or their power, well, God shall increase
that power, and that wealth, and that learning, even in this world.

    You have seene *Sauls* sicknesse, and the exaltation of the disease,
Then when he breathed threatnings, and slaughter, Then when he
went in his triumph; And you have seen his death, The death of the

Ier. 51.17

I Cor. 3.18

[Acts. 9.17]

3 Part

righteous, His humiliation, *He fell to the earth;* And there remaines
yet his Resurrection; The Angel of the great Counsell, Christ Jesus,
with the Trumpet of his owne mouth, rayses him, with that, *Saul,
Saul, why persecutest thou mee?*

Vox   First, he affords him a call, *A voyce. Saul* could not see; Therefore
400 he deales not upon him by visions. He gives a voyce; and a voyce that
he might heare; God speaks often, when we doe not heare; He *heard
it,* and *heard it saying;* Not a voyce only, but a distinct, and intelligible
voyce; and *saying unto him,* that is, appliable to himselfe; and then,
that that the voyce said to him, was, *Saul, Saul, why persecutest thou
me?* We are unequall enemies, Thou seest I am too hard for thee,
Cur tu me? why wilt thou, thou in this weakenesse oppose me? And
then, we might be good friends, Thou seest I offer parly, I offer treaty,
Cur tu me? Why wilt thou oppose me, me that declare such a disposition to be reconciled unto thee? In this so great a disadvantage on
410 thy part, why wilt thou stirre at all? In this so great a peaceablenesse
on my part, why wilt thou stirre against me? *Cur tu me? Why
persecutest thou me?*

        First then, God speaks: For, beloved, we are to consider God, not
as he is in himselfe, but as he works upon us: The first thing that we
can consider in our way to God, is his Word. Our Regeneration is by
Luke 8.11   his Word; that is, by faith, which comes by hearing; *The seed is the
word of God,* sayes Christ himselfe; Even the seed of faith. Carry it
[Psa. 33.9]   higher, the Creation was by the word of God; *Dixit, & facta sunt,* God
spoke, and all things were made. Carry it to the highest of all, to
420 Eternity, the eternall Generation, the eternall Production, the eternall
Procession of the second Person in the Trinity, was so much by the
[Joh. 1.14]   Word, as that he is the Word; *Verbum caro,* It was that *Word,* that
was made *Flesh.* So that God, who cannot enter into bands to us, hath
given us security enough; He hath given us his Word; His written
Word, his Scriptures; His Essentiall Word, his Son. Our Principall,
and Radicall, and Fundamentall security, is his Essentiall Word, his
Son Christ Jesus. But how many millions of generations was this
Word in heaven, and never spoke? The Word, Christ himself, hath
been as long as God hath been: But the uttering of this Word, speak-
Iohn 6.68 430 ing hath been but since the Creation. *Peter* sayes to Christ, *To whom
shall we goe? Thou hast the words of eternall life.* It is not onely, Thou

art the word of eternall life; (Christ is so) But thou hast it; Thou hast
it, where we may come to thee for it; In thy Treasury, in thine Ordinance, in thy Church; Thou hast it, to derive it, to convey it upon us.
Here then is the first step of *Sauls* cure, and of ours, That there was not
onely a word, the Word, Christ himselfe, a Son of God in heaven, but
a Voyce, the word uttered, and preached; Christ manifested in his
Ordinance: *He heard a voyce.*

He heard it. How often does God speake, and nobody heares the   *Audivit*
440 voyce? He speaks in his Canon, in Thunder, and he speaks in our
Canon, in the rumour of warres. He speaks in his musique, in the
harmonious promises of the Gospel, and in our musique, in the temporall blessings of peace, and plenty; And we heare a noyse in his
Judgements, and wee heare a sound in his mercies; but we heare no
voyce, we doe not discern that this noyse, or this sound comes from
any certain person; we do not feele them to be mercies, nor to be
judgements uttered from God, but naturall accidents, casuall occur-
rencies, emergent contingencies, which as an Atheist might think,
would fall out though there were no God, or no commerce, no dealing,
450 no speaking between God and Man. Though *Saul* came not instantly
to a perfect discerning who spoke, yet he saw instantly, it was a Person
above nature, and therefore speakes to him in that phrase of submission, *Quis es Domine? Lord who art thou?* And after, with trembling
and astonishment, (as the Text sayes) *Domine quid me vis facere?*
Lord what wilt thou have me to do? Then we are truliest said to hear,
when we know from whence the voyce comes. Princes are Gods
Trumpet, and the Church is Gods Organ, but Christ Jesus is his voyce.
When he speaks in the Prince, when he speaks in the Church, there
we are bound to heare, and happy if we doe hear. Man hath a natural
460 way to come to God, by the eie, by the creature; So *Visible things* shew   Rom. 1.[20]
the *Invisible God:* But then, God hath super-induced a supernaturall
way, by the eare. For, though hearing be naturall, yet that faith in God
should come by hearing a man preach, is supernatural. God shut up
the naturall way, in *Saul,* Seeing; He struck him blind; But he opened
the super-naturall way, he inabled him to heare, and to heare him.
God would have us beholden to grace, and not to nature, and to come
for our salvation, to his Ordinances, to the preaching of his Word, and
not to any other meanes. Though hee were blinde, even that blind-

nesse, as it was a humiliation, and a diverting of his former glaring
470 lights, was a degree of mercy, of preparative mercy; yet there was a
voyce, which was another degree; And a voyce that he heard, which
was a degree above that; and so farre we are gone; And he heard it,
saying, that is distinctly, and intelligibly, which is our next Circumstance.

Dicentem

He heares him *saying,* that is, He heares him so, as that he knowes
what he sayes, so, as that he understands him; for, he that heares the
word, and understands it not, is subject to that which Christ sayes,

Mat. 13.19

That the wicked one comes, and catches away that that was sowne.
S. *Augustine* puts himselfe earnestly upon the contemplation of the
480 Creation, as *Moses* hath delivered it; he findes it hard to conceive, and

Confes.
L. xi. c. 3

he sayes, *Si esset ante me Moses,* If *Moses* who writ this were here,
Tenerem eum, & per te obsecrarem, I would hold him fast, and beg
of him, for thy sake, O my God, that he would declare this worke of
the Creation more plainly unto me. But then, sayes that blessed Father,
Si Hebræa voce loqueretur, If *Moses* should speake Hebrew to mee,
mine eares might heare the sound, but my minde would not heare the
voyce; I might heare him, but I should not heare what he said. This
was that that distinguished betweene S. *Paul,* and those who were in

Ver. 7
Acts 22.9

his company at this time; S. *Luke* sayes in this Chapter, *That they*
490 *heard the voyce,* and S. *Paul* relating the story againe, after sayes, *They*
heard not the voyce of him that spoke to me; they heard a confused
sound, but they distinguished it not to be the voyce of God, nor dis-

Ver. 28

cerned Gods purpose in it. In the twelfth of *Iohn, there came a voyce*
from Heaven, from God himselfe, *and the people said, It thundred.*
So apt is naturall man to ascribe even Gods immediate and miraculous
actions to naturall causes; apt to rest and determine in Nature, and
leave out God. The Poet chides that weaknesse, (as he cals it) to be
afraid of Gods judgements, or to call naturall accidents judgements;
Quo morbo mentem concusse? timore Deorum, sayes he; he sayes
500 The Conscience may be over-tender, and that such timerous men, are
sick of the feare of God; But it is a blessed disease The feare of God,
and the true way to true health. And though there be a morall constancy that becomes a Christian well, not to bee easily shaked with the
variations and revolutions of this world, yet it becomes him to establish his constancy in this, That God hath a good purpose in that action,

not that God hath no hand in that action; That God will produce good out of it, not that God hath nothing to doe in it. The Magicians themselves were forced to confesse *Digitum Dei,* The finger of God, in a small matter. Never thinke it a weakenesse, to call that a judgement
510 of God, which others determine in Nature; Doe so, so far as works to thy edification, who seest that judgement, though not so far, as to argue, and conclude the finall condemnation of that man upon whom that judgement is fallen. Certainely, we were better call twenty natu-rall accidents judgements of God, then frustrate Gods purpose in any of his powerfull deliverances, by calling it a naturall accident, and suffer the thing to vanish so, and God be left unglorified in it, or his Church unedified by it. Then we heare God, when we understand what he sayes; And therefore, as we are bound to blesse God, that he speakes to us, and heares us speake to him, in a language which wee
520 understand, and not in such a strange language, as that a stranger who should come in and heare it, would thinke the Congregation mad; So also let us blesse him for that holy tendernesse, to be apt to feele his hand in every accident, and to discerne his presence in every thing that befals us. *Saul heard the voyce, saying;* He understood what it said, and by that, found that it was directed *to him,* which is also another step in this last part.

This is an impropriation without sacriledge, and an enclosure of a Common without damage, to make God mine owne, to finde that all that God sayes is spoken to me, and all that Christ suffered was suf-
530 fered for me. And as *Saul* found this voyce at first, to be directed to him, so ever after he bends his eye the same way, and observes the working of God especially upon himselfe; As at the beginning, so in the way too; particularly there, *By the grace of God I am that I am;* and then, *His grace was bestowed on me, And not in vaine;* and againe, *I have laboured more abundantly then all;* And after all, still he consid-ers himselfe, and findes himselfe to be the greatest sinner, *Quorum ego maximus.* It is called a greatnesse of spirit, or constancy, but it is indeed an incorrigible height of pride, when a man will not beleeve that he is meant in a libel, if he be not named in that libel. It is a fearfull obdura-
540 tion, to be Sermon-proofe, or not to take knowledge, that a judgement is denounced against him, because he is not named in the denouncing of that judgement. Is not thy name *Simon Magus,* if thou buy and sell

Exod. 8.19

I Cor. 14.23

Sibi

I Cor.
15.[10]

[1 Tim.
1.15]

spirituall things thy selfe? and is not thy servants name *Gehazi,* if he exact after? Is not thy name *Cain,* if thou rise up against thy brother? And is not thy name *Zacheus,* if thou multiply thy wealth by oppression? Is not thy name *Dinah,* if thou gad abroad, to see who will solicite thee? And is not the name of *Putiphars* Wife upon thee, if thou stay at home and solicite thy servants? Postdate the whole Bible, and whatsoever thou hearest spoken of such, as thou art, before, beleeve
550 all that to be spoken but now, and spoken to thee. This was one happinesse here, that *Saul* found this voyce to be directed to him; And another (which is our last Consideration) is what this voyce said; it said, *Saul, Saul, why persecutest thou me?*

Saul   Here, to make sure of him, God cals him by his name, that hee should not be able to transfer the summons upon any other, or say it was not he. They say that our *Noctambulones,* men that walke in their sleepe, will wake if they be called by their names. To wake *Saul* out of this dreame, (for, to thinke to oppose Christ and his cause, is, in the highest person of the world, of what power or of what counsel soever,
560 but a vertiginous dreame, and a giddy vapour) to wake him, he cals him by his name, to let him know he meanes him; and to wake him
Saul, Saul   throughly, he cals him twice, *Saul,* and *Saul* againe. The great desolation which was to fall upon that land, God intimates, God intermi-
Ier. 22.29   nates, God intonates with such a vehemency, *Terra, terra, terra, Earth, earth, earth heare the word of the Lord.* God should be heard at first, beleeved at first; but such is his abundant goodnesse, as that he ingeminates, multiplies his warnings; And to this whole land he hath said, *Terra, terra, terra,* Earth, earth, earth heare the Word of the Lord; Once in an Invasion, once in a Powder-treason; and againe, and
570 againe in pestilentiall contagions; And to every one of us, he hath said oftner then so, Dust, dust, dust why doest thou lift up thy self against thy Maker? *Saul, Saul why persecutest thou mee?*

Me   Here Christ cals the afflictions of those that are his, in his purpose, his afflictions. Christ will not absolutely verifie his owne words, to his
[Joh. 19.30]   owne ease; He had said before this, upon the Crosse, *Consummatum est, All is finished;* But though all were finished in his Person, he hath a daily passion in his Saints still. This language which the Apostle
2 Cor. 11.29   learnt of Christ here, himselfe practised, and spake after, *Who is weake, and I am not weake? who is offended, and I burne not?* Since

580 Christ does suffer in our sufferings, be this our consolation, Till he be weary, we should not be weary, nor faint, nor murmur under our burdens; and this too, That when he is weary, he will deliver us even for his owne sake; for he, though he cannot suffer paine, may suffer dishonour in our sufferings; therefore attend his leisure.

We end all in this, *Cur tu me? Why doest Thou persecute Me?* Why *Saul* Christ? Put it upon a Nation, (what is any *Saul*, any one man to a Nation?) Put it upon all the Nations of the World, and you shall heare God aske with an indignation, *Quare fremuerunt Gentes?* *Why doe the heathen rage, why do the people imagine a vaine thing?* 590 why will they doe it? what can they get? *He that sitteth in the Heavens shall laugh; The Lord shall have them in derision.* Christ came into the Temple and disputed with the Doctors; but hee did not despise them, he did not laugh at them. When all the Midianites, and all the Amalekites, and all the Children of the East, were in a body against Israel, God did not laugh at them. *Gideon* his Generall, mustered two and thirty thousand against them. God would not imploy so many in the day of Battaile, yet he did not laugh at them, hee did not whip them out of the field, he made the face of an Army, though it were but three hundred. But when God can chuse his way, Hee can call in 600 Nation against Nation, he can cast a dampe upon any Nation, and make them afraid of one another, He can doe an execution upon them by themselves, (I presume you remember those stories in the Bible, where God did proceed by such wayes) or he can sit still in a scorne, and let them melt away of themselves; when he can cast downe *Saul* to the earth, and never appeare in the cause, benight his noone, frustrate his purposes, evacuate his hopes, annihilate him in the height of his glory, *Cur tu me?* why will any *Saul*, any Nation, any World of *Sauls* persecute Christ, any sinner tempt him, who is so much too hard for him?

610 *Cur me?* Why doest thou offer this to me, who being thus much too hard for thee, would yet faine be friends with thee? and therefore came to a parley, to a treaty? for, *verba hæc, non tam arguentis, quam defendentis,* sayes S. *Chrysostome:* These are not so much offensive as defensive words; He would not confound *Saul*, but he would not betray his own honour. To many Nations God hath never spoken; To the Jews he spoke, but suffered them to mistake him; To some whole

Tu me

Psal. 2.1
Ver. 4

Iudg. 6.33

Christian Churches he speaks, but he lets them speake too; he lets
them make their word equall to his; To many of us he hath spoken,
and chidden, but given over before we are cured; As he sayes of
⁶²⁰ Israel, in a manner, That she is not worth his anger, not worth his
punishing, *A people laden with sinnes, why should they any more be*
smitten? Why should I go about to recover them? But if God speake
to thee still, and speake in a mixt voyce, of Correction, and Consolation
too, *Saul, Saul, why persecutest thou me?* Him that receives so little
benefit by thee, and yet is so loath to lose thee, Him that can so easily
spare thee, and yet makes thy soule more precious then his own life,
Him that can resolve thee, scatter thee, annihilate thee with a word,
and yet afford so many words, so many houres conferences, so many
Sermons to reclaime thee, why persecutest Thou Him? Answer this
⁶³⁰ question, with *Sauls* answer to this question, by another question,
Domine quid me vis facere? Lord what wilt thou have me do? Deliver
thy selfe over to the will of God, and God shall deliver thee over, as he
did *Saul* to *Ananias;* provide thee by his Ministery in his Ordinance,
means to rectifie thee, in all dejection of spirit, light to cleare thee in all
perplexities of conscience, in the wayes of thy pilgrimage, and more
and more effectuall seals thereof, at the houre of thy transmigration
into his joy, and thine eternall rest.

Esay 1.4

Number 11.

Preached at White-hall,
March 4. 1624. [1624/5]

MAT. 19.17. *AND HE SAID UNTO HIM, WHY CALLEST THOU ME GOOD? THERE IS NONE GOOD BUT ONE; THAT IS, GOD.*

HAT WHICH God commanded by his Word, to be done at some times (that we should humble our soules by fasting) the same God commands by his Church, to be done now: In the Scriptures you have *Præceptum,* The thing it self, What; In the Church, you have the *Nunc,* The time, When. The Scriptures are Gods Voyce; The Church is his Eccho; a redoubling, a repeating of some particular syllables, and accents of the same voice. And as we harken with some earnestnesse, and some admiration at an Eccho, when perchance we doe not understand the voice that occasioned that Eccho; so doe the ¹⁰ obedient children of God apply themselves to the Eccho of his Church, when perchance otherwise, they would lesse understand the voice of God, in his Scriptures, if that voice were not so redoubled unto them. This fasting then, thus enjoyned by God, for the generall, in his Word, and thus limited to this Time, for the particular, in his Church, is indeed but a continuation of a great Feast: Where, the first course (that which we begin to serve in now) is Manna, food of Angels, plentifull, frequent preaching; but the second course, is the very body and blood of Christ Jesus, shed for us, and given to us, in that blessed Sacrament, of which himselfe makes us worthy receivers at that time. ²⁰ Now, as the end of all bodily eating, is Assimilation, that after all other concoctions, that meat may be made *Idem corpus,* the same body that I am; so the end of all spirituall eating, is Assimilation too, That after all Hearing, and all Receiving, I may be made *Idem spiritus cum Domino,* the same spirit, that my God is: for, though it be good to

223

Heare, good to Receive, good to Meditate, yet, (if we speake effectually, and consummatively) why call we these good? there is nothing
good but One, that is, Assimilation to God; In which perfect and consummative sense, Christ saies to this Man, in this Text, *Why callest
thou me good? there is none good but one, that is God.*

Divisio   30   The words are part of a Dialogue, of a Conference, betweene Christ,
and a man who proposed a question to him; to whom Christ makes
an answer by way of another question, *Why callest thou me good, &c.*
In the words, and by occasion of them, we consider the Text, the Context, and the Pretext: Not as three equall parts of the Building; but the
Context, as the situation and Prospect of the house, The Pretext, as the
Accesse and entrance to the house, And then the Text it selfe, as the
House it selfe, as the body of the building: In a word, In the Text,
the Words; in the Context, the Occasion of the words; In the Pretext,
the Pretence, the purpose, the disposition of him who gave the occasion.

1 Part.   40   We begin with the Context; the situation, the prospect; how it
Context   stands, how it is butted, how it is bounded; to what it relates, with
what it is connected. And in that, we are no farther curious, but onely
to note this, that the Text stands in that Story, where a man comes to
Christ, inquires the way to Heaven, beleeves himselfe to be in that
way already, and (when he heares of nothing, but keeping the Commandements) beleeves himselfe to be far gone in that way; But when
he is told also, that there belongs to it a departing with his Riches, his
beloved Riches, he breakes off the conference, he separates himselfe
from Christ; for, (saies the Story) *This Man had great possessions.*

50 And to this purpose, (to separate us from Christ) the poorest amongst
us, hath great possessions. He that starves, as well as he that surfets,
he that lies in the spitting places, and excrementall corners of the
streets, as well as he that sits upon carpets, in the Region of perfumes,
he that is ground and trod to durt, with obloquie, and contempt, as
well as he that is built up every day, a story and story higher with
additions of Honour, Every man hath some such possessions as possesse him, some such affections as weigh downe Christ Jesus, and
separate him from Him, rather then from those affections, those
possessions. Scarce any sinner but comes sometimes to Christ, in the
60 language of the man in this Text, *Good Master what good thing shall
I do, that I may have eternall life?* And if Christ would go no farther

with such men, but to say to the Adulterer, Do not thou give thy
money to usury; no more to the penurious Usurer, but, Do not thou
wast thy selfe in superfluous and expensive feasting; If Christ would
proceed no farther, but to say to the needy person, that had no money,
Do not thou buy preferment; or to the ambitious person that soares
up after all, Do not thou forsake thy selfe, deject thy selfe, undervalue
thy selfe, In all these cases, the Adulterer and the Usurer, The needy
and the ambitious man, would all say with the man in the Text, *All*
⁷⁰ *these things have we done from our youth*. But when Christ proceeds
to a *Vade, & vende,* to depart with their possessions, that which they
possesse, that which possesses them, this changes the case.

There are some sins so rooted, so riveted in men, so incorporated,
so consubstantiated in the soule, by habituall custome, as that those
sins have contracted the nature of Ancient possessions. As men call
Manours by their names, so sins have taken names from men, and
from places; *Simon Magus* gave the name to a sin, and so did *Gehazi,*
and *Sodom* did so: There are sins that run in Names, in Families, in
Blood; Hereditary sins, entailed sins; and men do almost prove their
⁸⁰ Gentry by those sins, and are scarce beleeved to be rightly borne, if
they have not those sins; These are great possessions, and men do
much more easily part with Christ, then with these sins. But then
there are lesse sins, light sins, vanities; and yet even these come to
possesse us, and separate us from Christ. How many men neglect this
ordinary meanes of their Salvation, the comming to these Exercises,
not because their undoing lyes on it, or their discountenancing; but
meerely out of levity, of vanity, of nothing; they know not what to do
else, and yet do not this. You heare of one man that was drowned in a
vessell of Wine; but how many thousands in ordinary water? And
⁹⁰ he was no more drowned in that precious liquor, then they in that
common water. A gad of steele does no more choake a man, then a
feather, then a haire; Men perish with whispering sins, nay with silent
sins, sins that never tell the conscience they are sins, as often as with
crying sins: And in hell there shall meet as many men, that never
thought what was sin, as that spent all their thoughts in the compassing
of sin; as many, who in a slack inconsideration, never cast a thought
upon that place, as that by searing their conscience, overcame the
sense and feare of that place. Great sins are great possessions; but

levities and vanities possesse us too; and men had rather part with
¹⁰⁰ Christ, then with any possessions; which is all we will note out of this
first part, The Context, the situation, and prospect of the house, the
coherence and connexion of the Text.

The second part, is the pretext; that is the pretense, the purpose, the
disposition of him that moved this question to Christ, and occasioned
this answer. Upon which we make this stop, because it hath been
variously apprehended by the Expositors; for some think he came in
an humble disposition to learn of Christ, and others think he came in
a Pharisaicall confidence in himself, with which *Epiphanius* first, and
then S. *Ierome* charge him. But in such doubtful cases in other mens
¹¹⁰ actions, when it appeares not evidently, whether it were well, or ill
done, where the balance is eaven, always put you in your charity, and
that will turne the scale the best way. Things which are in themselves,
but mis-interpretable, doe not you presently mis-interpret, you allow
some graines to your gold, before you call it light: allow some infirmities to any man, before you call him ill. For this man in the Text,
venit, sayes this Euangelist, he came to Christ, he came of himselfe.
S. *Peter* himself came not so, S. *Peter* came not, till his brother *Andrew*
brought him: none of the twelve Apostles came to Christ so, they came
not, till Christ called them: Here, we heare of no calling, no inviting,
¹²⁰ no mention of any motion towards him, no intimation of any intimation to him, and yet he came. Blessed are they that come to Christ
Jesus, before any collaterall respects draw them, before the Laws compell them, before calamities drive them to him: He onely comes hither,
that comes voluntarily, and is glad he is here; He that comes so, as that
he had rather he were away, is not here. *Venit,* sayes our Euangelist,

of this man: And then, sayes S. *Mark,* handling the same story, *Venit
procurrens, He came running. Nicodemus* came not so, *Nicodemus*
durst not avow his comming; and therefore he came creeping, and he
came softly, and he came seldome, and he came by night.
¹³⁰   Blessed are they who make haste to Christ, and publish their zeale
to the encouragement of others: For, let no man promise himself a
religious constancy in the time of his triall, that doth not his part in
establishing the religious constancy of other men. Of all proofes,
Demonstration is the powerfullest: when I have just reason to think
my superiours would have it thus, this is Musique to my soul; When

I heare them say they would have it thus, this is Rhetorique to my soule; When I see their Laws enjoyne it to be thus, this is Logick to my soul; but when I see them actually, really, clearely, constantly do thus, this is a Demonstration to my soule, and Demonstration is the
¹⁴⁰ powerfullest proofe: The eloquence of inferiours is in words, the eloquence of superiours is in action.

He came to Christ; hee ran to him; and when he was come, as S. *Mark* relates it, *He fell upon his knees to Christ.* He stood not then Pharisaically upon his own legs, his own merits, though he had been a diligent observer of the Commandements before. Blessed are they, who bring the testimony of a former zeale to Gods service, and yet make no excuse for their present, or future slacknesse; The benefit of our former goodnesse is, that that enables us to be the better still: For, as all example is powerfull upon us, so our own example most of all;
¹⁵⁰ in this case we are most immediately bound by our selves; still to be so good, as we our selves have been before: There was a time when I was nothing; but there shall never be any time, when I shall be nothing; and therefore I am most to respect the future. The good services that a man hath done to God by pen, or sword, are wings, and they exalt him if he would go forward; but they are waights and depresse him, and aggravate his condemnation, if his presumption upon the merit of those former services, retard him for the future. This man had done well, but he stood not upon that; he kneeled to Christ, and he said to him, *Magister bone, Good master.* He was no ignorant man,
¹⁶⁰ and yet he acknowledged that he had somewhat more to learn of Christ, then he knew yet. Blessed are they that inanimate all their knowledge, consummate all in Christ Jesus. The University is a Paradise, Rivers of knowledge are there, Arts and Sciences flow from thence. Counsell Tables are *Horti conclusi,* (as it is said in the Canticles) *Gardens that are walled in,* and they are *Fontes signati, Wells that are sealed up;* bottomlesse depths of unsearchable Counsels there. But those *Aquæ quietudinum,* which the Prophet speaks of, *The waters of rest,* they flow *à magistro bono,* from this good master, and flow into him again; All knowledge that begins not, and ends not with
¹⁷⁰ his glory, is but a giddy, but a vertiginous circle, but an elaborate and exquisite ignorance. He would learn of him, and what? *Quid boni faciam,* What good thing shall I do? Still he refers to the future; to do

[Cant. 4.12]

as well as to have done: and still to be doing so. Blessed are they that bring their knowledge into practise; and blessed again, that crown their former practise with future perseverance.

This was his disposition that came; His, though he were a yong man; (for so he is said to be, in the 22. ver.) and yong men are not often so forward in such wayes. I remember one of the Panegyriques celebrates and magnifies one of the Romane Emperors for this, That
[180] he would marry when he was yong; that he would so soon confine and limit his pleasures, so soon determine his affections in one person. When a yong man comes to Christ, Christ receives him with an extraordinary welcome; well intimated in that, that that disciple whom Christ loved most, came to him yongest. He came though he were yong; and he came though he were *Vnus è principibus,* (for so
Luke 18.18   he is qualified in S. *Luke*) A principall man, a great man; as we translate it, *One of the Rulers:* for so he is a reall and a personall answer
[Joh. 7.48]   and instance to that scornfull question of the Pharisees, *Nunquid è principibus, Do any of the Rulers,* any great men, *beleeve in Christ?*
I Cor. 1.26   [190] It is true that the Holy Ghost doth say, *Non multi nobiles,* few noble men come to heaven. Not out of *Panigorola,* the Bishop of Asti, his reason, *Pauci quia pauci,* There cannot come many noble men to heaven, because there are not many upon earth; for many times there are many. In calme and peaceable times, the large favours of indulgent Princes, in active and stirring times, the merit and the fortune of forward men, do often enlarge the number. But such is often the corrupt inordinatenesse of greatnesse, that it only carries them so much beyond other men, but not so much nearer to God; It only sets men at a farther, not God at a nearer distance to them; but because they are
I King.   [200] come to be called gods, they think they have no farther to go to God,
20.28   but to themselves. But *God is the God of the Mountains, as well as of the Valleyes:* Great and small are equall, and equally nothing in his
Esay 40.12   sight: for, when all the world is *In pugillo, in Gods fist,* (as the Prophet speaks) who can say then, This is the Ant, this is the Elephant? Our conversation should be in heaven; and if we look upon the men of this world, as from heaven, as if we looked upon this world it self, from thence, the hils would be no hils, but all one flat and equall plain; so are all men, one kinde of dust. Records of nobility are only from the book of Life, and your preferment is your interest in a place

²¹⁰ at the right hand of God. But yet, when those men whom God hath
raised in this world, take him in their armes, and raise him too, though
God cannot be exalted above himself, yet he is content to call this a
raising, and to thank them for it. Therefore when this man, a man of
this rank came to him, *Iesus beheld him,* sayes the Gospell, *and he
loved him, and he said, One thing thou lackest;* God knows, he lacked
many things; but because he had that one, zeale to him, Christ doth
not reproach to him his other defects: God pardons great men many
errors, for that one good affection, a generall zeale to his glory, and
his cause.

Mar. 10.21

²²⁰ His disposition then, (though it have seemed suspitious, and ques-
tionable to some) was so good, as that it hath afforded us these good
considerations. If it were not so good as these circumstances promise,
yet it affords us another as good consideration, That how bad soever
it were, Christ Jesus refused him not, when he came to him. When he
enquired of Christ after salvation, Christ doth not say, There is no
salvation for thee, thou Viper, thou Hypocrite, thou Pharisee, I have
locked an iron doore of predestination between salvation and thee;
when he enquired of him, what he should do to be sure of heaven,
Christ doth not say, There is no such art, no such way, no such assur-
²³⁰ ance here; but you must look into the eternall decree of Election first,
and see whether that stand for you or no: But Christ teaches him the
true method of this art: for, when he sayes to him, *Why callest thou
me good? There is none good but God,* he only directs him in the way
to that end, which he did indeed, or pretended to seek. And this direction of his, this method is our third part; In which, (having already
seen in the first, the Context) the situation and prospect of the house,
that is, the coherence and occasion of the words, And in the second,
(the Pretext) the accesse and entrance to the house, that is, the pretense
and purpose of him that occasioned the words, you may now be pleased
²⁴⁰ to look farther into the house it self, and to see how that is built; that is,
by what method Christ builds up, and edifies this new disciple of his;
which is the principall scope and intention of the Text, and that, to
which all the rest did somewhat necessarily prepare the way.

Our Saviour Christ thus undertaking the farther rectifying of this
thus disposed disciple, by a faire method leads him to the true end;
Good ends, and by good wayes, consummate goodnesse. Now Christs

3. Part

answer to this man is diversly read: We reade it, (as you have heard) *why callest thou me good?* The vulgat Edition in the Romane Church, reads it thus, *Quid me interrogas de bono? Why dost thou question*
250 *me concerning goodnesse?* Which is true? That which answers the Originall; and it can admit no question, but that ours doth so. But yet, *Origen,* to be sure, in his eighth Tractate upon this Gospell, reads it both wayes: And S. *Augustine,* in his 63. Chap. of the second book *De consensu Evangelistarum,* thinks it may very well be beleeved, that Christ did say both: That when this man called him *good master,* Christ said then, *There was none good but God;* and that when this man asked him, *what good thing he should do,* then Christ said, *Why dost thou ask me, me whom thou thinkest to be but a meere man, what is goodnesse? There is none good but God;* If thou look to un-
260 derstand goodnesse from man, thou must look out such a man as is God too. So that this was Christs method, by these holy insinuations, by these approaches, and degrees, to bring this man to a knowledge,

August.

that he was very God, and so the Messias that was expected. *Nihil est falsitas, nisi cum esse putatur, quod non est:* All error consists in this, that we take things to be lesse or more, other then they are. Christ was pleased to redeem this man from this error, and bring him to know truly what he was, that he was God. Christ therefore doth not rebuke this man, by any denying that he himself was good; for Christ doth

[Joh. 10.11]

assume that addition to himself, *I am the good Shepheard.* Neither
270 doth God forbid, that those good parts which are in men, should be celebrated with condigne praise. We see that God, as soon as he saw that any thing was good, he said so, he uttered it, he declared it, first of the Light, and then of other creatures: God would be no author, no example of smothering the due praise of good actions. For, surely that man hath no zeale to goodnesse in himself, that affords no praise to goodnesse in other men.

But Christs purpose was also, that this praise, this recognition, this testimony of his goodnesse, might be carried higher, and referred to the only true author of it, to God. So the Priests and the Elders come to

Judith 15.8

280 *Iudith,* and they say to her, Thou art the exaltation of Jerusalem, thou art the great glory of Israel, thou art the rejoycing of our Nation, thou hast done all these things by thy hand; And all this was true of *Iudith,* and due to *Iudith;* and such recognitions, and such acclamations God

requires of such people, as have received such benefits by such instruments: For as there is Treason, and petty-treason, so there is Sacriledge,
and petty-sacriledge; and petty-sacriledge is to rob Princes and great
persons of their just praise. But then, as we must confer this upon
them, so must they, and we, and all transfer all upon God: for so *Iudith*
proceeds there, with her Priests and Elders, Begin unto my God, with
²⁹⁰ Timbrels, sing unto the Lord with Cymbals, exalt him, and call upon
his name. So likewise *Elizabeth* magnifies the blessed Virgin *Mary*,
Blessed art thou amongst women: And this was true of her, and due   Luke 1.42
to her; and she takes it to her self, when she sayes there, *From hence-*
forth all Generations shall call me blessed; but first, she had carried
it higher, to the highest, *My soule doth magnifie the Lord, and my*
spirit doth rejoyce in God my Saviour. In a word, Christ forbids not
this man to call him good, but he directs him to know in what capacity that attribute of goodnesse belonged to him, as he was God:
That when this man beleeved before that Christ was good, and learnt
³⁰⁰ from him now, that none was good but God, he might by a farther
concoction, a farther rumination, a farther meditation of this, come
in due time to know that Christ was God; And this was his Method.
Now this leads us into two rich and fragrant fields; this sets us
upon the two Hemispheares of the world; the Western Hemispheare,
the land of Gold, and Treasure, and the Eastern Hemispheare, the
land of Spices and Perfumes; for this puts us upon both these considerations, first, that nothing is Essentially good, but God, (and
there is the land of Gold, centricall Gold, viscerall Gold, gremiall
Gold, Gold in the Matrice and womb of Gold, that is, Essentiall
³¹⁰ goodnesse in God himself) and then upon this consideration too,
That this Essentiall goodnesse of God is so diffusive, so spreading,
as that there is nothing in the world, that doth not participate of
that goodnesse; and there is the land of Spices and Perfumes, the
dilatation of Gods goodnesse. So that now both these propositions are
true, First, That there is nothing in this world good, and then this
also, That there is nothing ill: As, amongst the Fathers, it is in a good
sense, as truly said, *Deus non est Ens, Deus non est substantia,* God is
no Essence, God is no substance, (for feare of imprisoning God in a
predicament) as it is said by others of the Fathers, that there is no
³²⁰ other Essence, no other Substance but God.

First then, there is nothing good but God: neither can I conceive any thing in God, that concerns me so much as his goodnesse; for, by that I know him, and for that I love him. I know him by that, for, as *Damascen* sayes, *primarium Dei nomen, Bonitas;* Gods first name, that is, the first way by which God notified himself to man, was Goodness; for out of his goodnesse he made him. His name of Jehova we admire with a reverence; but we cannot expresse that name: not only not in the signification of it, but not confidently, not assuredly in the sound thereof; we are not sure that we should call it Jehova; 330 not sure that any man did call it Jehova a hundred yeares agoe. But,

August.   *ineffabili dulcedine teneor cum audio, Bonus Dominus;* I am, not transported with astonishment, as at his name of Jehova, but replenished with all sweetnesse, established with all soundnesse, when I hear of my God in that name, my good God. By that I know him, and for that I love him: For, the object of my understanding is truth; but the object of my love, my affection, my desire, is goodnesse. If my understanding be defective, in many cases, faith will supply it; if I beleeve it, I am as well satisfied, as if I knew it; but nothing supplies, nor fills, nor satisfies the desire of man, on this side of God; 340 Every man hath something to love, and desire, till he determine it in God; because God only hath *Imminuibilem bonitatem,* as they render *Dyonisius* the Areopagite, an inexhaustible goodnesse; a sea that no land can suck in, a land that no sea can swallow up, a forrest that no fire can waste, a fire that no water can quench. He is so good, good-

Aug.   nesse so, as that he is *Causa bonorum, & quæ in nos, & quæ in nobis,* the cause of all good either received by us, or conceived in us; of all, either prepared externally for us, or produced internally in us. In a

Idem   word, he is *Bonum cætera bona colorans, & amabilia reddens,* it is his goodnesse, that gilds and enamels all the good persons, or good actions 350 in this world. There is none good but God; and *quale bonum ille,* sayes that Father, what kinde of goodnesse God is, this doth sufficiently declare, *Quòd nulli ab eo recedenti bene sit,* That no man that ever went from him, went by good way, or came to good end; There is none good but God; there is centricall, viscerall, gremiall gold, goodnesse in the roote, in the tree of goodnesse, God.

[Mat. 7.17]   Now, *Arbor bona, bonos fructus,* sayes Christ; *If the tree be good, the fruit is good too.* The tree is God; What are the fruits of this tree?

What are the off-spring of God? S. *Ambrose* tells us, *Angeli & homines, & virtutes eorum;* Angels and men, and the good parts, and
360 good actions of Angels and men, are the fruit of this tree, they grow from God. Angels, as they fell, *Adam,* as he fell, the sins of Angels and men, are not fruits of this tree, they grow not radically, not primarily from God. *Nihil in se habet Deus semi-plenum,* saies *Damascen:* God is no half-god, no fragmentary God; he is an intire God, and not made of remnants; not good only so, as that he hath no roome for ill in himself, but good so too, as that he hath no roome for any ill will towards any man; no mans damnation, no mans sin, growes radically from this tree. When God had made all, sayes *Tertullian,* he blessed all; *Maledicere non norat, quia nec malefacere,* saies he:
370 God could no more meane ill, then doe ill; God can no more make me sin, then sin himself. It is the foole that saies, There is no God, saies *David;* And it is the other foole, sayes S. *Basil,* that saies, God produces any ill; *par precii scelus, quia negat Deum bonum;* It is as impiously done, to deny God to be intirely good, as to deny him to be God. For, we see the *Manichees,* and the *Marcionites,* and such other Heretiques in the Primitive Church, would rather admit, and constitute two Gods, a good God, and a bad God, then be drawn to think, that he that was the good God indeed, could produce any ill of himself, or meane any ill to any man, that had done none.
380   And therefore even from *Plato* himself, some Christians might learn more moderation in expressing themselves in this point; *Plato* says, *Creavit quia bonus,* therefore did God create us, that he might be good to us; and then he addes, *Bono nunquam inest invidia,* certainly that God, that made us out of his goodnesse, does not now envy us that goodnesse which he hath communicated to us; certainly he does not wish us worse, that so he might more justly damne us, and therefore compell us, by any positive decree, to sin, to justifie his desire of damning us: Much lesse did this good God hate us, or meane ill to us, before he made us, and made us only therefore, that he might have
390 glory in our destruction. There is nothing good but God, there is nothing but goodnesse in God.

How abusively then doe men call the things of this world, Goods? They may as well call them (so they do in their hearts) Gods, as Goods; *for there is none good but God.* But how much more abu-

sively do they force the word, that call them *Bona quia beant,* Goods because they make us good, blessed, happy? In which sense, *Seneca* uses the word shrewdly, *Insolens malum beata uxor,* a good wife, a blessed wife, sayes he, that is, a wife that brings a great estate, is an insolent mischiefe. If we doe but cast our eye upon that title in the
⁴⁰⁰ Law, *Bonorum,* and *De bonis,* of Goods, we shall easily see, what poor things they make shift to cal Goods. And if we consider (if it deserve a consideration) how great a difference their Lawyers make (*Baldus* makes that, and others with him) between *Bonorum possessio,* and *possessio bonorum,* that one should amount to a right and propriety in the goods, and the other but to a sequestration of such goods, we may easily see, that they can scarce tell what to call, or where to place such Goods. Health, and strength, and stature, and comelinesse, must be called Goods, though but of the body; The body it self is in the substance it self, but dust; these are but the accidents of that dust,
⁴¹⁰ and yet they must be Goods. Land, and Money, and honor must be called Goods, though but of fortune; Fortune her self, is but such an Idol, as that S. *Augustine* was ashamed ever to have named her in his works, and therefore repents it in his Retractations; her self is but

[1 Cor. 8.4] an Idol, and an *Idol is nothing,* these, but the accidents of that nothing, and yet they must be Goods. Are they such Goods, as make him necessarily good that hath them? Or such, as no man can be good, that is without them? How many men make themselves miserable, because they want these Goods? And how many men have been made miserable by others, because they had them? Except thou see the face
⁴²⁰ of God upon all thy money, as well as the face of the King, the hand of God to all thy Patents, as well as the hand of the King, Gods *Amen,* as well as the Kings *fiat,* to all thy creations, all these reach not to the title of Goods, for *there is none good but God.*

Nothing in this world; not if thou couldst have it all; carry it higher, to the highest, to heaven; heaven it self were not good, without God. For, in the Schoole, very many and very great men, have thought and taught, That the humane nature of Christ, though united Hypostatically to the Divine Nature, was not meerly by that Union, impeccable, but might have sinned, if besides that Union, God had not
⁴³⁰ infused, and super-induced other graces, of which other graces, the Beatificall vision, the present sight of the face and Essence of God,

was one: Because, (say they) Christ had from his Conception, in his Humane Nature, that Beatificall Vision of God, which we shall have in the state of Glory, therefore he could not sin. This Beatificall Vision, say they, which Christ had here, and which, (as they suppose, and not improbably, in the problematicall way of the Schoole) God, of his absolute power, might have with-held, and yet the Hypostaticall Union have remained perfect; (for, say they, the two Natures, Humane and Divine, might have been so united, and yet the Humane
440 not have so seen the Divine) This Beatificall Vision, this sight of God, was the Cause, or Seal, or Consummation of Christs Perfection, and impeccability in his Humane Nature. Much more is this Beatificall Vision, this sight of God in Heaven, the Cause or Consummation of all the joyes and glory which we shall receive in that place: for howsoever they dispute, whether that kinde of Blessednesse consist in seeing God, *formaliter,* or *causaliter,* that is, whether I shall see all things in God, as in a glasse, in which the species of all things are, or whether I shall see all things, by God, as by the benefit of a light, which shall discover all things to me, yet they all agree, (though they
450 differ *de modo,* of the manner, how) that howsoever it be, the substance of the Blessednesse is in this, that I shall see God: *Blessed are the pure in heart,* sayes Christ, *for they shall see God;* If they should not see God, they were not blessed. And therefore they who place children that die unbaptised, in a roome, where though they feele no torment, yet they shall never see God, durst never call that roome a part of heaven, but of hell rather; Though there be no torment, yet, if they see not God, it is hell. There is nothing good in this life, nothing in the next, without God, that is, without sight and fruition of the face, and presence of God; which is that, which S. *Augustine* intends,
460 when he sayes, *Secutio Dei est appetitus Beatitatis, consecutio Beatitas;* our looking towards God, is the way to Blessednesse, but Blessednesse it self is only the sight of God himself.

That therefore thou maist begin thy heaven here, put thy self in the sight of God, put God in thy sight, in every particular action. We cannot come to the body of the Sun, but we can use the light of the Sun many waies: we cannot come to God himself here, but yet here we can see him by many manifestations: so many, as that S. *Augustine,* in his 20. Chapt. *De moribus Ecclesiæ Catholicæ,* hath collected

aright places of Scripture, where every one of our senses is called a
470 Seeing; there is a *Gustate & videte,* and *audite,* and *palpate; tasting,*
and *hearing,* and *feeling,* and all, to this purpose, are called *seeing;*
In all our senses, in our faculties, we may see God if we will: God sees
us at midnight; he sees us, then, when we had rather he looked off. If
we see him so, it is a blessed interview. How would he that were come
abroad at mid-night, to doe a mischiefe, sneak away, if he saw the
watch? what a damp must it necessarily cast upon any sinner, in the
nearest approach to his sin, if he can see God? See him before thou
sinnest; then he looks lovingly: After the sin, remember how fain
Adam would have hid himself from God: He that goes one step out
480 of Gods sight, is loath to come into it againe: If you will sit at the right
hand of God hereafter, you must walk with God here; So *Abraham,*
so *Enoch walked with God, and God took him.* God knowes, God
takes not every man that dies: God sayes to the rich secure man, *Foole,*
this night they shall fetch away thy soule; but he does not tell him
who. That then you be no strangers to God then, see him now; and
remember, that his last judgement is expressed in that word, *Nescio*
vos, I know you not; not to be known by God, is damnation; and God
knows no man there, with whom he was not acquainted here. There
is none good but God; the fruition of that God, is in seeing him; The
490 way to see him there, is to look towards him here. And so we have
gone as far as the first of our two propositions carried us, That in this
world there is nothing good.

The other that remains, is, That there is nothing ill; that this goodnesse of God is so spread over all, (all actions, all persons) as that
there is nothing ill. *Seneca,* whom *Tertullian* calls still *Senecam*
nostram, our *Seneca,* that is, that Christian *Seneca,* as though he had
read that of S. *Paul,* (between whom and him, it hath been thought,
there passed Epistles) *Quid habes, quod non accepisti? what hast*
thou, that thou hast not received from God? and meant to say more
500 then that, sayes *quid non dedit?* what is there, that were good for thee,
that God hath not given thee? And he, whom they call so often
Platonem Hebræorum, the Jews *Plato,* that is, *Philo Iudæus,* sayes well,
Nihil boni sterile creavit Deus; God hath made nothing, in which he
hath not imprinted, and from which he hath not produced some good:
He follows it so far, (and justly) as to say, that God does good, where

Gen. 5.24

[Luke
12.20]

[Luke
13.25]

[1 Cor. 4.7]

that good does no good: He takes his examples from Gods raining in
the Sea; that rain does no good in the Sea: And from Gods producing
fresh springs in the desart Land, where, not only no beasts come to
drink, but where the very salt tide overflows the fresh spring. He
510 might have added an example from Paradise, that God would plant
such a garden, for so few houres; that God would provide man such
a dwelling, when he knew he would not dwell a day in it. And he
might have added an example from the Light too; That God would
create light, and say it was good, then when it could be good for
nothing, for there was nothing made to see it, nor to be seen by it: so
forward, so early was God, in diffusing his goodnesse. Of every particular thing, God said *it was good,* and of all together, that *it was*   [Gen. 1.31]
very good; there was, there is nothing ill. For, when it is ordinarily
inquired in the Schoole, whether any thing be essentially good, it is
520 safely answered there, that if by essentially we mean independantly,
so good as that it can subsist of it self, without dependance upon, or
relation to any other thing, so there is nothing essentially good: But if
by essentially good, we mean that whose essence, and beeing is good,
so every thing is essentially good. And therefore when the *Manichees*
pressed S. *Augustine* with that, *Vnde malum?* If there be not an ill
God, as wel as a good, *unde malum,* from whom, or from whence
proceed all that ill that is in the world? S. *Augustine* saies, *Vnde
malum? Quid malum?* From whence comes evill? Why, what is
there, that you can call evill? I know no such thing; so that, if there
530 be such a God, that God hath no creature. For, as poisons conduce to
Physick, and discord to Musick, so those two kinds of evill, into which
we contract all others, are of good use, that is, *malum pœnæ,* the evill
of punishment, affliction, adversity, and *malum culpæ,* even sin it selfe,
from which, the punishment flowes.

Be pleased to stop a little, upon each of these. First, *malum pœnæ,*
affliction, poverty, sicknesse, imprisonment, banishment, and such, are
not evill. The blood of Christ Jesus only is my cordiall; that restores
me, repaires me; but affliction is my Physick; that purges, that cleanses
me. *Hostiliter se opponit medicus,* saies *Tertullian,* The Physitian
540 comes in like an enemy, with a knife to launce, with fire to cauterize,
but *opponit se morbo,* he is but an enemy to the disease, he means the
patient no harm; no more does God to me, in all his medicinall cor-

rections. But how if these afflictions hang long upon me? If they do so,

that is *Ægrotantium animarum diæta;* God enters into another course of Physick, and finds it better for me to spend my disease by a diet; and long sicknesses are such diets: God will recover my soul by a consumption of the body, and establish everlasting health, by long sicknesse. Howsoever, let Gods corrections go as high as they can go in this world, *Etsi novum videtur, quod dicere volo,* saies *Origen, dicam*
550 *tamen;* Though it be strange that I will say, I wil say it, *Etiam bonitas Dei est, qui dicitur furor ejus;* That which we cal the anger of God,

the wrath of God, the fury of God, is the goodnesse of God. *Correct me not O Lord, in thy wrath,* saies *David;* but, rather then leave me uncorrected, correct me any way. We call God, Just, and we call him

Mercifull, according to our present taste of God, and use of God, *Cum unicam habeat affectionem Deus, nempe bonitatem,* when as God hath but one affection in himself, that is, goodnesse, nor but one purpose upon us, that is, to doe us good.

So then, this which we call *Malum pœnæ,* Affliction, Adversity, is
560 not evill; That which occasions this, *Malum culpæ,* sin it self, is not evill; not evill so, as that it should make us incapable of this diffusive goodnesse of God. You know, I presume, in what sense we say in the Schoole, *Malum nihil,* and *Peccatum nihil,* that evill is nothing, sin is nothing; that is, it hath no reality, it is no created substance, it is but a privation, as a shadow is, as sicknesse is; so it is nothing. It is wittily argued by *Boethius,* God can do all things; God cannot sin; Therefore sin is nothing. But it is strongly argued by S. *Augustin,* If there be any thing naturally evill, it must necessarily be contrary to that which is naturally good; and that is God. Now *Contraria æqualia,* saies he;
570 whatsoever things are contrary to one another, are equall to one another; so, if we make any thing naturally evill, we shall slide into the Manichees error, to make an Evill God. So farre doth the Schoole follow this, as that there, one Archbishop of Canterbury, out of another, that is, *Bradwardin* out of *Anselme,* pronounces it *Hæreticum esse dicere, Malum esse aliquid,* To say that any thing is naturally evill, is an heresie.

But if I cannot finde a foundation for my comfort, in this subtilty of the Schoole, That sin is nothing, (no such thing as was created or induced by God, much lesse forced upon me by him, in any coactive

⁵⁸⁰ Decree) yet I can raise a second step for my consolation in this, that be sin what it will in the nature thereof, yet my sin shall conduce and cooperate to my good. So *Ioseph* saies to his Brethren, *You thought* Gen. 50.20 *evill against me, but God meant it unto good:* which is not onely good to *Ioseph,* who was no partaker in the evill, but good even to them, who meant nothing but evill. And therefore, as *Origen* said, *Etsi novum,* Though it be strangely said, yet I say it, That Gods anger is good; so saies S. *Augustine, Audeo dicere,* Though it be boldly said, yet I must say it, *Vtile esse cadere in aliquod manifestum peccatum,* Many sinners would never have beene saved, if they had not com- ⁵⁹⁰ mitted some greater sin at last, then before; for, the punishment of that sin, hath brought them to a remorse of all their other sins formerly neglected. If neither of these will serve my turne, neither that sin is nothing in it selfe, and therefore not put upon me by God, nor that my sin, having occasioned my repentance, hath done me good, and estab-lished me in a better state with God, then I was in before that sin, yet this shall fully rectifie me, and assure my consolation, that in a pious sense I may say, Christ Jesus is the sinner, and not I. For, though in the two and twentieth Session of the Councell of Basil, that proposition were condemned as scandalous, in the mouth of a Bishop of Nazareth, ⁶⁰⁰ *Augustinus de Roma, Christus quotidie peccat,* That Christ does sin every day, yet *Gregory Nazianzen* expresses the same intention, in equivalent termes, when he saies, *Quamdiu inobediens ego, tamdiu, quantum ad me attinet, inobediens Christus:* As long as I sin, for so much as concernes me, me, who am incorporated in Christ, me, who by my true repentance have discharged my selfe upon Christ, Christ is the sinner, even in the sight, and justice of his Father, and not I.

And as this consideration, That the goodnesse of God, in Christ, is thus spread upon all persons, and all actions, takes me off from my aptnesse to mis-interpret other mens actions, not to be hasty to call ⁶¹⁰ indifferent things, sins, not to call hardnesse of accesse in great Persons, pride, not to call sociablenesse of conversation in women, prostitution, not to call accommodation of Civill businesses in States, prevarication, or dereliction and abandoning of God, and toleration of Religion; as it takes me off from this mis-interpreting of others; so, for my selfe, it puts me upon an ability, to chide, and yet to cheare my soule, with those words of *David, O my Soule, why art thou so sad? why art thou so dis-* [Psa. 42.11] *quieted within me?* Since sin is nothing, no such thing as is forced upon thee by God, by which thy damnation should be inevitable, or thy reconciliation impossible, since of what nature soever sin be in it

620 selfe, thy sins being truly repented, have advanced, and emproved thy state in the favour of God, since thy sin, being by that repentance discharged upon Christ, Christ is now the sinner, and not thou, *O my Soule, why art thou so sad? why art thou disquieted within me?* And this consideration of Gods goodnesse, thus derived upon me, and made mine in Christ, ratifies and establishes such a holy confidence in me, as that all the morall constancy in the world, is but a bulrush, to this bulwark; and therefore, we end all, with that historicall, but yet usefull note, That that Duke of Burgundy, who was sirnamed *Carolus Audax,* Charles the Bold, was Son to that Duke, who was sirnamed

630 *Bonus,* The Good Duke; A Good one produced a Bold one: True

Prov. 28.1   confidence proceeds onely out of true Goodnesse: for, *The wicked shall flye, when no man pursueth, but the righteous are bold as a Lion.* This constancy, and this confidence, and upon this ground, Holy courage in a holy feare of him, Almighty God infuse and imprint in you all, for his Son Christ Jesus sake. And to this glorious Son of God, &c.

Number 12.

The First Sermon Preached to King Charles, at Saint James: 3°. April. 1625.

PSALME 11.3. *IF THE FOUNDATIONS BE DESTROYED, WHAT CAN THE RIGHTEOUS DOE?*

WEE ARE still in the season of *Mortification;* in *Lent:* But wee search no longer for *Texts* of *Mortification;* The Almightie hand of *God* hath shed and spred a *Text* of *Mortification* over all the land. The last *Sabboth* day, was his *Sabboth* who entred then into his everlasting *Rest;* Be this our *Sabboth,* to enter into a holy and thankfull acknowledgement of that *Rest,* which *God* affords us, in continuing to us our *Foundations;* for, *If foundations be destroyed, what can the righteous doe?*

I scarse know any word in the Word of *God,* in which the *Originall* [10] is more ambiguous, and consequently the *Translations* more various, and therfore, necessarily also, the *Expositions* more divers, then in these words. There is one thing, in which all agree, that is, the *Argument,* and *purpose,* and *scope* of the *Psalme;* And then, in what sense, the words of the *Text* may conduce to the scope of the *Psalme,* wee rest in this Translation, which our Church hath accepted and authorized, and which agrees with the first Translation knowen to us, by way of Exposition, that is the *Chalde Paraphrase, If Foundations bee destroyed, what can the righteous doe?*

The Church of *God* ever delighted herselfe in a holy officiousnesse [20] in the Commemoration of *Martyrs:* Almost all their solemne, and extraordinarie Meetings, and Congregations, in the Primitive Church, were for that, for the honourable Commemoration of Martyrs: And for that, they came soone to institute and appoynt certaine *Liturgies,* certaine *Offices* (as they called them) certaine *Services* in the Church,

which should have reference to that, to the Commemoration of *Martyrs;* as wee have in our Booke of Common Prayer, certaine *Services* for *Marriage,* for *Buriall,* and for such other holy Celebrations; And in the Office and Service of a *Martyr,* the Church did use this *Psalme;* This *Psalme,* which is in generall, a Protestation of *David,*
30 That though hee were so vehemently pursued by *Saul,* as that all that wished him well, sayd to his Soule, *Flie as a Bird to the Mountaine,* as it is in the first verse; Though hee saw, *That the wicked had bent their Bowes, and made ready their Arrowes, upon the string, that they might privily shoot at the upright in heart,* as it is in the second verse: Though he take it almost as granted, that *Foundations are destroyed,* (*And then, what can the righteous doe?*) as it is in the third verse which is our *Text,* yet in this distresse he findes what to doe. For as hee begunne in the first verse, *In thee Lord, put I my trust:* So after he had passed the enumeration of his dangers, in the second and third
40 verses, in the fourth he pursues it as he begun, *The Lord is in his holy Temple, the Lords Throane is in Heaven.* And in the fifth hee fixes it thus, *The Lord tryeth the Righteous,* (he may suffer much to be done for their triall) *but the wicked, and him that loveth violence, his soule hateth.* This then is the *Syllogisme,* this is the *Argumentation* of the righteous Man; In Collaterall things, in Circumstantiall things, in things that are not fundamentall, a righteous Man, a constant Man should not bee shaked at all, not at all Scandalized; Thats true; But then, (in a second place) sometimes it comes to that, *That Foundations are destroyd, and what can the Righteous doe then?* Why even then,
50 this is a question, not of desperation, that nothing can bee done, but of Consultation with God, what should be done. I know, sayes *David,* I should not be, and thou knowest, O God, I have not beene mov'd with ordinary trialls; not though my Friends have dis-avowed mee, and bid *mee flye to the Mountaine as a Bird,* not though mine enemies prepare, and *prepare Arrowes,* and shoote, and *shoote privily,* (bestowe their labour, and their cost, and their witts, to ruine mee) yet these have not moov'd mee, because I had fixed my selfe upon certaine *Foundations,* Confidences, and Assurances of Deliverance from thee. But if, O Lord, I see these foundations destroyed, if thou put mee into
60 mine Enemies hand, if thou make them thy Sword, if their furie draw that Sword, and then, thy Almightie Arme, sinewed even with thine

owne indignation, strike with that sword, what can I, how righteous soever I were, doe? So then, for the *Explication,* and *Application* of these words, there will need no more, but to spread them by way of *Paraphrase* upon these three considerations: First, That the righteous is bolde as a *Lyon,* not easily shaked; But then, *Foundations* themselves may bee destroyed, and so hee may bee shaked; If hee bee, yet hee knowes what to doe, or where to aske Counsell, for these are not wordes of *Desperation,* but of *Consultation, If Foundations bee de-* 70 *stroyed, &c.*

Divisio

First then, wee fixe our selves upon this consideration, that the Prophet in proposing this thus, *If Foundations bee destroyed,* intimates pregnantly, that except there bee danger of destroying *Foundations,* it is the part of the righteous Man, the godly man to bee quiet. *Studie to bee quiet,* sayes the *Apostle; Studie,* that is an action of the Minde; and then, *Operam detis,* sayes the *Vulgate Edition, Labour to bee quiet,* and *Labour* is an action of the bodie: Indeed it is the proper businesse of the *Minde* and *Bodie* too, of *Thoughts* and *Actions* too, to bee quiet: And yet, alas, how many breake their sleepe in the night, 80 about things that disquiet them in the day too, and trouble themselves in the day, about things that disquiet them all night too? Wee disquiet our selves too much, in beeing over tender, over sensible of imaginarie injuries. *Transeant iniuriæ,* sayes the Morall man; *Let many injuries passe over;* for, *Plærasque non accipit, qui nescit; Hee that knowes not of an injurie, or takes no knowledge of it, for the most part, hath no injurie. Qui inquirunt, quid in se dictum est,* sayes hee, They that are too inquisitive, what other men say of them, they disquiet themselves; for that which others would but *whisper,* they *publish.* And therefore that which hee addes there, for *Morall,* and *Civill* matters, holds in a 90 good proportion, in things of a more *Divine* Nature, in such parts of the religious worship and service of *God,* as concerne not *Foundations, Non expedit omnia videre, non omnia audire;* we must not too jealously suspect, not too bitterly condemne, not too peremptorily conclude, that what soever is not done, as wee would have it done, or as wee have seene it done in former times, is not well done: for there is a large Latitude, and, by necessitie of Circumstances, much may bee admitted, and yet no *Foundations destroyed;* and till *Foundations bee destroyed, the righteous should bee quiet.*

1. *Part*

1 Thess. 4.11

Seneca

Now this should not prepare, this should not incline any man, to
100 such an indifferencie, as that it should bee all one to him, what became
of all things; all one, whether wee had one, or two, or tenne, or no
Religion; or that hee should not bee awake, and active, and diligent,
in assisting trueth, and resisting all approaches of Errour. For, *God*
hath sayd of all, into whose hand hee hath committed power, *You are
Gods.* Now, they are not *Gods,* but *Idoles,* if, as the *Prophet* sayes,

Psal. 115.6   *They have Eyes and see not, Eares and heare not, Hands and strike
not;* nay, (as hee addes there) *if they have Noses and smell not;* if they
smell not out a mischievous practise, before it come to execution. For,

Iob 34.21   *Gods eyes are upon the wayes of man, and hee sees all his goings:*
110 Those, who are in the number of them, of whome *God* hath said, they
are *Gods,* must have their eyes upon the *wayes* of men, and not upon
their *Ends* onely; upon the *pathes* of mischiefe, and not upon the *bed*
of mischiefe onely; upon the *Actors* of mischiefe, and not upon the *Act*
onely. *Gods eye sees our wayes,* sayes *David* too; that is, hee can see

Iere. 32.19   them, when hee will; but there is more in the other *Prophet, Gods
eyes are open upon all our wayes;* always open, and hee cannot chuse
but see: So that, a wilfull shutting of the eye, a winking, a connivencie,

Abac. 1.13   is not an assimilation to *God.* And then, *Gods eyes are purer, then to
beholde evill, and they cannot looke upon iniquitie:* So that in an in-
120 differencie, whether Times, or Persons bee good or badd, there is not

Hebr. 4.13   this assimilation to *God.* Againe, *All things are naked and open to the
eyes of God:* So that in the disguising, and palliating, and extenuating
the faults of men, there is not this assimilation to *God.* Thus farre they
falsifie *Gods* Word, who hath sayd, *They are Gods;* for *they are Idoles,
and not Gods, if they have eyes, and see not.* So is it also in the con-

Psal. 94.9   sideration of the *Eare* too: for, as *David* sayes, *Shall not hee that
planted the Eare, heare?* So wee may say, Shall hee upon whom *God*
hath planted an Eare, bee deafe? *Gods* eares are so open, so tender, so

Psal. 39.12   sensible of any motion, as that *David* formes one Prayer thus, *Auribus
130 percipe lachrimas meas,* O Lord, heare my teares; hee puts the office
of the *Eye* too, upon the *Eare.* And then, if the *Magistrate* stop his
Eares with *Wooll,* (with staple bribes, profitable bribes) and with
Cyvet in his wooll, (perfumes of pleasure and preferment in his
bribes) hee falsifies *Gods* Word, who hath said, they are *Gods,* for
they are Idoles, and not Gods, if they have eares, and heare not. And

so it is also of the hand too; In all that *Iob* suffered, he sayes no more, but that *the Hand of God had touched him;* but *touched* him, in respect of that hee could have done: for, when *Iob* sayes to men, *Why persecute you mee, as God?* hee meanes, as *God* could doe, so vehe-
140 mently, so ruinously, so destructively, so irreparably. There is no *phrase* oftner in the *Scriptures,* then that *God* delivered his people, in the *hand* of *Moses,* and the *hand* of *David,* and the *hand* of the *Prophets:* all their Ministeriall office is called the *Hand:* and therfore, as *David* prayes to *God, That hee would pull his hand out of his bosome, and strike:* so must wee ever exhort the *Magistrate,* That hee would plucke his hand out of his pocket, and forget what is there, and execute the Lawes committed to him. For, as wee, at last, shall commend our Spirits, into the hands of *God, God* hath commended our Spirits, not onely our civill peace, but our Religion too, into the *hand*
150 of the *Magistrate.* And therefore, when the *Apostle* sayes, *Studie to bee quiet,* it is not quiet in the blindnesse of the *Eye,* nor quiet in the *Deafenesse* of the *Eare,* nor quiet in the *Lamenesse* of the *Hand;* the just discharge of the dueties of our severall places, is no *disquieting* to any man. But when *private* men will spend all their thoughts upon their *Superiours* actions, this must necessarily disquiet them; for they are off of their owne *Center,* and they are *extra Sphæram Activitatis,* out of their owne *Distance,* and *Compasse,* and they cannot possibly discerne the *Ende,* to which their *Superiours* goe. And to such a jealous man, when his jealousie is not a tendernesse towards his owne actions,
160 which is a holy and a wholesome jealousie, but a suspition of his *Superiours* actions, to this Man, every *Wheele* is a *Drumme,* and every *Drumme* a *Thunder,* and every *Thunder-clapp* a dissolution of the whole frame of the World: If there fall a broken tyle from the house, hee thinkes *Foundations are destroyed;* if a crazie woman, or a disobedient childe, or a needie servant fall from our *Religion,* from our *Church,* hee thinkes the whole *Church* must necessarily fall, when all this while there are no *Foundations destroyed;* and *till foundations bee destroyed, the righteous should be quiet.*

Hence have wee just occasion, first to *condole* amongst *our selves,*
170 who, for matters of *Foundations* professe one and the same *Religion,* and then to complaine of our *Adversaries,* who are of another. First, that amongst our selves, for matters not *Doctrinall,* or if *Doctrinall,*

Iob 19.22

yet not *Fundamentall*, onely because wee are sub-divided in divers *Names*, there should bee such Exasperations, such Exacerbations, such Vociferations, such Ejulations, such Defamations of one another, as if all *Foundations* were destroyed. Who would not tremble, to heare those *Infernall* words, spoken by men, to men, of one and the same Religion fundamentally, as *Indiabolificata, Perdiabolificata,* and *Super-diabolificata,* that the *Devill,* and all the *Devills* in Hell, and worse

180 then the *Devill* is in their *Doctrine,* and in their *Divinitie,* when, *God* in heaven knowes, if their owne uncharitablenesse did not exclude him, there were roome enough for the *Holy Ghost,* on both, and on either side, in those *Fundamentall* things, which are unanimely professed by both: And yet every *Mart,* wee see more Bookes written by these men against one another, then by them both, for *Christ.*

But yet though this *Torrent* of uncharitablenesse amongst them, bee too violent, yet it is within some bankes; though it bee a *Sea,* and too tempestuous, it is limitted within some bounds; The poynts are certaine, knowen, limitted, and doe not grow upon us every yeare, and

190 day. But the uncharitablenesse of the *Church* of *Rome* towards us all, is not a *Torrent,* nor it is not a *Sea,* but a *generall Flood,* an universall *Deluge,* that swallowes all the world, but that *Church,* and *Church-yard,* that *Towne,* and *Suburbes,* themselves, and those that depend upon them; and will not allowe possibilitie of Salvation to the whole *Arke,* the whole *Christian Church,* but to one *Cabin* in that *Arke,* the *Church* of *Rome;* and then denie us this Salvation, not for any *Positive* Errour, that ever they charged us to affirme; not because wee affirme any thing, that they denie, but because wee denie some things, which they in their afternoone are come to affirme.

200 If they were *Iusti,* Righteous, right and just dealing men, they would not raise such dustes, and then blind mens eyes with this dust of their own raysing, in things that concerne no *Foundations.* It is true, that all *Heresie* does concerne *Foundations:* there is no *Heresie* to bee called little: Great *Heresies* proceeded from things, in apparance, small at first, and seem'd to looke but towards small matters. There were great *Heresies,* that were but *Verball, Heresies* in some Word. That great Storme, that shaked the *State,* and the *Church,* in the *Councell* of *Ephesus,* and came to Factions, and Commotions in the *Secular* part, and to Exautorations, and Excommunications amongst

²¹⁰ the *Bishops*, so farre, as that the *Emperour* came to declare both sides
to bee *Heretiques;* All this was for an Errour in a *Word,* in the word
Deipara, whether the *Blessed Virgine Marie* were to bee called the
Mother of God, or no. There have beene *Verball Heresies,* and *Heresies* that were but *Syllabicall;* little *Præpositions* made *Heresies;* not
onely *State-præpositions,* Precedencies, and Prerogatives of *Church*
above *Church,* occasioned great *Schismes,* but *Literall Præpositions,*
Præpositions in *Grammar,* occasioned great *Heresies.* That great
Heresie of the *Acephali,* against which *Damascene* bendes himselfe in
his Booke, *De Natura Composita,* was grounded in the *Præposition,*
²²⁰ *In;* They would confesse *Ex,* but not *In,* That *Christ* was made *of* two
Natures, but that hee did not consist *in* two Natures. And wee all
know, what differences have beene raysed in the *Church,* in that one
poynt of the *Sacrament,* by these three Prepositions, *Trans, Con,* and
Sub. There have beene great *Heresies,* but *Verball,* but *Syllabicall;*
and as great, but *Litterall;* The greatest *Heresie* that ever was, that of
the *Arrians,* was but in one Letter. So then, in *Heresie,* there is nothing
to bee called little, nothing to bee suffered. It was excellently sayde of
Heretiques, (though by one, who, though not then declared, was then
an *Heretique* in his heart,) *Condolere Hereticis crimen est;* It is a   *Nestorius*
²³⁰ fault, not onely to bee too indulgent to an *Heretique,* but to bee too
compassionate of an *Heretique,* too sorrie for an *Heretique.* It is a
fault to say, Alas, let him alone, hee is but an *Heretique;* but, to say,
Alas, hope well of him, till you bee better sure, that hee is an Heretique,
is charitably spoken. *God* knowes, the sharpe and sowre Name of
Heretique, was too soone let loose, and too fast spread in many places
of the world. Wee see, that in some of the first *Catalogues,* that were
made of *Heretiques,* men were Registred for *Heretiques,* that had but
expounded a place of *Scripture,* otherwise then that place had beene
formerly expounded, though there were no harme, in that newe Ex-
²⁴⁰ position. And then, when once that infamous Name of *Heretique*
was fastened upon a man, nothing was too heavie for, any thing was
beleeved of that man. And from thence it is, without question, that
wee finde so many so absurd, so senselesse Opinions imputed to those
men, who were then called *Heretiques,* as could not, in trueth, with
any possibilitie, fall into the imagination or fancie of any man, much
lesse bee *Doctrinally,* or *Dogmatically* delivered. And then, upon this,

there issued *Lawes,* from particular *States,* against particular *Here-sies,* that troubled those *States* then, as namely, against the *Arrians,* or *Macedonians,* and such; and in a short time, these *Lawes* came to
²⁵⁰ bee extended, to all such *Opinions,* as the passion of succeeding times, called *Heresie.* And at last, the *Romane Church* having constituted that *Monopolie,* That Shee onely should declare what should bee *Heresie,* and having declared that to bee *Heresie,* which opposed, or retarded the dignitie of *that Church,* now they call in *Brachium Spir-ituale,* All those Sentences of *Fathers,* or *Councells* that mention *Heresie,* and they call in *Brachium Sæculare,* all those *Lawes* which punish *Heresie,* and whereas these *Fathers,* and *Councells,* and *States,* intended by *Heresie,* Opinions that destroyed *Foundations,* they bend all these against every poynt, which may endammage, not the *Church*
²⁶⁰ of *God,* but the *Church* of *Rome;* nor the *Church* of *Rome,* but the *Court* of *Rome;* nor the *Court* of *Rome,* but the *Kitchin* of *Rome;* not for the *Heart,* but for the *Bellie;* not the *Religion,* but the *Policie;* not the *Altar,* but the *Exchequer* of *Rome.*

But the Righteous lookes to *Foundations,* before hee will be scan-dalized himselfe, or condemne another. When they call Saint *Peter* their first *Pope,* and being remembred, how hee denied his *Master,* say then, that was but an Acte of *Infirmitie,* not of *Infidelitie,* and there were no *Foundations* destroyed in that; wee presse not that evi-dence against *Saint Peter,* wee forbeare, and wee are quiet. When
²⁷⁰ wee charge some of *Saint Peters* imaginary Successors, some of their *Popes,* with actuall, and personall *Sacrificing* to *Idoles,* some with *subscribing* to formall *Heresies,* with their owne hand, many with so enormous an ill life, as that their owne Authors will say, that for many yeares together, there lived not one *Pope,* of whose Salvation, any hope could bee conceived; and they answere to all this, that all these were but *Personall* faults, and destroyed no *Foundations;* wee can bee content to bury their faultes with their persons, and wee are quiet. When wee remember them, how many of the *Fathers* excused *officious Lyes,* and thought some kinde of *Lying* to bee no *Sinne,*
²⁸⁰ how very many of them hearded in the *heresie* of the *Millenarians,* That the *Saints* of *God* should enjoy a thousand yeares of temporall felicity in this world, after their *Resurrection,* before they ascended into Heaven; And that they say to all this, The *Fathers* said these

things before the *Church* had decreed any thing to the contrary, and till that, it was lawfull for any man to say, or thinke what hee would, wee do not load the memory of those blessed *Fathers* with any heavier pressings, but wee are quiet. Yet wee cannot chuse but tell them, that tell us this, that they have taken a hard way, to make that saying true, that all things are growen deare in our times; for they have
290 made *Salvation* deare; Threescore yeares agoe, a man might have beene sav'd at halfe the price hee can now: Threescore yeares agoe, he might have beene saved for beleeving the *Apostles Creed;* now it will cost him the *Trent Creed* too. Evermore they will presse for all, and yeeld nothing; and there is indeed their *Specification,* there's their *Character,* that's their *Catholique,* their *Vniversall;* To *have all;* As, in *Athanasius* his time, when the *Emperour* pressed him to affoord the *Arrians* one *Church* in *Alexandria,* where hee was *Bishop,* and hee asked but one *Church* in *Antioch,* where the *Arrians* prevayled, not doubting but hee should draw more to the true *Church* in *An-*
300 *tioch,* then they should corrupt in *Alexandria,* yet this would not bee granted; It would not be granted at *Rome,* if we should aske a *Church* for a *Church.* In a word, wee charge them with *uncharitablenesse,* (and *Charitie* is without all Controversie, a *Foundation* of *Religion*) that they will so peremptorily exclude us from Heaven, for matters that doe not appertaine to *Foundations.* For, if they will call all *Foundations,* that that *Church hath,* or *doth,* or *shall* decree, wee must learne our *Catechisme* upon our *Death-bedd,* and inquire for the Articles of our Faith, when wee are going out of the world, for they may have decreed something that Morning. No one *Author* of
310 theirs denied *Pope Ioane,* till they discerned the *Consequence,* That by confessing a *Woman Pope,* they should disparage that *Succession* of *Bishops,* which they pretend, And this *Succession* must bee *Foundation.* No Author of our side denied *Saint Peters* beeing at *Rome,* till wee discerned the *Consequence,* That upon his *personall* being there, they grounded a *Primacie* in that *Sea,* And this *Primacie* must bee *Foundation.* Much might bee admitted in cases of *Indifferencie,* even in the *Nature of the things,* Much in cases of *Necessitie,* for the *importance of Circumstances,* much in cases of *Conveniency,* for the suppling of boysterous, and for the becalming of tempestuous
320 humours; but when every thing must be called *Foundation,* we shall

never knowe where to stop, where to consist. If wee should beleeve their *Sacrificium incruentum*, their unbloody Sacrifice in the *Masse*, if wee did not beleeve their *Sacrificium Cruentum* too, that there was a power in that *Church*, to sacrifice the Blood of *Kings*, wee should bee sayde to bee defective in a *fundamentall Article*. If wee should admitt their *Metaphysiques*, their transcendent *Transubstantiation*, and admitt their *Chimiques*, their *Purgatorie* Fires, and their *Mythologie*, and *Poetrie*, their apparitions of *Soules* and *Spirits*, they would binde us to their *Mathematiques* too, and they would not let us bee
330 saved, except wee would reforme our *Almanackes* to their *tenne dayes*, and reforme our *Clockes* to their *foure and twentie:* for who can tell when there is an ende of *Articles of Faith*, in an *Arbitrarie*, and in an *Occasionall Religion?* When then this *Prophet* says, *If Foundations bee destroyed, what can the righteous doe*, hee meanes, that till that, the righteous should bee *quiet:* Except it were in *fundamentall Articles* of Faith, our selves should not bee so bitter towards one another, our Adversarie should not bee so uncharitable against us all. And farther wee need not extend this first Consideration.

2. *Part* The second is, to Survay some such *Foundations*, as fall within the
340 frayltie, and suspition, and possibilitie of this Text, that they may bee destroyed: for when the Prophet sayes, *If they bee*, they may bee. Now *Fundamentum proprie de ædificijs dicitur*, sayes the *Lawe:* when wee speake of *Foundations*, wee intend a *house:* and heere, wee extend this *House* to foure Considerations; for in foure *Houses* have every one of us a dwelling. For, first, *Ecclesia Domus*, the *Church* is a *House*, it is *Gods house;* and in that House, wee are *of the house-*
Hebr. 3.5 *holde of the faithfull*, if (as it is testified of *Moses*) *wee bee faithfull in all his House, as Servants*. You see there is a faithfulnesse required in every man, in *all the house of God*, not in any one roome; a dis-
350 position required to doe good to the whole *Church* of *God* every where, and not onely at *home*. Secondly, *Respublica Domus*, The *Commonwealth*, the *State*, the *Kingdome* is a *House;* and this is that which is called so often, *Domus Israel, The house of Israel*, the State, the Government of the *Iewes:* And in this *House*, God dwells, as well as in the other; In the *State*, as well as in the *Church:* For, these
Psa. 132.13 words, *The Lord hath chosen Sion, hee hath desired it for a habitation*, are spoken of the whole Bodie, *Church*, and *State*. Thirdly,

there is *Domus Habitationis, Domus quæ Domicilium,* a House to
dwell in, and to dwell with, a *Family:* and in this House *God* dwells
360 too; for, as *David* sayes of the *Building,* wee may say of the *Dwelling,
Except the Lord build the House, they labour in vaine:* So except
the Lord dwell in the House, it is a desolate Habitation. And then
lastly, there is *Domus quæ Dominus,* a house which is the *Master* of
the *House;* for as every Man is a little World, so every man is his
owne House, and dwels in himselfe: And in this *House God* dwells
too; for the *Apostle* seemes so much to delight himselfe in that *Metaphore,* as that hee repeats it almost in all his *Epistles, Habitat in nobis,*
That the Holy Ghost dwells in us. Now, of all these foure *Houses,*
that *house* which hath no walles, but is spread over the face of the
370 whole Earth, the *Church,* And that *House,* which with us, hath no
other walls, but the *Sea,* the *State,* the *Kingdome,* And that *house*
which is walled with *drie Earth,* our dwelling house, our family, and
this *house* which is wall'd with *wet Earth,* this loame of flesh, our
selfe, Of all these foure houses, those three, of which, and in which
we are, and this fourth, which wee our selfe are, *God* is the *Foundation,* and so *foundations* cannot be destroyed; But, as, though the
common foundation of all buildings bee the *Earth,* yet wee make
particular foundations for particular buildings, of Stone, or Brick,
or Piles, as the Soyle requires; so shall wee also heere consider such
380 particular Foundations of these foure houses, as may fall within the
frailtie, and suspition, within the possibilitie, and danger of the Text,
of being *destroyed.*

Of the first *House* then, which is the *Church,* the foundation is
*Christ, Other foundation can no man lay, then that which is layd,
which is Iesus Christ. Non propterea dicimus,* sayes Saint *Augustine,*
Wee doe not say that our *Church* is *Catholique* therefore, because
Optatus sayes so, and because *Ambrose* sayes so, (and yet *Optatus,*
and *Ambrose,* the *Fathers,* are good Witnesses) neither do we say
it, (sayes he) *Quia Collegarum nostrorum Conciliis prædicta est,*
390 Because some *Synodes* and *Councells* of men of our owne Religion
have said it is *Catholique* (And yet a *Harmony of Confessions* is good
Evidence,) *Nec quia tanta fiunt in ea mirabilia,* sayes hee, wee call
it not *Catholique,* because so many *Myracles* are wrought in it, (for
wee oppose *Gods* many miraculous Deliverances of this *State* and

Psal. 127.1

*Ecclesia
Domus*
1 Cor. 3.11
De unita

Eccles. C. 16

Church, to all their *imaginary miracles* of *Rome*) *Non ideo mani-festatur Catholica,* sayes still that *Father,* All this does not make our Church *Catholique,* nay, *non manifestatur,* all this does not declare it to bee *Catholique,* all these are no infallible marks thereof, but onely this one, sayes hee, *Quia ipse Dominus Iesus, &c.* because the *Lord* 400 *Iesus* himselfe is the *Foundation* of this Church. But may not this be subject to reasoning, to various Disputation, Whether wee have that

De Moribus foundation, or no? It may; but that will goe farre in the clearing
Eccles. Cat. thereof, which the same Father sayes in another *Booke, Nihil in Ec-*
C. 25 *clesia catholica salubrius fit, quam ut Rationem præcedat Autoritas:* Nothing is safer for the finding of the *Catholique* Church, then to preferre *Authoritie* before my *Reason,* to submit and capivate my *Reason* to *Authoritie.* This the *Romane Church* pretends to embrace; but *Apishly;* like an *Ape,* it kills with embracing, for it evacuates the right *Authoritie;* The *Authority* that they obtrude, is the *Decretals* 410 of their owne *Bishops,* The *authoritie,* which *Saint Augustine* liter-ally and expressely declares himselfe to meane, is the *authoritie* of the *Scriptures.*

    Christ then, that is, the *Doctrine of Christ,* is the *foundation* of this
2 Chro. 3.3 first *House,* the *Church. Hæc sunt fundamenta quæ jecit Salomon,* sayes the *vulgate Edition,* These are the *foundations* that *Salomon* layde; and then our *Translation* hath it, *These are the things in which Salomon was instructed;* One calls it *Foundations,* the other *Instruc-tions;* All's one; The *Instructions* of *Christ,* the *Doctrine* of *Christ,* the *Word,* the *Scriptures* of *Christ,* are the *Foundation* of this *House.*
Ephes. 2.20 420 For, when the Apostle sayes, *Christ Iesus himselfe is the chiefe corner Stone,* yet hee addes there, *Yee are built upon the Prophets and Apos-tles:* for the *Prophets* and *Apostles,* had their part in the *foundation;* in the *laying,* though not in the *beeing* of the *Foundation. The wall*
Apoc. 21.14 *of the citie,* sayes Saint *Iohn, had twelve Foundations, and in them, the Names of the twelve Apostles:* But still, in that place, they are *Apostles of the Lambe,* still they have relation to *Christ:* For, they, who by inspiration of the *Holy Ghost,* writt of *Christ,* and so made up the Bodie of the Scriptures, have their parts too, in this *Founda-tion.* Besides these, it is sayd, in the building of the *Materiall Temple,*
1 Reg. 5.17 430 *The King commaunded, and they brought great Stones, and costly Stones, and hewed Stones, to lay the foundations of the House:* The

care of the *King,* the labours of men conduce to the *foundation.* And besides this, in that place of the *Revelation,* The *foundation* of the Wall, is sayde to bee *garnished with all manner of precious stones; Garnished,* but not *made* of that kinde of precious stones. So then *Salomons* hewed Stones, and costly stones, may, in a faire accommodation, bee understood to bee the *Determinations,* and *Resolutions, Canons,* and *Decrees* of generall *Councels:* And Saint *Iohns* garnishment of precious stones, may, in a faire accommodation, bee understood to bee the Learned and Laborious, the zealous and the pious *Commentaries* and *Expositions* of the *Fathers;* For *Councells* and *Fathers* assist the *Foundation;* But the *foundation* it selfe is Christ himselfe in his *Word;* his *Scriptures.* And then, certainely they love the *House* best, that love the *foundation* best: not they, that impute to the *Scriptures* such an *Obscuritie,* as should make them *in-intelligible* to us, or such a defect as should make them *insufficient* in themselves. To denie us the use of *Scriptures* in our vulgar Translations, and yet to denie us the use of them, in the *Originall* Tongues too, To tell us we must not trie *Controversies* by our *English,* or our *Latine Bibles,* nor by the *Hebrew Bibles* neither, To put such a Majestie upon the *Scriptures,* as that a Lay man may not touch them, and yet to put such a diminution upon them, as that the writings of men shall bee equall to them; this is a wrinching, a shrinking, a sinking, an undermining, a destroying of *Foundations,* of the *foundation* of this first *House,* which is the *Church,* the *Scriptures.*

.Enter wee now into a Survay of the second *House,* The *State,* the *Kingdome,* the *Common-wealth;* and of this *House,* the *foundation* is the *Law.* And therefore Saint *Hierome* referres this Text, in a litterall and primary signification to that, to the *Law:* for so, in his *Commentaries* upon the *Psalmes,* he translates this Text, *Si dissipatæ Leges,* Hee makes the evacuating of the *Law,* this destroying of *foundations. Lex communis Reipub. sponsio,* says the *Law* it selfe: The *Law* is the mutuall, the reciprocall Suretie betweene the *State* and the *Subject.* The *Lawe* is my *Suretie* to the *State,* that I shall pay my Obedience, And the *Lawe* is the States *Suretie* to mee, that I shall enjoy my Protection. And therefore, therein did the *Iewes* justly exalt themselves above all other Nations, That *God was come so much nearer to them then to other Nations, by how much they had*

Respub.
Domus

[Deut. 4.7 and 8]

Lawes and Ordinances more righteous then other Nations had. Now,
470 as it is sayd of the *Foundations* of the other *House,* the *Temple, The King commaunded in the laying thereof,* the *King* had his hand in the *Church,* so is it also in this *House,* the *State,* the *Common-wealth,* the *King* hath his hand *in,* and *upon* the *foundation* here also, which is the *Lawe:* so farre, as that every *forbearing* of a *Lawe,* is not an *Evacuating* of the *Law;* every *Pardon,* whether a *Post-pardon,* by way of mercy, after a Lawe is broken, or a *Præ-pardon,* by way of *Dispensation,* in wisedome before a Lawe bee broken, is not a *Destroying of this foundation.* For, when such things as these are done, *Non astu Mentientis, sed affectu compatientis,* not upon colourable disguises, 480 nor private respects, but truely for the *Generall good,* all these *Pardons,* and *Dispensations* conduce and concurre to the *Office,* and contract the *Nature* of the *Foundation* it selfe, which is, that the whole Bodie may bee the better supported. But where there is an inducing of a *super-Soveraigne,* and a *super-Supremacie,* and a *Sea* above our *foure Seas,* and a *Horne* above our *Head,* and a *forraine Power* above our *Native* and *naturall Power,* where there are dogmaticall, Positive Assertions, that men borne of us, and living with us, and by us, are yet none of us, no *Subjects,* owe no *Allegeance,* this is a wrinching, a shrinking, a sinking, an undermining, a destroying of *Foundations,* 490 the *Foundation* of this second *House,* which is the *State,* the *Law.*

The third *House* that falles into our present Survay, is *Domus quæ Domicilium, Domus habitationis,* our *Dwelling house,* or *Family,* and of this *house,* the *foundation* is *Peace:* for *Peace* compacts all the peeces of a *family* together; Husband and Wife, in Love and in Obedience, Father and Sonne, in Care and in Obedience, Master and Servant, in Discipline and in Obedience: Still *Obedience* is one Ingredient in all *Peace;* there is no *Peace* where there is no *Obedience.* Now every smoke does not argue the house to bee on fire; Every domestique offence taken or given, does not destroy this *Foundation,* this *Peace,* 500 within doores. There may bee a *Thunder* from above, and there may bee an *Earth-quake* from below, and yet the *foundation* of the House safe: From above there may bee a defect in the *Superiour,* in the Husband, the Father, the Master; and from below, in the Wife, the Sonne, the Servant; There may bee a *Iealousie* in the Husband, a *Morositie* in the Father, an *Imperiousnesse* in the Master; And there may bee

Ivo

*Domus Do-
micilium*

an *inobsequiousnesse* and an *indiligence* in the Wife, there may bee *levitie* and *inconsideration* in the Sonne, and there may bee *unreadinesse, unseasonablenesse* in a Servant, and yet *Foundations* stand, and *Peace* maintayned, though not by an exquisite performing of all du-
510 ties, yet by a mutuall support of one anothers infirmities. This destroyes no *Foundation;* But if there bee a windowe opened in the house, to let in a *Iesuiticall firebrand,* that shall whisper, though not proclaime, deliver with a *non Dominus sed Ego,* that though it bee not a declared *Tenet* of the *Church,* yet hee thinkes, that in case of *Heresie,* Civill and Naturall, and Matrimoniall duties cease, no Civill, no Naturall, no Matrimoniall Tribute due to an *Heretique;* Or if there bee such a fire kindled within doores, that the Husbands jealousie come to a *Substraction* of necessary meanes at home, or to *Defamation* abroad, or the Wives levitie induce just *Imputation* at home, or *scan-*
520 *dall* abroad, If the Fathers wastfulnesse amount to a *Disinheriting,* because hee leaves nothing to bee inherited, Or the Sonnes incorrigiblenesse occasion a just *disinheriting,* though there bee enough, If the Master make *Slaves* of Servants, and macerate them, or the Servants make *prize* of the Master, and prey upon him, in these cases, and such as these, there is a wrinching, a shrinking, a sinking, an undermining, a destroying of *Foundations,* the *Foundation* of this third *House,* which is the *family, Peace.*

There remains yet another *House,* a fourth House, a poore and wretched *Cottage;* worse then our *Statute Cottages;* for to them the
530 *Statute* layes out certaine *Acres;* but for these *Cottages,* wee measure not by *Acres,* but by *Feete;* and five or sixe foote serves any *Cottager:* so much as makes a *Grave,* makes up the best of our *Glebe,* that are of the *Inferiour,* and the best of their *Temporalties,* that are of the *Superiour Cleargie,* and the best of their *Demeanes* that are in the greatest *Soveraigntie* in this world: for this *house* is but *our selfe,* and the *foundation* of this *House* is *Conscience.* For, this proceeding with a good *Conscience* in every particular action, is that, which the *Apostle* calles, *The laying up in store for our selves, a good foundation, against the time to come:* The *House* comes not till the time to come, but the
540 *Foundation* must bee layde heere. *Abraham looked for a Citie;* that was a *future* expectation; but, sayes that Text, it was a *Citie that hath a foundation;* the *foundation* was layd alreadie, even in this life, in

Domus Dominus

I Tim. 6.19

Heb. 11.10

a good *Conscience:* For no interest, no mansion shall that Man have in the upper-roomes of that *Ierusalem,* that hath not layd the *foundation* in a good *Conscience* heere. But what is *Conscience? Conscience* hath but these two *Elements, Knowledge,* and *Practise;* for *Conscientia presumit Scientiam;* Hee that does any thing with a good *Conscience,* knowes that hee should doe it, and why hee does it: Hee that does *good* ignorantly, stupidly, inconsiderately, implicitely, does
550 *good,* but hee does that good *ill. Conscience* is, *Syllogismus practicus;* upon certaine premisses, well debated, I conclude, that I should doe it, and then I doe it. Now for the destroying of this *foundation,* there are *sinnes,* which by *Gods* ordinary grace exhibited in his *Church,* proove but *Alarums,* but *Sentinells* to the *Conscience:* The very sinne, or something that does naturally accompany that sinne, *Povertie,* or *Sickenesse,* or *Infamie,* calls upon a man, and awakens him to a remorse of the sinne. Which made Saint *Augustine* say, *That a man got by some sinnes;* some sinnes helpe him in the way of repentance for sinne; and these sinnes doe not *destroy the foundation.* But there
560 are sinnes, which in their nature preclude repentance, and batter the *Conscience,* devastate, depopulate, exterminate, annihilate the *Conscience,* and leave no sense at all, or but a sense of *Desperation,* And

Sap. 17.11   then, the case being reduc'd to that, *That wickednes condemned by her owne wickednes, becomes very timerous,* (so as the *Conscience* growes afrayd, that the promises of the *Gospell* belong not to her) And (as it is added there) *beeing pressed with Conscience, always forecasteth grievous things,* that whatsoever *God* layes upon him heere, all that is but his *earnest* of future worse torments, when it

Ver. 12   comes to such a *Feare,* as (as it is added in the next verse) *Betrayes the*
570 *succours that Reason offers him,* That whereas in reason a man might argue, *God* hath pardoned greater sinnes, and greater sinners, yet hee can finde no hope for himselfe; this is a shrinking, a sinking, an undermining, a destroying of this *Foundation* of this fourth *House,* the *Conscience:* And farther wee proceed not in this *Survay.*

3. *Part*   Wee are now upon that which we proposed for our last Consideration; Till *foundations* are shaked, the righteous stirres not; In some cases some *foundations* may be shaked; if they be, *what can the righteous doe?* The *holy Ghost* never askes the question, what the *unrighteous,* the wicked can doe: They doe well enough, best of all,

⁵⁸⁰ in such cases: Demolitions and Ruines are their raisings; Troubles are their peace, Tempests are their calmes, Fires and combustions are their refreshings, Massacres are their harvest, and Destruction is their Vintage; All their Rivers runne in Eddies, and all their Centers are in wheeles, and in perpetuall motions; the wicked do well enough, best of all then; *but what shall the righteous do?* The first entrance of the *Psalme* in the first verse, seemes to give an answere; *The righteous may flie to the Mountaine as a Bird;* he may *retire,* withdraw himselfe. But then the generall *scope* of the *Psalme,* gives a *Reply* to the *Answere;* for all *Expositors* take the whole *Psalme* to bee an answere from *David,* ⁵⁹⁰ and given with some indignation against them, who perswaded him to flie, or retire himselfe. Not that *David* would constitute a *Rule* in his *Example,* that it was unlawfull to flie in a time of danger or persecution, (for it would not bee hard to observe at least nine or ten severall flights of *David*) but that in some cases such circumstances of *Time,* and *Place,* and *Person,* may accompany and invest the action, as that it may bee inconvenient for *that Man,* at *that Time,* to retire himselfe. As oft, as the retyring amounts to the *forsaking of a Calling,* it will become a very disputable thing, how farre a retyring may bee lawfull. Saint *Peters* vehement zeale in disswading *Christ* from going   Mat. 16.21 ⁵⁰⁰ up to *Ierusalem,* in a time of danger, was so farre from retarding *Christ* in that purpose, as that it drew a more bitter increpation from *Christ* upon *Peter,* then at any other time.

So then, in the *Text,* we have a *Rule* implyed, *Something is left to the righteous to doe, though some Foundations bee destroyed;* for the words are words of *Consultation,* and *consultation* with *God;* when Man can afford no Counsayle, *God* can, and will direct those that are his, the righteous, what to doe. The words give us the *Rule,* and *Christ* gives us the *Example* in himselfe. First, hee continues his *Innocencie,* and *avowes* that; the destroying of *Foundations,* does not destroy his ⁵¹⁰ *Foundation, Innocence:* still hee is able to confound his adversaries, with that, *Which of you can convince mee of sinne?* And then, hee   Ioh. 8.46 *prayes* for the remooving of the persecution, *Transeat Calix,* let this   [Mat. 26.39] Cup passe. When that might not bee, hee *prayes* even for them, who inflicted this persecution, *Pater ignosce,* Father forgive them; And   [Luke when all is done, hee *suffers* all that can bee done unto him: And hee   23.34] calls his whole Passion, *Horam suam,* it spent *nights* and *dayes;* his whole life was a continuall Passion; yet how long soever, he calls it but an *Houre,* and how much soever it were *their* act, the act of their malignitie that did it, yet hee calls it *his,* because it was the act of his 620 owne *Predestination* as *God,* upon himselfe as *Man;* And hee calles it by a more acceptable Name then that, hee calles his Passion *Calicem suum,* his Cup, because hee brought not onely a patience to it, but a delight and a joy in it; for, *for the joy that was set before him, hee endured the Crosse.* All this then the righteous can doe, though *Foundations bee destroyed;* Hee can *withdrawe* himselfe, if the duties of his place make not his residence necessarie; If it doe, hee can *pray;* and then hee can *suffer;* and then hee can *rejoyce* in his sufferings; and hee can make that *protestation, Our God is able to deliver us, and hee will deliver us; but if not, wee will serve no other Gods.* For, the righteous 630 hath evermore this refuge, this assurance, that though some *Foundations* bee destroyed, all cannot bee: for first, *The foundation of God stands sure, and hee knowes who are his;* Hee is safe in *God;* and then he is safe in his owne *Conscience,* for, *The Righteous is an everlasting foundation;* not onely that he *hath* one, but *is* one; and not a temporary, but an everlasting *Foundation:* So that *foundations* can never bee so destroyed, but that hee is safe in *God,* and safe in *himselfe.*

For such things then, as concerne the *foundation* of the first *House,* the *Church,* Bee not apt to call *Super-Edifications, Foundations;* Collaterall Divinitie, Fundamentall Divinitie; Problematicall, Disputable, 640 Controvertible poynts, poynts Essentiall, and Articles of Faith. Call not *Super-Edifications, Foundations,* nor call not the *furniture* of the *House, Foundations;* Call not *Ceremoniall,* and *Rituall* things, *Essentiall* parts of Religion, and of the worship of *God,* otherwise then as they imply *Disobedience;* for *Obedience* to lawfull Authoritie, is alwayes an *Essentiall* part of Religion. Doe not *Anti-date* Miserie; doe not *Prophesie* Ruine; doe not *Concurre* with Mischiefe, nor *Contribute* to Mischiefe so farre, as to *over-feare* it before, nor to misinterprete their *wayes,* whose *Ends* you cannot knowe; And doe not call the cracking of a pane of glasse, a *Destroying of foundations.* But 650 every man doing the particular duties of his distinct Calling, for the preservation of *Foundations, Praying,* and *Preaching,* and *Doing,* and *Counsailing,* and *Contributing* too, *Foundations* beeing never destroyed, the Righteous shall doe still, as they have done, enjoy *God*

Hebr. 12.2

Dan. 3.17

2 *Tim.* 2.19

Pro. 10.25

Domus Ecclesia

manifested in *Christ,* and *Christ* applyed in the *Scriptures,* which is the *foundation* of the first *House,* the *Church.*

For things concerning the *Foundation* of the second *House,* the *Commonwealth,* which is the *Lawe,* Dispute not *Lawes,* but obey them when they are made; In those *Councells,* where *Lawes* are made, or reformed, dispute; but there also, without particular interest, with-
⁶⁶⁰ out private affection, without personall relations. Call not every en-
trance of such a *Iudge,* as thou thinkest insufficient, a *corrupt* entrance; nor every *Iudgement,* which hee enters, and thou understandest not, or likest not, a *corrupt* Judgement. As in *Naturall* things, it is a weake-
nesse to thinke, that every thing that I knowe not how it is done, is done by *Witch-craft,* So is it also in *Civill* things, if I know not why it is done, to thinke it is done for *Money.* Let the *Law* bee sacred to thee, and the Dispensers of the *Law,* reverend; Keepe the *Lawe,* and the *Lawe* shall keepe thee; And so *Foundations* being never destroyed, the Righteous shall doe still, as they have done, enjoy their Possessions,
⁶⁷⁰ and Honours, and themselves, by the overshadowing of the *Lawe,* which is the *Foundation* of the second *House,* the *State.*

For those things which concerne the *Foundations* of the third *House,* the *Family,* Call not light faults by heavie Names; Call not all sociablenesse, and Conversation, Disloyaltie in thy Wife; Nor all levitie, or pleasurablenesse, Incorrigiblenesse in thy Sonne; nor all negligence, or forgetfulnesse, Perfidiousnesse in thy Servant; Nor let every light disorder within doores, shut thee out of doores, or make thee a stranger in thine owne House. In a smoakie roome, it may bee enough to open a Windowe, without leaving the place; In Domestique
⁶⁸⁰ unkindnesses, and discontents, it may bee wholesomer to give them a Concoction at home in a discreete patience, or to give them a vent at home, in a moderate rebuke, then to thinke to ease them, or put them off, with false divertions abroad. As *States* subsist in part, by keeping their weakenesses from being knowen, so is it the quiet of *Families,* to have their *Chauncerie,* and their *Parliament* within doores, and to compose and determine all emergent differences there: for so also, *Foundations* beeing kept undestroyed, the righteous shall doe, as they should doe, enjoy a *Religious* Unitie, and a *Civill* Unitie, the same Soule towards *God,* the same heart towards one another, in a holy,
⁶⁹⁰ and in a happy *Peace,* and *Peace* is the *foundation* of this third *House,* The *Family.*

Respub.
Domus

Domus
Domicilium

Domus
Dominus

Lastly, for those things which concerne the *Foundations* of the fourth *House, Our selves,* Mis-interprete not *Gods* former Corrections upon thee, how long, how sharpe soever: Call not his Phisicke, poyson, nor his Fish, Scorpions, nor his Bread, Stone: Accuse not *God,* for that hee hath done, nor suspect not *God,* for that hee may doe, as though *God* had made thee, onely because hee lacked a man, to damne. In all

[Ioh. 6.68]

scruples of *Conscience,* say with Saint *Peter, Domine quo vadam, Lord, whither shall I goe, thou hast the Word of eternall life,* And *God*

⁷⁰⁰ will not leave thee in the darke: In all oppression from potent Ad-

[Ps. 51.4]

versaries, say with *David, Tibi soli peccavi: Against thee, O Lord, onely have I sinned,* And *God* will not make the malice of another man his Executioner upon thee. Crie to him; and if hee have not heard thee, crie lowder, and crie oftner; The first way that *God* admitted thee to him was by Water, the water of *Baptisme;* Goe still the same

[Isa. 38.5.
The Vul-
gate has
lacrymas]

way to him, by Water, by repentant *Teares:* And remember still, that when *Ezechias* wept, *Vidit lachrymam, God saw his Teare,* His Teare in the *Singular: God* sawe his first teare, every severall teare: If thou thinke *God* have not done so by thee, Continue thy teares, till thou

⁷¹⁰ finde hee doe. The first way that *Christ* came to thee, was in *Blood;* when hee submitted himselfe to the *Lawe,* in *Circumcision;* And the last thing that hee bequeathed to thee, was his *Blood,* in the Institution of the Blessed *Sacrament;* Refuse not to goe to him, the same way too, if his glorie require that *Sacrifice.* If thou pray, and hast an apprehen-sion that thou hearest *God* say, hee will not heare thy prayers, doe not beleeve that it is hee that speakes; If thou canst not chuse but beleeve that it is hee, let mee say, in a pious sense, doe not beleeve him: *God* would not bee beleeved, in denouncing of Judgements, so absolutely, so peremptorily, as to bee thought to speake unconditionally, illim-

⁷²⁰ itedly: *God* took it well at *Davids* hands, that when the *Prophet* had

[2 Sam.
12.14]

tolde him, *The childe shall surely die,* yet hee beleeved not the *Prophet* so peremptorily, but that hee proceeded in Prayer to *God,* for the life

Psal. 61.4
62.7 [Vulg.
reading]

of the childe. Say with *David, Thou hast beene a strong Tower to mee; I will abide in thy Tabernacle, Et non Emigrabo,* I will never goe out, I know thou hast a *Church,* I know I am in it, and I will never depart from it; and so *Foundations* beeing never destroyed, the righteous shall doe, as the righteous have alwayes done, enjoy the *Evidence,* and the *Verdict,* and the *Iudgement,* and the *Possession* of a good *Con-*

science, which is the *Foundation* of this fourth *House.* First, governe
730 this first *House, Thy selfe,* well; and as *Christ* sayde, hee shall say
againe, *Thou hast beene faithfull in a little, take more;* Hee shall enlarge thee in the next House, Thy *Family,* and the next, The *State,*
and the other, The *Church,* till hee say to thee, as hee did to *Ierusalem,*
after all his other Blessings, *Et prosperata es in Regnum, Now I have
brought thee up to a Kingdome,* A Kingdome, where not onely no
Foundations can bee destroyed, but no stone shaked; and where the
Righteous know alwayes what to doe, to glorifie *God,* in that incessant
Acclamation, *Salvation to our God, who sits upon the Throne, and to
the Lambe;* And to this *Lambe of God,* who hath taken away the
740 *sinnes* of the world, and but changed the *Sunnes* of the world, who
hath complicated two wondrous workes in one, To make *our Sunne*
to set at Noone, and to make *our Sunne* to rise at Noone too, That hath
given him *Glorie,* and not taken away our *Peace,* That hath exalted
him to Upper-roomes, and not shaked any *Foundations* of ours, To this
Lambe of God, the glorious *Sonne of God,* and the most Almightie
Father, and the *Blessed Spirit* of Comfort, three Persons and one *God,*
bee ascribed by us, and the whole *Church,* the *Triumphant Church,*
where the *Father* of blessed *Memorie* raignes *with God,* and the *Militant Church,* where the *Sonne* of blessed *Assurance* raignes *for God,*
750 All Power, Praise, Might, Majestie, Glory, and Dominion, now, and
for ever.

Amen.
FINIS.

[Luke
19.17]

[Ezek.
16.13]

[Apoc. 7.10]

Number 13.

Preached at S. Pauls, in the Evening,
upon Easter-day. 1625.

JOHN 5.28 and 29. *MARVELL NOT AT THIS; FOR*
THE HOURE IS COMMING, IN THE WHICH,
ALL THAT ARE IN THE GRAVES, SHALL
HEARE HIS VOICE; AND SHALL COME
FORTH, THEY THAT HAVE DONE GOOD,
UNTO THE RESURRECTION OF LIFE; AND
THEY THAT HAVE DONE EVILL, UNTO
THE RESURRECTION OF DAMNATION.

As THE Sun works diversly, according to the diverse disposition of
the subject, (for the Sun melts wax, and it hardens clay) so
do the good actions of good men: upon good men they
work a vertuous emulation, a noble and a holy desire to imitate, upon
bad men they work a vicious, and impotent envy, a desire to disgrace,
and calumniate. And the more the good is that is done, and the more
it works upon good men, the more it disaffects the bad: for so the
Pharisees expresse their rancor and malignity against Christ, in this
Gospel, *If we let him thus alone, all men will beleeve in him;* And that
[10] they foresaw would destroy them in their reputation. And therefore
they enlarged their malice, beyond Christ himselfe, to him, upon
whom Christ had wrought a Miracle, to *Lazarus, They consulted to*
put him to death, because by reason of him, many beleeved in Iesus.
Our Text leads us to another example of this impotency in envious
men; Christ, in this Chapter had, by his only word, cured a man that
had been eight and thirty yeares infirm; and he had done this work
upon the Sabbath. They envyed the work in the substance, but they

John 11.48

John 12.10

262

quarrell the circumstance; And they envy Christ, but they turn upon
the man, who was more obnoxious to them; and they tell him, *That it*
²⁰ *was not lawfull for him to carry his bed that day.* He discharges himself upon Christ; I dispute not with you concerning the Law; This
satisfies me, *He that made me whole, bad me take up my bed and walk.*
Thereupon they put him to finde out Jesus; And when he could not
finde Jesus, Jesus found him, and in his behalf offers himself to the
Pharisees. Then they direct themselves upon him, and (as the Gospell
sayes) *They sought to slay him, because he had done this upon the*
Sabbath: And, as the patient had discharged himself upon Christ,
Christ discharges himself upon his Father; doth it displease you that
I work upon the Sabbath? be angry with God, be angry with the
³⁰ Father, for the Father works when I work. And then this they take
worse then his working of Miracles, or his working upon the Sabbath,
That he would say, that God was his Father; And therfore in the
averring of that, that so important point, *That God was his Father,*
Christ grows into a holy vehemence, and earnestnesse, and he repeats
his usuall oath, *Verily, verily,* three severall times: First, ver. 19. *That*
whatsoever the Father doth, He, the Son, doth also, And then ver. 24.
He that beleeveth on me, and him that sent me, hath life everlasting.
And then again, ver. 25. *The houre is comming, and now is, when the*
dead shall heare the voice of the Son of God, and they that heare it shall
⁴⁰ *live.* At this, that the dead should live, they marvelled; But because
he knew that they were men more affected with things concerning the
body, then spirituall things, as in another story, when they wondered
that he would pretend to forgive sins, because he knew, that they
thought it a greater matter to bid that man that had the Palsie, take up
his bed and walk, then to forgive him his sins, therefore he took that
way which was hardest in their opinion, he did bid him take up his
bed and walk; So here, when they wondred at his speaking of a
spirituall Resurrection, to heare him say, that at his preaching, the dead
(that is, men spiritually dead in their sins) should rise again, to them
⁵⁰ who more respected the body, and did lesse beleeve a reall Resurrection
of the body, then a figurative Resurrection of the soul, he proceeds to
that which was, in their apprehension, the more difficult, *Marvell not*
at this, sayes he, here in our Text; not at that spirituall Resurrection by

John 5.10

Ver. 11

V. 16

V. 17

V. 18

preaching, *for the houre is comming, in the which, all that are in the graves, &c.* and so he establishes the Resurrection of the body.

That then which Christ affirmes and avows, is, That he is the Son of God; and that is the first thing, that ever was done in Heaven, The eternall generation of the Son: that, by which, he proves this, to these men, is, That by him, there shall be a resurrection of the body; and ⁶⁰ that is the last thing, that shall be done in Heaven, for, after that, there is nothing, but an even continuance in equall glory. Before that, saies he, that is, before the resurrection of the body, there shall be another resurrection, a spirituall resurrection of the soule from sin; but that shall be, by ordinary meanes, by Preaching, and Sacraments, and it shall be accomplished every day; but fix not upon that, determin not your thoughts upon that, marvaile not at that, make that no cause of extraordinary wonder, but make it ordinary to you, feele it, and finde the effect thereof in your soules, as often as you heare, as often as you receive, and thereby provide for another resurrection, *For, the houre* ⁷⁰ *is comming, in which, all that are in their graves, &c.*

Where we must necessarily make thus many steps, though but short ones. First, the dignity of the Resurrection, marvaile at nothing so much, as at this, nothing is so marvailous, so wonderfull as this; And secondly, the approach of the Resurrection, *The houre is comming;* And thirdly, The generality, *All that are in the graves;* And then the the instrument of the resurrection, *The voice of Christ, that shall be heard;* And lastly, the diverse end of the resurrection, *They shall come forth, they that have done good, &c.* God hath a care of the Body of man, that is first; And he defers it not, that is next; And he extends it ⁸⁰ to all, that is a third; And a fourth is, That he does that last act, by him, by whom he did the first, The Creation, and all betweene, the Redemption, that is, by his Son, by Christ; And then the last is, that this is an everlasting separation and divorce of the good and the bad, The bad shall never be able to receive good from the Good, nor to doe harme to the Good, after that.

First then, Christ saies, *Ne miremini, Marvaile not at this,* not at your spirituall resurrection, not that a Sermon should worke upon man, not that a Sacrament should comfort a man, make it not a miracle, nor an extraordinary thing, by hearing to come to repentance, ⁹⁰ and so to such a resurrection. For though S. *Augustine* say, That to

convert a man from sin, is as great a miracle, as Creation, yet S. *Augustine* speaks that of a mans first conversion, in which the man himselfe does nothing, but God all; Then he is made of nothing; but after God hath renewed him, and proposed ordinary meanes in the Church still to worke upon him, he must not looke for miraculous working, but make Gods ordinary meanes, ordinary to him. This is *Panis quotidianus,* The daily bread which God gives you, as often as you meet here, according to his Ordinances; *Ne miremini,* stand not to wonder, as though you were not sure, but come to enjoy Gods good-
100 nesse, in his ordinary way here.

But it is, *Ne miremini hoc, Wonder not at this;* but yet, there are things, which we may wonder at. *Nil admirari,* is but the Philosophers wisdome; He thinks it a weaknesse, to wonder at any thing, That any thing should be strange to him: But Christian Philosophy that is rooted in humility, tels us, in the mouth of *Clement* of *Alexandria, Principium veritatis est res admirari,* The first step to faith, is to wonder, to stand, and consider with a holy admiration, the waies and proceedings of God with man: for, Admiration, wonder, stands as in the midst, betweene knowledge and faith, and hath an eye towards
110 both. If I know a thing, or beleeve a thing, I do no longer wonder: but when I finde that I have reason to stop upon the consideration of a thing, so, as that I see enough to induce admiration, to make me wonder, I come by that step, and God leads me by that hand, to a knowledge, if it be of a naturall or civill thing, or to a faith, if it be of a supernaturall, and spirituall thing.

And therefore be content to wonder at this, That God would have such a care to dignifie, and to crown, and to associate to his own ever-lasting presence, the body of man. God himself is a Spirit, and heaven is his place; my soul is a spirit, and so proportioned to that place;
120 That God, or Angels, or our Soules, which are all Spirits, should be in heaven, *Ne miremini,* never wonder at that. But since we wonder, and justly, that some late Philosophers have removed the whole earth from the Center, and carried it up, and placed it in one of the Spheares of heaven, That this clod of earth, this body of ours should be carried up to the highest heaven, placed in the eye of God, set down at the right hand of God, *Miramini hoc,* wonder at this; That God, all Spirit, served with Spirits, associated to Spirits, should have such an affection,

Hoc

such a love to this body, this earthly body, this deserves this wonder.
The Father was pleased to breathe into this body, at first, in the Crea-
130 tion; The Son was pleased to assume this body himself, after, in the
Redemption; The Holy Ghost is pleased to consecrate this body, and

[Gen. 1.26]   make it his Temple, by his sanctification; In that *Faciamus hominem,*
Let us, all us, *make man,* that consultation of the whole Trinity in
making man, is exercised even upon this lower part of man, the dignifying of his body. So far, as that amongst the ancient Fathers, very
many of them, are very various, and irresolved, which way to pronounce, and very many of them cleare in the negative, in that point,
That the soule of man comes not to the presence of God, but remaines
in some out-places till the Resurrection of the body: That observation,
140 that consideration of the love of God, to the body of man, withdrew
them into that error, That the soul it self should lack the glory of
heaven, till the body were become capable of that glory too.

They therefore oppose God in his purpose of dignifying the body of
man, first, who violate, and mangle this body, which is the Organ in
which God breathes; And they also which pollute and defile this body,
in which Christ Jesus is apparelled; and they likewise who prophane
this body, which the Holy Ghost, as the high Priest, inhabites, and
consecrates.

Transgressors in the first kinde, that put Gods Organ out of tune,
150 that discompose, and teare the body of man with violence, are those
inhumane persecutors, who with racks, and tortures, and prisons, and
fires, and exquisite inquisitions, throw downe the bodies of the true
Gods true servants, to the Idolatrous worship of their imaginary Gods;
that torture men into hell, and carry them through the inquisition
into damnation. S. *Augustine* moves a question, and institutes a disputation, and carries it somewhat problematically, whether torture be
to be admitted at all, or no. That presents a faire probability, which he
sayes against it: we presume, sayes he, that an innocent man should
be able to hold his tongue in torture; That is no part of our purpose in
160 torture, sayes he, that hee that is innocent, should accuse himselfe, by
confession, in torture. And, if an innocent man be able to doe so, why
should we not thinke, that a guilty man, who shall save his life, by
holding his tongue in torture, should be able to doe so? And then,
where is the use of torture? *Res fragilis, & periculosa quæstio,* sayes

that Lawyer, who is esteemed the law, alone, *Vlpian:* It is a slippery triall, and uncertaine, to convince by torture: For, many times, sayes S. *Augustine* againe, *Innocens luit pro incerto scelere certissimas pœnas;* He that is yet but questioned, whether he be guilty or no, before that be knowne, is, without all question, miserably tortured. 70 And whereas, many times, the passion of the Judge, and the covetousnesse of the Judge, and the ambition of the Judge, are calamities heavy enough, upon a man, that is accused, in this case of torture, *Ignorantia Iudicis est calamitas plerumque innocentis,* sayes that Father, for the most part, even the ignorance of the Judge, is the greatest calamity of him that is accused: If the Judge knew that he were innocent, he should suffer nothing; If he knew he were guilty, he should not suffer torture; but because the Judge is ignorant, and knowes nothing, therefore the Prisoner must bee racked, and tortured, and mangled, sayes that Father.

80 There is a whole Epistle in S. *Hierome,* full of heavenly meditation, and of curious expressions: It is his forty ninth Epistle, *Ad Innocentium:* where a young man tortured for suspition of adultery with a certaine woman, *ut compendio cruciatus vitaret,* sayes he, for his ease, and to abridge his torment, and that he might thereby procure and compasse a present death, confessed the adultery, though false: His confession was made evidence against the woman: and shee makes that protestation, *Tu testis Domine Iesu,* Thou Lord Jesus be my Witnesse, *Non ideo me negare velle, ne peream, sed ideo mentiri nolle, ne peccem:* I doe not deny the fact for feare of death, but I dare not 90 belie my selfe, nor betray mine innocence, for feare of sinning, and offending the God of Truth; And, as it followes in that story, though no torture could draw any Confession, any accusation from her, she was condemned; and one Executioner had three blowes at her with a Sword, and another foure, and yet she could not be killed.

And therefore, because Storie abounds with Examples of this kinde, how uncertaine a way of tryall, and conviction, torture is, though S. *Augustine* would not say, that torture was unlawfull, yet he sayes, It behoves every Judge to make that prayer, *Erue me Domine à necessitatibus meis,* If there bee some cases, in which the Judge must neces100 sarily proceed to torture; O Lord, deliver me, from having any such case brought before me.

But what use soever there may be for torture, for Confession, in the Inquisition they torture for a deniall, for the deniall of God, and for the renouncing of the truth of his Gospell: As men of great place, think it concernes their honour, to doe above that which they suffer, to make their revenges, not only equall, but greater then their injuries; so the Romane Church thinks it necessary to her greatnesse, to inflict more tortures now, then were inflicted upon her in the Primitive Church; as though it were a just revenge, for the tortures she received

²¹⁰ then, for being Christian, to torture better Christians then her selfe, for being so. In which tortures, the Inquisition hath found one way, to escape the generall clamour of the world against them, which is to torture to that heighth, that few survive, or come abroad after, to publish, how they have been tortured. And these, first, oppose Gods purpose, in the making, and preserving, and dignifying the body of man.

Transgressors herein, in the second kinde, are they, that defile the garment of Christ Jesus, the body in which he hath vouchsafed to invest and enwrap himselfe, and so apparell a Harlot in Christs cloathes, and make that body, which is his, hers. That Christ should take my

²²⁰ body, though defiled with fornication, and make it his, is strange; but that I, in fornication, should take Christs body, and make it hers, is

I Cor. 6.15   more. *Know ye not,* says the Apostle, *that your bodies are the mem-*
V. 16   *bers of Christ?* And againe, *Know you not, that he that is joyned to a harlot, is one body?* Some of the Romane Emperours, made it treason, to carry a Ring, that had their picture engraved in it, to any place in the house, of low Office. What Name can we give to that sin, to make the body of Christ, the body of a harlot? And yet, the Apostle there, as taking knowledge, that we loved our selves better then Christ, changes the edge of his argument, and argues thus, ver. 18. *He that*

²³⁰ *committeth fornication, sinneth against his own body;* If ye will be bold with Christs body, yet favour your own: No man ever hated his own body; and yet, no outward enemy is able so to macerate our body, as our owne licentiousnesse. Christ, who tooke all our bodily infirmities upon him, Hunger, and Thirst, and Sweat, and Cold, tooke no bodily deformities upon him, he tooke not a lame, a blinde, a crooked body; and we, by our intemperance, and licentiousnesse, deforme that body which is his, all these wayes. The licentious man, most of any, studies bodily handsomenesse, to be comely, and gracious, and acceptable, and

yet, soonest of any, deformes, and destroyes it, and makes that loath-
40 some to all, which all his care was to make amiable: And so they
oppose Gods purpose of dignifying the body.

Transgressors in a third kinde are they, that sacrilegiously prophane
the Temple of the Holy Ghost, by neglecting the respect and duties,
belonging to the dead bodies of Gods Saints, in a decent and comely
accompanying them to convenient Funerals. Heires and Executors are
oftentimes defective in these offices, and pretend better employments
of that, which would be, (say they) vainly spent so. But remember
you, of whom (in much such a case) that is said in S. *Iohn, This he*   John 12.6
said, not because he cared for the poore, but because he was a Thiefe,
50 *and had the bagge, and bore that which was put therein:* This Executors say, not because they intend pious uses, but because they beare,
and beare away the bagges. Generally, thy opinion must be no rule
for other mens actions; neither in these cases of Funerals, must thou
call all too much, which is more then enough; That womans Ointment
poured upon Christs feet, that hundred pound waight of perfumes to
embalme his one body, was more then enough, necessarily enough;
yet it was not too much, for the dignity of that person, nor for the
testimony of their zeale, who did it, in so abundant manner.

Now, as in all these three waies, men may oppose the purpose of
60 God, in indignifying the body, so in concurring with Gods purpose,
for the dignifying thereof, a man may exceed, and goe beyond Gods
purpose, in all three. God would not have the body torne, and mangled
with tortures, in those cases; but then, hee would not have it pampered
with wanton delicacies, nor varnished with forraigne complexion. It
is ill, when it is not our own heart, that appeares in our words; it is ill
too, when it is not our own blood, that appeares in our cheekes; It may
doe some ill offices of blood, it may tempt, but it gives over, when it
should doe a good office of blood, it cannot blush. If when they are
filling the wrinkles, and graves of their face, they would remember,
70 that there is another grave, that calls for a filling with the whole body,
so, even their pride would flow into a mortification. God would not
have us put on a sad countenance, nor disfigure our face, not in our
fastings, and other disciplines; God would not have us marre his
work; nor God would not have us goe about to doe his last work,
which he hath reserved to himselfe in heaven, here upon earth, that is,

to glorifie our bodies, with such additions here, as though we would
need no glorification there.

So also in the second way of giving due respect to the body of man,
a man may exceed Gods purpose. God would not have the body cor-
²⁸⁰ rupted and attenuated, shrunk and deformed with incontinency, and
licentiousnesse; But God would not have that sparing of the body, to
dishonour, or undervalue, or forbeare mariage, nor to frustrate that,
which was one of Gods purposes, in the institution of mariage, procreation of children. Mariage without possibility of children, lacks one
halfe of Gods purpose in the institution of mariage; for, the third
reason of mariage, after the other two, (which two were, for a Helper,
and for Children) which is, that mariage should be for a Remedy, that
third came in after; for at the time of the institution of mariage, man
was not fallen into any inordinate concupiscencies, and so, at that time,
²⁹⁰ needed no remedy. Mariage without possibility of children, lacks one
of Gods two reasons for children; but mariage with a contract against
children, or a practice against children, is not (sayes S. *Augustine*) a
mariage, but a solemne, an avowed, a dayly Adultery. To choose to be
ill in the sight of God, rather then to look ill, in the sight of men, is a
perverse, and a poysonous Physick. The sin of *Er,* and *Onan,* in maried
men; the sin of procured abortions, in maried women, doe, in many
cases, equall, in some, exceed, the sin of Adultery; To rob a husband,
or a wife, of a future child, may be in the wife, or husband, as great a
sin, as to bring a supposititious, or a spurious child, into the Fathers
³⁰⁰ inheritance. God would not have the comelinesse, the handsomenesse
of the body defaced by incontinency, and intemperance, but he would
not have the care of that comelinesse, and handsomenesse frustrate his
purpose of children in mariage.

And as in those two, (God would not have the body tortured, nor
mangled, God would not have the body deformed by licentiousnesse)
so, in his third respect to mans body, God would not have the bodies of
his dead Saints neglected, Gods purpose may be exceeded too. Gods
purpose therein is, that all men should be Decently, and Honourable
persons, Honourably buried; but his purpose herein is exceeded, when
³¹⁰ any ragge of their skin, or chip of their bones, or lock of their haire, is
kept for a Relique, and made an Universall balme, and Amulet, and
Antidote, against all temporall, and all spirituall diseases, and calam-

ities, not onely against the rage of a Feaver, but of hell it selfe. What their counterfait Reliques may doe, against their counterfait hell, against their Purgatory, I know not: That powerfull, and precious, and onely Relique, which is given to us, against hell it selfe, is onely the Communion of the body, and blood of Christ Jesus, left to us by him, and preserved for us, in his Church, though his body be removed out of our sight.

To end this, *Miramini hoc,* marvell at this, at the wonderfull love of God to the body of man, and thou wilt favour it so, as not to macerate thine owne body, with uncommanded and inhumane flagellations, and whippings, nor afflict their bodies, who are in thy charge, with inordinate labour; thou wilt not dishonour this body, as it is Christs body, nor deforme it, as it is thine owne, with intemperance, but thou wilt behave thy selfe towards it so, as towards one, whom it hath pleased the King to honour, with a resurrection, (which was our first) and not to deferre that resurrection long, which is our next step, *Venit hora, The houre is comming.*

Non talem Deum tuum putes, qualis nec tu debes esse, is excellently said by S. *Augustine:* Never presume upon any other disposition in God, then such as thou findest in thine own heart, that thou art bound to have in thy selfe; for we finde in our hearts, a band of conformity, and assimilation to God, that is, to be as like God as we can. Therefore whatsoever thou findest thy selfe bound to doe to another, thou maist expect at Gods hand. Thou art bound to help up another that is fallen, therefore thou maist assure thy selfe, that God will give thee a Resurrection: so, thou findest in thy heart, that the soul of an almes, the soule of a benefit, that that gives it life, is the speedy, the present doing of it; Therefore thou maist be sure, that God will make speed to save thee, that he will not long deferre this thy resurrection, *hora venit.* S. *Augustine* comparing the former resurrection, which is the spirituall resurrection of the soule, ver. 25. with this in the Text, which is the resurrection of the body, observes, that there Christ sayes, *hora venit, & nunc est, the houre is comming, and now is;* because in every private inspiration of the Holy Ghost, in every Sermon, in every meeting of the Congregation, the dead may heare, and live; *nunc est,* they may doe it now. But that in this resurrection in the Text, the resurrection of the body, it is not said, *nunc est,* that the houre is now; for, the

Venit hora

³⁵⁰ Son of Man who sayes it, (as hee is the Son of Man) knowes not when it shall bee; But hee sayes *Hora venit, It is comming,* and comming apace, and comming quickly, shortly.

As soone as God had made man, he gave him his patent, *Domi-namini,* Dominion over the Creature; As soone as Man was fallen, God gave him the promise of a Messias; And of his second comming, [Apoc. 22.7] himselfe sayes, *Ecce, venio citò, Behold, I come speedily: Venit,* he comes, he is upon the way; and *Ecce, venit,* Behold, he comes, he is within sight, you may see him in his fore-running tokens; and *Ecce citò,* as little way as he hath to goe, he makes haste, And there is a Maldon. ³⁶⁰ Jesuit that makes the haste so great, as that he sayes, Howsoever S. *Augustine* make use of that note, that it is not said in the Text, *Nunc est,* That the houre of the Resurrection is now, yet he does beleeve, that Christ did say so, though the Euangelist left it out. We need not say so; we doe not; so much lesse liberty doe we take in departing from the Fathers, then the Romane Authors doe: But yet, so as S. I Joh. 2.18 *Iohn* speaks, *Hora novissima,* This is the last time, (*Now there are many Antichrists, whereby we know that this is the last time*) And so, 2 Pet. 3.8 as S. *Peter* speaks, *Be not ignorant of this one thing, that one day is with the Lord as a thousand yeares, and a thousand yeares as one day:* ³⁷⁰ So as this *Nunc* may signifie *Vltimum statum,* The last course of times, the time not of Nature, nor of Law, but of Grace; so we admit that addition in this Resurrection too, *Hora venit, & nunc est, The houre is comming, and now is,* because there are no other meanes to be here-after instituted for the attaining of a happy Resurrection, then those that now are established in the Church, especially at a mans death, may we very properly say, *Nunc est,* Now is the Resurrection come to him, not onely because the last Judgement is involved in the first, (for that Judgment which passeth upon every man at his death, stands for ever without Repeal, or Appeal, or Error) but because after the death of ³⁸⁰ the Body, there is no more to be done with the Body, till the Resurrec-tion; for as we say of an Arrow, that it is over shot, it is gone, it is beyond the mark, though it be not come to the mark yet, because there is no more to be done to it till it be; so we may say, that he that is come to death, is come to his Resurrection, because he hath not another step to make, another foot to goe, another minute to count, till he be at the Resurrection.

The Resurrection then, being the Coronation of man, his Death, and lying downe in the grave, is his enthroning, his sitting downe in that chayre, where he is to receive that Crown. As then the Martyrs, under the Altar, though in heaven, yet doe cry out for the Resurrection; so let us, in this miserable life, submit our selves cheerfully to the hand of God, in death, since till that death we cannot have this Resurrection, and the first thing that we shall doe after this death, is to rise againe. To the child that is now borne, we may say, *Hora venit,* The day of his Resurrection is comming; To him that is old, we may say, The hour is come; but to him that is dead, The minute is come, because to him there are no more minutes till it doe come.

Miramini hoc, Marvail at this, at the descent of Gods love, He loves the Body of Man, And *Miramini hoc,* Mervaile at his speed, He makes haste to expresse this love, *Hora venit,* And then *Miramini hoc,* Marvaile at the Generality, it reaches to all, all that are in the Grave; *All that are in the graves shall heare his voice, &c.* God hath made the Body as a House for the soule, till he call her out, and he hath made the Grave as a House for the body, till he call it up. The misery, and poore estate that Christ submitted himselfe unto for man, was not determined in that, *That foxes had holes, but he no where to lay his head,* while he lived; but he had no grave that he could claime, when he was dead. It is some discontinuance of the Communion of Saints, if I may not be buried with the Saints of God. Every man that hath not devested Humanity, hath a desire to have his bones lie at rest, and we cannot provide for that so well, any way, as to bury them in Consecrated places, which are, in common entendment, safest from prophane violences. Even that respect, that his bones might lye at rest, seems to have mov'd one Prophet, to enjoyne his Sons, to bury him, in the Sepulcher, where the other Prophet was buried. He knew that *Iosiah* would burne the bones of all the other graves, upon the Altar of *Bethel,* as was prophecied; and he presum'd that he would spare the bones of that Prophet, and so his bones should be safe, if they were mingled with the other. God expressed his love to *Moses,* in that particular, *That he buried him;* And, to deliver, and remove him, from the violence of any that lov'd him not, and so might dishonor his memory, and from the superstition of any that over-lov'd him, and so might over-honour his memory, God buried him in secret. In more then one place doth *David*

Omnes

Mat. 8.20

I King.
13.31

Deut. 34.6

complaine, *That there was none to bury Gods Saints;* And the Dignity that is promised here in the Text, is appropriated to them, *who are in the graves,* who are buried.

But then, was that generall? Is it simply, plainly, literally of them, and them onely, who are in graves, who are buried? Shall none enjoy a Resurrection, that have not enjoy'd a Grave? Still I say, it is a comfort ⁴³⁰ to a dying man, it is an honour to his memory, it is a discharge of a duty in his friends, it is a piece of the Communion of Saints, to have a consecrated grave: But the word here is, *In monumentis,* All that are in Monuments; that is, in Receptacles of Bodies, of what kind soever they be: wheresoever the hand of God layes up a dead Body, that place

Psal. 34.20

is the Receptacle, so the monument, so the grave of that Body. *God keeps all the bones of the righteous, so that none of them are broken:* Though they be trod to dust in our sight, they are intire in his, because he can bid them be whole againe in an instant. Some Nations burnt their dead, there the fire is the grave; some drowned their dead, there ⁴⁴⁰ the sea is the grave; and some hung them up upon trees, and there the ayre is their grave: Some Nations eat their dead themselves, and some

Herod.
Strabo

maintained dogs to eat the dead; and as they called those dogs, *Canes Sepulchrales,* Sepulchrall dogs, so those men were sepulchrall men,

Apoc. 20.13

those men and those dogs were graves. *Death and hell shall deliver up their dead,* sayes S. *Iohn:* That is, the whole state, and mansion of the dead, shall be emptied: The state of the dead is their grave, and upon all that are in this state, shall the testimony of Gods love, to the body of man, fall; And that is the Generality, *All that are in the grave, &c.*

Audient

Our next step, is, The Instrument, the Means, by which, this, first so ⁴⁵⁰ speedy, and then so generall love of God, to man, to man in his lowest part, his body, is accomplished unto him; These, All these, All these that are in graves, in all these kinds of graves, *shall heare his voice,* and that is the Meanes. First, whose voice? That is expressed immediately before, *The Son of man.* In the other Resurrection, in that of the dead soule, *ver. 25.* there it is said, *The dead shall heare the voyce of the Son of God.* In this, which is the Resurrection to Judgement, it is *The Son of man.* The former Resurrection (that of a sinner to repentance by preaching) is wrought by a plaine, and ordinary meanes here in the Church; where you doe but heare a man in a Pew, read prayers, and ⁴⁶⁰ pronounce Absolution, and a man in a Pulpit preach a Sermon, and a man at a Table consecrate, and administer a Sacrament; And because all this, though it be the power of life, and the meanes of your spirituall resurrection, is wrought by the Ministery of man, who might be contemptible in your eye, therefore the whole worke is referred to God, and not the son of man, but *the Son of God,* is said to do it.

In this Resurrection of the Text, which is a Resurrection to Judgement, and to an account with God, that God whom we have displeased, exasperated, violated, wounded in the whole course of our life, lest we should be terrified, and dejected at the presence of that God, the whole worke is referred to *the Son of Man,* which hath himselfe formerly felt all our infirmities, and hath had as sad a soule at the approach of death, as bitter a Cup in the forme of Death, as heavy a feare of Gods forsaking him in the agony of death, as we can have: And for sin it self, I would not, I do not extenuate my sin, but let me have fallen, not seven times a day, but seventy seven times a minute, yet what are my sins, to all those sins that were upon Christ? The sins of all men, and all women, and all children, the sins of all Nations, all the East and West, and all the North and South, the sins of all times and ages, of Nature, of Law, of Grace, the sins of all natures, sins of the body, and sins of the mind, the sins of all growth, and all extentions, thoughts, and words, and acts, and habits, and delight, and glory, and contempt, and the very sin of boasting, nay of our belying our selves in sin; All these sins, past, present and future, were at once upon Christ, and in that depth of sin, mine are but a drop to his Ocean; In that treasure of sin, mine are but single money to his Talent; And therefore, that I might come with a holy reverence to his Ordinance, in this place, though it be but in the Ministery of man, that first Resurrection is attributed to the Son of God, to give a dignity to that Ministery of man, which otherwise might have beene under-valued, that thereby we might have a consolation, and a cheerefulnesse towards it; It is He, that is, the Son of God, and the Son of man, Christ; which remembers us also, that all that belongs to the expressing of the Law of God to man, must be received by us, who professe our selves Christians, in, and by, and for, and through Christ.

We use to ascribe the Creation to the Father, but the Father created by the Word, and his Word, is his Son, Christ; *When he prepared the Heavens, I was there,* (saies Christ, of himselfe in the person of Wis-

Prov. 8.27

dome) *and when he appointed the foundations of the earth, then was I by him, as one brought up with him;* It is not, as one brought in to
500 him, or brought in by him, but with him; one as old, that is, as eternall, as much God as he. We use to ascribe Sanctification to the Holy Ghost; But the Holy Ghost sanctifies in the Church, And the Church was purchased by the blood of Christ, and Christ remaines Head of the Church, *usque in consummationem,* till the end of the world. I looke upon every blessing that God affords me, and I consider whether it be temporall, or spirituall; and that distinguishes the metall; the temporall is my silver, and the spirituall is my Gold; but then I looke againe upon the Inscription, *Cujus Imago,* whose Image, whose inscription it beares, and whose Namè; and except I have it, in, and for,
510 and by Christ Jesus, Temporall, and Spirituall things too, are but imaginary, but illusory shadows; for God convayes himselfe to us, no other way, but in Christ.

Christum   The benefit then in our Text, the Resurrection, is by him; but it is limited thus, It is by hearing him, *They that are in their Graves shall heare, &c.* So it is in the other Resurrection too, the spirituall resurrection, *v.* 25. There, they must *heare* him, that will *live.* In both resurrections, That in the Church, now, by Grace, And that in the Grave hereafter, by Power, it is said, *They shall heare him.* They shall, which seemes to imply a necessity, though not a coaction; But that necessity,
520 not of equall force, not equally irresistible in both: In the Grave, *They shall;* Though they be dead, and senslesse as the dust, (for they are dust it selfe) though they bring no concurrence, no cooperation, *They shall heare,* that is, They shall not chuse but heare. In the other resurrection, which is, in the Church, by Grace, in Gods Ordinance, *They shall heare too,* that is, There shall be a voice uttered so, as that they may heare, if they will, but not whether they will or no, as in the other case, in the grave. Therefore when God expresses his gathering of his
Zecha. 10.8   Church, in this world, it is *Sibilabo & congregabo, I will hisse, or chirpe for them, and so gather them:* He whispers in the voyce of the
530 Spirit, and he speaks a little louder, in the voice of a man; Let the man be a *Boanerges,* a Son of thunder, never so powerfull a speaker, yet no thunder is heard over all the world. But for the voyce that shall be
Mat. 24.31   heard at the Resurrection, *He shall send his Angels, with a great sound of a Trumpet;* A great sound, such as may be made by a Trumpet,

such as an Angell, all his Angels can make in a Trumpet, and more
then all that, *The Lord himselfe shall descend from Heaven,* and that, I Thes. 4.16
with a shout, and with the voice of an Archangel, that is, saies S.
Ambrose, of Christ himselfe, *And in the Trumpet of God,* that is also,
Christ himselfe.

⁴⁰   So then, you have the Person, Christ; The meanes, A Voyce, And
the powerfulnesse of that voyce, in the Name of an Archangell, which
is named but once more in all the Scriptures: And therefore, let no
man, that hath an holy anhelation and panting after the Resurrection,
suspect that he shall sleepe in the dust, for ever; for, this is a voyce that
will be heard, he must rise. Let no man, who because he hath made
his course of life like a beast, would therefore be content his state in
death might be like a beast too, hope that he shall sleepe in the dust,
for ever, for this is a voice, that must be heard, *And all that heare shall
come forth, they that have done good, &c.*

⁵⁰   *He shall come forth;* even he that hath done ill, and would not, shall   *Procedent*
come forth. You may have seene morall men, you may have seen
impious men, go in confidently enough: not afrighted with death, not
terrified with a grave; but when you shall see them come forth againe,
you shall see them in another complexion. That man that dyed so,
with that confidence, thought death his end; It ends his seventy yeares,
but it begins his seventy millions of generations of torments, even to
his body, and he never thought of that: Indeed, *Iudicii, nisi qui vitæ
æternæ prædestinatus est, non potest reminisci,* saies S. *Ambrose,* No
man can, no man dares thinke upon the last Judgement, but he that
⁶⁰ can thinke upon it with comfort, he that is predestinated to eternall
life. Even the best, are sometimes shaked with the consideration of the
Resurrection, because it is impossible to separate the consideration of
the Resurrection, from the consideration of the Judgement; and the
terrors of that may abate the joy of the other: *Sive comedo, sive bibo,*
saies S. *Hierom,* Whether I eate, or drink, still me thinks I heare this
sound, *Surgite mortui, & venite ad Iudicium,* Arise you dead, and
come to Judgement: When it cals me up from death, I am glad, when
it cals me to Judgement, that impaires my joy. Can I thinke that God
will not take a strict account; or, can I be without feare, if I thinke he
⁷⁰ will? *Non expavescere requisiturum est dicere, non requiret,* is excellently said by S. *Bernard,* If I can put off all feare of that Judgement,

I have put off all imagination, that any such Judgement shall be. But, when I begin this feare, in this life, here, I end this feare, in my death, and passe away cheerefully: But the wicked begin this feare, when the Trumpet sounds to the Resurrection, and then shall never end it; but, as a man condemned to be halfe hang'd, and then quartered, hath a fearfull addition in his quartering after, and yet had no ease in his hanging before; so they that have done ill, when they have had their hanging, when they have suffered in soule, the torments of Hell, from 580 the day of their death, to the day of Judgement, shall come to that day with feare, as to an addition to that, which yet, was infinite before. And therefore the vulgat Edition hath rendred this well, *Procedent, They shall proceed,* they shall go farther and farther in torment.

Conclusio   But this is not the object of our speculation, the subject of our meditation, now: we proposed this Text, for the Contemplation of Gods love to man, and therefore we rather comfort our selves with that branch, and refresh our selves with the shadow of that, *That they who have done good, shall come forth unto the Resurrection of life.* Alas, the others shall live as long as they; *Lucifer* is as immortall as *Michael,*
August. 590 and *Iudas* as immortall as S. *Peter:* But *Vita damnatorum, mors est,* That which we call immortality in the damned, is but a continuall dying; howsoever it must be called life, it hath all the qualities of death, saving the ease, and the end, which death hath, and damnation hath not. They must come forth; they that have done evill, must do so too: Neither can stay in their house, their grave; for, their house (though that house should be the sea) shall be burnt downe; all the world dissolv'd with fire. But then, They who have done evill, shall passe from that fire, into a farther heat, without light, They who have done good, into a farther light, without heat.

600   But fix upon the Conditions, and performe them; They must *have done Good;* To have knowne Good, to have beleeved it, to have intended it, nay to have preached it to others, will not serve, They must have done good. They must be rooted in faith, and then bring forth fruit, and fruit in season; and then is the season of doing good, when another needs that good at thy hands. God gives the evening raine, but he gave the morning rain before; A good man gives at his death, but he gives in his life time too. To them belongs this Resurrection of the body to life; upon which, since our Text inclines us to marvell rather

then to discourse, I will not venture to say with David, *Narrabo omnia*   Psal. 9.1
mirabilia tua, I will shew all thy wondrous works, (an Angels tongue
could not shew them) but I will say with him, *Mementote mirabilium,*   Psal. 105.5
Remember the marvellous works he hath done, And by that, God will   Psal. 119.18
open your eyes, that you may behold the wondrous things that he will
do: Remember with thankfulnesse the severall resurrections that he
hath given you; from superstition and ignorance, in which, you, in
your Fathers lay dead; from sin, and a love of sin, in which, you, in
the dayes of your youth, lay dead; from sadnesse, and dejection of
spirit, in which, you, in your worldly crosses, or spirituall tentations,
lay dead; And assure your self, that that God that loves to perfect his
own works, when you shall lye dead in your graves, will give you that
Resurrection to life, which he hath promised to all them that do good,
and will extend to all them, who having done evill, do yet truly repent
the evill they have done.

Number 14.

Preached at Denmark house, some few days before the body of King James, was removed from thence, to his buriall, Apr. 26. 1625.

CANT. 3.11. *GOE FORTH YE DAUGHTERS OF SION, AND BEHOLD KING SOLOMON, WITH THE CROWN, WHEREWITH HIS MOTHER CROWNED HIM, IN THE DAY OF HIS ES-POUSALS, AND IN THE DAY OF THE GLAD-NESSE OF HIS HEART.*

[Gen. 1.26]

IN THE Creation of man, in that one word, *Faciamus, let Vs make man,* God gave such an intimation of the *Trinity,* as that we may well enlarge, and spread, and paraphrase that one word, so farre, as to heare therein, a councell of all the *three Persons,* agreeing in this gracious designe upon Man, *faciamus,* let us make him; *make* him, and *mend* him, and make him *sure:* I, the Father, will make him by my power; if he should fall, Thou the Sonne shalt repayr him, re-edify him, *redeem* him; if he should distrust, that this Re-demption belonged not to him, Thou, the *Holy Ghost,* shalt apply to his particular soule, and conscience, this *mercy* of mine, and this *merit* of the Sonnes; and so let *us make him.* In our Text there is an intima-tion of another *Trinity.* The words are spoken but by *one,* but the

Divisio persons in the text, are *Three;* For first, The *speaker,* the Director of all, is the *Church,* the *spouse* of Christ, she says, *Goe forth ye daughters of Sion;* And then the *persons* that are *called up,* are, as you see, *The Daughters of Sion,* the obedient children of the Church, that hearken to her voice: And then lastly, the *person* upon whom they are directed, is *Solomon* crowned, That is, Christ invested with the royall dignity

280

of being *Head of the Church;* And in this, especially, is this applyable
20 to the occasion of our present meeting (All our meetings now, are, to
confesse, to the glory of God, and the rectifying of our own consciences, and manners, the uncertainty of the prosperity, and the assurednesse of the adversity of this world) That this *Crown of Solo-*
mons in the text, will appear to be Christs crown of *Thornes,* his
Humiliation, his *Passion;* and so these words will dismisse us in this
blessed consolation, That then we are nearest to our crown of Glory,
when we are in *tribulation* in this world, and then enter into full possession of it, when we come to our *dissolution* and *transmigration* out
of this world: And these three persons, The *Church,* that calls, The
30 *children* that hearken, and *Christ in his Humiliation,* to whom they
are sent, will be the three parts, in which we shall determine this
Exercise.

First then, the person that directs us, is *The Church; no man hath*   1 Part
seen God, and lives; but no man lives till he have *heard God;* for God   *Ecclesia*
spake to him, in his *Baptisme,* and called him by his *name,* then. Now,
as it were a contempt in the *Kings house,* for any servant to refuse any
thing, except he might heare the King in person command it, when
the King hath already so established the government of his house, as
that his commandements are to be signifyed by his great Officers: so
40 neither are we to look, that God should speak to us *mouth to mouth,*
spirit to spirit, by *Inspiration,* by *Revelation,* for it is a large mercy, that
he hath constituted an Office, and established a Church, in which we
should heare him. When Christ was baptized by *John,* it is sayd by
all those three Evangelists, that report that story, in particular circumstances, that *there was a voice heard from heaven saying, This is*   [Mat. 3.17]
my beloved Son in whom I am well pleased: and it is not added in any
of those three Evangelists, that that voice added, *Hear him:* for, after
that Declaration, that he, who was visibly and personally come
amongst them, was the *Sonne of God,* there was no reason to doubt
50 of mens willingnesse to hear him, who went forth in person, to preach
unto them, in this world; As long as he was to stay with them, it was
not likely that they should need provocation, to hear him, therefore
that was not added at his *Baptism,* and *entrance* into his *personall*
ministery: But when Christ came to his *Transfiguration,* which was a
manifestation of his *glory,* in *the next world,* and an intimation of the

approaching of the time of his going away, to the possession of that glory, out of this world, there that voyce from heaven sayes, *This is my beloved Sonne, in whom I am well pleased, heare him:* When he was gone out of this world, men needed a more particular solicitation ⁶⁰ to heare him; for, *how,* and *where,* and *in whom* should they heare him, when he was *gone?* In the *Church,* for the same testimony that *God* gave of *Christ,* to authorize and justifie his preaching, hath *Christ* given *of the Church,* to justifie her power: The *holy Ghost* fell upon *Christ,* at his *Baptisme,* and the *holy Ghost* fell upon the *Apostles,* (who were the *representative Church*) at *Whitsontide:* The holy Ghost *tarried* upon Christ then, and the holy Ghost shall tarry with the Church, *usque ad consummationem, till the end of the world.* And

therefore, as we have that institution from Christ, *Dic Ecclesiæ,* when men are refractary and perverse, to complaine to the Church, so have ⁷⁰ they who are complained of to the Church, that institution from Christ also, *Audi Ecclesiam,* Hearken to the voyce of God, in the Church; and they have from him that commination, *If you disobey them, you disobey God;* in what fetters soever they *binde* you, you shall rise bound in those fetters; and, as he who is *excommunicated* in one Diocese, should not be received in another; so let no man presume of a better state, in the Triumphant Church, then he holds in the Militant, or hope for *communion* there, that despises *excommunication* here. That which the *Scripture* says, *God* sayes, (says St. *Augustine*) for the Scripture is his word; and that which the *Church* says, ⁸⁰ the *Scriptures* say, for she is their word, they speak *in her;* they authorize her, and she explicates them; The *Spirit* of God *inanimates* the Scriptures, and makes them *his* Scriptures, the *Church actuates* the Scriptures, and makes them *our Scriptures: Nihil salubrius,* says the same Father, There is not so wholsome a thing, no soule can live in so good an aire, and in so good a diet, *Quàm ut Rationem præcedat authoritas,* Then still to submit a mans owne particular reason, to the authority of the Church expressed in the Scriptures: For, certainly it is very truly (as it is very usefully) said by *Calvin, Semper nimia morositas, est ambitiosa,* A frowardnesse, and an aptnesse to quarrell ⁹⁰ at the proceedings of the Church, and to be delivered from the obligations, and constitutions of the Church, is ever accompanied with an ambitious pride, that they might enjoy a licentious liberty; It is

not because the Church doth truly take *too much* power, but because
they would be under *none;* it is an ambition, to have all government
in their own hands, and to be absolute Emperors of themselves, that
makes them refractary: But, if they will pretend to *believe in God,*
they must believe in God so, as God hath manifested himself to
them, they must *believe in Christ;* so if they will pretend to *heare*
Christ, they must heare him there, where he hath promised to speake,
100 they must *heare him in the Church.*

  The first reason then in this *Trinity,* the person that directs, is *the*
Church; the *Trumpet* in which God sounds his *Judgements,* and the
Organ, in which he delivers his *mercy;* And then the persons of the
second place, the persons *to whom* the Church speakes here, are *Filiæ*
Sion, The daughters of Sion, her owne daughters. We are not called,
Filii Ecclesiæ, sonnes of the Church: The name of *sonnes* may imply
more *virility,* more manhood, more sense of our owne strength, then
becomes them, who professe an obedience to the Church: Therefore,
as by a name, importing more *facility,* more supplenesse, more appli-
110 cation, more *tractablenesse,* she calls her children, *Daughters.* But
then, being *a mother,* and having the dignity of a *Parent* upon her,
she does not proceed *supplicatorily,* she does not pray them, nor intreat them, she does not say, *I would you would go forth,* and *I would*
you would looke out, but it is *Egredimini, & videte, imperatively,*
authoritatively, *Do it, you must do it:* So that she showes, what, in
important and *necessary cases,* the power of the Church is, though
her *ordinary* proceedings, by us, and our Ministery, be, *To pray you,*
in Christs stead, to be reconciled to God. In your *baptisme,* your
soules became daughters of the Church; and they must continue so,
120 as long as they continue in you; you cannot devest your *allegiance*
to the *Church,* though you would; no more then you can to the *State,*
to whom you cannot say, *I will be no subject.* A father may *dis-inherit*
his son, upon reasons, but even that dis-inherited *childe* cannot *re-*
nounce his father. That Church which *conceived thee,* in the *Cove-*
nant of God, made to Christians, and their seed, and *brought thee*
forth in *baptisme,* and *brought thee up* in *catechizing,* and *preaching,*
may yet, for thy misdemeanor to God in her, separate thee, *à Mensa*
& Toro, from bed and board; from that sanctuary of the soule, the
Communion Table, and from that *Sanctuary* of the body, *Christian*

2 Part

[2 Cor.
5.20]

¹³⁰ *buriall,* and even that *Christian buriall* gives a man a good rise, a good helpe, a good advantage, even at the last resurrection, to be laid down in *expectation* of the Resurrection, in *holy ground,* and in a place *accustomed to Gods presence,* and to have been found worthy *of that Communion of Saints,* in the very body, is some earnest, and some kinde of first-fruits, of the joyfull resurrection, which we attend: God can call our dead bodies from the sea, and from the fire, and from the ayre, for every element is his; but *consecrated ground* is our *element.* And therefore you daughters of Sion, holy and religious souls, (for to them onely this indulgent mother speaks here)
¹⁴⁰ hearken ever to her voice; quarrell not your mothers honor, nor her discretion: Despise not her person, nor her apparell; Doe not say, *she is not the same woman, she was heretofore, nor that she is not so well dressed, as she was then;* Dispute not her *Doctrine,* Despise not her *Discipline;* that as you *sucked her breasts* in your *Baptism,* and in the *other Sacrament,* when you entred, and whilst you stayd in this life, so you may *lie in her bosome,* when you goe out of it. *Hear her;* and a good part of that, which you are to hear from her, is envolv'd and inwrapped in that which we have propos'd to you, for our third part, *Goe forth, and behold Solomon, &c.*

3 Part   ¹⁵⁰   Here are two duties enjoyn'd; at least two steps, two degrees; *Egredimini, Go forth,* and then, *Videte, Behold,* contemplate; And, after the duty, or wrap'd in the duty, we have *the Object,* which we are to

Egredimini   look upon, and in that, divers things to be considered; as we shall see in their order. First, when we are bid to *Go forth,* it is not to go so far, as *out* of that Church, in which God hath given us our station; for,

[Deut. 30.13]   as *Moses* says, That *the word of God is not beyond Sea;* so the Church of God, is not so *beyond Sea,* as that we must needs seek it *there,* either in a *painted Church,* on one side, or in *a naked Church,* on another; a Church in a *Dropsie,* overflowne with *Ceremonies,* or a
¹⁶⁰ Church in a *Consumption,* for want of such Ceremonies, as the primitive Church found usefull, and beneficiall for the advancing of the glory of God, and the devotion of the Congregation. That which Christ says to the Church it selfe, the Church says to every soule in

Cant. 1.8   the Church: *Goe thy way forth, by the footsteps of the flocke;* Associate thy selfe to the true shepheard, and true sheep of Christ Jesus, and stray not towards *Idolatrous Chappels,* nor towards *schismaticall*

Conventicles, but goe by the footsteps of the flock; there must be *footsteps,* some must have gone that way before, take heed of *Opin-ions,* that begin in thy selfe; and the whole flock must have gone that way, take heed of opinions vented by a *few new men,* which have not had the establishment of a Church. And truly the best way to discerne footsteps, is *Daniels way, Daniels* way was to *straw ashes,*   [Bel v. 14] and so their footsteps that had been there, were easily discerned: Walke in thine own *ashes,* in the meditation of thine own death, or in the *ashes of Gods Saints,* who are dead before thee, in the contem-plation of their example, and thou wilt see some *footsteps of the flock,* some impressions, some directions, how they went, and how thou art to follow, to the heavenly Jerusalem. In conversing evermore, with them which tread upon *Carpets,* or upon *Marbles,* thou shalt see no footsteps, Carpets and Marbles receive no impressions; Amongst them that tread in *ashes,* in the ways of holy sorrow, and *religious humilia-tion,* thou shalt have the way best marked out unto thee. *Goe forth,* that is, *goe farther then thy selfe,* out of thy selfe; at least out of the *love of thy self,* for that is but a short, a giddy, a vertiginous walk; how little a thing is the greatest man? If thou have many rooms in thy selfe, many capacities to contemplate thy selfe in, if thou walke over the consideration of thy selfe, as thou hast such a title of *Honour,* such an Office of Command, such an *Inheritance,* such a pedigree, such a *posterity,* such an *Allyance,* if this be not a short walke, yet it is a round walke, a giddy, a vertiginous proceeding. Get beyond thine own circle; consider thy selfe at thine end, at thy death, and then *Egredere,* Goe further then that, *Go forth and see* what thou shalt be after thy death.

Still that which we are to look upon, is especially *our selves,* but it is   *Videte* *our selves,* enlarg'd and extended into the *next world;* for till we see, what we shall be then, we are but *short-sighted.* Wouldst thou say, thou knew'st a man, because thou hadst seen him in *his Cradle?* no more canst thou be said, to have known thy self, because thou knowest the titles, and additions, which thou hast received in this world; for all those things which we have here, are but *swadling clouts,* and all our *motions,* and preferments, from place, to place, are but the *rock-ing of a cradle.* The first thing that Christ says to his spouse in the Canticles, is, *If thou know not thy selfe,* (for so all the Ancients read   1.8

it, and so the Originall beares it) *If thou know not thy selfe, O thou fairest of women;* she might know, that she was the fairest of women, and yet not know her selfe; Thou mayst know, that thou art the happyest of men, in this world, and yet not know thy self. All this life is but a *Preface,* or but an *Index* and *Repertory* to the book of *life;* There, at that book beginnes thy study; To grow perfect in that
²¹⁰ book, to be dayly conversant in that book, to find what be the marks of them, whose names are written in that book, and to finde those marks, ingenuously, and in a rectified conscience, in thy selfe, To finde that no murmuring at Gods corrections, no disappointing of thy hopes, no interrupting of thy expectations, no frustrating of thy possibilities in the way, no *impatience in sicknesse,* and in the agony of death, can deface those marks, this is to goe *forth,* and see thy self, beyond thy self, to see what thou shalt be in the next world. Now, we cannot see our own face, without a glasse: and therefore in the

Exod. 38.8   old Temple, *In, or about that laver of brasse,* where the water, for the
²²⁰ uses of the Church was reserved, *Moses* appointed *looking-glasses* to be placed; that so, at the entring into the Temple, men might see themselves, and make use of that water, if they had contracted any foulnesse, in any part about them. Here, at your coming hither now, you have *two glasses,* wherein you may see your selves from head to foot; One in the Text, your *Head, Christ Jesus,* represented unto you, in the name and person of *Solomon, Behold King Solomon crowned, &c.* And another, under your feet, in the dissolution of this great *Monarch,* our *Royall Master,* now layd lower by death then any of us, his Subjects and servants.

Solomon   ²³⁰   First then, behold your selves in that first glasse, *Behold King Solomon; Solomon* the sonne of *David,* but not the Son of *Bathsheba,* but of a better mother, the most blessed *Virgin Mary.* For, *Solomon,* in this text, is not a *proper* Name, but an *Appellative;* a significative word: *Solomon* is *pacificus,* the *Peacemaker,* and our peace is made in, and by Christ Jesus: and he is that *Solomon,* whom we are called

[1 Cor. 2.2]   upon to see here. Now, as Saint *Paul* says, that *he would know nothing but Christ,* (that's his first abridgement) and then he would know nothing of Christ, but *him crucifyed,* (and that's the re-abridgement) so we seek no other glasse, to see our selves in, but Christ, nor any
²⁴⁰ other thing in this glasse, but his *Humiliation.* What need we? Even

that, his lowest humiliation, his death, is expressed here, in three words of exaltation, It is a *Crown,* it is a *Mariage,* it is the *gladnesse of heart: Behold King Salomon crowned,* &c.

The Crown, which we are called to see him crowned with, *his mother* put upon him; The Crown which his *Father gave him,* was that glory, wherewith he was glorifyed, with the Father, *from all eternity,* in his *divine nature:* And the Crown wherewith his Father crowned his *Humane nature,* was the glory given to that, in his *Ascension. His Mother* could give him no such Crown: she her selfe ⁵⁰ had no Crown, but that, which *he* gave her. The Crown that *she* gave him, was that substance, that he received from her, *our flesh,* our nature, our *humanity;* and this, *Athanasius,* and this, Saint *Ambrose,* calls the *Crown,* wherewith *his Mother crowned him,* in this text, his infirm, his humane nature. Or, *the Crown wherewith his Mother crowned him,* was that Crown, to which, that infirme nature which he tooke from her, submitted him, which was his *passion,* his *Crown of thornes;* for so *Tertullian,* and divers others take this Crown of his, from her, to be his *Crown of thorns: Woe to the Crown of pride, whose beauty is a fading flower,* says the Prophet; But blessed be ⁶⁰ this Crown of Humiliation, whose flower cannot fade. Then was there truly a *Rose* amongst *Thorns,* when through his Crown of *Thorns,* you might see his title, *Jesus Nazarenus:* for, in that very name *Nazarenus,* is involved the signification of a *flower;* the very word signifies a *flower. Esay's* flower in the Crown of pride fades, and is removed; This flower in the Crown of Thornes fades not, nor could be removed; for, for all the importunity of the Jews, *Pilate* would not suffer *that title* to be removed, or to be changed; still *Nazarenus* remained, and still a rose amongst thorns. You know the curse of the earth, *Thorns and thistles shall it bring forth unto thee;* It did so to our ⁷⁰ *Solomon* here, it brought forth thornes to Christ, and he made a *Crown* of those thorns, not onely for *himself,* but for us too, *Omnes aculei mortis, in Dominici Corporis tolerantia, obtusi sunt,* All the thorns of life and death, are broken, or blunted upon the head of our *Solomon,* and now, even our *thorns,* make up *our Crown,* our tribulation in life, our dissolution in death, conduce to our glory: *Behold him crowned with his Mothers Crown,* for even that brought him to his *Fathers Crown,* his humiliation to exaltation, his passion to glory.

Corona

Esa. 28.1

Gen. 3.18

Tertul.

Behold your *Solomon, your Saviour* again, and you shall see an-

Desponsatio

other *beam* of Comfort, in your tribulations from his; for even this
280 *Humiliation* of his, is called his *Espousals,* his *marriage, Behold him
crowned in the day of his Espousals.* His Spouse is the *Church,* His
marriage is the *uniting* of himselfe to this Spouse, in his becomming
Head of the Church. The great City, the heavenly Jerusalem, is called

21.9

The Bride, and *The Lambs wife,* in the *Revelation:* And he is the
Head of this body, the *Bridegroom* of this Bride, the Head of this

[1.5]

Church, as he is *The first-borne of the Dead;* Death, that dissolves
all ours, made up this marriage. His Death is his Marriage, and upon
his Death flowed out from his side, those two *Elements of the Church,*

[Ioh. 19.34]

water and *bloud;* The Sacraments of *Baptisme,* and of the *Com-*
290 *munion* of himself. Behold then this *Solomon crowned* and *married;*
both words of *Exaltation,* and *Exultation,* and both by *Death;* and
trust him for working the same effects upon thee; That thou (*though
by Death*) shalt be *crowned* with a Crown of Glory, and *married*
to him, in whose right and merit thou shalt have that Crown.

Lætitia

And *Behold* him once again, and you shall see not a *beam,* but a
stream of comfort; for this day, which is the day of his death, he calls
here *The day of the gladnesse of his heart. Behold him crowned in
the day of the gladnesse of his heart.* The fulnesse, the compasse, the
two *Hemispheres* of Heaven, are often designed to us, in these two
300 names, *Joy* and *Glory:* If the *Crosse* of Christ, the *Death* of Christ,
present us both these, how neare doth it bring, how fully doth it deliver Heaven it self to us in this life? And then we heare the Apostle

Heb. 2.9

say, *We see Jesus, for the suffering of Death, crowned with Honour
and Glory:* There is *half* Heaven got by *Death, Glory.* And then,

12.2

for the joy that was set before him, he indured the Crosse; There is
the *other half, Joy;* All Heaven purchased by Death. And therefore,

1 Pet. 4.16

if any man suffer as a Christian, let him not be ashamed, saith the
Apostle; but *let him glorifie God, In isto Nomine,* as the *vulgate*
read it; *In that behalfe,* as *we* translate it. But, *In isto Nomine,* saith
310 S. *Augustine:* Let us glorifie God, in that Name; *Non solum in
nomine Christiani, sed Christiani patientis,* not onely because he is
a *Christian* in his *Baptisme,* but a Christian in a *second Baptisme,* a
Baptisme of bloud; not onely as he hath received Christ, in accepting
his *Institution,* but because he hath conformed himself to Christ, in
fulfilling his *sufferings.* And therefore, though we admit *naturall*

and *humane sorrow,* in the calamities which overtake us, and sur-
round us in this life: (for as *all glasses* will gather drops and tears
from externall causes, so this very glasse which we looke upon now,
our *Solomon* in the Text, our *Saviour,* had those *sadnesses of heart*
²⁰ toward his Passion, and *Agonies* in his passion) yet *count it all Joy*
when you fall into tentations, saith the Apostle: *All Joy,* that is, both
the *interest,* and the *principall,* hath the *earnest* and the *bargain;* for
if you can conceive joy in your tribulations in this world, how shall
that joy be multiplied unto you, when no tribulation shall be mingled
with it? There is not a better evidence, nor a more binding earnest
of everlasting Joy in the next world, then to find *Joy of heart* in the
tribulations of this; fixe thy self therefore upon this first glasse, this
Solomon, thy Saviour, *Behold King Solomon crownd,* &c. and by
conforming thy self to his *holy sadnesse,* and *humiliation,* thou shalt
³⁰ also become like him, in his Joy, and Glory.

But then the hand of God, hath *not set up,* but *laid down another*
Glasse, wherein thou maist see thy self; a glasse that reflects thy self,
and nothing but thy selfe. Christ, who was the other glasse, *is like*
thee in every thing, but not absolutely, for *sinne* is *excepted;* but in
this glasse presented now (*The Body of our Royall,* but *dead Master*
and Soveraigne) we cannot, we doe not except sinne. Not onely the
greatest man is subject to *naturall infirmities,* (Christ himself was so)
but the holiest man is subject to *Originall and Actuall sinne,* as thou
art, and so a fit glasse for thee, to see thyself in. *Jeat* showes a man his
⁴⁰ face, as well as *Crystall;* nay, a Crystall glasse will not show a man
his face, except it be steeled, except it be darkned on the backside:
Christ as he was a pure *Crystall* glasse, as he was *God,* had not been
a glasse for us, to have seen ourselves in, except he had been *steeled,*
darkened with our humane nature; Neither was he ever so throughly
darkened, as that he could present us wholly to our selves, because
he had no *sinne,* without seeing of which we do not see our selves.
Those therefore that are like thee in all things, subject to humane
infirmities, subject to *sinnes,* and yet are translated, and *translated* by
Death, to everlasting *Joy,* and *Glory,* are nearest and clearest glasses
⁵⁰ for thee, to see thy self in; and such is this glasse, which God hath
proposed to thee, in this house. And therefore, change the word of
the Text, in a letter or two, from *Egredimini,* to *Ingredimini;* never
go forth to see, but *Go in and see a Solomon crowned with his mothers*

Matth. 26.38
Luc. 22.44
Jam. 1.2

Rex

[Heb. 2.17]

crown, &c. And when you shall find that hand that had signed to one of you a *Patent* for *Title*, to another for *Pension*, to another for *Pardon*, to another for *Dispensation, Dead:* That hand that settled Possessions by his *Seale*, in the *Keeper*, and rectified *Honours* by the *sword*, in his *Marshall*, and distributed relief to the *Poore*, in his *Almoner*, and *Health* to the *Diseased*, by his *immediate Touch*, Dead:
360 That Hand that ballanced his *own three Kingdomes* so equally, as that none of them complained of one another, nor of him, and carried the *Keyes* of all the Christian world, and locked up, and let out *Armies* in their due season, Dead; how poore, how faint, how pale, how momentany, how transitory, how empty, how frivolous, how Dead things, must you necessarily thinke *Titles*, and *Possessions*, and *Favours*, and all, when you see that Hand, which was the *hand of Destinie*, of *Christian Destinie*, of the *Almighty God*, lie dead? It was not so *hard* a hand when we touched it last, nor so *cold* a hand when we kissed it last: That hand which was wont *to wipe all teares*
370 *from all our eyes*, doth now but presse and squeaze us as so many spunges, filled one with one, another with another cause of teares. Teares that can have no other banke to bound them, but the declared and manifested *will of God:* For, till our teares flow to that heighth, that they might be called a *murmuring* against the declared will of God, it is against our Allegiance, it is *Disloyaltie*, to give our teares any stop, any termination, any measure. It was a great part of *Annaes*

Luc. 2.37

prayse, That she departed not from the Temple, day nor night; visit Gods Temple often in the day, meet him in his owne House, and depart not from his *Temples,* (The *dead bodies* of his Saints are his
380 Temples still) even at *midnight;* at midnight remember them, who resolve into dust, and make them thy glasses to see thy self in. Looke now especially upon him whom God hath presented to thee now, and with as much cheerfulnesse as ever thou heardst him say, *Remember my Favours, or remember my Commandements;* heare him

Ecclus. 38.22

say now with the wise man, *Remember my Iudgement, for thine also shall be so; yesterday for me, and to day for thee;* He doth not say *to morrow*, but *to Day, for thee.* Looke upon him as a beame of that Sunne, as an abridgement of that *Solomon* in the Text; for every Christian truely reconciled to God, and *signed* with his hand in the
390 *Absolution*, and *sealed* with his bloud in the *Sacrament*, (and this was his case) is a beame, and an abridgement of *Christ* himselfe.

Behold him therefore *Crowned with the Crown that his Mother gives him: His Mother, The Earth.* In antient times, when they used to reward Souldiers with particular kinds of *Crowns,* there was a great dignity *in Corona graminea,* in a Crown of Grasse: That denoted a Conquest, or a Defence of that land. He that hath but *Coronam Gramineam,* a turfe of grasse in *a Church yard,* hath a Crown from his *Mother,* and even in that buriall taketh *seisure* of the *Resurrection,* as by a turfe of grasse men give seisure of land. *He is crowned in the day of his Marriage;* for though it be a day of *Divorce* of us from him, and of *Divorce* of his body from his soul, yet neither of these Divorces breake the Marriage: His *soule* is married to him that made it, and his body and soul shall meet again, and all we, both then in that Glory where we shall acknowledge, that there is no way to this *Marriage,* but this *Divorce,* nor to *Life,* but by *Death.* And lastly, he is *Crowned in the day of the gladnesse of his heart:* He leaveth that heart, which was accustomed to the halfe joyes of the earth, in the earth; and he hath enlarged his heart to a greater capacity of Joy, and Glory, and God hath filled it according to that new capacity. And therefore, to end all with the Apostles words, *I would not have you to be ignorant, Brethren, concerning them, which are asleepe, that ye sorrow not, as others that have no hope; for if ye beleeve that Jesus died, and rose again, even so, them also, which sleepe in him, will God bring with him.* But when you have performed this *Ingredimini,* that you have gone in, and mourned upon him, and performed the *Egredimini,* you have gone forth, and laid his Sacred body, in Consecrated Dust, and come then to another *Egredimini,* to a going forth in many severall wayes: some to the service of their *new Master,* and some to the enjoying of their Fortunes conferred by their old; some to the raising of new *Hopes,* some to the burying of old, and all; some to new, and busie endeavours in Court, some to contented retirings in the Countrey; let none of us, goe so farre from him, or from one another, in any of our wayes, but that all we that have served him, may meet once a day, the first time we see the Sunne, in the eares of almighty God, with humble and hearty prayer, that he will be pleased to hasten that day, in which it shall be *an addition,* even to the joy of that place, as perfect as it is, and as infinite as it is, to see that face againe, and to see those eyes open there, which we have seen closed here. Amen.

1 Thess. 4.13

Number 15.

Preached at S. Pauls,
May 8. 1625.

The first of the Prebend of Cheswicks *five Psalmes; which five are appointed for that Prebend; as there are five other, for every other of our thirty Prebendaries.*

PSAL. 62.9. *SURELY MEN OF LOW DEGREE ARE VANITY, AND MEN OF HIGH DEGREE ARE A LIE; TO BEE LAID IN THE BALANCE, THEY ARE ALTOGETHER LIGHTER THEN VANITY.*

WE CONSIDER the dignity of the Booke of Psalmes, either in the whole body together, or in the particular limmes and distribution thereof. Of the whole Body, it may be enough to tell you that which S. *Basil* saith, That if all the other bookes of Scripture could perish, there remained enough in the booke of Psalmes for the supply of all: And therefore he cals it *Amuletum ad profligandum dæmonem;* Any Psalme is Exorcisme enough to expell any Devill, Charme enough to remove any tentation, Enchantment enough to ease, nay to sweeten any tribulation. It is abundantly enough that our Saviour Christ himselfe cites the Psalmes, not onely as Canonicall Scripture, but as a particular, and entire, and noble limme of that Body; *All must be fulfilled of me,* (saith he) *which is written in the Law, in the Prophets, and in the Psalmes.* The Law alone was the Sadduces Scripture, they received no more: The Law and the Prophets were (especially) the Scribes Scripture, they interpreted that: The Christians Scripture, in the Old Testament, is especially the Psalmes. For (except the Prophecy of *Esay* be admitted into the comparison) no booke of the Old Testament is so like a Gospel, so particular in all things concerning Christ, as the Psalmes.

Basil.

10

Luk. 24.44

²⁰ So hath the Booke of Psalmes an especiall dignity in the intire Body, all together. It hath so also in divers distributions thereof into parts. For even amongst the Jewes themselves, those fifteen Psalmes which follow immediatly and successively after the 119. Psalme, were especially distinguished, and dignified by the name of *Graduall Psalmes;* Whether because they were sung upon the Degrees and staires ascending to the Altar, Or because hee that read them in the Temple, ascended into a higher and more eminent place to reade them, Or because the word *Graduall* implies a degree of excellency in the Psalmes themselves, I dispute not; But a difference those fifteen ³⁰ Psalmes ever had above the rest, in the Jewish and in the Christian Church too. So also hath there beene a particular dignity ascribed to those seven Psalmes, which we have ever called the *Penitentiall Psalmes;* Of which S. *Augustine* had so much respect, as that he commanded them to be written in a great Letter, and hung about the curtaines of his Death-bed within, that hee might give up the ghost in contemplation, and meditation of those seven Psalmes. And it hath beene traditionally received, and recommended by good Authors, that that *Hymne,* which Christ and his Apostles are said to have sung after the Institution and celebration of the Sacrament, was a *Hymne* com-⁴⁰ posed of those six Psalmes, which we call the *Allelujah Psalmes,* immediatly preceding the hundred and nineteenth.

So then, in the whole Body, and in some particular limmes of the Body, the Church of God hath had an especiall consideration of the booke of Psalmes. This Church in which we all stand now, and in which my selfe, by particular obligation serve, hath done so too. In this Church, by ancient Constitutions, it is ordained, That the whole booke of Psalmes should every day, day by day bee rehearsed by us, who make the Body of this Church, in the eares of Almighty God. And therefore every Prebendary of this Church, is by those Constitu-⁵⁰ tions bound every day to praise God in those five Psalmes which are appointed for his Prebend. And of those five Psalmes which belong to mee, this, out of which I have read you this Text, is the first. And, by Gods grace, (upon like occasions) I shall here handle some part of every one of the other foure Psalmes, for some testimony, that those my five Psalmes returne often into my meditation, which I also assure

August.

Matt. 26.30

my selfe of the rest of my brethren, who are under the same obligation in this Church.

Psalmus integer

For this whole Psalme, which is under our present consideration, as *Athanasius* amongst all the Fathers, was most curious, and most
60 particular, and exquisite, in observing the purpose, and use of every particular Psalm, (for to that purpose, he goes through them all, in this maner; If thou wilt encourage men to a love, and pursuit of goodnesse, say the first Psalme, and 31. and 140, &c. If thou wilt convince the Jewes, say the second Psalme; If thou wilt praise God for things past, say this, and this, And this, and this if thou wilt pray for future things) so for this Psalme, which we have in hand, he observes in it a summary abridgement of all; For of this Psalme he sayes in generall, *Adversus insidiantes,* Against all attempts upon thy body, thy state, thy soule, thy fame, tentations, tribulations, machinations, defama-
70 tions, say this Psalme. As he saith before, that in the booke of Psalmes, every man may discerne *motus animi sui,* his owne sinfull inclinations expressed, and arme himselfe against himselfe; so in this Psalme, he may arme himselfe against all other adversaries of any kinde. And therefore as the same Father entitles one Sermon of his, *Contra omnes hæreses,* A Sermon for the convincing of all Heresies, in which short Sermon he meddles not much with particular heresies, but onely establishes the truth of Christs Person in both natures, which is indeed enough against all Heresies, and in which (that is the consubstantiality of Christ with the Father, God of God) this Father *Athanasius,* hath
80 enlarged himselfe more then the rest (insomuch, that those heretiques which grow so fast, in these our dayes, The Socinians, (who deny the Godhead of Christ) are more vexed with that Father, then with any other, and call him for *Athanasius, Sathanasius*) As he cals that Sermon, a sermon against all Heresies, so he presents this Psalme against all Tentations, and Tribulations; Not that therein *David* puts himselfe to waigh particular tentations, and tribulations, but that he puts every man, in every triall, to put himselfe wholly upon God, and to know, that if man cannot helpe him in this world, nothing can; And, for man, *Surely men of low degree are vanity, and men of high degree*
90 *are a lie; To be laid in the balance, they are altogether lighter then vanity.*

Divisio

We consider in the words, The maner, and the matter, How it is

spoken, And what is said. For the first, the maner, this is not absolutely spoken, but comparatively, not peremptorily, but respectively,
not simply, but with relation. The Holy Ghost, in *Davids* mouth, doth
not say, That man can give no assistance to man; That man may looke
for no helpe from man; But, that God is alwayes so present, and so
all-sufficient, that wee need not doubt of him, nor rely upon any other,
otherwise then as an instrument of his. For that which he had spread
100 over all the verses of the Psalme before, he summes up in the verse immediatly before the Text, *Trust in God at all times, for hee is a*
refuge for us; and then, hee strengthens that with this, What would
yee prefer before God, or joyne with God? man? what man? *Surely*
men of low degree are vanity, and men of high degree are a lie; To
be laid in the balance, they are altogether lighter then vanity.

Which words being our second part, open to us these steps: First,
that other Doctrins, morall or civill Instructions may be delivered to
us possibly, and probably, and likely, and credibly, and under the like
termes, and modifications, but this in our Text, is Assuredly, un-
110 doubtedly, undeniably, irrefragably, *Surely men of low degree, &c.* For
howsoever when they two are compared together, with one another, it
may admit discourse and disputation, whether men of high degree, or
of low degree doe most violate the lawes of God; that is, whether
prosperity or adversity make men most obnoxious to sin, yet, when
they come to bee compared, not with one another, but both with God,
this asseveration, this *surely* reaches to both; *Surely, The man of low*
degree is vanity, and, as *Surely, The man of high degree is a lie.* And
though this may seeme to leave some roome, for men of middle ranks,
and fortunes, and places, That there is a mediocrity, that might give an
120 assurance, and an establishment, yet there is no such thing in this case,
for (as *surely* still) *to be laid in the balance, they are all,* (not all of
low, and all of high degree, all rich, and all poore, but) All, of all conditions, *altogether lighter then vanity.*

Now, all this doth not destroy, not extinguish, not annihilate that
affection in man, of hope, and trust, and confidence in any thing; but
it rectifies that hope, and trust, and confidence, and directs it upon the
right object: Trust not in flesh, but in spirituall things, That wee
neither bend our hopes downeward, to infernall spirits, to seeke help
in Witches; nor mis-carry it upward, to seeke it in Saints, or Angels,

¹³⁰ but fix it in him, who is nearer us then our owne soules, our blessed, and gracious, and powerfull God, who in this one Psalme is presented unto us, by so many names of assurance and confidence, *My expectation, my salvation, my rocke, my defence, my glory, my strength, my refuge,* and the rest.

First then these words, *Surely men of low degree, and men of high degree are vanity,* are not absolutely, simply, unconditionally spoken; Man is not nothing: Nay, it is so farre from that, as that there is nothing but man. As, though there may bee many other creatures

living, which were not derived from *Eve,* and yet *Eve* is called *Mater* ¹⁴⁰ *viventium,* The Mother of all that live, because the life of none but man, is considered; so there bee so many other Creatures, and Christ

sends his Apostles to preach, *Omni Creaturæ,* to every creature, yet he meanes none but Man. All that God did in making all other creatures, in all the other dayes, was but a laying in of Materials; The setting up of the work was in the making of Man. God had a picture of himselfe

from all eternity; from all eternity, the Sonne of God was the *Image of the invisible God;* But then God would have one picture, which should bee the picture of Father, Sonne, and Holy Ghost too, and so made man to the Image of the whole Trinity. As the Apostle argues,

¹⁵⁰ *Cui dixit, To whom did God ever say, This day have I begotten thee,* but to Christ? so we say, for the dignity of man, *Cui dixit,* of what creature did God ever say, *Faciamus,* Let us, us make it, All, all, the Persons together, and to imploy, and exercise, not onely Power, but Counsaile in the making of that Creature? Nay, when man was at worst, he was at a high price; man being fallen, yet then, in that undervalue, he cost God his own and onely Son, before he could have him. Neither became the Son of God capable of redeeming man, by any lesse, or any other way, then by becomming man. The Redeemer must be better then he whom he is to redeeme; and yet, he must abase ¹⁶⁰ himselfe to as low a nature as his; to his nature; else he could not redeeme him. God was aliened from man, and yet God must become man, to recover man.

God joyned man in Commission with himselfe, upon his Creation, in the *Replete* and *Dominamini,* when he gave Man power to possesse the Earth, and subdue the Creature; And God hath made man so equall to himselfe, as not onely to have a soule endlesse and immortall, as God himselfe, (though not endlesse and immortall as himselfe, yet endlesse and immortall as himselfe too, though not immortall the same way, (for Gods immortality is of himselfe) yet as certainly, and as infallibly Immortall as he) but God hath not onely given man such an immortall soule, but a body that shall put on Incorruption and Immortality too, which he hath given to none of the Angels. In so much, that howsoever it be, whether an Angel may wish it selfe an Archangel, or an Archangel wish it selfe a Cherubin; yet man cannot deliberately wish himselfe an Angel, because he should lose by that wish, and lacke that glory, which he shall have in his body. *We shall be like the Angels,* says Christ; In that wherein we can be like them, we shall be like them, in the exalting and refining of the faculties of our soules; But they shall never attaine to be like us in our glorified bodies. Neither hath God onely reserved this treasure and dignity of man to the next world, but even here he hath made him *filium Dei,* The Sonne of God, and *Semen Dei,* The seed of God, and *Consortem divinæ naturæ,* Partaker of the divine Nature, and *Deos ipsos,* Gods themselves, for *Ille dixit Dii estis,* he hath said we are Gods. So that, as though the glory of heaven were too much for God alone, God hath called up man thither, in the ascension of his Sonne, to partake thereof; and as though one God were not enough for the administration of this world, God hath multiplied gods here upon Earth, and imparted, communicated, not onely his power to every Magistrate, but the Divine nature to every sanctified man. *David* asks that question with a holy wonder, *Quid est homo? What is man that God is so mindfull of him?* But I may have his leave, and the holy Ghosts, to say, since God is so mindfull of him, since God hath set his minde upon him, What is not man? Man is all.

Since we consider men in the place that they hold, and value them according to those places, and aske not how they got thither, when we see Man made The Love of the Father, The Price of the Sonne, The Temple of the Holy Ghost, the Signet upon Gods hand, The Apple of Gods eye, Absolutely, unconditionally we cannot annihilate man, not evacuate, not evaporate, not extenuate man to the levity, to the vanity, to the nullity of this Text (*Surely men altogether, high and low, are lighter then vanity.*) For, man is not onely a contributary Creature, but a totall Creature; He does not onely make one, but he is all; He is

Marke 12.25

Luke 6.35
I Joh. 3.9
2 Pet. 1.4
[Psa. 82.6]

[Psa. 8.4]

not a piece of the world, but the world it selfe; and next to the glory

of God, the reason why there is a world.

But we must not determine this consideration here, That man is something, a great thing, a noble Creature, if we refer him to his end, to his interest in God, to his reversion in heaven; But when we consider man in his way, man amongst men, man is not nothing, not un-

²¹⁰ able to assist man, not unfit to be relyed upon by man; for, even in that respect also, God hath made *Hominem homini Deum,* He hath made one man able to doe the offices of God to another, in procuring his regeneration here, and advancing his salvation hereafter; As he sayes,

Obad. 21

Saviours shall come up on Mount Sion; which is the Church. Neither hath God determined that power of assisting others, in the Character of Priesthood onely, (that the Priest should be a god, that is, doe the offices and the work of God to the people, by delivering salvation unto them) but he hath also made the Prince, and the secular Magistrate, a god, that is able to doe the offices, and the works of God, not onely to

²²⁰ the people, but to the Priest himselfe, to sustaine him, yea, and to countenance, and favour, and protect him too, in the execution and exercise of his priestly office; As we see in the first plantation of those two great Cedars, The Secular, and the Ecclesiasticall Power, (which, that they might alwayes agree like brethren, God planted at first in those two brethren, *Moses* and *Aaron*) There, though *Moses* were the temporall, and *Aaron* the spirituall Magistrate, yet God sayes to *Moses,*

Exod. 7.1

I have made thee a God to Pharaoh, (but not onely to *Pharaoh*) but *Aaron thy brother shall be thy Prophet;* for, (as he had said before)

Exod. 4.16

Thou shalt be to him in stead of a God. So usefull, so necessary is man

²³⁰ to man, as that the Priest, who is of God, incorporated in God, subsists

Isidor

also by man; for, *Principes hujus seculi rationem reddituri sunt,* The Princes of this world must give God an account, *Propter Ecclesiam, quam à Christo tuendam susceperunt,* for that Church, which Christ hath committed to their protection. In spirituall difficulties, and for spirituall duties, God sends us to the Priest; but to such a *Priest* as is a

Heb. 4.15

man; and (as our comfort is expressed) *A Priest which was touched with the feeling of our infirmities, and was in all points tempted like as we are:* for the businesses of this world, Rights, and Titles, and

Deut. 16.18

Proprieties, and Possessions, God sends us still to the Judge; (*Iudges*

²⁴⁰ *and officers shalt thou make in all thy gates*) Judges to try between

man and man; And the sword in battaile tryes between State and State, Prince and Prince; And therefore God commands and directs the levying of men to that purpose, in many places of the history of his people; particularly God appoints *Gideon* to take a certaine pro- Judg. 7.[7] portion of the army, a certaine number of Souldiers. And in another place, there goes out a presse for Souldiers from *Moses* mouth; He Exod. 32.26 presses them upon their holy allegeance to God, when he sayes, *Who is on the Lords side, let him come unto me.* So, in infirmities, in sick- nesses of the body, we aske with the Prophet, *Is there no balme in* Jer. 8.22 ²⁵⁰ *Gilead? Is there no Physitian there?* God does not reprove *Asa* for 2 Chro. 16.12 seeking of helpe of the Physitians; but the increpation lyes onely upon this, *That he sought to the Physitian, and not to the Lord.* God sends man to the Priest, to the Prince, to the Judge, to the Physitian, to the Souldier, and so, (in other places) to the Merchant, and to cunning Artificers, (as in the building of the Temple) that all that man needs might be communicated to man by man.

So that still, simply, absolutely, unconditionally, we cannot say, Surely men, men altogether, high or low, or meane, all are lesse then vanity. And surely they that pervert and detort such words as these, ²⁶⁰ to such a use, and argue from thence, Man is nothing, no more then a worme or a fly, and therefore what needs this solemne consideration of mans actions, it is all one what he does, for all his actions, and him- selfe too are nothing; They doe this but to justifie or excuse their own lazinesse in this world, in passing on their time, without taking any Calling, embracing any profession, contributing any thing to the spirituall edification, or temporall sustentation of other men. But take the words, as the Holy Ghost intends them, comparatively, what man compared with God, or what man considered without God, can doe any thing for others, or for himselfe? When the Apostle sayes, *That* Phil. 3.8 ²⁷⁰ *all the world is but dung,* when the Prophet sayes, *That all the* Esay 40.17 *Nations of the world are lesse then nothing,* when the Apostle sayes even of himselfe, *that he is nothing,* all this is nothing in comparison 2 Cor. 12.11 of that expression in the same Apostle, *That even the preaching of the* I Cor. 1.21 *Gospel is foolishnesse,* That that which is the *savour of life unto life,* Gods owne Ordinance, *Preaching,* is but *foolishnesse;* Let it be a *Paul* that plants, and an *Apollo* that waters, if God give not increase, all is but frivolousnesse, but foolishnesse; And therefore boldly, confidently,

uncontroulably we may proceed to the propositions of our Text, which
constitute our second part, Man, any man, every man, all men, col-
²⁸⁰ lectively, distributively, considered so, (comparatively with God, or
privatively without God) is but a *lie,* but *vanity, lesse then vanity.*

2 Part
Surely

To make our best use of the words, (as our translation exhibits
them) we make our entrance, with this word of confidence, and infallibility, which onely becomes the holy Ghost, in his asseverations,
and in which he establishes the propositions following; Surely, surely
men of low degree, and as surely, men of high, and, surely still all men
together, are lighter then vanity. Men deliver their assertions otherwise
modified, and under other qualifications. They obtrude to us miraculous doctrines of Transubstantiation, and the like, upon a possibility
²⁹⁰ onely; It may be done, say they, It is possible, God can doe it. But that
is far from the assurednesse of the Holy Ghost, Surely it is so; for

Chrysost.

Asylum hæreticorum, est omnipotentia Dei, is excellently said, and by
more then one of the Fathers, The omnipotence of God is the Sanctuary of Heretiques, Thither they fly, to countenance any such error;
This God can doe, why should you not beleeve it? Men proceed in
their asseverations farther then so, from this possibility to a probability; It will abide argument, it hath been disputed in the Schoole,
and therefore is probable; why should not you beleeve it? And so they
offer us the doctrine of the immaculate conception of the blessed
³⁰⁰ Virgin without Originall sinne; But this probability reaches not to this
assurednesse of our text, *surely.* They will goe farther then this probability, to a verisimilitude, it is more then meerly possible, more then
fairly probable, it is likely to be so; some of the ancient Fathers have
thought so; and then, why should not you beleeve it? and so they offer
us prayer for the dead. Farther then this verisimilitude they goe too;
They goe to a *Piè creditur,* It may be piously beleeved, and it is fit to
beleeve it, because it may assist and exalt devotion to thinke so; And
then why should you not beleeve it? And so they offer us the worship
of Images and Reliques. But still, all this comes short of our assured-
³¹⁰ nesse, *Surely,* undoubtedly, undisputably it is so.

And when the Romane Church would needs counterfeit the language of the Holy Ghost, and pronounce this surenesse upon so many
new Articles in the Councell of Trent, it hath not prospered well with
them; for we all know, they have repented that forwardnesse since,

and wished they had not determined so many particulars to be matter of faith; because after such a determination by a Councell, they have bound themselves not to recede from those doctrines, how unmaintenable soever they be in themselves, or how inconvenient soever they fall out to be to them. And therefore we see, that in all the solicitations that can be used, even by Princes, to whom they are most affected, they will not come now to pronounce so surely, to determine so positively upon divers points that rest yet in perplexity amongst them. Which hath raysed them so many commotions in the kingdome of Spaine, and put more then one of their later Kings, to send divers Ambassages to Rome, to solicite a cleare declaration in that point, but could never, nor can yet attaine it, that is, The immaculate conception of the blessed Virgin without Originall sinne. So also, for the obligation that the lawes of secular Magistrates lay upon the Conscience, so also for the Concurrence of Grace, and Free-will, and divers others; in which they will not be drawne to this, Surely, to determine and declare of either side; for, indeed that is the language of the Holy Ghost.

It hath been observed amongst Philosophers, that *Plato* speaks probably, and *Aristotle* positively; *Platoes* way is, It may be thus, and *Aristotles,* It must be thus. The like hath been noted amongst Divines, between *Calvin,* and *Melanchton; Calvin* will say, *Videtur,* It seemes to be thus, *Melanchton,* It can be no otherwise but thus. But the best men are but Problematicall, Onely the Holy Ghost is Dogmaticall; Onely he subscribes this *surely,* and onely he seales with Infallibility. Our dealings are appointed to be in yea, yea, and nay, nay, and no farther; But *all the promises of God are yea, and Amen,* that is, surely, verily; for that is his Name; These things saith *The Amen,* He that is Amen. And it is not (I hope) an impertinent note, That that Euangelist S. *Iohn,* who considers the Divinity of Christ, more then the other Euangelists doe, does evermore, constantly, without any change, double that which was Christs ordinary asseveration, *Amen.* As oft as the other Euangelists mention it in Christs mouth, still they expresse it with one *Amen, verily I say;* S. *Iohn* always, *Amen, Amen, verily, verily,* it is thus and thus. The nearer we come to the consideration of God, the farther we are removed from all contingencies, and all inclination to Error, and the more is this *Amen, verily, surely,* multiplied and established unto us.

2 Cor. 1.20
Rev. 3.14

It is in doctrines and opinions, as it is in designes and purposes; *Goe*

[Jam. 4.13] *to,* (sayes the Prophet, by way of reprehension) *Goe to, you that say, we will goe to such a City, and trade thus and thus there, &c.* So, goe to, you that pronounce upon every invention, and Tradition of your own, a *Quicunque vult salvus esse,* Whosoever will be saved, must beleeve this, and clogge every problematicall proposition with an *Anathema,* Cursed be he, Excommunicated he that thinks the contrary to this; Goe to, you that make matters of faith of the passions of men.
³⁶⁰ So also, goe to, you that proceed and continue in your sinnes, and say, Surely I shall have time enough to repent hereafter. Goe to, you that in a spirituall and irreligious melancholy and diffidence in Gods mercy, say, Surely the Lord hath locked up his mercy from me, surely I shall never see that Sunne more, never receive, never feele beame of his mercy more, but passe through this darknesse into a worse. This word, *surely,* in such cases, in such senses, is not your mothers tongue, not the language of the Christian Church. She teaches you, to condition all in Christ; In him you are enabled to doe all things, and without him nothing. But absolutely, unconditionally, this *surely* is appropriated to
³⁷⁰ the propositions, to the assertions of God himselfe; And some of those follow in this text.

Comparatio Divitis & Pauperis

Now that which the Holy Ghost presents here upon this assurednesse, is, *That men of low degree are vanity, and that men of high degree are a lie;* These are both sure, and alike sure. It is true that it constitutes a Probleme, that it admits a Discourse, it will abide a debatement, whether men of high degree, or of low degree be worst; whether riches or poverty, (both considered in a great measure, very rich, and very poore) Prosperity or Adversity occasion most sinnes. Though God call upon us in every leafe of the Scripture, to pity the
³⁸⁰ poore, and relieve the poore, and ground his last Judgement upon our

Mat. 25.34 works of mercy, *(Because you have fed and clothed the poore, inherit the kingdome)* yet, as the rich and the poore stand before us now, (as it were in Judgement) as we inquire and heare evidence, which state is most obnoxious, and open to most sinnes, we embrace, and apply to

Exod. 23.3 our selves that law, *Thou shalt not countenance a poore man in his*
Levit. 19.15 *cause;* And (as it is repeated) *Thou shalt not respect the person of the poore in Iudgement.*

There is then a poverty, which, without all question, is the direct

way to heaven; but that is spirituall; *Blessed are the poore in spirit.* Mat. 5.3
This poverty is humility, it is not beggary. A rich man may have it, and
a beggar may be without it. The Wiseman found not this poverty, (not
humility) in every poore man. He found three sorts of men, whom his
soule hated; And one of the three, *was a poore man that is proud.* And Ecclus. 25.2
when the Prophet said of Jerusalem in her afflictions, *Paupercula es &*
ebria, Thou are poore, and miserable, and yet drunke, though (as he Esay 51.21
addes there) *it were not with wine,* (which is now, in our dayes an
ordinary refuge of men of all sorts, in all sadnesses and crosses to relieve themselves upon wine and strong drinke, which are indeed strong
illusions) yet, though Jerusalems drunkennesse were not with wine, it
was worse; It was a staggering, a vertiginousnesse, an ignorance, a
blindnesse, a not discerning the wayes to God; which is the worst
drunkennesse, and fals often upon the poore and afflicted, That their
poverty and affliction staggers them, and damps them in their recourse
to God, so far, as that they know not, *That they are miserable, and* Revel. 3.17
wretched, and poore, and blinde, and naked. The Holy Ghost alwaies
makes the danger of the poore great, as well as of the rich. *The rich* Pro. 10.15
mans wealth is his strong City. There is his fault, his confidence in that;
But *Pavor pauperum, The destruction of the poore is his poverty;*
There is his fault, Desperation under it. *Solomon* presents them, as
equally dangerous, *Give me neither poverty, nor riches.* So does *Booz* Pro. 30.8
to *Ruth, Blessed be thou of the Lord, my daughter, in as much as thou* Ruth 3.10
followedst not young men, whether poore, or rich. That which *Booz*
intended there, Incontinency, and all vices that arise immediately out
of the corruption of nature, and are not induced by other circumstances,
have as much inclination from poverty, as from riches. May we not
say, more? I doubt we may. He must be a very sanctified man, whom
extreame poverty, and other afflictions, doe not decline towards a jealousie, and a suspicion, and a distrusting of God; And then, the sins
that bend towards desperation, are so much more dangerous, then
those that bend towards presumption, that he that presumes, hath still
mercy in his contemplation, He does not thinke, that he needs no
mercy, but that mercy is easily had; He beleeves there is mercy, he
doubts not of that; But the despairing man imagines a cruelty, an
unmercifulnesse in God, and destroyes the very nature of God himselfe. Riches is the Metaphor, in which, the Holy Ghost hath delighted

Rom. 2.4
11.33
Ephes. 3.8
ver. 16

to expresse God and Heaven to us; *Despise not the riches of his good-nesse,* sayes the Apostle; And againe, *O the depth of the riches of his wisdome;* And so, after, *The unsearchable riches of Christ;* And for the consummation of all, *The riches of his Glory.* Gods goodnesse
[430] towards us in generall, our Religion in the way, his Grace here, his Glory hereafter, are all represented to us in Riches. With poverty God ordinarily accompanies his comminations; he threatens feeblenesse, and warre, and captivity, and poverty every where, but he never threatens men with riches.

Ordinary poverty, (that is a difficulty, with all their labors and in-dustry, to sustaine their family, and the necessary duties of their place) is a shrewd, and a slippery tentation. But for that street-beggery, which is become a Calling, (for Parents bring up their children to it, nay they doe almost take prentises to it, some expert beggers teach others what
[440] they shall say, how they shall looke, how they shall lie, how they shall cry) for these, whom our lawes call Incorrigible, I must say of them

Matt. 15.26

(in a just accommodation of our Saviours words, *It is not meet to take the childrens bread, and to cast it to dogs*) It is not meet, that this vermin should devoure any of that, which belongs to them who are truely poore. Neither is there any measure, any proportion of riches, that exposes man naturally to so much sin, as this kinde of beggery doth. Rich men forget, or neglect the duties of their Baptisme; but of these, how many are there, that were never baptized? Rich men sleepe out Sermons, but these never come to Church: Rich men are negligent
[450] in the practise, but these are ignorant in all knowledge.

It would require a longer disquisition, then I can afford to it now, whether Riches, or Poverty (considered in lesser proportions, ordinary riches, ordinary poverty) open us to more, and worse sins; But con-sider them in the highest and in the lowest, abundant riches, beggerly poverty, and it will scarce admit doubt, but that the incorrigible vaga-bond is farther from all wayes of goodnesse, then the corruptest rich man is. And therefore labour wee all earnestly in the wayes of some lawfull calling, that we may have our portion of this world by good meanes. For first, the advantages of doing good to others in a reall
[460] reliefe of their wants, is in the rich onely, whereas the best way of a good poore man, to doe good to others, is but an exemplary patience, to catechize others by his suffering; And then, all degrees of poverty

are dangerous and slippery, even to a murmuring against God, or an invading of the possessions, and goods of other men, but especially the lowest, the desperate degree of beggery, and then especially, when we cannot say it is inflicted by the hand of God, but contracted by our owne lazinesse, or our owne wastfulnesse.

This is a problematicall, a disputable case, Whether riches or poverty occasion most sins. And because on both sides there arise good doctrines of edification, I have thus far willingly stopped upon that disputable consideration. But now, that which wee receive here, upon *Davids,* upon the Holy Ghosts security, Surely it is thus, It is surely so, is this, That we shall be deceived, if we put our trust in men; for, what sort of men would we trust? *Surely men of low degree are vanity.* And this, if it be taken of particular men, needs no proving, no illustrating, no remembring. Every man sees and acknowledges, that to rely upon a man of no power, of no place, no blood, no fortune, no friends, no favour, is a vanity, *Surely men of low degree are vanity.* The first younger brother that was borne in the world, because he was lesse then another, is called by the very name of *vanity;* The eldest brother *Cain* signifies *possession,* but *Abel* is *vanity.*

But take it of a whole body of such men, Men of low degree, and it is so too; the Applause of the people is vanity, Popularity is vanity. At how deare a rate doth that man buy the peoples affections, that payes his owne head for their hats? How cheaply doth he sell his Princes favour, that hath nothing for it, but the peoples breath? And what age doth not see some examples of so ill merchants of their owne honours and lives too? How many men, upon confidence of that flattering gale of winde, the breath and applause of the people, have taken in their anchors, (that is, departed from their true, and safe hold, The right of the Law, and the favour of the Prince) and as soone as they hoysed their sailes, (that is, entred into any by-action) have found the wind in their teeth, that is, Those people whom they trusted in, armed against them. And as it is in Civill, and Secular, so it is in Ecclesiasticall, and Spirituall things too. How many men, by a popular hunting after the applause of the people, in their manner of preaching, and humouring them in their distempers, have made themselves incapable of preferment in the Church where they tooke their Orders, and preached themselves into a necessity of running away into for-

⁵⁰⁰ raine parts, that are receptacles of seditious and schismaticall Sepa-
ratists, and have been put there, to learne some trade, and become
Artificers for their sustentation? The same people that welcommed
Christ, from the Mount of Olives, into Jerusalem, upon Sunday, with
their *Hosannaes to the Sonne of David,* upon Friday mocked him in
Jerusalem, with their *Haile King of the Iewes,* and blew him out of
Jerusalem to Golgotha, with the pestilent breath, with the tempestu-
ous whirlwind of their *Crucifige's.* And of them, who have called the
Master Beelzebub, what shall any servant looke for? *Surely men of
low degree are vanity.*

⁵¹⁰   And then, under the same oath, and asseveration, *Surely,* as surely
as the other, *men of high degree are a lie.* Doth *David* meane these
men, whom he calls a *lie,* to be any lesse then those whom hee called
vanity? Lesse then vanity, then emptinesse, then nothing, nothing
can be; And low, and high are to this purpose, and in this consideration, (compared with God, or considered without God) equally nothing. He that hath the largest patrimony, and space of earth, in the
earth, must heare me say, That all that was nothing; And if he ask,
But what was this whole Kingdom, what all Europe, what all the
World? It was all, not so much as another nothing, but all one and
⁵²⁰ the same nothing as thy dung-hill was. But yet the Holy Ghost hath
beene pleased to vary the phrase here, and to call *Men of high degree,*
not *vanity,* but *a lie,* because the poore, men of low degree, in their
condition promise no assistance, feed not men with hopes, and therefore cannot be said to *lie,* but in the condition of men of high degree,
who are of power, there is a tacit promise, a naturall and inherent assurance of protection, and assistance, flowing from them. For, the
Magistrate cannot say, That he never promised me Justice, never
promised mee Protection; for in his assuming that place, he made me
that promise. I cannot say, that I never promised my Parish, my
⁵³⁰ service; for in my Induction, I made them that promise, and if I
performe it not, I am a lie; for so this word *Chasab* (which we translate *a lie*) is frequently used in the Scriptures, for that which is defective in the duty it should performe; *Thou shalt bee a spring of water,*
(sayes God in *Esay*) *Cujus aquæ non mentiuntur, whose waters never
lie,* that is, never dry, never faile.

  So then, when men of high degree doe not performe the duties of
their places, then they are a lie of their owne making; And when I

Matt. 21.9

Matt. 10.25

High degree

Esay 58.11

over-magnifie them in their place, flatter them, humor them, ascribe more to them, expect more from them, rely more upon them, then I should, then they are a lie of my making. But whether the lie be theirs, That they feare greater men then themselves, and so prevaricate in their duties; Or the lie be mine, that canonize them and make them my God, they, and I shall be disappointed; for, *Surely men of high degree are a lie.* But we are upon a Sermon, not upon a Satyr, therefore we passe from this.

And, for all this, there may seeme to be roome left for the Middle-state, for a mediocrity; when it is not so low as to be made the subject of oppression, nor so high as to be made the object of ambition, when it is neither exposed to scorne and contempt, nor to envy, and under-mining, may we not then trust upon, not rest in such a condition? Indeed, this mediocrity seemes (and justly) the safest condition; for this, and this onely enjoyes it selfe: The lazy man gets not up to it; The stirring man stayes not at it, but is gone beyond it. From our first Themes at Schoole, to our Texts in the Pulpit, we continue our praysing and perswading of this mediocrity. A man may have too much of any thing; *Anima saturata, A full soule will tread hony under his feete;* He may take in knowledge till he be ignorant; Let the Prophet *Ieremy* give the Rule, *Stultus factus est omnis homo à scientia, Every man becomes a foole by knowledge,* by over-weening, and over-valuing his knowledge; And let *Adam* be the example of this Rule, His eyes were opened by eating the fruit, and he knew so much, as he was ashamed of it; Let the Apostle be the Physitian, the moderator, *Sapere ad sobrietatem,* not to dive into secrets, and un-revealed mysteries. There is enough of this doctrine involved in the fable, *Acteon* saw more then he should have seene, and perished. There is abundantly enough expressed in the Oracle of Truth, *Vzza* was over-zealous in an office that appertained not to him, in assisting the Arke, and suffered for that.

We may quickly exceed a mediocrity, even in the praise of Medi-ocrity. But all our diligence will scarce finde it out. What is medi-ocrity? Or where is it? In the Hierarchy of the Roman Church they never thought of this mediocrity; They go very high, and very low, but there is no meane station; I meane no denomination of any Order from meannesse, from mediocrity. In one degree you finde em-broydered shooes, for Kings to kisse, and in another degree bare feet;

Mediocrity

Prov. 27.7

Ier. 10.14

Rom. 12.3

2 Sam. 6.6

we finde an Order of the *Society of Iesus;* and that is very high, for, Society implies community, partnership; And we finde low descents, *Minorits,* men lesse then others, and *Minims,* least of all men; and lower then all them, *Nullans,* men that call themselves, *Nothing;* And 580 truly, this Order, best of all others hath answered and justified the name, for, very soone, they came to nothing. Wee finde all extreames amongst them, even in their names, but none denominated from this mediocrity.

But to passe from names to the thing; indeed what is Mediocrity? where is it? Is it the same thing as Competency? But what is competency? or where is that? Is it that which is sufficient for thy present degree? perchance thy present degree is not sufficient for thee; Thy charge perchance, perchance thy parts and abilities, or thy birth and education may require a better degree. God produced plants in Para- 590 dise therefore, that they might grow; God hath planted us in this world, that we might grow; and he that does not endeavour that by all lawfull meanes, is inexcusable, as well as he that pursues unlawfull. But, if I come to imagine such a mediocrity, such a competency, such a sufficiency in my selfe, as that I may rest in that, that I thinke I may ride out all stormes, all dis-favours, that I have enough of mine owne, wealth, health, or morall constancy, if any of these decay, this is a verier vanity, then trusting in men of low degree, and a verier lye, then men of high degree; for, this is to trust to our selves; this is a

Habbak.　　*sacrificing* to our owne *nets,* our owne industry, our owne wisdome,
1.16　　600 our owne fortune; And of all the Idolatries of the Heathen, who made Gods of every thing they saw or imagined, of every thing, in, and betweene Heaven and hell, we reade of no man that sacrificed to himselfe. Indeed no man flatters me so dangerously, as I flatter my selfe, no man wounds me so desperately, as I wound myselfe; And therefore, since this which we call Mediocrity, and Competency is conditioned so, that it is enough to subsist alone, without relation to others, dependency upon others, feare from others, induces a confidence, a relying upon my selfe; As, that which we imagine to be the middle region of the ayre, is the coldest of all, So this imagined mediocrity, 610 that induces a confidence in our selves, is the weakest rest, the coldest comfort of all, and makes me a lye to my selfe. Therefore may the Prophet well spread, and safely extend his asseveration, his *Surely,* upon all, high, and low, and meane; *Surely to be laid in the balance, they are altogether lighter then vanity.*

Here then, upon a full enumeration of all parts, the Prophet concludes upon all. If therefore thou have the favour of great ones, the
applause of the people, confidence in thy selfe, in an instant, the power
of those great ones may be overthrowne, or their favour to thee with-
drawne from thee, (and so, that bladder is pricked, upon which thou
²⁰ swommest) The applause of the people may be hushed and silenced,
(either they would not, or they dare not magnifie thee) And, thine
owne constancy may be turned into a dejection of spirit, and consternation of all thy faculties. Put all together, (which fals out seldome, that any man can do so) but if he can do that, (which is the
best state of man, that can be imagined in this world, that he hath
all these together, the favour of High and low, and of himselfe, that
is, his owne testimony in his conscience, (though perchance an erring,
a mistaking conscience) yet, the Prophet had delivered the same assurance before (even of that state of man, which is rather imagined,
³⁰ then ever possest) *Surely every man, at his best state, is altogether*
vanity; And here, he adds, *lighter then vanity.* Vanity is nothing, but
there is a condition worse then nothing. Confidence in the things, or
persons of this world, but most of all, a confidence in our selves, will
bring us at last to that state, wherein we would faine be nothing, and
cannot. But yet, we have a balance in our text; And all these are but
put together in one balance. In the other scale there is something put
to, in comparison whereof all this world is so light. God does not leave
our great and noble faculty, and affection of hope, and trust, and
confidence, without something to direct it selfe upon, and rectifie it
⁴⁰ selfe in. He does not; for, for that he proposes himselfe; The words
immediately before the text, are, *God is a refuge;* and in comparison
of him, *To be laid in the balance, Surely they are altogether lighter*
then vanity.

So then, it is not enough not to trust in the flesh (for, for that, *Cursed*
be man, that trusted in man, or maketh flesh his arme; Their flesh
cannot secure thee, neither is thine owne *flesh brasse,* that thou canst
endure the vexations of this world, neither can *flesh* and *blood* reveale unto thee the things of the next world) It is not enough not to
trust in flesh, but thou must trust in that that is Spirit. And when thou
⁵⁰ art to direct thy trust upon him, who is spirit, the spirit of power, and
of consolation, stop not, stray not, divert not upon evill spirits, to
seeke advancement, or to seeke knowledge from them, nor upon good

Lighter then
vanity

Psal. 39.5

Deus omnia
Ier. 17.5
Iob 6.12
Mat. 16.17

spirits, the glorious saints of GOD in Heaven, to seeke salvation from them, nor upon thine owne spirit, in an over-valuation of thy purity, or thy merits. For, there is a pestilent pride in an imaginary humility, and an infectious foulenesse in an imaginary purity; but turne onely to the onely invisible and immortall God, who turnes to thee, in so many names and notions of power, and consolation, in this one Psalme. In the last verse but one of this Psalme, *David* sayes, 660 *God hath spoken once, and twice have I heard him.* God hath said enough at once; but twice, in this Psalme, hath he repeated this, in the second, and in the sixt verse, *He onely is my Rocke, and my Salvation, and my Defence,* And, (as it is inlarged in the seventh verse) *my Refuge, and my Glory.* If my *Refuge,* what enemy can pursue me? If my *Defence,* what tentation shall wound me? If my *Rock,* what storme shall shake me? If my *Salvation,* what melancholy shall deject me? If my *Glory,* what calumny shall defame me?

I must not stay you now, to infuse into you, the severall consolations of these severall names, and notions of God towards you. But, goe 670 your severall wayes home, and every soule take with him that name, which may minister most comfort unto him. Let him that is pursued with any particular tentation, invest God, as God is a *Refuge,* a Sanctuary. Let him that is buffeted with the messenger of Satan, battered with his owne concupiscence, receive God, as God is his *Defence* and target. Let him that is shaked with perplexities in his understanding, or scruples in his conscience, lay hold upon God, as God is his *Rock,* and his anchor. Let him that hath any diffident jealousie or suspition of the free and full mercy of God, apprehend God, as God is his *Salvation;* And him that walks in the ingloriousnesse and contempt 680 of this world, contemplate God, as God is his *Glory.* Any of these notions is enough to any man, but God is all these, and all else, that all soules can thinke, to every man. Wee shut up both these Considerations, (man should not, (that is not all) God should be relied upon) Mic. ult. 5 with that of the Prophet, *Trust ye not in a friend, put not your confidence in a guide, keepe the doores of thy mouth from her that lies in thy bosome;* (there is the exclusion of trust in man) and then he adds in the seventh verse, because it stands thus betweene man and man, *I will looke unto the Lord, I will looke to the God of my Salvation, my God will heare me.*

Number 16.

Preached upon **Whitsunday** *[? 1625]*

JOHN 16.8, 9, 10, 11. *AND WHEN HE IS COME, HE WILL REPROVE THE WORLD OF SIN, AND OF RIGHTEOUSNESSE, AND OF JUDGEMENT. | OF SIN, BECAUSE YE BELEEVE NOT ON ME. | OF RIGHTEOUSNESSE, BECAUSE I GOE TO MY FATHER, AND YE SEE ME NO MORE. | OF JUDGEMENT, BECAUSE THE PRINCE OF THIS WORLD IS JUDGED.*

OUR *Panis quotidianus,* Our daily bread, is that *Iuge sacrificium,* That daily sacrifice of meditating upon God; Our *Panis hodiernus,* This dayes bread, is to meditate upon the holy Ghost. To day if ye will heare his voice, to day ye are with him in Paradise; For, wheresoever the holy Ghost is, he creates a Paradise. The day is not past yet; As our Saviour said to *Peter, Hodie, in nocte hac,* This day, even in this night thou shalt deny me, so, *Hodie in nocte hac,* Even now, though evening, the day-spring from on high visits you, God carries back the shadow of your Sun-dyall, as to *Heze-* ¹⁰ *chias;* And now God brings you to the beginning of this day, if now you take knowledge, that he is come, who, when he comes, *Reproves the world of sin, &.*

    The solemnity of the day requires, and the method of the words offers for our first consideration, the Person; who is not named in our text, but designed by a most emphaticall denotation, *Ille, He,* He who is all, and doth all. But the word hath relation to a name, proper to the holy Ghost: for, in the verse immediatly preceding, our Saviour tels his disciples, *That he will send them the Comforter.* So, forbear-

Luk. 23.43

Mar. 14.30

Esay 38.8

Divisio

311

ing all other mysterious considerations of the holy Ghost, we receive
²⁰ him in that notion, and function in which Christ sends him, *The Comforter.* And therefore, in this capacity, as *The Comforter,* we must consider his action, *Arguet, He shall reprove;* Reprove, and yet Comfort; nay, therefore comfort, because reprove: And then the subject of his action, *Mundum, The world,* the whole world; no part left unreproved, yet no part left without comfort: And after that, what he reproves the world of; That multiplies; *Of sin, of righteousnesse, of judgement.* Can there be comfort in reproofe for sin? Or can there lie a reproofe upon righteousnesse, or upon judgement? Very justly; Though the evidence seem at first, as strange as the crime; for, though
³⁰ that be good evidence against the sin of the world, That they beleeve not in Christ, (*Of sin, because ye beleeve not on me*) yet to be *Reproved of righteousnesse, because Christ goes to his Father, and they see him no more,* And to be *Reproved of judgement, because the Prince of this world is judged,* this seemes strange, and yet this must be done, and done to our comfort; For, this must be done, *Cum venerit,* Then when the holy Ghost, and he in that function, as the Comforter, *is come,* is present, is working.

Beloved, Reproofes upon others without charity, rather to defame them, then amend them, Reproofes upon thy selfe, without shewing
⁴⁰ mercy to thine own soule, diffidences, and jealousies, and suspitions of God, either that he hated thee before thy sin, or hates thee irremediably, irreconciliably, irreparably for thy sin, These are Reproofes, but they are *Absente spiritu,* In the absence of the holy Ghost, before he comes, or when he is gone; *When he comes,* and stayes, *He shall reprove,* and *reprove all the world,* and all the world of those errours, *sin, and righteousnesse, and judgement,* and those errours upon those evidences, *Of sin, because ye beleeve not on me, &c.* But, in all this proceeding he shall never devest the nature of a Comforter; In that capacity he is sent, in that he comes, and works. I doubt I shall see an
⁵⁰ end of my houre, and your patience, before I shall have passed those branches, which appertaine most properly to the celebration of this day, the Person, the Comforter, his action, Reproofe, the subject thereof, the world, and the Time, *Cum venerit,* When he comes. The inditement, of what the accusation is, and the evidence, how it is proved, may exercise your devotion at other times. This day, the holy

Acts 2.2

Ghost is said to have come suddenly, and therefore in that pace we proceed, and make haste to the consideration of the Person, *Ille, When he,* He the holy Ghost, the Comforter, *is come.*

    Ille, Ille alone, *He,* is an emphaticall denotation; for to this purpose
60 *Ille* and *Ipse* is all one; And then, you know the Emphasis of that *Ipse; Ipse conteret, He* or *It shall bruise the Serpents head,* denotes the Messias, though there be no Messias named: This *Ipse* is so emphaticall a denotation, as that the Church of Rome, and the Church of God strive for it; for they will needs reade it *Ipsa,* and so refer our salvation, in the bruising of the Serpents head, to the Virgin *Mary;* we refer it according to the truth of the doctrine, and of the letter, to Christ himselfe, and therefore reade it *Ipse, He.* If there were no more but that in *David, It is He that hath made us,* every man would conclude, that that He is God. And if S. *Paul* had said *Ipse* alone, and not *Ipse*
70 *spiritus,* That *He,* and not *He the Spirit beares witnesse with our spirit,* every spirit would have understood this to be the holy Spirit, the holy Ghost. If in our text there had been no more, but such a denotation of a person that should speak to the hearts of all the world, that that *Ille,* that *He* would proceed thus, we must necessarily have seen an Almighty power in that denotation; But because that denotation might have carried terrour in it, being taken alone, therefore we are not left to that, but have a relation to a former name, and specification of the holy Ghost, *The Comforter.*

    For the establishment of Christs divinity, Christ is called *The mighty*
80 *God;* for his relation to us, he hath divers names. As we were all *In massa damnata,* Forfeited, lost, he is *Redemptor,* A Redeemer, for that that is past, *The Redeemer shall come to Sion,* sayes the Prophet, and so *Iob* saw *His Redeemer,* one that should redeem him from those miseries that oppressed him. As Christ was pleased to provide for the future, so he is, *Salvator,* A Saviour, Therefore the Angel gave him that name *Iesus, For he shall save his people from their sins.* So, because to this purpose Christ consists of two natures, God and man, he is called our Mediator, *There is one Mediator between God and man, the man Christ Iesus.* Because he presents those merits which are his, as ours,
90 and in our behalfe, he is called an Advocate, *If any man sin, we have an Advocate with the Father, Iesus Christ the righteous.* And because every man is to expect according to his actions, he is called the Judge,

Spiritus sanctus

Gen. 3.15

Psal. 100.3

Rom. 8.16

Esay 9.6

Esay 59.20
Job 19.2 [5]

Mat. 1.21

1 Tim. 2.5

1 John 2.1

Rom. 2.6

We testifie that it is he, that is ordained of God to bee the Iudge of
quick and dead. Now, for Christs first name, which is the roote of all,
which is, *The mighty God, No man can say that Iesus is the Lord, but*
by the holy Ghost; And there is our first comfort, in knowing that
Christ is God; for, he were an Intruder for that which is past, no
Redeemer, he were a weak Saviour for the future, an insufficient
Mediator, a silenced Advocate, and a Judge that might be misinformed,
¹⁰⁰ if he were not God. And though he were God, he might be all these
to my discomfort, if there were not a holy Ghost to make all these
offices comfortable unto me. To be a Redeemer and not a Saviour, is
but to pay my debts, and leave me nothing to live on. To be a Mediator,
a person capable by his composition of two natures, to intercede between God and man, and not to be my Advocate, is but to be a good
Counsellor, but not of counsell with me; To be a Judge of quick and
dead, and to proceed out of outward evidence, and not out of his
bosome mercy, is but an acceleration of my conviction; I were better
lie in Prison still, then appeare at that Assize; better lye in the dust of
¹¹⁰ the grave for ever, then come to that judgement. But, as there is *Mens*
in anima, There is a minde in the soule, and every man hath a soule,
but every man hath not a minde, that is, a Consideration, an Actuation,
an Application of the faculties of the soule to particulars; so there is
Spiritus in Spiritu, a Holy Ghost in all the holy offices of Christ, which
offices, being, in a great part, directed upon the whole world, are made
comfortable to me, by being, by this holy Spirit, turned upon me, and
appropriated to me; for so, even that name of Christ, which might
most make me afraid, The name of Judge, becomes a comfort to me.
To this purpose does S. *Basil* call the holy Ghost, *Verbum Dei, quia in-*
¹²⁰ *terpres filii:* The Son of God is the word of God, because he manifests
the Father, and the Holy Ghost is the word of God, because he applies
the Son. Christ comes with that loud Proclamation, *Ecce auditum fecit,*
Behold the Lord hath proclaimed it, to the end of the world, *Ecce*
Salvator, and *Ecce Merces,* Behold his Salvation, Behold thy Reward,
(This is his publication in the manifest Ordinances of the Church)
And then the Holy Ghost whispers to thy soule, as thou standest in the
Congregation, in that voyce that he promises, *Sibilabo populum*
meum, I will hisse, I will whisper to my people by soft and inward
inspirations. Christ came to tell us all, *That to as many as received him,*

Acts 10.42

1 Cor. 12.3

Basil.

Esay 62.11

Zach. 10.8

Iohn 1.12

30 *he gave power to become the Sons of God,* The Holy Ghost comes to
tell thee, that thou art one of them. The Holy Ghost is therefore
Legatus, and *Legatum Christi,* He is Christs Ambassadour sent unto
us, and he is his Legacy bequeathed unto us by his Will; his Will made
of force by his death, and proved by his Ascension.

Now, when those dayes were come, that the *Bridegroome was to bee*   Mat. 9.15
taken from them, Christ Jesus to be removed from their personall
sight, and conversation, and therefore even the *children of the mariage*
Chamber were to mourne, and fast; when that Church that mourned,
and lamented his absence, when she was but his *Spouse,* must neces-   Cant.
40 sarily mourn now in a more vehement manner, when she was to be,
(in some sense) his *Widow;* when that *Shepheard* was not onely to be   Mat. 26.31
smitten, and so *the flock dispersed,* (this was done in his passion) but
he was to be taken away, in his Ascension; what a powerfull Comforter had that need to be, that should be able to recompence the absence of Christ Jesus himselfe, and to infuse comfort into his Orphans,
the children of his mariage Chamber, into his Widow, the desolate,
and disconsolate Church, into his flock, his amazed, his distressed, and,
(as we may, properly enough, say in this case) his beheaded Apostles
and Disciples? *Quantus ergo Deus, qui dat Deum?* Lesse then God   Aug.
50 could not minister this comfort; How great a God is he, that sends a
God to comfort us? and how powerfull a Comforter hee, who is not
onely sent by God, but is God? Therefore does the Apostle inlarge, and
dilate, and delight his soule upon this comfort, *Blessed be God, even*   2 Cor. 1.3
the Father of our Lord Iesus Christ, the Father of mercies, and the
God of all comfort, who comforteth us in all our tribulations, that we
may be able to comfort them which are in any affliction, by that com-
fort, wherewith our selves are comforted of God. The Apostle was
loath to depart from the word, *Comfort;* And therefore, as *God, be-*   Heb. 6.13
cause he could sweare by no greater, sware by himselfe, So, because
60 there is no stronger adjuration, then the comfort it selfe, to move you
to accept this comfort, as the Apostle did, so we intreat you by that, *If*   Phil. 2.1
there be any consolation in Christ, if any comfort of love, if any fellow-
ship of the Spirit, if any bowels, and mercie, Lay hold upon this true
comfort, the comming of the Holy Ghost, and say to all the deceitfull
comforts of this world, not onely *Vanè consolati estis,* Your comforts   Zach. 10.2
are frivolous, but *Onerosi consolatores,* Your comforts are burden-   Job 16.2

Acts 4.36

Esay 66.11

Ver. 13

some; there is not onely a disappointing of hopes, but an aggravating of sin, in entertaining the comforts of this world. As *Barnabas,* that is, *Filius consolationis, The son of consolation,* that he might bee capable ¹⁷⁰ of this comfort, devested himselfe of all worldly possessions, so, as such sons, *Suck and be satisfied, at the breasts of this consolation, that you may milke out, and be delighted with the abundance of his glory; And as one whom his mother comforteth, so will I comfort you, and you shall be comforted in Ierusalem.* Heaven is Glory, and heaven is Joy; we cannot tell which most; we cannot separate them; and this comfort is joy in the Holy Ghost. This makes all *Iobs* states alike; as rich in the first Chapter of his Booke, where all is suddenly lost, as in the last, where all is abundantly restored. This Consolation from the Holy Ghost makes my mid-night noone, mine Executioner a Physitian, a ¹⁸⁰ stake and pile of Fagots, a Bone-fire of triumph; this consolation makes a Satyr, and Slander, and Libell against me, a Panegyrique, and an Elogy in my praise; It makes a *Tolle* an *Ave,* a *Væ* an *Euge,* a *Crucifige* an *Hosanna;* It makes my death-bed, a mariage-bed, And my Passing-Bell, an Epithalamion. In this notion therefore we receive this Person, and in this notion we consider his proceeding, *Ille, He,* He the Comforter, *shall reprove.*

Arguet

Psal. 6.1

2 Tim. 4.2
August.

This word, that is here translated *To reprove, Arguere,* hath a double use and signification in the Scriptures. First to reprehend, to rebuke, to correct, with Authority, with Severity; So *David, Ne in furore* ¹⁹⁰ *arguas me, O Lord rebuke me not in thine anger:* And secondly, to convince, to prove, to make a thing evident, by undeniable inferences, and necessary consequences; So, in the instructions of Gods Ministers, the first is *To reprove,* and then *To rebuke;* So that reproving is an act of a milder sense, then rebuking is. S. *Augustine* interprets these words twice in his Works; and in the first place he followes the first signification of the word, That the Holy Ghost should proceed, when he came, by power, by severity against the world. But though that sense will stand well with the first act of this Reproofe, (That he shall *Reprove,* that is, reprehend *the world of sin*) yet it will not seeme so properly ²⁰⁰ said, To reprehend the world of Righteousnesse, or of Judgement; for how is Righteousnesse, and Judgement the subject of reprehension? Therefore S. *Augustine* himselfe in the other place, where he handles these words, imbraces the second sense, *Hoc est arguere mundum,*

ostendere vera esse, quæ non credidit; This is to reprove the world, to
convince the world of her errours, and mistakings; And so (scarce any
excepted) doe all the Ancient Expositors take it, according to that, *All
things are reproved of the light, and so made manifest;* The light does
not reprehend them, not rebuke them, not chide, not upbraid them;
but to declare them, to manifest them, to make the world see clearly
what they are, this is to reprove.

That reproving then, which is warrantable by the Holy Ghost, is not
a sharp increpation, a bitter proceeding, proceeding onely out of power,
and authority, but by inlightning, and informing, and convincing the
understanding. The signification of this word, which the Holy Ghost
uses here for reproofe, *Elenchos,* is best deduced, and manifested to us,
by the Philosopher who had so much use of the word, who expresses it
thus, *Elenchus est Syllogismus contra contraria opinantem;* A reproofe, is a proofe, a proofe by way of argument, against another man,
who holds a contrary opinion. All the pieces must be laid together:
For, first it must be against an opinion, and then an opinion contrary
to truth, and then such an opinion held, insisted upon, maintained,
and after all this, the reproofe must lie in argument, not in force, not
in violence.

First it must come so farre, as to be an opinion; which is a middle
station, betweene ignorance, and knowledge; for knowledge excludes
all doubting, all hesitation; opinion does not so; but opinion excludes
indifferency, and equanimity; I am rather inclined to one side then
another, when I am of either opinion. *Id opinatur quisque quod nescit:*
A man may have an opinion that a thing is so, and yet not know it. S.
Bernard proposes three wayes for our apprehending Divine things;
first, understanding, which relies upon reason; faith, which relies upon
supreme Authority; and opinion, which relies upon probability, and
verisimilitude. Now there may arise in some man, some mistakings,
some mis-apprehensions of the sense of a place of Scripture, there may
arise some scruple in a case of conscience, there may arise some inclinations to some person, of whose integrity and ability I have otherwise
had experience, there may arise some Paradoxicall imaginations in my
selfe, and yet these never attaine to the setlednesse of an opinion, but
they float in the fancy, and are but waking dreames; and such imaginations, and fancies, and dreames, receive too much honour in the

Ephes. 5.13

Elenchus

Opinio

Lactant.

Bernard.

things, and too much favour in the persons, if they be reproved, or questioned, or condemned, or disputed against. For, often times, even a condemnation nourishes the pride of the author of an opinion; and besides, begets a dangerous compassion, in spectators and hearers; and then, from pitying his pressures and sufferings, who is condemned, men come out of that pity, to excuse his opinions; and from excusing them, to incline towards them; And so that which was but straw at first, by being thus blown by vehement disputation, sets fire upon timber, and drawes men of more learning and authority to side, and
250 mingle themselves in these impertinencies. Every fancy should not be so much as reproved, disputed against, or called in question.

Contra   As it must not be only a fancy, an imagination, but an opinion, (in which, though there be not a *Certò,* yet there is a *Potiùs,* Though I be not sure, yet I doe rather thinke it) so we consider *Contraria opinan-tem,* That it must be an opinion contrary to something that we are sure of; that is, to some received article, or to some evident religious duty; contrary to religion, as religion is matter of faith, or as religion is matter of obedience, to lawfull Authority. Though fancies grow to be opinions, that men come to thinke they have reasons for their opinions,
260 and to know they have other men on their side, in those opinions; yet, as long as these are but opinions of a little too much, or a little too little, in matter of Ceremony and Circumstance, as long as they are but deflectings, and deviations upon collaterall matters, no foundation shaked, no corner-stone displaced, as long as they are but preteritions, not contradictions, but omissions, not usurpations, they are not worthy of a reproofe, of a conviction, and there may be more danger then profit in bringing them into an over-vehement agitation. Those men whose end is schisme, and sedition, and distraction, are brought so neare their owne ends, and the accomplishment of their owne desires,
270 if they can draw other men together by the eares: As some have all they desire, if they can make other men drunke, so have these if they can make sober men wrangle.

Tenenda   They must be Opinions, not fancies, and they must have a con-trariety, an opposition to certaine truths, and then they must be held, persisted in, before it be fit to give a reproofe, either by calling in question, or by confutation. As some men are said to have told a lye so often, as that at last, they beleeve it themselves, so a man admits

sometimes an opinion to lodge so long, as that *Transit in intellectum,* It fastens upon his understanding, and that that he did but think be-
280 fore, now he seems to himself to know it, and he beleeves it. And then, *Fides si habet hæsitationem, infirma est,* As that faith that admits a scruple is weake, and so, without scruple he comes peremptorily to beleeve it. But so, *Opinio si habet assertionem, temeraria est,* When that which is but an opinion comes to be published and avowed for a certaine, and a necessary truth, then it becomes dangerous; And that growes apace; for scarcely does any man beleeve an opinion to be true, but he hath a certaine appetite and itch to infuse it into others too.

Now when these pieces meet, when these atomes make up a body, a body of Error, that it come to an Opinion, a halfe-assurance, and that
290 in some thing contrary to foundations, and that it be held stiffely, pub- liquely persisted in, then enters this reproofe; but yet even then re- proofe is but *Syllogismus,* it is but an argument, it is but convincing, it is not destroying; it is not an Inquisition, a prison, a sword, an axe, a halter, a fire; It is a syllogisme, not a syllogisme, whose *major* is this, Others, your Ancestors beleeved it, and the *minor* this, We that are your Superiours beleeve it, *Ergo* you must, or else be banisht or burnt. With such syllogismes the Arians abounded, where they prevailed in the Primitive Church, and this is the Logique of the Inquisition of Rome. But our syllogisme must be a syllogisme within our Authors
300 definition, when out of some things which are agreed on all sides, other things that are controverted, are made evident and manifest. Hell is presented to us by fire, but fire without light: Heaven by light, and light without any ill effect of fire in it. Where there is nothing but an Accuser, (perchance not that) and fire, citation and excommunica- tion, here is Satan, (who is an Accuser, but an invisible one) and here is Hell it selfe, a devilish and a darke proceeding. But when they, to whom this reproofe belongs, take Christs way, not to *tread out smoak- ing flaxe,* that a poore soule, mis-led by ignorant zeale, and so easily combustible and apt to take fire, be not troden downe with too much
310 power, and passion, when they doe not *breake a bruised reed,* that is, not terrifie a distracted conscience, which perchance a long ill conversa- tion with schismaticall company, and a spirituall melancholy, and over-tender sense of sin hath cast too low before, then does this reproofe worke aright, when it is brought in with light before fire, with con- venient instruction, and not hasty condemnation.

Bernard.

Idem

Syllogismus

We may well call this *Viam Christi,* and *Viam Spiritus sancti,* Christs way, and the Holy Ghosts way, for he had need be a very good Christian, and a very sanctified man, that can walke in that way; *Perfectorum est, nihil in peccatore odisse præter peccata:* He that hates nothing in an Heretique, or in a Schismatique, but the Schisme, or the Heresie, He that sets bounds to that sea, and hath said to his affections, and humane passions, Stay there, go no farther, hath got far in the steps of Christian perfection. The slipperinesse, the precipitation is so great on the other side, that commonly we begin to hate the person first, and then grow glad, when he growes guilty of any thing worthy our hate; and we make God himselfe the Devils instrument, when we pretend zeale to his service, in these reproofes and corrections, and serve onely our owne impotent passion, and inordinate ambition. For therein *Plerumque cum tibi videris odisse inimicum, fratrem odisti, & nescis;* Thou thinkest or pretendest to hate an enemy, and hatest thine owne brother, and knowest it not; Thou knowest not, considerest not, that he, by good usage and instruction, might have beene made thy Brother, a fellow-member in the Visible Church, by outward conformity, and in the Invisible too, by inward. *Etiam fictilia vasa confringere, Domino soli concessum,* If thou be a vessell of gold or silver, and that other of clay, thou of a cleere, and rectified, he of a darke and perverted understanding, yet even vessels of clay are onely in the power of that Potters hand that made them, or bought them, to breake, and no bodies else: Still, as long as it is possible, proceed we with the moderation of that blessed Father, *Sic peccata Hæreticorum compesce, ut sint quos pœniteat peccasse,* Take not away the subject of the error, (the perversenesse of the man) so, as that thou take away the subject of repentance, the man himselfe; If thou require fruit, leave a tree; If thou wouldst have him repent, take not away his life, sayes he. We see the leasurely pace that Gods Justice walks in: When *Daniel* had told *Nebuchadnezzar* his danger, yea *the Decree of God upon him,* (as hee cals it) yet he told him a way how to revoke it; *by workes of mercy to the poore, and breaking off his sinnes;* And after all this, hee had a yeares space to consider himselfe, before the judgement was executed upon him.

But now beloved, all that we have said, or can be said to this purpose, conduces but to this, That though this reproof, which the Holy Ghost leads us to, be rather in convincing the understanding by argument,

Marginal notes:

August.

320

August.

330

Cyprian.

August. 340

Dan. 4.24

27

Voluntas
perversa

350

and other perswasions then by extending our power to the destruction
of the person, yet this hath a modification, how it must be, and a
determination where it must end, for, there are cases in which we may,
we must go farther. For, for the understanding, we know how to
worke upon that; we know what arguments have prevayled upon us,
with what arguments we have prevailed upon others, and those we can
use: so far, *Vt nihil habeant contra, & si non assentiantur,* That though
360 they will not be of our minde, yet they shall have nothing to say
against it. So far we can go upon that faculty, the understanding. But
the will of man is so irregular, so unlimited a thing, as that no man
hath a bridle upon anothers will, no man can undertake nor promise
for that; no Creature hath that faculty but man, yet no man understands that faculty. It hath beene the exercise of a thousand wits, it
hath beene the subject, yea the knot and perplexity of a thousand
disputations, to find out, what it is that determines, that concludes the
will of man so, as that it assents thereunto. For, if that were absolutely
true which some have said, (and yet perchance that is as far as any
370 have gone) that *Vltimus actus intellectus est voluntas,* That the last
act of the Understanding is the Will, then all our labour were still to
worke upon the Understanding, and when that were rectified, the Will
must follow. But it is not so; As we feele in our selves that we doe
many sins, which our understanding, and the soule of our understanding, our conscience, tels us we should not doe, so we see many others
persist in errors, after manifest convincing, after all reproofe which
can be directed upon the understanding.

When therefore those errors which are to be reproved, are in that
faculty, which is not subject to this reproofe by argument, in a per-
380 verted will, because this wilfull stubbornnesse is alwaies accompanied
with pride, with singularity, with faction, with schisme, with sedition,
we must remember the way which the Holy Ghost hath directed us
in, *If the iron be blunt, we must either put to more strength, or whet*   Eccles. 10.10
the edge. Now, when the fault is in the perversenesse of the will, we
can put to no more strength, no argument serves to overcome that;
And therefore the holy Ghost hath admitted another way, *To whet*
the iron; And in that way does the Apostle say, *Vtinam abscindantur,*   Gal. 5.12
I would they were even cut off which trouble you. There is an incor-
rigibility, in which, when the reproofe cannot lead the will, it must

390 draw blood; which is, where pretences of Religion are made, and Treasons, and Rebellions, and Invasions, and Massacres of people, and Assasinates of Princes practised. And this is a reproofe (which, as we shall see of the rest, in the following branches is) from the Holy Ghost, in his function in this text, as he is a Comforter; This therefore is our comfort, That our Church was never negligent in reproving the Adversary, but hath from time to time strenuously and confidently maintained her truths against all oppositions, to the satisfying of any understanding, though not to the reducing of some perverse wils. So *Gregory de Valentia* professes of our arguments, I confesse these reasons would 400 conclude my understanding, *Nisi didicissem captivare intellectum meum ad intellectum Ecclesiæ,* But that I have learnt to captivate my understanding to the understanding of the Church, and, say what they will, to beleeve as the Church of Rome beleeves; which is *Maldonats* profession too, upon divers of *Calvins* arguments, This argument would prevaile upon me, but that he was an Heretique that found it. So that here is our comfort, we have gone so far in this way of Reproofe. *Vt nihil habeant contra, etsi nobiscum non sentiant.* This is our comfort, that as some of the greatest Divines in forraine parts, so also, in our Church at home, some of the greatest Prelates, who have beene tra-410 duced to favour Rome, have written the most solidly and effectually against the heresies of Rome of any other. But it must be a comfort upon them that are reproved. And this is their comfort, that the State never drew drop of blood for Religion; But then, this is our comfort still, that where their perversnesse shall endanger either Church or State, both the State and Church may, by the holy Ghosts direction, and will return to those means which God allows them for their preservation, that is, *To whet the edge of the Iron,* in execution of the laws. And so we passe from our second consideration, The Action, Reproofe, to the subject of Reproofe, The world, *He shall reprove the world.*

Mundus 420   It is no wonder that this word *Mundus* should have a larger signification then other words, for it containes all, embraces, comprehends all: But there is no word in Scripture, that hath not only not so large, but so diverse a signification, for it signifies things contrary to one another. It signifies commonly, and primarily, the whole frame of the world; and more particularly all mankinde; and oftentimes only John 3.16   wicked men; and sometimes only good men, As *Dilexit mundum,*

God loved the world, And *Hic est verè salvator mundi, This is the Christ, the Saviour of the world;* And *Reconciliatio mundi, The casting away of the Iews, is the reconciliation of the world:* The Jews were
430 a part of the world, but not of this world. Now in every sense, the world may well be said to bee subject to the reproofe of God, as reproof is a rebuke: for *He rebuked the winde, and it was quiet;* And, *He rebuked the red Sea, and it was dryed up;* He rebuked the earth bitterly in that *Maledicta terra,* for *Adams* punishment, *Cursed be the ground for thy sake;* And for the noblest part of earth, man, and the noblest part of men, Kings, *He rebuked even Kings for their sakes, and said, Touch not mine anointed.* But this is not the rebuke of our Text; for ours is a rebuke of comfort, even to them that are rebuked; Whereas the angry rebuke of God carries heavy effects with it. *In-*
440 *crepat, & fugiunt, God shall rebuke them, and they shall flie far off;* He shall chide them out of his presence, and they shall never return to it. *Increpasti superbos, & maledicti isti: Thou hast rebuked the proud,* and thy rebuke hath wrought upon them as a *malediction,* not physick, but poyson; As it is in another Psalme, *Increpasti, & periit, Thou hast rebuked them, and they perished.* In these cases, there is a working of the holy Ghost; and that, as the holy Ghost is a Comforter; for it is a comfort to them, for whose deliverances God executes these judgements upon others, that they are executed; but we consider a rebuke, a reproofe that ministers comfort even to them upon whom it fals; and
450 so in that sense, we shall see that *this Comforter reproves the world,* in all those significations of the word which wee named before.

As the world is the whole frame of the world, God hath put into it a reproofe, a rebuke, lest it should seem eternall, which is, a sensible decay and age in the whole frame of the world, and every piece thereof. The seasons of the yeare irregular and distempered; the Sun fainter, and languishing; men lesse in stature, and shorter-lived. No addition, but only every yeare, new sorts, new species of wormes, and flies, and sicknesses, which argue more and more putrefaction of which they are engendred. And the Angels of heaven, which did so familiarly
460 converse with men in the beginning of the world, though they may not be doubted to perform to us still their ministeriall assistances, yet they seem so far to have deserted this world, as that they do not appeare to us, as they did to those our Fathers. S. *Cyprian* observed this in his

Marginal references:
John 4.42
Rom. 11.15

Luk. 8.24
Psal. 106.9
Gen. 3.17

Psal. 105.14

Esay 17.13

Psal. 119.21

Psal. 9.6

Mundus magnus

Cyprian.

time, when writing to *Demetrianus,* who imputed all those calamities which afflicted the world then, to the impiety of the Christians who would not joyne with them in the worship of their gods, *Cyprian* went no farther for the cause of these calamities, but *Ad senescentem mundum,* To the age and impotency of the whole world; And therefore, sayes he, *Imputent senes Christianis, quòd minùs valeant in* 470 *senectutum;* Old men were best accuse Christians, that they are more sickly in their age, then they were in their youth; Is the fault in our religion, or in their decay? *Canos in pueris videmus, nec ætas in senectute desinit, sed incipit à senectute;* We see gray haires in children, and we do not die old, and yet we are borne old. Lest the world (as the world signifies the whole frame of the world) should glorifie it selfe, or flatter, and abuse us with an opinion of eternity, we may admit usefully (though we do not conclude peremptorily) this observation to be true, that there is a reproofe, a rebuke born in it, a sensible decay and mortality of the whole world.

Consolatio   480   But is this a reproofe agreeable to our Text? A reproofe that carries comfort with it? Comfort to the world it selfe, that it is not eternall?
Rom. 8.19   Truly it is; As S. *Paul* hath most pathetically expressed it; *The creature* (that is, the world) *is in an earnest expectation, The creature waiteth, The whole creation groaneth, and travelleth in pain.* Therefore the creature (that is, the world) receives a perfect comfort, in being delivered at last, and an inchoative comfort, in knowing now, that *it shall*
Ver. 20.   *be delivered;* From what? *From subjection to vanity, from the bond-*
and 21   *age of corruption;* That whereas the world is now subject to mutability and corruption, at the Resurrection it shall no longer be so, but in that
Ver. 21   490 measure, and in that degree which it is capable of, *It shall enter into the glorious liberty of the children of God,* that is, be as free from corruption, or change in that state, wherein it shall be glorified, as the
Esay 30.26   Saints shall be in the glory of their state; for, *The light of the Moon shall be as the light of the Sun, and the light of the Sun shall be seven-*
2 Pet. 3.13   *fold; And there shall be new heavens, and new earth;* Which is a state, that this world could not attaine to, if it were eternally to last, in that condition, in which it is now, a condition subject to vanity, impotency, corruption, and therefore there is a comfort in this reproofe, even to
Mundus,   this world, That it is not eternall; This world is the happier for that.
homines   500   As the world, in a second sense, signifies all the men of the world,

(so it is, Wo unto the world, because of offences) There is a reproofe Mat. 18.7
born in every man; which reproofe is an uncontrollable sense, and an
unresistible remorse, and chiding of himselfe inwardly, when he is
about to sin, and a horrour of the Majesty of God, whom, when he is
alone, he is forced (and forced by himselfe) to feare, and to beleeve,
though he would fain make the world beleeve, that he did not beleeve
in God, but lived at peace, and subsisted of himselfe, without being
beholding to God. For, as in nature, heavy things will ascend, and
light descend rather then admit a vacuity, so in religion, the devill will
510 get into Gods roome, rather then the heart of man shall be without the
opinion of God; There is no Atheist; They that oppose the true, do
yet worship a false god; and hee that sayes there is no God, doth for
all that, set up some God to himselfe. Every man hath this reproofe
borne in him, that he doth ill, that he offends a God, that he breaks a
law when he sins. And this reproofe is a reproofe within our Text, for
it hath this comfort with it, That howsoever some men labour to over- *Consolatio*
come the naturall tendernesse of the conscience, and so triumph over
their own ruine, and rejoyce when they can sleep, and wake again
without any noise in their conscience, or sense of sin, yet, in truth this
520 candle cannot be blowne out, this remorse cannot be overcome; But
were it not a greater comfort to me if I could overcome it? No. For
though this remorse (which is but a naturall impression, and common
to all men) be not grace, yet this remorse, which is the naturall reproofe
of the soule, is that, that grace works upon. Grace doth not ordinarily
work upon the stifnesse of the soule, upon the silence, upon the frowardnesse, upon the aversnesse of the soule, but when the soule is
soupled and mellowed, and feels this reproofe, this remorse in it self,
that reproofe, that remorse becomes as the matter, and grace enters as
the form, that becomes the body, and grace becomes the soule; and that
530 is the comfort of this naturall reproofe of the world, that is, of every
man: First, that it will not be quenched in it selfe, and then, that
ordinarily it induces a nobler light then it selfe, which is effectuall and
true Repentance. Mundus,
mali
    As the world, in a third sense, signifies only the wicked world (so it
is, *Noah in preparing an Ark, condemned the world;* And so, *God* Heb. 11.7
spared not the old world) That world, the world of the wicked suffer 2 Pet. 2.5
many reproofes, many rebukes in their hearts, which they will not

discover, because they envy God that glory. We reade of divers great actors in the first persecutions of the Christians, who being fearefully ⁵⁴⁰ tormented in body and soule, at their deaths, took care only, that the Christians might not know what they suffered, lest they should receive comfort, and their God glory therein. Certainly *Herod* would have been more affected, if he had thought that we should have knowne how his pride was punished with those sudden wormes, then with the punishment it selfe. This is a self-reproofe; even in this, though he will not suffer it to break out to the edification of others, there is some kinde of chiding himself for some thing mis-done. But is there any comfort in this reproofe? Truly, beloved, I can hardly speak comfortably of such a man, after he is dead, that dyes in such a ⁵⁵⁰ dis-affection, loath that God should receive glory, or his servants edification by these judgements. But even with such a man, if I assisted at his death-bed, I would proceed with a hope to infuse comfort, even from that dis-affection of his: As long as I saw him in any acknowledgement (though a negligent, nay though a malignant, a despitefull acknowledgement) of God, as long as I found him loath that God should receive glory, even from that loathnesse, from that reproofe, from that acknowledgement, That there is a God to whom glory is due, I would hope to draw him to glorifie that God before his last gasp; My zeale should last as long as his wives officiousnesse, or his ⁵⁶⁰ childrens, or friends, or servants obsequiousnesse, or the solicitude of his Physitians should; as long as there were breath, they would minister some help; as long as there were any sense of God, I would hope to do some good. And so much comfort may arise even out of this reproofe of the world, as the world is only the wicked world.

In the last sense, the world signifies the Saints, the Elect, the good men of the world, beleeving and persevering men. Of those Christ sayes, *The world shall know that I love the Father;* And, *That the world may beleeve that thou hast sent me.* And this world, that is, the godliest of this world, have many reproofes, many corrections upon ⁵⁷⁰ them. That outwardly they are the prey of the wicked, and inwardly have that *Stimulum carnis,* which is the devils Solicitor, and round about them they see nothing but profanation of his word, mis-imployment of his works, his creatures, mis-constructions of his actions, his judgements, blasphemy of his name, negligence and under-valuation

Acts 12.23

Consolatio

Mundus,
sancti

John 14.31
John 17.21

[2 Cor.
12.7]

of his Sacraments, violation of his Sabbaths, and holy convocations.
O what a bitter reproofe, what a manifest evidence of the infirmity,
nay of the malignity of man, is this, (if it be put home, and throughly
considered) That even the goodnesse of man gets to no higher a
degree, but to have been the occasion of the greatest ill, the greatest
580 cruelty that ever was done, the crucifying of the Lord of life! The
better a man is, the more he concurred towards being the cause of
Christs death; which is a strange, but a true and a pious consideration.
Dilexit mundum, He loved the world, and he came to save the world;
That is, most especially, and effectually, those that should beleeve in
him, in the world, and live according to that beliefe, and die according
to that life. If there had been no such, Christ had not died, never been
crucified. So that impenitent men, mis-beleeving men have not put
Christ to death, but it is we, we whom he loves, we that love him, that
have crucified him.

590   In what rank then, of opposition against Christ, shall we place our
sins, since even our faith and good works have been so farre the cause
why Christ died, that, but for the salvation of such men, Beleevers,
Workers, Perseverers, Christ had not died? This then is the reproofe
of the world, that is, of the Saints of God in the world, that though *I*   Psal. 84.10
had rather be a doore-keeper in the house of my God, I must *dwell*
in the tents of wickednesse, That though *my zeale consume me, be-*   Psal. 119.139
cause mine enemies have forgotten thy words, I must stay amongst
them that have forgotten thy words; But this, and all other reproofes,
that arise in the godly, (that we may still keep up that consideration,
600 that he that reproves us, is *The Comforter*) have this comfort in them,
that these faults that I indure in others, God hath either pardoned in
me, or kept from me: and that though this world be wicked, yet
when I shall come to the next world, I shall finde *Noah,* that had been   Gen. 9.21
drunk; and *Lot,* that had been incestuous; and *Moses,* that murmured   Gen. 19.33
at Gods proceedings; and *Iob,* and *Ieremy,* and *Ionas,* impatient, even   Numb.
to imprecations against themselves; Christs owne Disciples ambitious   11.11
of worldly preferment; his Apostles forsaking him, his great Apostle
forswearing him; And *Mary Magdalen* that had been, I know not
what sinner; and *David* that had been all; I leave none so ill in this
610 world, but I may carry one that was, or finde some that had been as
ill as they, in heaven; and that blood of Christ Jesus, which hath

brought them thither, is offered to them that are here, who may be successors in their repentance, as they are in their sins. And so have you all intended for the Person, the Comforter, and the Action, Reproofe, and the Subject, the World; remaines only (that for which there remaines but a little time) the Time, *Cum venerit, When the Comforter comes he will proceed thus.*

Cum venerit   We use to note three Advents, three commings of Christ. An Advent of Humiliation, when he came in the flesh; an Advent of glory, [620] when he shall come to judgement; and between these an Advent of grace, in his gracious working in us, in this life; and this middlemost Advent of Christ, is the Advent of the Holy Ghost, in this text; when Christ works in us, the Holy Ghost comes to us. And so powerfull is his comming, that whereas he that sent him, Christ Jesus himself, John 1.11   *Came unto his own, and his own received him not;* The Holy Ghost never comes to his owne but they receive him; for, onely by receiving him, they are his owne; for, besides his title of Creation, by which we are all his, with the Father, and the Son, as there is a particular title accrewed to the Son by Redemption, so is there to the Holy Ghost, [630] of certaine persons, upon whom he sheds the comfort of his applica- [John 3.8]   tion. The Holy Ghost picks out and chooses whom he will; *Spirat ubi vult;* perchance me that speake; perchance him that heares; perchance him that shut his eyes yester-night, and opened them this morning in the guiltinesse of sin, and repents it now: perchance him that hath been in the meditation of an usurious contract, of an ambitious supplantation, of a licentious solicitation, since he came hither into Gods house, and deprehends himselfe in that sinfull purpose now. This is his Advent, this is his Pentecost. As he came this day with a Manifestation, so, if he come into thee this evening, he comes with a Declaration, a Decla- John 5.17 [640] ration in operation. *Pater meus usque modo operatur, & ego operor, My Father works even now, and I work,* was Christs answer, when he was accused to have broken the Sabbath day; that the Father wrought that day as well as he. So also Christ assignes other reasons of work- Luke 14.5   ing upon the Sabbath; *Cujus Bos,* Whose Oxe is in danger, and the owner will not relieve him? *Nonne legistis,* Have ye not read how Mat. 12.3   *David* ate the Shew-bread? And *Annon legistis,* Did not the Priests and 5   breake the Sabbath, in their service in the Temple? But the Sabbath is the Holy Ghosts greatest working day: The Holy Ghost works

more upon the Sunday, then all the week. In other dayes, he picks
and chooses; but upon these days of holy Convocation, I am surer
that God speakes to me, then at home, in any private inspiration. For,
as the Congregation besieges God in publique prayers, *Agmine facto,*
so the Holy Ghost casts a net over the whole Congregation, in this
Ordinance of preaching, and catches all that break not out.

If he be come into thee, he is come to reprove thee; to make thee
reprove thy selfe; But doe that, *Cum venerit, when the Holy Ghost
is come.* If thou have beene slack in the outward acts of Religion, and
findest that thou art the worse thought of amongst men, for that
respect, and the more open to some penall Laws, for those omissions,
and for these reasons onely beginnest to correct, and reprove thy selfe,
this is a reproofe, *Antequam Spiritus venerit,* before the Holy Ghost
is come into thee, or hath breathed upon thee, and inanimated thine
actions. If the powerfulnesse, and the piercing of the mercies of thy
Saviour, have sometimes, in the preaching thereof, entendered and
melted thy heart, and yet upon the confidence of the readinesse, and
easinesse of that mercy, thou returne to thy vomit, to the re-pursuite
of those halfe-repented sins, and thinkest it time enough to goe forward upon thy death-bed, this is a reproofe *Postquam abierit Spiritus,*
After the Holy Ghost is departed from thee. If the burden of thy sins
oppresse thee, if thou beest ready to cast thy selfe from the Pinacle
of the Temple, from the participation of the comforts afforded thee
in the Absolution, and Sacraments of the Church, If this appeare to
thee in a kinde of humility, and reverence to the Majesty of God,
That thou darest not come into his sight, not to his table, not to speake
to him in prayer, whom thou hast so infinitely offended, this is a reproofe, *Cum Spiritus Sanctus simulatur,* when the Holy Ghost is
counterfaited, when Satan is transformed into an Angel of light, and
makes thy dismayed conscience beleeve, that that affection, which
is truly a higher Treason against God, then all thy other sins, (which
is, a diffident suspecting of Gods mercy) is such a reverend feare, and
trembling as he looks for.

Reprove thy selfe; but doe it by convincing, not by a downe-right
stupefaction of the conscience; but by a consideration of the nature
of thy sin, and a contemplation of the infinite proportion between
God and thee, and so between that sin and the mercy of God; for, thou

Tertul.

canst not be so absolutely, so intirely, so essentially sinfull, as God
is absolutely, and intirely, and essentially mercifull. Doe what thou
canst, there is still some goodnesse in thee; that nature that God made,
is good still; Doe God what hee will, hee cannot strip himselfe, not
690 devest himselfe of mercy. If thou couldst doe as much as God can
pardon, thou wert a Manichæan God, a God of evill, as infinite as the
God of goodnesse is. Doe it, *Cum venerit Spiritus,* when the Holy
Ghost pleads on thy side; not *cum venerit homo,* not when mans
reason argues for thee, and sayes, It were injustice in God, to punish
one for another, the soule for the body: Much lesse *Cum venerit
inimicus homo,* when the Devill pleads, and pleads against thee, that
thy sins are greater then God can forgive. Reprove any over-bold
presumption, that God cannot forsake thee, with remembring who
[Mat. 27.46]   it was that said, *My God, my God, why hast thou forsaken me?* Even
700 Christ himselfe could apprehend a dereliction. Reprove any distrust
[Luke   in God, with remembring to whom it was said, *Hodiè mecum eris
23.43]   in Paradiso;* Even the thiefe himselfe, who never saw him, never met
him, but at both their executions, was carried up with him, the first
day of his acquaintance. If either thy cheerefulnesse, or thy sadnesse
bee conceived of the Holy Ghost, there is a good ground of thy *Noli
[Mat. 1.20]   timere,* feare neither. So the Angel proceeded with *Ioseph, Feare not
to take Mary, for that which is conceived in her, is of the Holy Ghost.*
Feare not thou, that a chearefulnesse and alacrity in using Gods blessings, feare not that a moderate delight in musique, in conversation,
710 in recreations, shall be imputed to thee for a fault, for, it is conceived
by the Holy Ghost, and is the off-spring of a peacefull conscience.
Esay 26.12   Embrace therefore his working, *Qui omnia opera nostra operatus
est nobis, Thou, O Lord, hast wrought all our works in us;* And whose
43.13   working none shall be able to frustrate in us; *Operabitur, & quis
avertit? I will worke, and who shall let it?* And as the Son concurred
with the Father, and the Holy Ghost with the Son, in working in our
[Phil. 2.12]   behalfe, so *Operemur & nos,* let us also *worke out our Salvation with
feare and trembling,* by reproving the errors in our understanding,
and the perversenesses of our conversation, that way, in which the
720 Holy Ghost is our guide, by reproving, that is, chiding and convincing the conscience, but still with comfort, that is, stedfast application
of the merits of Christ Jesus.

Number 17.

Preached upon Christmas day, at
S. Pauls. 1625.

GALAT. 4.4 and 5. *BUT WHEN THE FULNESSE OF*
TIME WAS COME, GOD SENT FORTH HIS SON,
MADE OF A WOMAN, MADE UNDER THE LAW,
TO REDEEM THEM THAT WERE UNDER THE
LAW, THAT WE MIGHT RECEIVE THE ADOP-
TION OF SONNES.

WEE ARE met here to celebrate the generation of Christ Jesus;
but *Generationem ejus quis enarrabit*, sayes the Prophet, Esay 53.8
who shall declare his generation, his age? For, for his
essentiall generation, by which he is the Son of God, the Angels, who
are almost 6000. yeares elder then we, are no nearer to that generation
of his, then if they had been made but yesterday: Eternity hath no
such distinctions, no limits, no periods, no seasons, no moneths, no
yeares, no dayes; *Methusalem,* who was so long lived, was no elder
in respect of eternity, then *Davids* son by *Berseba,* that dyed the first
10 week. The first *Fiat* in the Creation of *Adam,* and the last note of the
blowing of the Trumpets to judgement, (though there be between
these (as it is ordinarily received) 2000. yeares of nature, between the
Creation, and the giving of the Law by *Moses,* and 2000. yeares of the
Law between that, and the comming of Christ, and 2000. yeares of
Grace and Gospell between Christs first, and his second comming)
yet this Creation and this Judgement are not a minute asunder in
respect of eternity, which hath no minutes. Whence then arises all
our vexation and labour, all our anxieties and anguishes, all our suits
and pleadings, for long leases, for many lives, for many yeares pur-
20 chase in this world, when, if we be in our way to the eternall King

of the eternall kingdome, Christ Jesus, all we are not yet, all the world shall never be a minute old; *Generationem ejus quis enarrabit,* what tongue can declare, what heart can conceive his generation which was so long before any heart or tongue was made? But we come not now to consider that eternall generation, not Christ meerly as the Son of God, but the Son of *Mary* too: And that generation the Holy Ghost hath told us, was in *the fulnesse of time: When the fulnesse of time was come, God sent forth, &.*

Divisio

In which words, we have these three considerations; First, the time of Christs comming, and that was *the fulnesse of time;* And then, the maner of his comming, which is expressed in two degrees of humiliation, one, that he was *made of a woman,* the other, that he was *made under the Law;* And then, the third part is the purpose of his comming, which also was twofold; for first, he came *to redeem them who were under the Law,* All; And secondly he came, that we (we the elect of God in him) might receive adoption; *When the fulnesse of time was come, &c.*

1 Part

For the full consideration of this *fulnesse of time,* we shall first consider this fulnesse in respect of the Jews, and then in respect of all Nations, and lastly in respect of our selves: The Jews might have seen *the fulnesse of time,* the Gentiles did ·(in some measure) see it, and we must (if we will have any benefit by it) see it too. It is an observation of S. *Cyril,* That none of the Saints of God, nor such as were noted to be exemplarily religious, and sanctified men did ever celebrate with any festivall solemnity, their own birth-day. *Pharaoh*

Gen. 40.22

celebrated his own Nativity, but who would make *Pharaoh* his example? and besides, he polluted that festivall with the bloud of one

[Mat. 14.6]

of his servants. *Herod* celebrated his Nativity, but who would think it an honor to be like *Herod?* and besides, he polluted that festivall with the blood of *Iohn Baptist.* But the just contemplation of the miseries and calamities of this life, into which our birth-day is the doore, and the entrance, is so far from giving any just occasion of a festivall, as it hath often transported the best disposed Saints and servants of God to a distemper, to a malediction, and cursing of their

Jer. 20.[14]

birth-day. *Cursed be the day wherein I was born, and let not that day*

Job

wherein my mother bare me be blessed. Let the day perish wherein

3.[3 and 4]

I was born, let that day be darknesse, and let not God regard it from

above. How much misery is presaged to us, when we come so generally weeping into the world, that, perchance, in the whole body
⁶⁰ of history we reade but of one childe, *Zoroaster,* that laughed at his birth: What miserable revolutions and changes, what downfals, what break-necks, and precipitations may we justly think our selves ordained to, if we consider, that in our comming into this world out of our mothers womb, we doe not make account that a childe comes right, except it come with the head forward, and thereby prefigure that headlong falling into calamities which it must suffer after? Though therefore the dayes of the Martyrs, which are for our example celebrated in the Christian Church, be ordinarily called *natalitia Martyrum,* the birth-day of the Martyrs, yet that is not intended of their
⁷⁰ birth in this world, but of their birth in the next; when, by death their soules were new delivered of their prisons here, and they newly born into the kingdome of heaven; that day, upon that reason, the day of their death was called their birth-day, and celebrated in the Church by that name. Onely to Christ Jesus, *the fulnesse of time* was at his birth; not because he also had not a painfull life to passe through, but because the work of our redemption was an intire work, and all that Christ said, or did, or suffered, concurred to our salvation, as well his mothers swathing him in little clouts, as *Iosephs* shrowding him in a funerall sheete; as well his cold lying in the
⁸⁰ Manger, as his cold dying upon the Crosse; as well the *puer natus,* as the *consummatum est;* as well his birth, as his death is said to have been *the fulnesse of time.*

First we consider it to have been so to the Jews; for this was *that fulnesse,* in which all the prophecies concerning the Messias, were exactly fulfilled; That he must come whilest the Monarchy of Rome flourished; And before the Temple of Jerusalem was destroyed; That he must be born in Bethlem; That he must be born of a Virgin; His person, his actions, his passion so distinctly prophecyed, so exactly accomplished, as no word being left unfulfilled, this must necessarily
⁹⁰ be a *fulnesse of time.* So fully was the time of the Messias comming, come, that though some of the Jews say now, that there is no certain time revealed in the Scriptures when the Messias shall come, and others of them say, that there was a time determined, and revealed, and that this time was the time, but by reason of their great sins he

Iudæis

Dan. 2
Hagg. 2
Mich. 5
Esay 7

did not come at his time, yet when they examine their own supputations, they are so convinced with that evidence, that this was that *fulnesse of time,* that now they expresse a kind of conditionall acknowledgement of it, by this barbarous and inhumane custome of theirs, that they alwayes keep in readinesse the blood of some Chris-
100 tian, with which they anoint the body of any that dyes amongst them, with these words, if Jesus Christ were the Messias, then may the blood of this Christian availe thee to salvation: So that by their doubt, and their implyed consent, in this action, this was *the fulnesse of time,* when Christ Jesus did come, that the Messias should come.

Gentibus It was so to the Jews, and it was so to the Gentiles too; It filled those wise men which dwelt so far in the East, that they followed the star from thence to Jerusalem. *Herod* was so full of it, that he filled the Countrey with streames of innocent bloud, and lest he should spare that one innocent childe, killed all. The two Emperours of
110 Rome, *Vespasian* and *Domitian* were so full of it, that in jealousie of a Messias to come then, from that race, they took speciall care for the destruction of all, of the posterity of *David.* All the whole people were so full of it, that divers false-Messiahs, *Barcocab,* and *Moses* of Crete, and others rose up, and drew, and deceived the people, as if they had been the Messiah, because that was ordinarily knowne, and received to be the time of his comming. And the Devill himself was so full of it, as that in his Oracles he gave that answer, That an Hebrew childe should be God over all gods, and brought the Emperour to erect an Altar, to this Messiah Christ Jesus, though he
120 knew not what he did. This was the fulnesse that filled Jew and Gentile, Kings and Philosophers, strangers and inhabitants, counterfaits and devils to the expectation of a Messiah; and when comes this *fulnesse of time* to us, that we feele this Messiah born in our selves?

Nobis In this fulnesse, in this comming of our Saviour into us, we should finde a threefold fullnesse in our selves; we should finde a fulnesse of nature (because not only of spirituall, but of naturall and temporall things, all the right which we have in this world, is in, and for, and by Christ, for so we end all our prayers of all sorts, with that clause, *per Dominum nostrum Iesum Christum, Grant this O Lord,*
130 *for our Lord and Saviour Christ Iesus sake.*) And we should finde a fulnesse of grace, a daily sense of improvement, growth in grace, a

filling of all former vacuities, a supplying of all emptinesses in our
soules, till we came to *Stephens* fulnesse, *Full of the holy Ghost and
wisdome, and full of the holy Ghost and Faith, and full of faith and
power:* And so we should come to finde a fulnesse of glory, that is
an apprehension and inchoation of heaven in this life; for the glory
of the next world, is not in the measure of that glory, but in the
measure of my capacity; it is not that I shall have as much as any
soule hath, but that I shall have as much as my soul can receive; it
⁴⁰ is not in an equality with the rest, but in a fulnesse in my self; And
so, as I shall have a fulnesse of nature, that is, such an ability and
such a use of naturall faculties, and such a portion of the naturall
things of this world as shall serve to fill up Gods purpose in me:
And as I shall have a fulnesse of grace, that is, such a measure of
grace as shall make me discern a tentation, and resist a tentation, or
at least repent it, if I have not effectually resisted it, so even here, I
shall have a fulnesse of glory, that is, as much of that glory as a
way-faring soul is capable of in this world; All these fulnesses I
shall have, if I can finde and feele in my selfe this birth of Christ.
⁵⁰ His eternall birth in heaven is unexpressible, where he was born
without a mother; His birth on earth is unexpressible too, where
he was born without a father; but thou shalt feele the joy of his
third birth in thy soul, most inexpressible this day, where he is born
this day (if thou wilt) without father or mother; that is, without
any former, or any other reason then his own meere goodnesse that
should beget that love in him towards thee, and without any matter
or merit in thee which should enable thee to conceive him. He had
a heavenly birth, by which he was the eternall Son of God, and
without that he had not been a person able to redeem thee; He had
⁶⁰ a humane birth, by which he was the Son of *Mary,* and without
that he had not been sensible in himself of thine infirmities, and
necessities; but, this day (if thou wilt) he hath a spirituall birth in
thy soul, without which, both his divine, and his humane birth are
utterly unprofitable to thee, and thou art no better then if there had
never been Son of God in heaven, nor Son of *Mary* upon earth. Even
*the Stork in the aire knoweth her appointed time, and the Turtle, and
the Crane, and the Swallow observe the time of their comming, but
my people knoweth not the judgements of the Lord.* For, if you doe

Acts 6.3
ver. 5. and 8

Jer. 8.[7]

know your time, you know that now is your *fulnesse of time;* This
[170] is your particular Christmas-day; when, if you be but as carefull to
cleanse your soules, as you are your houses, if you will but follow
that counsell of S. *Augustine, Quicquid non vis inveniri in domo
tua, non inveniat Deus in anima tua.* That uncleannesse which you
would be loth your neighbour should finde in your houses, let not
God nor his Angels finde in your soules, Christ Jesus is certainly
born, and will as certainly grow up in your soules.

2 Part

We passe from this, to our second part, The manner of his comming; where we proposed two degrees of Christs humiliation, That
he was *made of a woman,* and *made under the Law.* In the first alone,

Mulieris
non Dei

[180] are two degrees too, that he takes the name of the Son of a woman,
and waives the glorious name of the Son of God; And then, that he
takes the name of the son of a woman, and waives the miraculous
name of the son of a Virgin. For the first; Christ ever refers himself

Joh. 12.[49]

to his Father; As he sayes, *The Father which sent me, gave me a
commandement what I should say, and what I should speak,* so, for

Joh. 4.[34]
Joh. 16.[28]

all that which he did or suffered, he sayes, *My meate is to doe his
will that sent me, and to finish his work:* And so, though he say, *I am
come out from the Father, and am come into the world;* yet, be
where he will, still, *Ego & pater unum sumus,* He and his Father
[190] were all one. But devesting that glory, or slumbring it in his flesh,
till the Father glorifie him againe with that glory, which he had
with him from the beginning, in his Ascension, he humbles himselfe
here to that addition, *The Son of a woman, made of a woman.*

Non
Virginis

Christ waived the glorious Name of Son of God, and the miraculous Name of Son of a Virgin to; which is not omitted to draw
into doubt, the perpetuall Virginity of the Blessed Virgin, the Mother
of Christ; she is not called a woman, as though she were not a Maid;
when it is said, Joseph *knew her not, donec peperit, till she brought
forth her Son,* this did not imply his knowledge of her after, no more,
[200] then when God sayes to Christ, *donec ponam,* sit at my right hand,
till I make thine enemies thy footstoole, that imports, that Christ
should remove from his right hand after: For, here is a perpetuall
donec in both places; for evermore the ancient Expositors have understood that place of *Ezekiel,* to be intended of the perpetuall Virginitie

Ezek. 44.2

of *Mary, This gate shall be shut, and shall not be opened, and no man shall enter by it. Solomon* hath an exclamation, *Is there any thing whereof a man may say, Behold this is new?* and he answers himselfe immediately before, *There is no new thing under the Sun.* But behold here is a greater then *Solomon,* and he sayes now in action, by being borne of a Virgin, as he had said, long before, in Prophesie, *The Lord hath created a new thing upon earth, a woman shall compasse a man.* If this had been spoken of such a woman, as were no Maid, this had been no new thing: As it was, it was without example, and without naturall reason; *si ratio reddi posset,* (sayes St. *Bernard*) *non esset mirabile, si exempla haberemus, non esset singulare;* If there were reason for it, it were no miracle, if there were precedents for it, it were not singular; and God intended both, that it should be a miracle, and that it should be done but once; we see in Nature, trees do bud out, and there is an emission, and emanation of flowers, and fruits, without any help of man, or any act done by him, to that tree; we reade in *Genesis,* That the earth had produced all plants and herbs, before eyther any raine fell upon it, or any man tilled it. And these are good helps, and illustrations to us, after we have beleeved that a Virgin brought forth a Son; but nothing deduced out of nature, could prove this at first, to any man, except he beleeved it before. And therefore blessed be God, that hath given us that strength, which the Egyptian Mid-wives said the women of Israel had, that they brought forth children, without the help of Mid-wives: That we can humbly beleeve these mysteries of our religion, by faith, without the hand, and help of Reason; *Si nondum mens idonea, abstrusa investigare, sine hæsitatione credantur,* sayes St. *Augustine,* In things which are not subject to any faculty of ours, to be discerned by reason, there is a present exercise of our faith. As we know it to be true, that the bush, in which God spake to *Moses,* was full of fire, and did burne, but not consume, because God hath said so, in his booke, but yet we doe not know, how that was done: so we know, (by the same evidence) that the Mother of our Saviour, was a Virgin; but for the manner of this Mystery, we rest upon *Epiphanius* Rule, *Quæcunque dicit Deus, credamus quòd sint; quomodo, Soli Deo cognitum:* whatsoever God, in his word, sayes, was done, let us beleeve it to be done; how it was done, as we know that God knowes, so we are content not to inquire more then it hath been his pleasure to communicate to us.

[Eccles. 1.9 and 10]

Jer. 31.[22]

She was then, and she was alwaies a Virgin; but because this Text is of his Humiliation, he leaves that Name that proceeds from miracle, and descends to that lower name of nature, *Made of a woman.* The Spirit of God fore-saw, that the issue betweene the Church, and the Heretiques would not be *Virgin or no Virgin,* but whether Christ were *made of a woman.* Some Heretiques did question the first; 250 The *Helvidians* denied her perpetuall Virginitie: But that Heresie, and some others that opposed her Virginitie, vanished in a short time. But the *Manichees,* that lasted long, and spred farre in the old times, and the *Anabaptists,* which abound yet, deny that Christ was made of a woman; They say, that Christ passed through her, as water through a Pipe, but tooke nothing of her substance; and then, if he took not the nature of mankinde, he hath not redeemed mankinde. And therefore in that Prophesie of *Ieremy,* that Christ should be borne, and in this Gospel, in our Text, that Christ was borne, the Holy Ghost maintaines and continues that phrase, *Made of a woman:* 260 And where he begins to expresse his Divinitie in miracles, at the marriage in *Cana,* there Christ himselfe calls her, by no other name,

Joh. 2.[4]   *Woman, what have I to doe with thee?* And when he had drawne all his miracles to a glorious *consummatum est,* upon the *Crosse,* he

Joh. 19.[26]   cals her there, by that name too, *Woman, behold thy Son.* Here then was no such curious insisting upon Styles and Titles, and names of Dignities, no unkindnesse, no displeasure taken; [as] if one should leave out a Right Honourable, or Right Worshipfull, or an addition of an Office or Dignity; The powerfulnesse of Christs birth, consists in this, That he is made of God; The miraculousnesse of Christs birth, 270 consisted in this, that he was made of a Virgin, and yet the Prophet and the Apostle, two principall Secretaries of the Holy Ghost, present him with this addition, *made of a woman.* Christ had one priviledge in his birth, which never any Prince had, or shall have, that is, that he chose what Mother he would have, and might have been borne of what woman he would have chosen. And in this large and universall choyce, though he chose a woman full of grace to be his Mother, yet that he might give spirituall comfort to all sorts of women, first to those, who should be unjustly suspected, and insimulated of sin and incontinency, when indeed they were innocent, hee was content 280 to come of a Mother, who should be subject to that suspicion, and

whom her husband should think to be with child, before he marryed
her, and thereupon purpose to put her away; And then, to fill those
women, who had been guilty of that sinne, with reliefe in their consciences against the wrath of God, and with reparation of their reputation and good name in the world, it was his unsearchable will and
pleasure, that in all that Genealogie, and pedigree, which he, and
his spirit hath inspired the Euangelists to record of his Ancestors,
there is not one woman named, of whom Christ is descended, who
is not dangerously noted in the Scriptures, to have had some asper-
10 sion of incontinence upon her; as both St. *Hierome,* and St. *Ambrose,*
and St. *Chrysostome* observe, of *Thamar,* of *Berseba,* and of *Ruth*
also.

So then, Christ Jesus who came onely for the reliefe of sinners, is
content to be known to have come, not onely of poore parents, but
of a sinfull race; and though he exempted his Blessed Mother, more
then any, from sin, yet he is now content to be born again of sinful
Mothers: In that soul, that accuses it self most of sin; In that soul,
that cals now to mind, (with remorce, and not with delight) the
severall times, and places, and waies, wherein she hath offended God;
20 In that soul that acknowledgeth it self to have bin a sink of uncleannesse, a Tabernacle, a Synagogue of Satan; In that soul, that hath
been as it were possessed with *Mary Magdalens* seven Devils, yea
with him, whose name was Legion, with all Devils; In that sinful
soul would Christ Jesus fain be born, this day, and make that soul,
his Mother, that he might be a regeneration to that soul. We cannot
afford Christ, such a birth in us, as he had, to be born of a Virgin;
for every one of us wel-nigh hath married himself to some particular
sin, some beloved sin, that he can hardly divorce himselfe from; nay,
no man keepes his faith, to that one sin, that he hath marryed him-
30 selfe to, but mingles himselfe with other sins also. Though Covetousnesse, whom he loves, as the wife of his bosome, have made him rich,
yet he will commit adultery with another sin, with Ambition; and
he will part, even with those riches, for Honour: Though Ambition
be his wife, his marryed sin, yet he will commit adultery with another
sin, with Licentiousnesse, and he will endanger his Honour, to fulfill his Lust; Ambition may be his wife, but Lust is his Concubine.
We abandon all spirituall chastity, all virginitie, we marry our par-

ticular sinnes, and then we divide our loves with other sins too: *Thou
hast multiplyed thy fornications, and yet art not satisfied,* is a com-
³²⁰ plaint, that reaches us all, in spirituall fornications, and goes very
farre, in carnall. And yet, for all this, we are capable of this Conception, Christ may be borne in us, for all this: As God said unto the
Prophet, *Take thee a wife of fornications, and children of fornications;*
so is Christ Jesus content to take our soules, though too often mothers
of fornications: As long as we are united, and incorporated in his
beloved Spouse, the Church, conforme our selves to her, grow up in
her, hearken to his word in her, feed upon his Sacraments in her,
acknowledge a seale of reconciliation, by the absolution of the Minister in her, so long, (how unclean soever we have bin, if wee abhorre
³³⁰ and forsake our uncleannesse now) wee participate of the chastity
of that Spouse of his, the Church, and in her, are made capable of
this conception of Christ Jesus, and so, it is as true this houre of us,
as it was when the Apostle spoke these words, *This is the fulnesse
of time, when God sent his Son, &c.*

Now you remember, that in this second part, (the manner of Christs
comming) we proposed two degrees of humiliation; One which we
have handled, in a double respect, as he is made, *filius mulieris, non
Dei,* the son of a woman, and not the Son of God; the other, as he
is *filius mulieris, non Virginis,* The son of a woman, and not called the
³⁴⁰ son of a Virgin.

Sub Lege

The second remaines, that he was *sub lege, under the law;* now,
this phrase, to be *under the law,* is not alwayes so narrowly limited
in the Scriptures, as to signifie onely the law of *Moses;* for, so, onely
the Jews were under the law, and so, Christs comming for them, who
were under the law, his Death, and Merits should belong onely to
the Jews. But St. *Augustine* observes, that when Christ sent the message of his birth, to the wise men, in the East, by a starre, and to the
shepheards, about *Bethlem,* by an Angel, *In pastoribus, Iudæi; in
magis, Gentes vocatæ;* The Jews had their calling in that manifesta-
³⁵⁰ tion to the shepheards, and the Gentiles in that, to the wise men in
the East. But besides that Christ did submit himselfe, to all the waight
even of the Ceremoniall law of *Moses,* he was under a heavyer law,
then that, under that *lex decreti,* the contract and covenant with God
the Father, under that *oportuit pati, This he ought to suffer, before*

he could enter into glory. So that his being under the law, may be accounted not a part of his Humiliation, as his being made of a woman was, but rather the whole history, and frame of his humiliation, All that concernes his obedience, even to that law, which the Father had laid upon him; for, the life and death of Christ, from the
50 *Ave Maria,* to the *consummatum est,* from his comming into this World, in his Conception, to his transmigration upon the Crosse, was all under this law, heavier then any law, that any man is under, the law of the contract, and covenant between the Father, and him.

Though therefore we may think, judging by the law of reason, that since Christ came to gather a Church, and to draw the world to him, it would more have advanced that purpose of his, to have been borne at *Rome,* where the seat of the Empire, and the confluence of all Nations, was, then in *Iury,* and (if he would offer the Gospel first to the Jews) better to have been borne at *Ierusalem,* where all the out-
70 ward, publique, solemne worship of the Jews was, then at obscure *Bethlem,* and in *Bethlem,* in some better place then in an Inne, in a Stable, in a Manger; though we may think thus, in the law of reason, yet, *non cogitationes meæ cogitationes vestræ,* sayes God in the Prophet, *My thoughts are not your thoughts, nor my lawes your lawes,* for I am *sub lege decreti,* under another manner of law, then falls within your reading, under an obedience to that covenant, which hath passed betweene my Father, and me, and by those Degrees, and no other way, was my humiliation, for your Redemption, to be expressed. Though we may thinke in the law of Reason, that his work
80 of propagating the Gospel, would have gone better forward, if he had taken for his Apostles, some *Tullies,* or *Hortensii,* or *Senecaes,* great, and perswading Orators, in stead of his *Peter,* and *Iohn,* and *Matthew,* and those Fishermen, and tent-makers, and toll-gatherers; Though we might think in reason, and in piety too, that when he would humble himselfe to take our salvation into his care, it had beene enough, to have beene under the law of *Moses,* to live innocently, and righteously, without shedding of his bloud; If he would shed bloud, it might have beene enough to have done so in the Circumcision, and scourging, without dying; If he would die, it might have been enough
90 to have dyed some lesse accursed, and lesse ignominious death, then the death of the Crosse; though we might reasonably enough, and

Esay 55.[8]

piously enough, think thus, yet, *non cogitationes vestræ, cogitationes meæ,* sayes the Lord, *your way is not my way, your law is not my law;* for, Christ was *sub lege decreti,* and *thus,* as he did, and no other

[Mat. 3.15] way, *it became him to fulfill all righteousnesse,* that is, all that Decree of God, which he had accepted, and acknowledged as Righteous. He was so much under *Moses* law, as he would be: so much under that law, as that he suffered that law, to be wrested against him, and to bee pretended to be broken by him, and to be endited, and con-

Exod. ⁴⁰⁰ demned by that law. The Jews pressed that law, *non sines veneficum*
22.[18] *vivere, Thou shalt not suffer a witch to live,* when they attributed all his glorious miracles, to the power of the devil: and the Romans were incensed against him, for treason, and sedition, as though he aliened and withdrew the people from *Cæsar.* But he was under a heavyer law, then Jews or Romanes, the Law of his Father, and his owne eternall Decree, so farre, as that he came to that sense of the

[Mat. 27.46] waight thereof, *Eli, Eli, My God, My God, why hast thou forsaken me?* and was never delivered from the burden of this law, till he pleaded the performance of all conditions between his Father, and

[Luke ⁴¹⁰ him, and delivered up all the evidence thereof, in those words, *In*
23.46] *manus tuas, Into thy hands, O Lord I give my spirit,* and so presented both the righteousnesse of his soule, which had fulfilled the law, and the soule it selfe, which was under the law. He dyed in Execution, and so discharged all; And so we have done with our second part, The manner of his comming.

3. Part   We are come now, in our Order, to our third part, The purpose of Christs comming; and in that we consider two objects, that Christ had, and two subjects to work upon, two kindes of work, and two kindes of persons; First, to Redeeme, and then to Adopt; Those are
⁴²⁰ his works, his objects; And then, *To redeeme those that were under the law,* that is, all, but to Adopt those whom he had chosen, us; And those are the persons, the subjects, that he works upon, by his comming.

Sub Lege   First then, (to begin with the persons) those of the first kinde, *those that were under the Law:* for them, (as we told you before) the law must not be so narrowly restrained here, as to be intended onely of *Moses* Law, for Christs purpose was not onely upon the

2 Reg. 5 Jews; for else, *Naaman* the Syrian, by whom God fought great bat-

tailes, before he was cured of his leprosie, and who, when he was
° cured, was so zealous of the worship of the true God, that he would
needs carry holy earth, to make Altars of, from the place, where the
Prophet dwelt: And else, *Iob,* who though he were of the land of
Hus, hath good testimony of being an upright and just man, and
one that feared God; And else, the Widow of Sarepta, whose meale,   1 Reg. 17
and oyle God preserved unwasted, and whose dead sonne, God raised
againe, at the prayer of *Eliah;* All these, and all others, whom the
searching Spirit of God, seales to his service, in all the corners of the
earth, because they are strangers in the land of Israel, should not be
under the Law, and so should have no profit by Christs being made
° under the Law, if the Law should be understood, onely of the Law
of *Moses.* And therefore to be *under the Law,* signifies here, thus
much, To be a debter to the law of nature, to have a testimony in
our hearts and consciences, that there lyes a law upon us, which we
have no power in our selves to performe; that to those lawes, *To love
God with all our powers,* and *to love our neighbour as our selves,*
and *to doe, as we would be done to,* we finde our selves naturally
bound, and yet wee finde our selves naturally unable to performe
them, and so to need the assistance of another, which must be Christ
Jesus, to performe them for us; And so, all men, Jews and Gentiles
° are under the Law, because naturally they feele a law upon them,
which they breake. And therefore wheresoever our power becomes
defective, in the performance of this law, if our will be not defective
too, if we come not to say, God hath given us an impossible Law, and
therefore it is lost labour, to goe about to performe it, or God hath
given us another to performe this Law for us, and therefore nothing
is required at our hands; If we abstaine from these quarrels to the
law, and these murmurings at our owne infirmity, wee shall finde,
that the fulnesse of time is this day come, this day Christ is come to
all that are under the Law, that is, to all mankinde; to all, because
° all are unable to performe that Law, which they all see, by the light
of nature to lye upon them.

These then be the persons of the first kinde, All, all the world;   *Redemit*
Dilexit mundum, God so loved the world, that he gave his Son for it,   [Joh. 3.16]
for all the world; And, accordingly, *venit salvare mundum,* the obedience of the Son, was as large as the love of the Father, Hee came to

save all the world, and he did save all the world; God would have all men, and Christ did save all men. It is therefore fearefully (and scarce allowably said) that Christ did contrary to his Fathers will, when he called those to grace, of whom he knew his Fathers pleasure
470 to bee, that they should have no grace; It is fearefully and dangerously said, *Absurdum non esse, Deum interdum falsa loqui, & falsum loquenti credendum,* that it is not absurd to say, (that is, that it may truly be said) that God does sometimes speake untruly, and that we are bound to beleeve God, when he does so: for, if we consider the soveraigne balme of our soules, the blood of Christ Jesus, there is enough for all the world; if we consider the application of this physick, by the Ministers of Christ Jesus in the Church, hee hath given us that spreading Commission, To goe and preach to every creature, we are bid to offer, to apply, to minister this to all the world: Christ hath
480 excommunicated no Nation, no shire, no house, no man: Hee gives none of his Ministers leave to say to any man, thou art not Redeemed, he gives no wounded nor afflicted conscience leave, to say to it selfe, I am not Redeemed. There may be meat enough brought into the house, for all the house, though some be so weake, as they cannot, (which is the case of the Gentiles) some so stubborne, as they will not eate, (which is the case of the carnall man, though in the Christian Church.)

He came to all, There are the persons, and *to Redeeme all,* there is his errand; but how to Redeeme? S. *Hierome* saies, *Gentes non*
490 *Redimuntur, sed emuntur:* The Gentiles, saies hee, are not properly Christs, by way of Redeeming, but by an absolute purchase: To which purpose those words are also applied, which the Apostle saies to the

1 Cor. 6.20　　Corinthians, *Ye are bought with a price,* S. *Hieroms* meaning therein, is, that if we compare the Jews and the Gentiles, though God permitted the Jews, in punishment of their rebellions, to bee captivated by the devill in Idolatries, yet the Jews were but as in a mortgage, for they had beene Gods peculiar people before; But the Gentiles were as the devils inheritance, for God had never claimed them, nor owned

Ps. 2.8　　them for his; and therefore God sayes to Christ, *Postula à me, Aske*
500 *of me, and I will give thee the nations for thine inheritance;* as though they were not his yet, or not his by that title, as the Jews were. So that, in S. *Hieromes* construction, the Jewes, which were Gods people

before, were properly Redeemed, the Gentiles, to whom God made no title before, are rather bought, then redeemed. But, *Nullum tempus occurrit Regi,* against the King of Kings there runnes no prescription; no man can devest his Allegeance to his Prince, and say he will be subject no longer; And therefore, since the Gentiles, were his by his first title of Creation, (for, *it is he that hath made us, and not we our selves,* nor the devill neither) when all we, by our generall revolt, and prevarication, (as we were all collectively in *Adams* loynes) came to be under that law, *morte morieris, Thou shalt dye the death,* when Christ came in the fulnesse of time, and delivered us from the sharpest, and heaviest clause of that Law, which is the second death, then he *Redeemed* us properly, because, (though not by the same title of Covenant, as the Jews were) yet we were his, and sold over to his enemy. These then were the persons, All, (none can say that he did not need him, none can say, that he may not have him) And this was his first worke, *to Redeeme,* to vindicate them from the usurper, to deliver them from the intruder, to emancipate them from the tyran, to cancell the covenant betweene hell, and them, and restore them so far to their liberty, as that they might come to their first Master, if they would; this was *Redeeming.*

But in his other worke, which is *Adoption,* and where the persons were more particular, not all, but wee, Christ hath taken us to him, in a straiter and more peculiar title, then Redeeming. For, *A servando Servi,* men who were, by another mans valour, saved and redeemed from the enemy, or from present death, they became thereby, servants to him that saved and redeemed them: Redemption makes us (who were but subjects before, for all are so, by creation) servants; but it is but servants; but Adoption makes us, who are thus made servants by Redemption, sons: for, *Adoption* is *verbum forense,* though it be a word which the Holy Ghost takes, yet he takes it from a civill use, and signification, in which, it expresses in divers circumstances, our Adoption into the state of Gods children. First, he that adopted another, must by that law, be a man, who had no children of his owne; And this was Gods case towards us; Hee had no children of his owne, wee were all *filii iræ, The children of wrath,* not one of us could be said to bee the child of God, by nature, if we had not had this *Adoption* in Christ. Secondly, he, who, by that law, might

Adoptio

Eph. 2.[3]

⁵⁴⁰ Adopt, must be a Man, who had had, or naturally might have had
children; for an Infant under yeares, or a man, who by nature was
disabled from having children, could not Adopt another; And this
was Gods case towards us too; for God had had children without
Adoption; for by our creation in Innocence, we were the sons of God
till we died all in one transgression, and lost all right, and all life,
and all meanes of regaining it, but by this way of *Adoption* in Christ
Jesus. Againe, no man might adopt an elder man then himselfe; and
so, our Father by *Adoption,* is not onely *Antiquus dierum,* The ancient of Daies, but *Antiquior diebus* ancienter then any Daies, before
⁵⁵⁰ Time was; he is (as *Damascene* forces himselfe to expresse it) *Super-
principale principium,* the Beginning, and the first Beginning, and
before the first beginning; He is, saies he, *æternus,* and *præ-æternus,*
Eternall, and elder then any eternity, that we can take into our
imagination. So likewise no man might adopt a man of better quality
then himselfe, and here, we are so far from comparing, as that we
cannot comprehend his greatnesse, and his goodnesse, of whom, and
to whom, S. *Augustin* saies well, *Quid mihi es?* If I shall goe about
to declare thy goodnesse, not to the world in generall, but *Quid mihi
es,* how good thou art to me, *Miserere ut loquar,* saies he, I must have
⁵⁶⁰ more of thy goodnesse, to be able to tell thy former goodnesse, Be
mercifull unto me againe, that I may bee thereby able to declare how
mercifull thou wast to me before, except thou speake in me, I cannot
declare what thou hast done for me. Lastly, no man might be adopted,
into any other degree of kindred, but into the name, and right of a
son; he could not be an adopted Brother, nor cosin, nor nephew: And
[Rom. 8.15]　　this is especially our dignity; wee have *the Spirit of Adoption, whereby
we cry Abba, Father.* So that, as here is *a fulnesse of time* in the text,
so there is a fulnesse of persons, *All,* and a fulnesse of the worke belonging to them, *Redeeming,* Emancipation, delivering from the
Esa. 52.[3]　⁵⁷⁰ chaines of Satan, (we were his by Creation, we sold our selves for
nothing, and he redeemed us, without money, that is, without any
cost of ours) but because for all this generall Redemption, we may
turne from him, and submit our selves to other services, therefore
he hath *Adopted us,* drawne into his family and into his more especiall
care, those who are chosen by him, to be his. Now that Redemption
reached to all, there was enough for all; this dispensation of that Re-

demption, this Adoption reaches onely to us, all this is done, *That wee might receive the Adoption of Sonnes.*

But who are this *Wee?* why, they are the elect of God. But who are they, who are these elect? *Qui timidè rogat, docet negare:* If a man aske me with a diffidence, Can I be the adopted son of God, that have rebelled against him, in all my affections, that have troden upon his Commandements, in all mine actions, that have divorced my selfe from him, in preferring the love of his creatures before him-selfe, that have murmured at his corrections, and thought them too much, that have undervalued his benefits, and thought them too little, that have abandoned, and prostituted my body, his Temple, to all uncleannesse, and my spirit to indevotion, and contempt of his Ordinances; can I be the adopted son of God, that have done this? *Ne timidè roges,* aske me not this, with a diffidence and distrust in Gods mercy, as if thou thoughtst with *Cain* thy iniquities were greater then could be forgiven; But aske me with that holy confidence, which belongs to a true convert, Am not I, who, though I am never without sinne, yet am never without hearty remorce and repentance for my sinnes; though the weaknesse of my flesh sometimes betray mee, the strength of his Spirit still recovers me; though my body be under the paw of that lion, that seekes whom hee may devoure, yet the lion of Judah raises againe and upholds my soule; though I wound my Saviour with many sinnes, yet all these, bee they never so many, I strive against, I lament, confesse, and forsake as farre as I am able. Am not I the child of God, and his adopted son in this state? *Roga fidenter,* aske me with a holy confidence in thine and my God, *& doces affirmare,* thy very question gives me mine answer to thee, thou teachest me to say, thou art; God himselfe teaches me to say so, by his Apostle, *The foundation of God is sure,* and this is the Seale, *God knoweth who are his,* and let them that *call upon his name, depart from all iniquity:* He that departs so far, as to repent former sinnes, and shut up the wayes, which he knows in his conscience, doe lead him into tentations, he is of this *quorum,* one of us, one of them, who are adopted by Christ, to be the sonnes of God. I am of this *quorum,* if I preach the Gospell sincerely, and live thereafter, (for hee preaches twice a day, that followes his owne doctrine, and does as he saies) And you are of this *quorum,* if you preach over the Ser-

Nos

[2 Tim. 2.19]

mons which you heare, to your owne soules in your meditation, to your families in your relation, to the world in your conversation. If you come to this place, to meet the Spirit of God, and not to meet one another, If you have sate in this place, with a delight in the Word of God, and not in the words of any speaker, If you goe out of this place, in such a disposition, as that, if you should meet the last Trum-
620 pets at the gates, and Christ Jesus in the clouds, you would not intreat him to goe back, and stay another yeare: To enwrap all in one, if you have a religious and sober assurance, that you are his, and walke according to your beleefe, you are his, and, as the fulnesse of time, so the fulnesse of grace is come upon you, and you are not onely within the first commission, of those who were under the Law, and so Redeemed, but of this *quorum* who are selected out of them, the adopted sons of that God, who never disinherits those that forsake not him.

Number 18.

A Sermon Preached at St. Dunstans
January 15. 1625. [*1625/6*]

The First Sermon after Our Dispersion, by the Sickness.

EXOD. 12.30. *FOR THERE WAS NOT A HOUSE WHERE THERE WAS NOT ONE DEAD.*

GOD INTENDED life and immortality for man; and man by sin induc'd death upon himself at first: When man had done so, and that now man was condemned, man must die; yet God gave him, though not an absolute pardon, yet a long reprieve; though not a new immortality, yet a life of seven and eight hundred years upon earth: And then, misery by sin growing upon man, and this long life which was enlarged in his favour being become a burden unto him, God abridged and contracted his seven hundred to seventy, and his eight hundred to eighty years, the years of his life came to be threescore and ten; and if misery do suffer him to exceed those, even the exceeding it self is misery. Death then is from our selves, it is our own; but the executioner is from God, it is his, he gives life; no man can quicken his own soul, but any man can forfeit his own soul: And yet when he hath done so, he may not be his own executioner; for as God giveth life, so he killeth, says *Moses* there: not as the cause of death, for death is not his creature; but because he employs what person he will, and executes by what instrument it pleases him to chuse, age or sickness, or justice, or malice, or (in our apprehension) fortune. In that History from whence we deduce this Text, which was that great execution, the sodain death of all the first-born of *Egypt;* it is very large, and yet we may usefully, and to good purpose enlarge it, if we take into our consideration spiritual death, as well as bodily: for so in our houses from whence we came hither, if we left but a servant, but a child in the cradle at home, there

[Deut. 32.39]

349

is one dead in that house. If we have no other house but this which we carry about us, this house of clay, this tabernacle of flesh, this body, yet if we consider the inmate, the sojourner within this house, the state of our corrupt and putrified soul, there is one dead in this house too. And though we be met now in the House of God, and
³⁰ our God be the God of Life, yet even in this house of the God of Life, and the ground enwrapped in the same consecration; not only of every such house, but let every mans length in the house be a house; of every such space this Text will be verified, *There is not a house where there is not one dead.*

God is abundant in his mercies to man, and as though he did but learn to give by his giving, as though he did but practise to make himself perfect in his own Art, which Art is bountiful Mercy; as though all his former blessings were but in the way of earnest, and not of payment; as though every benefit that he gave, were a new obligation
⁴⁰ upon him, and not an acquittance to him; he delights to give where he hath given, as though his former gifts were but his places of memory, and marks set upon certain men, to whom he was to give more. It is not so good a plea in our prayers to God, for temporal or for spiritual blessings, to say, *Have mercy upon me now, for I have loved thee heretofore,* as to say, *Have mercy upon me, for thou hast loved me heretofore.* We answer a Beggar, I gave you but yesterday; but God therefore gives us to day, because he gave us yesterday: and

[Mat. 6.11]   therefore are all his blessings wrap'd up in that word, *Panis quotidianus, Give us this day our daily bread:* Every day he gives; and early
[Lam. 3.23]   ⁵⁰ every day; his Manna falls before the Sun rises, and his mercies are new every morning. In this consideration of his abounding in all ways of mercy to us, we consider justly how abundant he is in instructing us. He writes his Law once in our hearts, and then he repeats that Law, and declares that Law again in his written Word, in his Scriptures. He writes his Law in stone-Tables once; and then those Tables being broken, he repeats that Law, writes that Law again in other Tables. He gives us his Law in *Exodus* and *Leviticus,* and then he gives us a *Deuteronomy,* a repetition of that Law, another time in another Book. And as he abounds so in instructing us, in going the
⁶⁰ same way twice over towards us, as he gives us the Law a second time, so he gives us a second way of instructing us; he accompanies, he

seconds his Law with examples. In his Legal Books we have Rules; in the Historical, Examples to practise by. And as he is every way abundant, as he hath added Law to Nature, and added Example to Law, so he hath added Example to Example; and by that Text which we have read to you here, and by that Text which we have left at home, our house and family, and by that Text which we have brought hither, our selves, and by that Text which we finde here, where we stand, and sit, and kneel upon the bodies of some of our dead friends or neigh-
⁷⁰ bors, he gives to us, he repeats to us, a full, a various, a multiform, a manifold Catechism, and Institution, to teach us that it is so absolutely true, that *there is not a house in which there is not one dead,* as that (taking spiritual death into our consideration) there is not a house in which there is one alive.

That therfore we may take in light at all these windows that God opens for us, that we may lay hold upon God by all these handles which he puts out to us, we shall make a brief survey of these four Houses; of that in *Egypt,* where the Text places it; of that at home, in which we dwell; of this, which is our selves, where we always are, or
⁸⁰ always should be within; and of this in which we are met, where God is in so many several Temples of his, as are above and under ground: So that this Sermon may be a general Funeral Sermon, both for *them that are dead in the flesh,* and for our selves, that *are dead in our sins;* for of all these four houses it is true, and by useful accommodation, applyable to all, *There is not a house where there is not one dead.*

First then to survey the first House, the House in *Egypt, Pharaoh,* by drawing upon himself and his Land this last and heaviest plague of the ten, the universal, the sodain, the midnight destruction of all, *all the firstborn of* Egypt, hath made himself a Monument, and a
⁹⁰ History, and a Pillar everlasting to the end of the world, to the end of all place in the world, and to the end of all time in the world, by which all men may know, that man, how perverse soever, cannot weary God; that man cannot add to his Rebellions so many heavy circumstances, but that God can add as many, as heavy degrees to his Judgements. First, *God turns their Rivers into blood; Pharaoh* sits that proces, and more, many more; and then in this bloody massacre of *all their firstborn,* God brings *blood out of the channels of their Rivers, into their chambers, into all their Chambers;* not only to *cut off their children*

Divisio

Part I

[Exod.7.20]

Jer. 9.21

from without, and the young men from the streets (as the Prophet
100 speaks) but (as he says also there) *Death came in at their windows,*

and entred into their Palaces. As Christ says of *Mary Magdalens* devotion, That *wheresoever* his *Gospel should be preached in the world, there* should *also this which this woman* had *done, be told for a memorial of her:* So we may say of mans obduration, Wheresoever the Book of God shall be read, *Pharaoh* shall be an example, that God will have his ends, let man be possest with the spirit of contradiction as furiously, with the spirit of rebellion as ragefully as he will. *Fremuerunt Gentes,* says *David* in the beginning of the second *Psalm, The Heathen Rage, and they break their sleep to contrive mischief.*
110 And within three verses more we finde, *The Lord sits still in heaven, and laughs, and hath them in derision.* The building of the Tower of *Babel* did not put God to build another Tower to confront it; God did nothing, and brought all their labours and their councels to nothing.

God took no hammer in hand to demolish and cast down *Nebuchadnezzars* Image, but a stone that *was cut out without hands, smote the image, and broke it in pieces. Si inceperit,* if God once set his work on

foot, *If I begin, I will also make an end,* says God to *Samuel;* if he have not begun, *si juraverit,* if the Lord have sworn it, it shall be, (those whom the Lord swore should not enter into his Rest, never entred into
120 his Rest.) If he have not sworn, *si locutus fuerit,* that's security enough, the security that the Prophet *Esay* gives through all his Prophecy, *os Domini,* thus and thus it must be, for the mouth of the Lord hath spoken it: if he have not gone so far, *si cogitaverit,* if he have *purposed*

it, as that word is used in *Esay;* if he have *determined* it, as the word is used in the *Chronicles;* if he have *devised* such a course, as the word is in *Jeremy; God will accomplish his work,* if he have begun it; his oath and word, if he have said or sworn it; his purpose and determination, if he have intended it; nothing shall frustrate or evacuate his purpose, he will atchieve his ends, though there be never a soul that
130 doth not sigh, never a heart that doth not ake, never a vein that doth not bleed, never a house in which there is not one dead.

In the building of the material Temple, there was no hammer, nor tool of noise used: In the fitting and laying of us, the living stones of the mystical Temple, God would use no hammer, no iron, no occasion of noise, or lamentation; but there are dispositions which will not be rectified without the hammer, and are not malleable neither, not fit to be rectified by the hammer, till a hot fire of vehement affliction have mollified them. *Thespesius* they say was a man desperately vicious, irrecoverably wicked; his friends asked the Oracle whether ever he would mend? The Oracle answered, he would when he was dead; he died of a sodain fall, at least to the eyes, and in the understanding of the world he died; but he recovered, and came to life again, and then reported such fearful visions which he had seen in the other world, upon the souls of some of his companions, and of his own father, as that out of the apprehension of those terrors in his extasie, in his second life, he justified the Oracle; and after he had been dead, lived well. Many such stories are in the Legends; but I take this at the fountain where they take most of theirs, that is, out of *Plutarch;* for *Plutarch* and *Virgil* are two principal Evangelists of the Legendaries. The Moral of them all is, *That God will imprint a knowledge of his Majesty, and a terror of his Judgements, though the heart be Iron:* He would bring the Egyptians to say with trembling, *We are dead men,* though they would not be brought to say it, till *there was not a house in which there was not one dead.*

Exod. 12
Vers. 33

But as in a River that is swelled, though the water do bring down sand and stones, and logs, yet the water is there still; and the purpose of Nature is to vent that water, not to pour down that sand, or those stones: so though God be put to mingle his Judgements with his mercies, yet his mercy is there still, and his purpose is, ever in those judgments, to manifest his mercy. Where the Channel is stopped by those Sands, and Stones, and Logs, the Water will finde another Channel; where the heart is hardned by Gods corrections, and thereby made incapable of his mercy, (as in some dispositions, even Gods corrections do work such obstructions and obdurations, as in *Pharaohs* case it was) yet the water will find a Channel, the mercy of God will flow out, and shew it self to others, though not to him; his mercy will take effect somewhere, as (in *Pharaohs* case) it did upon the Children of *Israel.* And yet God would not shew mercy to them, but so, as that at the same time they also might see his judgments, and thereby be brought to say, God hath a Treasury of both, *Mercy* and *Justice;* and God might have changed the persons, and made the *Egyptians* the objects of his *Mercies,* and us of his *Justice.*

The first act of Gods mercy towards me, when I see him execute a judgment upon another, is to confess, that that judgment belonged to me, and thereby to come to a *holy fear,* being under the same condemnation; as the one Thief said to the other, upon their several crosses; *Fearest not thou, being under the same condemnation?* At this time God delivered his Children out of *Egypt;* then was *fulness of mercy;* but God let them see his power and his powerful indignation ¹⁸⁰ upon others, for their instruction. God brought them out; there was *fulness* of mercy towards them: but he brought them out in the night. God would mingle some shadow, some signification of his *judgments* in his *mercies,* of adversity in prosperity, of night in day, of death in life. The persecuting Angel entred into none of their houses, God let them live; but God, though he let them live, would not let them be ignorant, that he could have thrown death in at their windows too: *For they came not into a house where there was not one dead.*

[Luke 23.40]

Part II
Domus Nostra

We stay no longer upon this first survey of the first house, *That in Egypt:* The next is, our own house, our habitation, our family. We have ¹⁹⁰ in the use of our Church, a short, and a larger *Catechism;* both instruct the same things, the same Religion, but some capacities require the one, and some the other. God would catechise us in the knowledge of our *mortality;* since we have devested our *immortality,* he would have us understand our *mortality;* since we have induced *death* upon our selves, God would raise such a benefit to us, out of *death,* as that by the continual *meditation* thereof, *death* might the less terrifie us, and the less damnifie us. First, His Law alone does that office, even his Common Law, *Morte morieris,* and *stipendium peccati Mors est: All have sinned, and all must die.* And so his Statute Law too, *Statutum* ²⁰⁰ *est,* It is enacted, *it is appointed to man once to die:* And then as a *Comment* upon that Law, he presents to us, either his great *Catechisms, Sennacheribs Catechism,* in which we see almost Two hundred thousand Soldiers, (more by many then both sides arm and pay, in these noiseful Wars of our Neighbors) slain in one night; or *Jeroboams Catechism,* where Twelve hundred thousand being presented in the field, (more by many, then all the Kings of Christendom arm and pay) Five hundred thousand men, chosen men, and men of *mighty valor,* (as the Text qualifies them) were slain upon one side in one day; or *Davids Catechism,* where Threescore and ten thousand were

[Rom. 6.23]

Heb. 9.27

Isai. 37.36

2 Chro.

13.[17]

2 Sam.
24.[15]

²¹⁰ devoured of the Pestilence, we know not in how few hours; or this *Egyptian Catechism,* of which we can make no conjecture, because we know no number of their houses; *and there was not a house, in which there was not one dead;* or God presents us his *Catechism* in the *Primitive Church,* where every day may be written in Red Ink, every day the Church celebrated Five hundred, in some Copies Five thousand Martyrs every day, that had writ down their names in their own blood, for the Gospel of *Christ Jesus;* or God presents us his *Catechism* in the later *Roman* Church; where, upon our attempt of the *Reformation,* they boast to have slain in one day Seventy Millions, in another ²²⁰ Two hundred Millions of them that attempted and assisted the *Reformation;* or else God presents his lesser *Catechisms,* the several Funerals of our particular Friends in the Congregation; or he abridges this *Catechism* of the Congregation to a less volume then that, to the consideration of every particular peece of our own Family at home: *For so, there is not a house, in which there is not one dead.*

Have you not left a dead son at home, whom you should have chastned, whilest there was hope, and have not? Whom you should have beaten with the rod, to deliver his soul from Hell, and have not? Whom you should have made an *Abel,* a Keeper of Sheep; or a *Cain,* ²³⁰ a Tiller of the Ground; that is, bestowed him, bound him, to some Occupation, or Profession, or Calling, and have not? You may believe God without an oath; but God hath sworn, *That because* Eli *restrained not the insolencies of his sons, no sacrifice should purge his house for ever.* And scarce shall you finde in the whole Book of God, any so vehement an intermination, any judgment so vehemently imprinted, as that upon *Eli,* for *not restraining the insolencies of his sons:* For in that case God says, *I will do a thing in Israel, at which, both the ears of every one that heareth it shall tingle:* That is, he would inflict a sudden death upon the Father, for his indulgence to his sons. Have ye ²⁴⁰ not left such a dead son, dead in contumacy, and in disobedience, at home? Have you not left a dead daughter at home? A daughter whom you should have kept at home, and have not; but suffered, with *Dinah,* to go out to see the daughters of the land, and so expose her self to dangerous tentations, as *Dinah* did? Have ye not left a dead servant at home, whom ye have made so perfect in deceiving of others, as that now he is able to take out a new lesson of himself, and deceive you?

Prov. 19.18

& 23.13
Gen. 4.2

1 Sam. 3.13

Gen. 34.1

Have you left no dead Inmates, dead Sojourners, dead Lodgers at home? Of whom, so they advance your profit, you take no care how vicious in themselves they be, or how dangerous to the State. *Gather*

Deut. 31.12   ²⁵⁰ *men, and women, and children, and strangers within thy gate,* says God, *that they may all learn the Law of the Lord.* If thy care spread not over all thy family, whosoever is dead in thy family by thy negligence, thou shalt answer the King that Subject, that is, the King of Heaven that Soul.

Part 3   We have (as we proposed to do) surveyed this House in *Egypt,* where the Text lays it, and the House at home where we dwell; there is a third House, which we are, this House of Clay, and of Mud-walls, our selves, these bodies. And is there none dead there? not within us? The House it self is ready to fall as soon as it is set up: The next thing ²⁶⁰ that we are to practise after we are born, is to die. The Timber of this

Ps. 32.3   House is but our Bones; and, *My bones are waxen old,* says *David;* and
Job. 20.11   perchance not with age, but as *Job* says, His *bones are full of the sins*
Job. 6.12   *of* his *youth.* The lome-walls of this House are but this flesh; and *Our strength is not the strength of stones, neither is our flesh brass;* and
Jer. 17.5   therefore, *Cursed is the man that trusteth in man, and maketh flesh his arm.* The windows of this House are but our eyes; and, *the light of*
[Psa. 38.10]   *mine eyes is gone from me,* says *David;* and we know not how, nor how soon. The foundation is but our feet; and, besides that *Our feet*
Esai. 59.10   *stumble at noon,* (as the Prophet complains) *David* found them so ²⁷⁰ cold, as that no art nor diligence could warm them. And the roof and covering of this House, is but this thatch of hair; and it is denounc'd
Esai. 15.2   by more then one of the Prophets, That *upon all heads shall fall bald-*
Jer. 48.37   *ness:* The House it self is always ready to fall; but is there not also always some dead in this House, in our selves? Is not our first-born dead? Our first-born (says St. *Augustin*) are the offspring of our beloved sin; for we have some Concubine-sins, and some one sin that we are married to: Whatsoever we have begot upon that wife, whatsoever we have got by that sin, that's our first-born, and that's dead: How much the better soever we make account to live by it, it is dead. ²⁸⁰ For, as it was the mischievous invention of a Persecutor in the Primitive Church, to tie living men to dead bodies, and let them die so; so men that tie the rest of their Estate to goods ill gotten, do but invent a way to ruine and destroy all. But that which is truly every mans first-

born-childe, is his zeal to the Religion and Service of God: As soon as we know that there is a Soul, that Soul knows that there is a God, and a Worship belonging to that God; and this Worship is Religion. And is not this first-born childe dead in many of us? In him that is not stirr'd, not mov'd, not affected for his Religion, his pulse is gone, and that's an ill sign. In him that dares not speak for it, not counsel, not preach
90 for it, his Religion lies speechless; and that's an ill sign. In him that feeds not Religion, that gives nothing to the maintenance thereof, his Religion is in a consumption. In a word, if his zeal be quenched, his first-born is dead. And so for these three Houses, That in *Egypt,* that at home, that in our selves, *There is not a house in which there is not one dead.*

The fourth House falling under this survey, is this House in which   *Part* 4
we are met now, the house of God; the Church and the ground wrapped up in the same consecration: and in this house you have seen, and seen in a lamentable abundance, and seen with sad eyes, that
100 for many moneths there hath scarce been one day in which there hath not been one dead. How should there be but multiplicity of deaths? why should it be, or be looked to be, or thought to be otherwise? The Master of the house, Christ Jesus, is dead before; and now it is not so much a part of our punishment, for the first *Adam,* as an imitation of the second *Adam,* to die; death is not so much a part of our debt to Nature, or Sin, or Satan, as a part of our conformity to him who died for us. If death were in the nature of it meerly evil to us, Christ would have redeemed us, even from this death, by his death. But as the death of Christ Jesus is the Physick of mankinde, so this natural death of the
110 body is the application of that Physick to every particular man, who only by death can be made capable of that glory which his death hath purchased for us. This Physick, all they whom God hath taken to him, have taken, and (by his grace) received life by it. Their first-born is dead; the body was made before the soul, and that body is dead. *Rachel*   [Jer. 31.15]
wept for her children, and would not be comforted, because they were not. If these children, and parents, and friends, and neighbours of ours were not, if they were resolved into an absolute annihilation, we could not be comforted in their behalf; but Christ, who says, he is *the Life,*   [Joh. 11.25]
lest we should think that to belong only to this life, says also that he is
120 *the Resurrection.* We were contracted to Christ in our Election, mar-

ried to him in our Baptism, in the Grave we are bedded with him, and in the Resurrection estated and put into possession of his Kingdom: And therefore, because these words do not only affect us with that sad consideration, That *there is* none of these houses *in which there is not one dead;* but minister withall that consolation, That there is none so dead, but may have a Resurrection, We shall pass another short survey over all these Houses.

330 Thus far we have survey'd these four Houses, *Egypt,* our families, our selves, and the Church, as so many places of Infection, so many temporal or spiritual Pesthouses, into which our sins had heaped powder, and Gods indignation had cast a match to kindle it. But now the very phrase of the Text, which is, *That in every house there was one dead, There was,* invites us to a more particular consideration of Gods mercy, in that, howsoever it were, it is not so now; in which we shall look how far this beam of mercy shines out in every of these houses, that it is not so now, There is not one dead in every house now; but the Infection, (Temporal and Spiritual Infection) is so far ceased, as that not only those that are alive, do not die, as before; but those whom we called dead, are not dead; they are alive in their spirits, *in Abrahams* 340 *bosome;* and they are alive in their very bodies, in their contract and inherence in Christ Jesus in an infallible assurance of a joyful Resurrection.

[Luke 16.22]

Egyptus   Now in the survey of the first sort of houses, of *Egypt,* herein we are interrupted. Here they were dead, and are dead still: We see clearly enough Gods indignation upon them; but we see neither of those beams of mercy, either that there die no more, or that we have the comfort of a joyful Resurrection in them who are dead: For this fearful calamity of the death of their first-born wrought no more upon them, but to bring them to that exclamation, that vociferation, that voice of

v. 33   350 despairful murmuring, *Omnes Moriemur, We are all dead men:* And they were mischievous Prophets upon themselves; for, proceeding in that sin which induc'd that calamity and the rest upon them, they pursued the children of *Israel* through the Red-sea, and perished in it; and then they came not to die one in a house, but as it is expressed in

Exod. 14.28   the Story, and repeated in the Psalms, *There remained not so much as*
Psal. 106.11   *one of them alive;* so that in their case there is no comfort in the first beam of mercy, that this phrase, *They were dead,* or *They did die,*

should intimate, That now they did not die, now Gods correction had
so wrought upon them, as that God withdrew that correction from
360 them, for it pursued them, and accompanied them to their final and
total destruction. And then for the other beam of mercy, of transferring
them which seemed dead in the eyes of the world, to a better life, by
that hand of death, to present happiness in their souls, and to an
assured resurrection to joy and glory in their bodies, in the communion
of Gods Saints, *Moses* hath given us little hope in their behalf; for thus
he encourageth his Countreymen in that place, *The Egyptians whom*   Exod. 14.13
you have seen this day, you shall see no more for ever: No more in this
world, no more in the world to come. Beloved, as God empayl'd a
Goshen in *Egypt,* a place for the righteous amongst the wicked; so
370 there is an *Egypt* in every *Goshen,* neasts of Snakes in the fairest
Gardens, and even in this City (which in the sense of the Gospel, we
may call, *The Holy City;* as Christ called *Jerusalem,* though she had
multiplied transgressions, *The Holy City,* because she had not cast
away his Law, though she had disobeyed it: So howsoever your sins
have provoked God, yet as you retain a zealous profession of the truth
of his Religion, I may in his name, and do in the bowels of his mercy,
call you, *The Holy City*) even in this City, no doubt but the hand of
God fell upon thousands in this deadly infection, who were no more
affected with it, then those *Egyptians,* to cry out, *Omnes Moriemur,*
380 We can but die, and we must die: And, *Edamus, & bibamus, cras*   [Isa. 22.13]
moriemur, Let us eat and drink, and take our pleasure, and make our
profits, *for to morrow we shall die,* and so were cut off by the hand of
God, some even in their robberies, in half-empty houses; and in their
drunkenness in voluptuous and riotous houses; and in their lusts and
wantonness in licentious houses; and so took in infection and death,
like *Judas's* sop, death dipt and soaked in sin. Men whose lust carried
them into the jaws of infection in lewd houses, and seeking one sore
perished with another; men whose rapine and covetousness broke into
houses, and seeking the Wardrobes of others, found their own wind-
390 ing-sheet, in the infection of that house where they stole their own
death; men who sought no other way to divert sadness, but strong
drink in riotous houses, and there drank up *Davids* cup of Malediction,
the cup of Condemned men, of death, in the infection of that place.
For these men that died in their sins, that sinned in their dying, that

sought and hunted after death so sinfully, we have little comfort of such men, in the phrase of this Text, *They were dead;* for they are dead still: As *Moses* said of the *Egyptians,* I am afraid we may say of these men, We *shall see them no more for ever.*

Domus nostra

⁴⁰⁰ But God will give us the comfort of this phrase in the next House; This next House is *Domus nostra,* our Dwelling-House, our Habitation, our Family; and there, *They were dead;* they were, but by Gods goodness they are not. If this savor of death have been the savor of life unto us; if this heavy weight of Gods hand upon us have awakened us to a narrower survey, and a better discharge of our duties towards all the parts of our Families, we may say, to our comforts and his glory, There was a son dead in disobedience and murmuring; there was a daughter dead in a dangerous easiness of conversation; there was a servant dead in the practice of deceit and falsifying; *there was,* but the Lord hath breath'd a new life into us, the Lord hath made even his ⁴¹⁰ tempest a refreshing, and putrefaction a perfume unto us. The same measure of wind that blows out a candle, kindles a fire; this correction that hath hardned some, hath entendred and mollified us; and howsoever there were dead sons, and dead daughters, and dead servants, this holy sense of Gods Judgements shall not only preserve for the future, that we shall admit no more such dead limbs into our Family, but even give to them who were (in these kindes) formerly dead, a new life, a blessed resurrection from all their sinful habits, by the power of his grace, though reached to them with a bloody hand, and in a bitter cup, in this heavy calamity; and as Christ said of himself, they

[Apoc. 1.18]
[1 Cor. 15.10]
Domus nos

⁴²⁰ shall say in him, *I was dead, but am alive;* and by that grace of God, I am that I am.

The same comfort also shall we have in this phrase of the Text, in our third House; the third House is not *Domus nostra,* but *Domus nos,* not the House we inhabit, but the House we carry; not that House which is our House, but that House which is our selves: There also, *They were dead;* they were, but are not. For beloved, we told you before in our former survey of these several Houses, That our firstborn, (for still ye remember, they were the first-born of *Egypt,* that induce all this application;) Our first-born in this House, in our selves, ⁴³⁰ is our Zeal; not meerly and generally our Religion, but our zeal to our Religion. For Religion in general, is natural to us; the natural man

hath naturally some sense of God, and some inclination to worship
that Power, whom he conceives to be God, and this Worship is Religion. But then the first thing that this general pious affection produces
in us, is Zeal, which is an exaltation of Religion. *Primus actus volun-*
tatis est Amor; Philosophers and Divines agree in that, That the will
of man cannot be idle, and the first act that the will of man produces,
is Love; for till it love something, prefer and chuse something, till
it would have something, it is not a Will; neither can it turn upon
440 any object, before God. So that this first, and general, and natural
love of God, is not begotten in my soul, nor produced by my soul,
but created and infus'd with my soul, and as my soul; there is
no soul that knows she is a soul, without such a general sense of
the love of God. But to love God above all, to love him with all my
faculties, this exaltation of this religious love of God, is the first
born of Religion, and this is Zeal. Religion, which is the Worship of
that Power which I call God, does but make me a man; the natural
man hath that Religion; but that which makes me a Father, and gives
me an off-spring, a first-born, that's Zeal: By Religion I am an *Adam,*
450 but by Zeal I am an *Abel* produced out of that *Adam.* Now if we consider times not long since past, there was scarce one house, scarce one
of us, in whom this first-born, this Zeal was not dead. Discretion is the
ballast of our Ship, that carries us steady; but Zeal is the very Fraight,
the Cargason, the Merchandise it self, which enriches us in the land
of the living; and this was our case, we were all come to esteem our
Ballast more then our Fraight, our Discretion more then our Zeal; we
had more care to please great men then God; more consideration of an
imaginary change of times, then of unchangeable eternity it self. And
as in storms it falls out often that men cast their Wares and their
460 Fraights over-board, but never their Ballast, so as soon as we thought
we saw a storm, in point of Religion, we cast off our Zeal, our Fraight,
and stuck to our Ballast, our Discretion, and thought it sufficient to
sail on smoothly, and steadily, and calmly, and discreetly in the world,
and with the time, though not so directly to the right Haven. So our
first-born in this House, in our selves, our Zeal, was dead. *It was;*
there's the comfortable word of our Text. But now, now that God
hath taken his fan into his hand, and sifted his Church, now that God
hath put us into a straight and crooked Limbeck, passed us through

narrow and difficult trials, and set us upon a hot fire, and drawn us
470 to a more precious substance and nature then before; now that God
hath given our Zeal a new concoction, a new refining, a new inanimation by this fire of tribulation, let us embrace and nurse up this new
resurrection of this Zeal, which his own Spirit hath begot and produced in us, and return to God with a whole and entire soul, without
dividing or scattering our affections upon other objects, and in the
sincerity of the true Religion, without inclinations in our selves, to
induce; and without inclinableness, from others, upon whom we may
depend, to admit, any dramms of the dregs of a superstitious Religion;
for it is a miserable extremity, when we must take a little poyson for
480 physick. And so having made the right use of Gods corrections, we
shall enjoy the comfort of this phrase, in this House, our selves, our
first-born, our Zeal was dead; it was, but it is not.

Lastly, in this fourth House, the House where we stand now, the
House of God, and of his Saints, God affords us a fair beam of this
consolation, in the phrase of this Text also, *They were dead.* How
appliable to you, in this place, is that which God said to *Moses, Put off
thy shoes, for thou treadest on holy ground;* put off all confidence, all
standing, all relying upon worldly assurances, and consider upon what
ground you tread; upon ground so holy, as that all the ground is made
490 of the bodies of Christians, and therein hath received a second consecration. Every puff of wind within these walls, may blow the father
into the sons eyes, or the wife into her husbands, or his into hers, or
both into their childrens, or their childrens into both. Every grain of
dust that flies here, is a piece of a Christian; you need not distinguish
your Pews by figures; you need not say, I sit within so many of such a
neighbour, but I sit within so many inches of my husbands, or wives,
or childes, or friends grave. Ambitious men never made more shift for
places in Court, then dead men for graves in Churches; and as in our
later times, we have seen two and two almost in every Place and Office,
500 so almost every Grave is oppressed with twins; and as at Christs resurrection some of the dead arose out of their graves, that were buried
again; so in this lamentable calamity, the dead were buried, and
thrown up again before they were resolved to dust, to make room for
more. But are all these dead? *They were,* says the Text; they were in
your eyes, and therefore we forbid not that office of the eye, that holy

[Exod. 3.5]

tenderness, to weep for them that are so dead. But there was a part in every one of them, that could not die; which the God of life, who breathed it into them, from his own mouth, hath suck'd into his own bosome. And in that part which could die, *They were dead,* but they are not. The soul of man is not safer wrapt up in the bosome of God, then the body of man is wrapt up in the Contract, and in the eternal Decree of the Resurrection. As soon shall God tear a leaf out of the Book of Life, and cast so many of the Elect into Hell fire, as leave the body of any of his Saints in corruption for ever. To what body shall Christ Jesus be loth to put to his hand, to raise it from the grave, then, that put to his very God-head, the Divinity it self, to assume all our bodies, when in one person, he put on all mankinde in his Incarnation? As when my true repentance hath re-ingraffed me in my God, and re-incorporated me in my Savior, no man may reproach me, and say, Thou wast a sinner: So, since all these dead bodies shall be restored by the power, and are kept alive in the purpose of Almighty God, we cannot say, *They are,* scarce that they were dead. When time shall be no more, when death shall be no more, they shall renew, or rather continue their being. But yet, beloved, for this state of their grave, (for it becomes us to call it a state; it is not an annihilation, no part of Gods Saints can come to nothing) as this state of theirs is not to be lamented, as though they had lost any thing which might have conduced to their good, by departing out of this world; so neither is it a state to be joyed in so, as that we should expose ourselves to dangers unnecessarily, in thinking that we want any thing conducing to our good, which the dead enjoy. As between two men of equal age, if one sleep, and the other wake all night, yet they rise both of an equal age in the morning; so they who shall have slept out a long night of many ages in the grave, and they who shall be caught up in the clouds, to meet the Lord Jesus in the aire, at the last day, shall enter all at once in their bodies into Heaven. No antiquity, no seniority for their bodies; neither can their souls who went before, be said to have been there a minute before ours, because we shall all be in a place that reckons not by minutes. Clocks and Sun-dials were but a late invention upon earth; but the Sun it self, and the earth it self, was but a late invention in heaven. God had been an infinite, a super-infinite, an unimaginable space, millions of millions of unimaginable spaces in heaven, before the Creation. And our afternoon shall be as long as Gods forenoon; for, as God never saw beginning, so we shall never see end; but they whom we tread upon now, and we whom others shall tread upon hereafter, shall meet at once, where, though we were dead, dead in our several houses, dead in a sinful *Egypt,* dead in our family, dead in our selves, dead in the Grave, yet we shall be received, with that consolation, and glorious consolation, you were dead, but are alive. *Enter ye blessed into the* [550] *Kingdom, prepared for you, from the beginning. Amen.*

Textual Notes to the Sermons
in Volume VI

Notes to Sermon No. 1

Notes to Sermon No. 2

Notes to Sermon No. 3

LINE

371–372   *Though ... instructors in Christ, yet ... for in Christ Jesus I* :
            Though ... instructors in Christ, *yet* ... for *in Christ Jesus I F*

382 *mg.*   3.5 : 3.6. *F*

415   *them* : *them, F*

431   preach : preach, *F*

464 *mg.*   2 *Tim.* 4.2 : 2 *Tim.* 4.3. *F*

481   out : our *F*

Notes to Sermon No. 4

83   all : All *F*

83   void; : void *F*

190   solemnly : solemly *F*

198   *if thou canst wake* : if thou *canst wake F*

200 *mg.*   NOTE: This reference, which is at the bottom of a page in *F*, is repeated in *F*, by error, at the top of the page following. We omit the repetition.

208   *Olive, F corr.* : Olive *F originally*

210   no [second "no"] *F corr.* : No *F originally*

257   *Hearkning, F corr* : Hearkning; *F originally*

272   *him;* : him. *F*

273   in *F corr.* : In *F originally*

273   Church. *Edd. conj.* : Church, *F corr.* : Church *F originally*

273   He *F corr.* : he *F originally*

278–279   perverse *F corr.* : pervers *F originally*

279   wil *F corr.* : will *F originally*

449   learn *F corr.* : leran *F originally*

456 *mg.*   *Fortitudo* : *Frtitudo F*

473 *mg.*   *Ps.* 53.5 : *Ps.* 53.6. *F*

514   *nocent iis* : *nocentiis F*

518   he as *F corr.* : he was *F originally*

519 *mg.*   *Prov.* 1.33 : Prov. 1.38. *F*

534 *mg.*   *Rom.* 11.20 : *Rom.* 11.02. *F*

548   *Vici* [Vulgate reading] : *vicit F*

552   but *F corr.* : bvt *F originally*

558   Devil appeared *F corr.* : Devill appeard *F originally*

571   enemies, : enemies) *F*

580 *mg.*   *Dan.* 3.25 : *Dan.* 3.2.25. *F*

654   *Timorous, or amorous;* : *Timorous;* or *amorous, F*

Notes to Sermon No. 5

LINE
20 *mg.* Col. 1.24 : Col. 1.14. *F*
24 *mg.* Numb. 13.23 : Numb. 13.24. *F*
154 *quo ei* : *quoei F*
191 unthankfull : unthanfull *F*
263 *mg.* Phil. 1.15 : Philem. 15. *F*
330 *in Phantasmate* : in *Phantasmate F*
347 *mg.* Dominus. : Dominus; *F*
425 *mg.* Esay 6.3 : Esay 6.2. *F*
439 *mg.* Iohn 13.13 : Iohn 13.14. *F*

Notes to Sermon No. 6

30–31 understanding : understannding *F*
68 have had : have have had *F*
173 *moriturum* : *morituturum F*
194 finde, it : finde. It *F*
194 deliberation; : deliberation, *F*
195 there, : there; *F*
311 blown *F corr. in errata* : blow *F originally*
394 *mg.* Rom. 10.18 : Rom. 10.17. *F*
470 πατήρ *Al* : πατρὸς *F*
470 Ὑιὸς : Ὑιὸς *F*
471 Ἅγιον : Αγιον *F*
NOTE: We have emended the faulty Greek in this passage, but Donne's knowledge of Greek was so limited that it is possible the errors in it were his, not the printer's.
561 *mg.* Esay 42 : Esay 41. *F*

Notes to Sermon No. 7

108–109 making : making, *F*
110 *Deos marinos* : *Deus marinos F*
155 *Angels* : *Angels, F*
172 yet *Born*..........*moneths, Circumcised* : *Born* ... *moneths,* yet *Circumcised F*
204 *mg.* 23 : 13 *F*
369–370 by ... *works Edd. conj.* : by a ... *works F* : by a ... work *Al*
375 otherwise, beloved : otherwise beloved *F*
403 and divers such : *and divers such F*

LINE

426 *mg.*   3.14   :   3.17. *F*
485 *mg.*   21.2   :   23.12. *F*
    508   *Non*   :   *Mon F*
530 *mg.*   Esai.   :   Esac. *F*
600 *mg.*   Esa. 63   :   Esa. 93. *F*

Notes to Sermon No. 8

123 *mg.*   Act. 19.15   :   Act 19.14. *F*
361 *mg.*   Esay 9   :   Esay 3. *F*
478–479   Heresies, ... *Augustine,*   :   Heresies; ... *Augustine F*
    554   innocencie?   :   innocencie. *F*

Notes to Sermon No. 9

    27   defer   :   differ *F*
 63, 93   *Monosillable*   :   *Monasillable F*
         NOTE: The spelling of *F* is not unknown (see *N.E.D.*), but it
         is ugly, and quite possibly here it is a misprint.
121 *mg.*   1 Sam. 15   :   1 Sam. 4. *F*
    130   *seven F corr.*   :   *even F originally*
143–144   unblameable)   :   unblameable: *F*
    187   *incontinency,*   :   *incontinency. F*
    214   abounds   :   abound *F*
    282   *hundred,*   :   *hundred F*   :   hundred and *Al*
    288   *Multitudinis*   :   *Multudinis F*
    289   *succession*   :   *successession F*
    445   *Restitution* [see line 543]   :   *Destitution* F
    485   Jesus,   :   Jesus: *F*
    537   *Formica*   :   *Formicæ F*
    572   circumcised,   :   circumcised; *F*
    620   *tribulation,* ... all;   :   *tribulation;* ... all, *F*
    626,
    627,   *Præsumimus ... præsumo ... præsumo ... præsumo ...*
    639,   *præsumo   :   presumimus ... presumo ... presumo ...*
    640   *presumo ... presumo F*
         NOTE: This quotation from St. Augustine is found with the
         correct spelling in Vol. I, Sermon No. 1, lines 180–184.

LINE

Notes to Sermon No. 10

12   *them,* (as   :   *them.* (as *F*
90 *mg.*   1 Cor. 15.8   :   1 Cor. 15.2. *F*
460 *mg.*   Rom. 1   :   Rom. 2 *F*
481 *mg.*   Confes. I. xi   :   Confes. l. 1. *F*
508 *mg.*   Exod. 8.19   :   Exod. 6.16. *F*

Notes to Sermon No. 11

76   Manours *corr. F in errata*   :   Manners *F originally*
309   Gold *Edd. conj.*   :   God *F*
      NOTE: Alford supports *F* in reading "God," but surely "the
      Matrice and womb of God" would be an extremely strained
      expression. We take "the Matrice and womb of Gold" as a
      development of the preceding words "centricall Gold, viscerall
      Gold, gremiall Gold," and as a reference to the theory that the
      precious metals were transmuted from baser elements in the
      womb of the earth.
394   [The semicolon following "Goods" is faint, and has failed to
      print properly in some copies of *F*.]
395   word   :   world *F*
482 *mg.*   Gen. 5.24   :   Gen. 5.25. *F*
497.   S.   :   S *F* [The stop has failed to print in the copies which we
      have seen.]
582 *mg.*   Gen. 50   :   Gen. 51. *F*

Notes to Sermon No. 12

76   sayes   :   say *Q*
109 *mg.*   *Iob* 34   :   *Iob* 33 *Q*
121   assimilation   :   assimulation *Q* [But cf. "assimulation" in lines
      118 and 123 of this sermon.]
147   Lawes *corr. Q in errata*   :   Cause *Q originally*
385   *Augustine,*   :   *Augustine.* Q ·
430 *mg.*   1 *Reg.*   :   2 *Reg. Q*
430   *brought*   :   *brought, Q*
489   undermining   :   vnderming *Q*
529   *Cottages*   :   *Co-/tages Q*
550   *Syllogismus corr. Q in errata*   :   *Syllagismus Q originally*
567   *things,*   :   *things) F*
693   Mis-interprete [In most copies the hyphen has failed to print.]
Errata   [The earlier-printed copies have only one line of errata, while
list   the later-printed ones have two lines.]

Notes to Sermon No. 13

LINE

105　*Alexandria,*　:　*Alexand. F*
126　*Miramini*　:　*Miremini F*
260　indignifying *corr. F in errata*　:　dignifying *F originally*
308　Decently,　:　Decently; *F*
398,
399, } *Miramini*　:　*Miremini F*
400
609 *mg.*　Psal. 9.1　:　Psal. 9.2. *F*

Notes to Sermon No. 14

17　*person*　:　*persons F*
284 *mg.*　21.9　:　21.19. *F*
311　*Christiani* [second in the line]　:　*Chri-/ani F*
352　two,　:　two' *F*
377 *mg.*　*Luc*　:　*Lue F*
380　remember　:　rememher F.
412　*for if*　:　for if *F*

Notes to Sermon No. 15

103　before God　:　before Cod *F*
136　simply　:　simple *F*
244 *mg.*　Judg. 7　:　Judg. 6. *F*
270 *mg.*　Esay 40.17　:　Esay 40.15. *F*
280　comparatively　:　comparatiuely *F*
342,
344, } Euangelist
346

Note: The recurrence of this form in these three lines, as also elsewhere in the 1640 Folio, shows the connection of the word with the Greek εὐαγγελιστής, whereas the form "evangelist" comes through the French "évangéliste." From the twelfth to the fourteenth century the usual form was "ewan(i)geliste" (*N.E.D.*). We have therefore retained "Eu," as its use here is evidently deliberate.

LINE

359	Goe to, you : Goe to you, *F* [See lines 352–353, 354–355.]	
360	goe to, : goe to *F*	
361	Goe to, : Goe to *F*	
429	*Glory.* : *Glory, F*	
435–436	labors and industry, : labors, and industry *F*	
442 *mg.*	Matt. 15 : Matt. 25. *F*	
534	*whose* : *mhose F*	

Notes to Sermon No. 16

6 *mg.*	Mar. 14.30 : Mat. 14.10. *F*
64	strive : strives *F*
141 *mg.*	Mat. 26.31 : Mat. 26.21. *F*
201	Righteousnesse : Righteonsnesse *F* [The "n" is a turned "u."]
347 *mg.*	27 : 26 *F*
432 *mg.*	Luk. 8.24 : Luk. 8.14. *F*
433 *mg.*	Psal. 106.9 : Psal. 106.17. *F*
451	word : world *F*
596 *mg.*	Psal. 119.139 : Psal. 119.138. *F*

Notes to Sermon No. 17

15	Christs : Christ *F*
181–182	waives … waives *corr. F in errata* : wanes … wanes *F originally*
194	waived *corr. F in errata* : waned *F originally*
266	[as] if : if *F*
291	observe : observes *F*
331	Church : Chnrch *F*
476	world; : world, *F*

Notes to Sermon No. 18

3	yet : yet/yet *F*
6	misery : misery, *F*
115	*was cut out* : was cut *out F*
188 *mg.*	*Part* II : *Part* I *F*
221	God : ~~Gods~~ *F*

LINE

255 *mg.*	*Part*	:	*Part.* F	
269 *mg.*	Esai	:	Essi F	
272 *mg.*	Esai. 15.2	:	Esai. 15.23. *F*	
283	destroy all	:	destroyall F	
326	dead	:	dad F	
327	Houses.	:	Houses.— F	
356 *mg.*	Psal. 106.11	:	Psal. 106.10. F	
505	your eyes	:	youreys F	